Science in the Service of Children

1893–1935

WANTED: A CHILD WELFARE BUREAU

Courtesy of the J. N. "Ding" Darling Foundation.

Science in the Service of Children, 1893–1935

Alice Boardman Smuts

With the assistance of Robert W. Smuts,
R. Malcolm Smuts, Barbara B. Smuts,
and P. Lindsay Chase-Lansdale

Yale University Press

New Haven and London

Published with assistance from the Louis Stern Memorial Fund.

frontispiece: From the Cora Bussey Hillis Scrapbook Inventory, Iowa State Historical Society, Iowa City. Courtesy of the J. N. "Ding" Darling Foundation.

Set in Garamond and Stone Sans types by The Composing Room of Michigan, Inc. Printed in the United States of America.

Library of Congress Cataloging-in-Publication Data
Smuts, Alice Boardman.
    Science in the service of children, 1893–1935 / Alice Boardman Smuts ; with the assistance of Robert W. Smuts . . . [et al.].
        p.   cm.
    Includes bibliographical references and index.
    ISBN-13: 978-0-300-10897-2 (alk. paper)
    ISBN-10: 0-300-10897-4 (alk. paper)
    1. Child development—Research—United States—History.   2. Children—Research—United States—History.   3. Child welfare—United States—History.   4. Child rearing—United States—History.   I. Smuts, Robert W. II. Title.
HQ787.85.S68   2005
362.7'0973'09041—dc22   2005023925

A catalogue record for this book is available from the Library of Congress and the British Library.

The paper in this book meets the guidelines for permanence and durability of the Committee on Production Guidelines for Book Longevity of the Council on Library Resources.

10 9 8 7 6 5 4 3 2

For my grandchildren, Robert Malcolm Smuts, Jr., and Felicia Alice Smuts.

And in memory of Ethel Sturges Dummer, Cora Bussey Hillis, Julia Lathrop, and Grace Abbott, who decided to find out what children really need, and for the men and women who have kept their quest alive.

Contents

Preface, ix

Acknowledgments, xi

Introduction: Three Movements, One Goal, 1

Part 1 **Preparing the Way, 1893–1910**

1 Save the Child and Save the Nation:
The Rise of Social Feminism and Social Research, 15

2 G. Stanley Hall and the Child Study Movement, 31

3 Scientific Child Rearing, Organized Motherhood,
and Parent Education, 49

4 Social Welfare Reformers and Reform-Minded
Scientists, 62

Part 2 **Creating the Models, 1910–1921**

5 The Children's Bureau under Julia Lathrop:
Government at Its Best, 81

6 From Juvenile Delinquency Research to Child Guidance, 103

7 Better Crops, Better Pigs, Better Children: The Iowa Child Welfare Research Station, 117

Part 3 **Breaking Through, 1922–1940**

8 The Children's Decade, 139

9 Child Development Research: Preventive Politics, 155

10 Out of Step with His Times: Arnold Gesell and the Yale Clinic, 173

11 The Child Guidance Movement: Another Approach to Preventive Politics, 191

12 Child Guidance Becomes Child Psychiatry, 207

13 The Children's Bureau under Grace Abbott: Uphill All the Way, 226

Epilogue: What Happened to the Early Movements? The Child Development Field after World War II, 252

Notes, 271
Index, 365

Preface

Admiring and envious comments from my mother about how I cared for my first baby, in 1949, eventually stimulated the research that is the basis for this book. She approved of my feeding my son when he was hungry and letting him sleep when he was tired. She had had to adhere to a fixed feeding and sleeping schedule when she was a new mother. Most of all, she liked my cuddling and soothing my baby when he cried. She had had to sit by my cradle, crying with frustration while I screamed, as she had been advised by her pediatrician neither to rock the cradle nor to hold me. Why, I wondered, had there been such a drastic change in child-rearing methods in twenty-five years? When, decades later, I suggested exploring this question to my Ph.D. advisor, Dr. Sidney Fine, he enthusiastically approved the idea.

Some colleagues were skeptical. What I was attempting, they insisted, was too ambitious for a thesis or a first book. It was "an old man's book." They were right. It became an "old lady's book," interrupted repeatedly by the demands and joys of family life. My children, who were in college when I began the research, are now middle-aged university professors, and my husband, whose faith and support were crucial to this undertaking, died in November 2003.

One difficulty, I discovered through reviews of the manuscript requested by potential publishers, was to strike a proper balance between information about historical events that influenced the founding of the field of child development and scientific information about the field itself. Historian reviewers wanted some of the historical information deleted. One of them wrote, for example, "Everyone knows about the land grant acts; no need to discuss them." In the same mail, a psychologist reviewer asked for additional historical information, particularly on the child labor movement. I concluded that I could not satisfy readers from both specialties, but I could hope that historians would skim the parts familiar to them and that developmentalists would consult the references if they wanted additional historical knowledge.

Finally, I hope that this book will stimulate other scholars to correct mistakes, challenge my interpretations, and carry the story forward through World War II into recent times. The effects of technological change on both the field of child study and the practice of child rearing are especially worthy of and fascinating to study. The social policy consequences derived from child study, in both the private and public sectors, constitute a huge subject that deserves continuing attention.

Acknowledgments

Without the financial support and enthusiastic participation of Robert W. Smuts, my late husband, this book would not have been written. He was an enormously helpful and delightful partner, a feminist's dream husband, who took over mundane housekeeping tasks to free me to complete the text. Without his formidable writing and editing skills, and his challenging questions and comments, it would have been a different and inferior history. He also participated in meetings of the Society for Research in Child Development (SRCD).

The book was very much a family affair. My son, R. Malcolm Smuts, professor of history at the University of Massachusetts, and my daughter, Barbara B. Smuts, professor of psychology at the University of Michigan, read and edited every chapter more than once and helped correct the proofs. Distinguished writers and scholars, they made substantial contributions.

This book would not have gone to press without the assistance of my cherished friend and colleague P. Lindsay Chase-Lansdale, professor in the School of Education and Social Policy and faculty fellow in the Institute for Policy Research at Northwestern University, and her capable assistants Renee Erline, Nicole Wong, and Barrie Leimer. Although the manuscript had been thoroughly edited, the care of my husband during the past six years prevented me from attending to the other tasks necessary to prepare a manuscript for publication. Lindsay, Ms. Erline, Ms. Wong, and Ms. Leimer took care of this formidable task. Lindsay and I have been friends for almost thirty years. Her devotion to this book, however, far exceeded what anyone might expect of even a very dear friend, and my gratitude to her knows no bounds.

When I began my research, I was totally ignorant of the field of child development. Dr. Harold Stevenson, professor emeritus of developmental psychology at the University of Michigan, more than any other individual, helped me to understand this field of child development. He shared his own vast knowledge and arranged for me to interview child development pioneers. His recommendation, I suspect, persuaded the William T. Grant Foundation to fund the interviews. Dr. Stevenson also introduced me to contemporary developmentalists from North America and abroad. As director of the University of Michigan Bush Center for Child Development and Social Policy, he appointed me as an associate to the center for five years from 1978 to 1983 There I learned at first hand of the problems involved in applying knowledge about children. John Hagen, executive director of the Society for Research in Child Development and chair of the department at the University of Michigan, enabled me to work with and learn from developmentalists by appointing me to the 1983 program committee for SRCD's fiftieth anniversary meeting. In addition, he has graciously answered literally hundreds of my questions over the past twenty years.

Dr. Dale Harris, former director of the Minnesota Institute of Child Development, instructed me about the early days of the field, in particular bringing to my attention the important relationship between agricultural research stations and developmental psychology. He later read and commented on the entire manuscript. Thanks also to Dr. Sheldon White, late professor of social psychology at Harvard University, for his encouragement and help.

Dr. Julius Richmond, former Surgeon General of the United States and former director of the Judge Baker Foundation, greatly enhanced my understanding of the child guidance movement. Dr. Arthur H. Parmelee, pediatrician and former director of the Child Development Institute at the University of California, through personal meetings and extensive correspondence shared his knowledge of early pediatrics and its relationship to the field of child development.

Dr. Edward Zigler, professor emeritus of psychology at Yale University, former director of the Children's Bureau, a founder and continuing advocate of Head Start, and former president of the American Orthopsychiatry Association, is unique in having participated in three of the child study efforts that are the primary focus of this book. No one has been more supportive of my efforts to tell a broad story nor more generous with help than Dr. Zigler.

I am grateful to many other developmentalists, whose contributions I acknowledge in the Notes.

Thus far, I have confined my gratitude to professionals in the field of child development, but I am an historian. The basis of this book is a two-volume University of Michigan Ph.D. dissertation in history (Alice Boardman Smuts, "Science Discovers the Child," 1995) . Professor Sidney Fine was chair of my committee. Although he had no knowledge of the founding of the child sciences, he urged me to explore their history. He became my friend as well as my mentor, always providing support and encouragement when I became disheartened. He validated his legendary reputation for devotion to his students, and his rigorous demands and high expectations drove me to accomplish more than I thought possible.

The other historians on my committee were Maris Vinovskis, a social historian and historian of education, and Martin Pernick, an historian of medicine. Dr. Vinovskis helped me with sources and interpretation of early nineteenth-century America and with organization. Dr. Pernick offered detailed and trenchant criticism and enlightened me about the eugenics movement. Since the nature-nurture conflict is a major theme of the history, his advice was significant. Dr. Harold Stevenson was the cognate member of the committee.

Dr. Robert M. Warner, archivist and University of Michigan historian, was director of the Bentley Historical Library when I began my research. He helped me to persuade the Governing Council of the Society for Research in Child Development to found a committee to locate and preserve the primary sources in its field. He was a consultant to the committee for several years and helped to raise the money to fund the project. Without this undertaking, valuable sources for this book and for many others would have been lost.

Dr. Elizabeth Lomax, an historian and close friend who has specialized in the history of British pediatrics, discussed with me differences and similarities between pediatrics in Britain and in the United States. She read the entire manuscript and offered many valuable suggestions. The late Dr. Myron Wegman, dean emeritus of the University of Michigan School of Public Health, suggested the book's title.

Gladys Topkis's charm and skill and her enthusiasm for this book persuaded me to offer it to Yale University Press. I am also grateful for her wonderful job of editing. My thanks are due also to subsequent editors at the press for their patience with me in spite of the long delay in submitting a finished manuscript and to Professor Zigler for what I suspect was his role in keeping the press patient. I especially wish to thank Cynthia Wells, freelance manuscript editor and Yale University Press editors Margaret Otzel and Keith Condon for their encouragement and help in preparing the book for publication.

Introduction: Three
Movements, One Goal

In 1918 only three psychologists and two psychiatrists were full-time scholars of childhood. By 1930 there were more than six hundred such professional researchers, and at the beginning of the twenty-first century there are an estimated eight thousand.[1] In this book I explore how female reformers, together with scientists and philanthropists, succeeded in launching the child sciences as we know them today. Unlike the establishment of the adult sciences of human nature, which took place over a relatively long period, the child sciences were institutionalized and professionalized in dramatic developments in the decade and a half following the end of World War I. During this brief period, the federal government under the leadership of President Herbert Hoover, philanthropic foundations, organized mothers, social welfare reformers, and behavioral scientists launched major independent and collaborative efforts to obtain more and better knowledge of children. Their ambitious goal was to inspire the study of *all* children—normal as well as damaged or deprived—in new ways, with new methods.

Their first goal was to establish systematically well-structured, well-funded organizations to investigate children and their lives in America. Then they would apply the new knowledge they acquired to child welfare reform and to the improvement of child rearing. Improving the child was perceived as the key to improving the nation. The 1920s, usually seen as the decade of the flapper and the bootlegger, was actually the decade of the child. More than in any other period of American history, before or since, trends in science and society converged to place the child at center stage.[2]

The new information that flowed from these scientific investigations reached an extremely receptive public, initiating a revolution in the ways in which we think about and treat our children. As soon as scientists released their findings, administrators and practitioners in the various fields of childcare and medicine rushed to apply them. A small but growing number of pediatricians offered to help keep children well, in addition to treating them when they were sick. Some tried to respond to parents' demands to help them cope with their children's behavioral problems. Parents enthusiastically welcomed the new child-rearing literature produced and distributed in unprecedented abundance. *Parents' Magazine*, established in 1926, became a thriving success and survived the Great Depression when many other popular magazines went under.[3] The new disciplines of child development and child-guidance psychiatry were founded at this time. The professional journals and societies that these new specialties established during the 1920s and 1930s thrive today.[4] The scientific revolution in child study is a neglected chapter in American history.

During the nineteenth century, most scientists had deemed children unsuitable subjects for scientific inquiry. A few occasionally turned their attention to children, but hardly any studied children exclusively. "Ten pages to the making of pots, ten lines to infancy," noted a writer in a review of anthropologist Ralph Linton's text *The Study of Man* (1936). Moreover, most American citizens were hostile to child study, believing it would be a threat to the primacy and privacy of the family, and possibly harmful to the children studied. During the 1890s parents objected even to the weighing and measuring of school children. The sparse knowledge of children that was disseminated in the United States was mostly imported from Europe. Consequently, most of what passed for child study before 1920 was adult science read backward and applied to the child. Even Sigmund Freud never actually studied a child. His famous deductions about the problems of Little Hans were based on discussions with the child's father.[5]

In the late 1890s the pioneer psychologist G. Stanley Hall launched the child study movement, paving the way for the founding of the child sciences that occurred rapidly after the end of World War I. Hall was foremost among the early behavioral scientists who were dissatisfied with academic advances alone and sought to promote social progress through the application of science to interactions with children. At first very popular, the movement declined by 1900 and was abandoned by Hall in 1910.

By 1917, however, women social reformers, organized mothers, and reform-minded scientists had worked to establish three new models for the study of children, each with a different approach: (1) the first child guidance clinic began its work in Chicago in 1909; (2) the United States Children's Bureau was founded in 1912; and (3) in 1917, the Iowa state legislature established the first institution in the world to study the normal child, called the Iowa Child Welfare Research Station.[6] In these efforts, women were the innovators, while male scientists were quick to cooperate with them.

The child guidance movement introduced the clinical study of emotional and behavioral troubles in children by an interdisciplinary team of psychiatrists, psychologists, and social workers who operated in the setting of community clinics, rather than hospitals. The second important model, the Children's Bureau, initiated the sociological study of children. It pioneered in applying to children the survey techniques developed by urban social reformers during the progressive era. The third program, the child development movement, springing from the Iowa Child Welfare Research Station, institutionalized research on the physical, mental, and emotional development of normal children from conception to maturity. The goal was to understand the child through the coordination and integration of research from numerous disciplines, including psychology, psychiatry, pediatrics, anatomy, nursing, dentistry, anthropology, sociology, nutrition, home economics, and education. As a result, most developmentalists worked in autonomous institutes, usually associated with universities, rather than in academic departments or scientific laboratories.

At first, the new organizations had little money or influence and a poor prospect of survival.[7] They nonetheless became the models for a nationwide network of child development and parent education institutes and for 350 child guidance clinics established after World War I. Private philanthropy invested millions of dollars to found and support these institutions. Shortly after the Armistice, philanthropic foundations shifted substantial support from adult to child programs and from charity to pioneering ventures in research, education, health, and welfare. Male foundation executives were strongly influenced by a utopian confidence in the possibility of creating a better society through the application of the social sciences and by the emphasis of the "new psychology" on the importance of childhood experience in the development of the adult. Using the child guidance clinic in Boston and the Iowa Child Welfare Research Station as models, they transformed prewar Progressive efforts to reform society for the benefit of the child into postwar efforts to reform the child for the benefit of society. Brand new human beings, they believed, would create a brave new world. "The adult is what the child was. Whoever can control the mental, physical, and moral life of the child can direct the child's future as an adult," declared a spokesman for the Commonwealth Fund. Lawrence K. Frank, the chief architect of the Laura Spelman Rockefeller Memorial child study programs, concurred. The outstanding development of the 1920s, he claimed, was the "growing belief in the possibility of directing and controlling social life through the care and nurture of children."[8]

The federal government also increased its commitment to child study after World War I. The 1931–1932 budget of the United States Children's Bureau was $395,000, more than fifteen times the 1912 sum. By 1934 the bureau had completed more than two hundred investigations of child life in the United States and was helping the federal government to incorporate the fruits of its research and experience in the Social Security Act, passed in 1935. Interest in child study had reached a climax in 1930, when President Herbert Hoover convened a White House Conference "to discover and summarize knowledge of and experience in the study of every phase of child life." The president diverted a half-million dollars to support the conference and professed to the delegates that "these questions of child health and protection are a complicated problem requiring much learning and much action. And we need have great concern over this matter. Let no one believe that these are questions that should not stir a nation; that they are below the dignity of statesmen or governments. If we could have one generation of properly born, trained, educated, and healthy children, a thousand other problems of government would vanish." The conference's findings were reported in thirty-two published volumes.[9]

Previous scholarship has been limited to the development of one or the other of the three child study movements—child guidance, sociological study, and child development—over a shorter time span or to the history of individual child study organizations. In this book I view these three new approaches to scientific child study not as isolated efforts but as related parts of a single broad movement. Their simultaneous trajectories along similar and sometimes intersecting pathways are summarized in table 1. Participants in each of the three

Table 1. Three Approaches to Science in the Service of Children

Date	Child Development	Child Guidance	Federal Government
1893	Hall's Child Study movement begins.		
1906			Campaign for U.S. Children's Bureau begins.
1909	Hall brings Freud to the United States	First child guidance clinic (Illinois Psychopathic Institute) founded. William Healy appointed Director.	White House Conference for Dependent Children
1910	Hall's Child Study movement ends.		
1912			U.S. Children's Bureau founded. Julia Lathrop appointed Chief.
1913–14			Children's Bureau publishes *Prenatal Care* (1913) and *Infant Care* (1914).
1915		*The Individual Delinquent* by William Healy is published.	
1917	Iowa State Child Welfare Research Station founded.	Judge Baker Clinic founded and William Healy appointed Director. It becomes the model for future child guidance clinics, with its team of psychiatrist, psychologist, and social worker.	
1918	Laura Spelman Rockefeller Memorial (LSRM) founded.	Commonwealth Fund founded.	President Wilson proclaims Children's Year.
1919			White House Conference on Child Welfare Standards
1921			Sheppard-Towner Act passed. Grace Abbott succeeds Julia Lathrop as Children's Bureau Chief.

continued

Table 1. (*continued*)

Date	Child Development	Child Guidance	Federal Government
1922–27		Commonwealth Fund sponsors first five-year child guidance program.	
1923–27	Child development research institutes founded by LSRM.		
1924		American Orthopsychiatry Association founded.	
1925	National Research Council Committee on Child Development founded.		
1927–32		Commonwealth Fund sponsors second five-year child guidance program.	
1929	LSRM dissolved.		Sheppard-Towner Act repealed.
1930	*Child Development* founded.	*American Journal of Orthopsychiatry* founded.	White House Conference on Child Health and Protection
1933	Society for Research in Child Development founded. Rockefeller's General Education Board begins support of child development.		
1934			Grace Abbott resigns as Children's Bureau Chief.

movements employed different strategies but all were united by a single fundamental goal: the discovery of new knowledge about children in order to better serve both children and the nation. During the Progressive Era before World War I, efforts to improve children's lives stemmed from humanitarian motives. After the war, the philanthropies that supported child study programs shifted their focus to improving the nation by improving its children. Science became the essential instrument through which child welfare reform was to be achieved.[10]

SCIENCE AS AN INSTRUMENT OF REFORM

Before the beginning of the twentieth century, social reformers had relied mainly on moral admonition, but Progressive reformers believed that scientifically validated facts were an essential preliminary to effective social action. Adherents of the child development movement hoped, through scientific research, to discover optimum child-rearing methods and, through parent education, to foster their application. Philanthropic sponsors of the child development research institutes believed that scientific child rearing would produce a new kind of child who would grow into a new kind of adult, free of most of the afflictions and deficiencies of their progenitors. Child guidance pioneers hoped that diagnosis and treatment of children's problems at an early stage in their development would nip in the bud incipient neurosis, psychosis, and criminal tendencies, and they predicted that their clinics would reduce the future need for mental hospitals and prisons. The staff of the Children's Bureau believed that research exposing the harmful effects of the conditions in which many children lived would arouse the American public to corrective action. Participants in all three movements pointed to what scientific research on crops and livestock had done for agriculture, what research on natural resources had done for conservation, and what medical and epidemiological research had done for public health. If science were applied to children as it had been to other areas of American life, they claimed, similar great benefits would ensue.

In their treatment of children, historians of the Progressive Era and the 1920s have focused on child welfare reform rather than child study. They have argued about the extent to which child welfare programs were motivated by humanitarian impulses or by social control goals, and they have emphasized the limited success and large failures of "child-saving" programs. Historians also have failed to notice that, although reform goals were seldom achieved, the means to that end—the new approaches to child study—took on a life of their own. Even with support curtailed, the child development research institutes survived the Depression, while the number of child guidance clinics actually increased. The Children's Fund of Michigan, established in 1929, invested a considerable portion of its ten million dollar endowment in child development research and child guidance programs, in spite of the pressing need to feed and shelter needy Michigan children during the Depression. Other foundations established new child development research institutes during the 1930s. After World War II, the federal government assumed an important role in both conducting and supporting child study. An unanticipated consequence of the movements to reform society by saving its children, the founding of scientific child study was a profoundly important development with enormous and continuing scientific and social consequences.

The social reform goal helped to overcome objections to research on children and shaped the character of the new child sciences by influencing the settings in which children were studied, their age and social class, the aspects of childhood examined, and the methods used. During the period of G. Stanley Hall's child study movement, when educational reform was dominant, scientists studied school-aged children and adolescents. After World War I, the new goal of influencing children's development and the importance assigned to early childhood shifted the attention of researchers to children between two and seven years of age. During the Progressive reform years before the war, investigators concentrated on poor, delinquent, and dependent children. After the war, philanthropy's utopian vision of reforming society by improving the lives of all children, not just the disadvantaged, led private foundations to focus on the study of "normal" middle-class children.

The social reform goal was also largely responsible for both the interdisciplinary approach and the location of child study outside the academic and medical establishments. These two characteristics of the new disciplines strongly influenced their research findings. The treatment and study of children in the guidance clinics led to conclusions very different from those of hospital psychiatry about the causes of children's emotional problems and to the emergence of a unique American child psychiatry. Child development in the institutes was not like the child psychology of academic departments, but was rather a distinct specialty with its own assumptions and methodology. The Children's Bureau, using a social rather than a medical approach to investigate infant mortality, correlated mortality rates with poverty. The powerful influence of the reform goal on the early history of scientific child study in America permeates this volume and is its central theme.[11]

FOUNDING MOTHERS AND FATHERS:
WOMEN SOCIAL REFORMERS AND
REFORM-MINDED SCIENTISTS

The establishment of all three new approaches to child study between 1909 and 1917 was the result of united efforts by women social reformers and reform-minded scientists. Until late in the nineteenth century, the United States imported most of its ideas about child rearing and child study from Europe. During the first two decades of the twentieth century, however, women social reformers, organized motherhood, and the first generation of American behavioral scientists worked together to create better ways of studying children. G. Stanley Hall was foremost among these early behavioral scientists who applied scientific knowledge to social reform. A new wave of college- and university-educated women joined with socially active clubwomen in rejecting confinement to hearth and home and setting forth to work in the larger world to improve life for women and children. Their efforts were necessary, they argued, because rapid industrialization, immigration, and other disruptive forces were harming mothers and children. Women reformers endorsed the use of science as a tool of reform. They therefore welcomed the validation and status conferred on their endeavors by their partnership with men of science, but women were the leaders, the innovators, and the driving force behind the new sciences of childhood.[12]

The contribution of women social reformers and professionals to the founding of scientific child study has never been sufficiently recognized. Two remarkable women who played crucial roles in the establishment of scientific child study have never been the subject of a scholarly article, nor are they included in the biographical dictionary *Notable American Women*. Cora Bussey Hillis organized and led mothers in a persistent campaign to create the Iowa Child Welfare Research Station, the model for the child development institutes established during the 1920s. The second of these remarkable women, Chicago philanthropist Ethel Dummer, helped to arrange and then funded William Healy's classic five-year study of eight hundred juvenile delinquents, undertaken in the first child guidance clinic. Dummer also helped Julia Lathrop, first chief of the Children's Bureau, through financial aid and personal participation in the bureau's research on maternal and child health and illegitimacy, and throughout her long life supported educational reform, mental hygiene, and child development programs. Lathrop is another remarkable woman whose achievements have not been adequately recognized.[13]

THE ROLE OF AMERICAN PHILANTHROPY

In addition to Dummer, other women philanthropists played important roles in founding scientific child study. Margaret Olivia Sage founded the Russell Sage Foundation, which supported survey research and some very early research on children. In 1918 Anna M. Richardson Harkness established the Commonwealth Fund "for the welfare of mankind" with an initial endowment of twenty million dollars, which she continued to augment until her death in 1926. The Commonwealth Fund became the founder and chief supporter of child guidance clinics. Also in 1918, John D. Rockefeller established the Laura Spelman Rockefeller Memorial to carry on his wife's charitable work, much of which had been directed toward aid for women and children. The memorial became the principal sponsor of child development studies. The childless widow of a Michigan senator who died in 1918, Lizzie Merrill-Palmer, bequeathed four million dollars to establish a school in Detroit to train young women for motherhood and homemaking. A home economist working there, Edna Noble White, transformed the "school" into the second child development research institute. Only three months after the Iowa Child Welfare Research Station established the first nursery school laboratory in 1922, at the insistence of the women who had led the campaign for the Iowa station, the Merrill-Palmer Institute established a similar school laboratory.[14]

A UNIQUE AMERICAN STORY

The founding of child study in the United States was a product of unique American attitudes, values, and circumstances. There were no counterparts in Europe for the reform-minded scientists, women social reformers, and parent-education enthusiasts who led the child study movements in this country or for the foundations that supported child study during the 1920s and early 1930s. No European woman acted remotely like Cora Bussey Hillis, the mother from Iowa who conceived the idea for the first institute in the world to study the normal child, spent years organizing the women of her state, and then led them in two campaigns to persuade the state legislature to establish the first child welfare research station. The model for the station was the American agricultural experiment station, and again it was this model that the Laura Spelman Rockefeller Memorial drew upon for its child development and parent education institutes in the 1920s. The memorial also used the networks of the agricultural extension service for its parent education programs. The nursery school laboratory was another American innovation, and nothing in Europe resembled the Children's Bureau studies of children in slums, factories, cotton fields, and juvenile courts. The child guidance team of psychiatrist, psychologist, and social worker was unique to the United States. Nor were there community child guidance clinics in Europe until 1929, when, at the British government's request, the Commonwealth Fund established a demonstration clinic in London and soon thereafter supported clinics in other parts of England. Unique American circumstances produced unique American child sciences.[15]

Although the three child study movements had slightly different timetables, their collective history falls roughly into three periods that provide the structure of this book. Part 1, Preparing the Way, 1893–1910, begins with a chapter on the responsibility of mothers to the nation in early America and then focuses on the rise and fall of G. Stanley Hall's child study movement and the growing involvement of women in child welfare reform and parent education. Part 2, Creating the Models, 1910–1921, describes the establishment and early years of the first child guidance clinic, the first child development research institute, and the Children's Bureau. Part 3, Breaking Through, 1922–1940, discusses the establishment and professionalization of the fields of child guidance and child development and the growing commitment of the federal government to child study. An epilogue offers a brief overview of postwar developments and some of the scientific and social consequences of the founding of child study. It also describes certain contemporary expressions of earlier themes and concludes with reflections on the contrast between the place of children in the hearts, minds, and institutions of the American people in the 1920s and at the beginning of the twenty-first century.

Part 1 Preparing the Way, 1893–1910

Chapter 1 Save the Child and Save the Nation: The Rise of Social Feminism and Social Research

A distinctly American ideology of domesticity originated during the earliest years of the republic and was embellished and expanded by evangelical Protestantism during the decades before the Civil War. A new nation with a sense of mission, the United States saw its destiny tied to its children. Children in early America were valued for their economic contributions to the family and nation. Boys were particularly valued also as future citizens who could fulfill the expectations of the democracy, whereas girls were prized as future mothers who could teach their own children to be responsible parents and citizens.[1] Children therefore required the kind of rearing that would produce adults morally dedicated to the democratic mission and trained to carry it out. Thus emerged early in the life of the new nation the concept of the Republican Mother, which enhanced women's status by linking it to the importance of the child for the future of the nation and justified education and participation in activities outside the home that were related to their unique stake in maintaining democracy.[2]

Linda Kerber points out that American post-Revolutionary ideology accomplished what the English and French Enlightenment had not: it justified and popularized a political role for women.[3] Although women could not vote or hold office, their domestic activities had an important political function because through them they molded sons and influenced husbands in the practice of civic virtue. Benjamin Rush, one of the theorists of the Republican Mother, urged American women to model themselves not on fashionable British woman-hood but on an ideal appropriate to democracy. According to Lois Meek Stolz, almost a century and a half after Rush wrote, Lawrence K. Frank, chief architect of the Laura Spelman Rockefeller Memorial child study programs, similarly urged American mothers not to imitate the Lady Bountiful activities of European women but to devote themselves to rearing their own children.[4]

DOMESTIC IDEOLOGY BEFORE THE CIVIL WAR

In early Puritan New England the father, as God's representative on earth, was held responsible for the education of his children. Although little is known about changes in the allocation of educational responsibility, it is clear that the educational role of fathers decreased as economic developments began to take men's work away from home and church membership became feminized.[5] By the 1830s and 1840s Protestant clergy and New England reformers were proposing that the remedy for the evils of materialism, the moral restoration of the nation, and the salvation of democracy depended on American mothers, who had the awesome task of instilling in young children the virtues and values essential to the republic. Mothers were asked to assume responsibility not only for their own children but also for all children in need. Single women and childless wives were expected to participate in this rescue mission.[6]

Before 1820 most child-rearing advice literature in the United States was imported from England. During the 1820s, however, a native, mass-circulation literature popularized the message that mothers had the power to change the course of the nation.[7] "When our land is filled with pious and patriotic mothers," John Abbott wrote in 1833, "then will it be filled with virtuous and patriotic men."[8] The exaltation of motherhood was linked to a belief in woman's special nature, untainted by the marketplace, which made her morally and spiritually superior to man. The doctrine of "separate spheres" emerged from these beliefs about the essential differences between males and females and the need to protect the home from the corruption of the world. Man's sphere was the world of business and politics; woman's, that of hearth and home. The cardinal virtues of "true womanhood," according to Barbara Welter, were piety, purity, submissiveness, and domesticity.[9]

Recent historical scholarship has challenged the validity of some of these views. Nancy Hewitt, for example, believes that the antebellum concept of "true womanhood" was not considered applicable to black and lower-class women and that middle- and upper-class women were divided along economic and social-interest lines more than they were united by domestic ideology.[10] Other scholars have shown that the reality of women's lives in the workplace and in reform activities did not conform to the rhetoric of the prescriptive literature. Laura McCall's content analysis of *Godey's Lady's Book* between 1830 and 1860 found that 37 percent of 234 fictional characters possessed none of Welter's four cardinal virtues, and no character possessed all four.[11] Mary P. Ryan also argues that Welter's four attributes, particularly "submissiveness," must be reconsidered.[12]

Although dispute continues over the extent to which the doctrine of separate spheres reflected antebellum reality, there is consensus that antebellum women had great power. "The question of political and civil rights for women," Anne Kuhn wrote, "paled into insignificance in the light of this great responsibility which made them moral agents for the carrying out of democratic purposes."[13]

European romanticism, introduced to the United States in the 1820s, meshed harmoniously with beliefs about the importance of childhood and motherhood. The Enlightenment's emphasis on the formal instruction of children in mental skills shifted during the early nineteenth century to an emphasis on the development of moral character, not through precept and instruction, but through intimate association with family members. Belief in the power of unconscious parental influence made early childhood a crucial period and led to increased reliance on the mother, who, because of her constant presence, was thought to be the single most important influence on the child.[14]

"By the time a child is three," cautioned the Reverend Horace Bushnell, the most influential dispenser of child-rearing advice during the two decades before the Civil War, "the parents will have done more than half of all they will ever do for his character." Preaching that God worked through domestic education and emphasizing the importance of parental example, Bushnell wrote that "the spirit of the house is in the members by nurture not by teaching, not by any attempt to communicate the same, but because it is in the air the children breathe. . . . The odor of the house will always be in his garments and the internal difficulties with which he has to struggle will spring of family seeds planted in his nature."[15] Since the child becomes virtuous before the age of reason by imitating the mother, she must be at all times an exemplary model. The mother's enormous power entailed comparable responsibility. She was not to entrust her child to servants and was expected to be energetic and active in discharging her parental obligations.[16]

Related to beliefs about how children acquired moral character was the veneration of the untutored mother. "The mother, whether wise or ignorant, learned or unlearned, healthy or sick," Bronson Alcott declared, "is the most efficient educator."[17] With respect to women of all classes, Cott pointed out, "Domesticity as a vocation began to mean for women what worldly occupations meant for men, and they staked their claims to social power on their 'vocations.'"[18] At mid-nineteenth century, Catherine Beecher popularized the idea that wife- and mother-hood was woman's "profession."[19]

THE SPREAD OF THE NEW
CHILD-REARING ADVICE

The new child-rearing advice enjoyed a wide circulation primarily through the efforts of local maternal associations and the periodicals they sponsored. Beginning in Portland, Maine, in 1815, maternal associations proliferated during the 1830s and 1840s. In 1836 two rural New Hampshire counties alone contained thirty-eight mothers' clubs with more than a thousand members. The purpose of maternal associations was to foster Christian motherhood and thereby transform the world. "Christian motherhood," Meckel explains, "represented a religious calling that superseded the boundaries of the organized church."[20]

Maternal associations encouraged mothers to share their experiences and learn from one another, but they also stressed the need to learn from experts; consequently, they distributed child-rearing literature. A member of the Utica, New York, maternal association sponsored the *Mother's Magazine,* a nonsectarian journal that was intended to reach beyond its Congregational and Presbyterian base. Founded in 1833, it had a circulation of ten thousand by 1837. Two more periodicals for mothers were established by 1841 and quickly rivaled the Utica magazine in circulation. In spite of their emphasis on early religious training and moral reform, the magazines contained, one historian notes, "surprisingly eclectic and inclusive material," including essays by Locke and Rousseau, articles on child health and the importance of maternal education, and even one on the early-childhood-education pioneer Pestalozzi before he had become well known to American educators. The maternal associations embraced a concept of children and a psychology of early child development that seemed "to seek a middle ground between Calvinist repression and romantic permissiveness." The magazines encouraged the establishment of new maternal associations that became effective channels for the widespread dissemination of child-rearing and maternal-reform literature. They reached and received much of their support from lower-middle-class women.[21]

Before the Civil War, the predominantly rural and relatively static character of American society and of women's lives encouraged a conservative interpretation of the ideology of domesticity. The changes in American society that later enticed women from their homes had not yet appeared. The mother's obligation to protect and provide for other people's children could be discharged through participation in local moral reform societies and maternal associations, and the demands of good motherhood and good wifehood left women with little energy or leisure for other interests.[22]

THE IDEOLOGY OF DOMESTICITY
AFTER THE CIVIL WAR

The Civil War launched women permanently into large-scale activity outside the home.[23] Drastic changes in American society during and after the war transformed the lives of middle-class women. Many women began to reject the conservative version of the ideology of domesticity because they believed that it would not allow them to fulfill their responsibilities to family and country. In meeting new challenges, these women did not draw on the egalitarian values that motivated women abolitionists and suffragists before the Civil War and that have dominated contemporary feminist ideology. Instead, they chose to radically reinterpret and extend the ideology of domesticity and the concept of separate spheres.[24] So ingeniously and effectively did they use the role of mother to justify their social reform agenda that they succeeded, during the decades just before and after World War I, in bestowing on the child an importance unsurpassed before or since. The "age of feminism" that emerged soon after the Civil War was in large part a reaction of numerous middle-class women to the harmful effects on women and children of urban-industrial life, and to the urgent need to help immigrant families adjust to life in the United States.[25] Women, they argued, must assume a greater role in the formulation of social policy affecting families. Although nineteenth-century women's movements culminated in the passage of the Nineteenth Amendment in 1920, the first demand of women reformers was not the vote but improvement in the lives of women and children. Many did not join the suffrage movement until the decade before World War I. They did so then not in a quest for equal rights, but because they thought the vote would be a powerful weapon for achieving maternal and child welfare reform.[26]

Social feminism is the term several historians have used to distinguish this particular form of feminism, which was dominant during the Progressive period.[27] The chief aim of social feminists was to protect and promote the welfare of women and children; few of them were feminists in the now-familiar sense of opposition to male dominance. They thought themselves above politics, pursuing reforms most women supported rather than questing for political and legal equality.[28] Noting that women would soon win the franchise, Chicago philanthropist and social reformer Ethel Dummer asked an all-female audience, Would women enjoy their new right selfishly, or would "the maternal instinct carry us to this great movement to secure justice for all children?" She added: "The finest feminism is that which seeks to solve this problem of motherhood."[29] According to Aileen Kraditor, many suffragists in the early twentieth century still believed that a woman's chief duty was to be a mother.[30]

Social feminists have generally been categorized by historians as more conservative than suffragists, but in 1914 Dummer called herself a "radical feminist." To her, and to many other women of her time, social feminism required a radical change of viewpoint and included female leadership and participation in many activities formerly undertaken only by men. Dummer said that, until 1906, she had lived in a sheltered world in which she assumed that all children were happy. Beginning in that year, her work with the Chicago Juvenile Protective Association exposed her to the shocking conditions of life for children in trouble with the law. She had stepped "from a trim and orderly garden . . . into a jungle." Until her death at the age of eighty, Dummer dedicated her life to helping children, partly through welfare activities, but primarily by organizing and funding scientific studies of children. In her humanitarian response to the plight of children in urban-industrial America, Dummer was typical of many upper-class and middle-class women of her time. Social feminism demanded recognition of the impact of social change on children's lives, a radical rethinking of how to discharge women's traditional obligations to home and children, and a willingness to leave home to venture into the once-forbidden public sphere.[31]

ACCOMMODATING THE IDEOLOGY OF DOMESTICITY TO NEW CONDITIONS IN LATE-NINETEENTH-CENTURY AMERICA

Redefining and expanding the ideology of domesticity, women mustered persuasive reasons to justify their participation in state and federal affairs in order to influence private and public policy affecting home and family. They pointed, first, to the magnitude of changes in post–Civil War American society that prevented the insulation of middle- and upper-class children from the problems of the rest of society. Relying on private benevolence or the local community would not safeguard society from the "dangerous classes," from exposure to disease caused by unsanitary conditions, nor from other perils brought about by rapid urbanization and industrialization and increased immigration.[32] Jane Addams told a receptive female audience that a mother's devotion to her family was no longer enough to protect her own children. Mothers were obligated to broaden the scope of their reform activities to encompass any and all issues that could affect their children's welfare.[33]

Muckraking articles and books, such as Jacob Riis's *Children of the Poor* and John Spargo's *Bitter Cry of the Children,* drew attention to the plight of many children.[34] At the first meeting of the National Congress of Mothers, Alice Birney, the founding president, called upon women to be good citizens as well as good mothers. Mothers had two responsibilities, she said: "We can work for our own salvation, but we must work for a better social order. . . . Just as man cannot live for himself alone nor can the mother live for the family alone. She must take into her heart all homes, all children, all motherhood."[35] Almost all women's organizations serving children in the late nineteenth and early twentieth centuries explicitly recognized this dual mission. But, they stated, a mother's first responsibility was to her own children. An Iowa manual on organizing and administering mothers' clubs, for example, urged clubs to disband before schools closed for summer vacation so that club work would not interfere with mothers' primary obligations to their own families. Cora Bussey Hillis, author of the Iowa mothers' club manual and leader of social welfare activities, declared, "I must do all this and yet be in my own home the kind of mother whose children will reflect honor on herself and her home."[36]

Even a professional woman like the renowned muckraker Ida Tarbell believed that the chief purpose of higher education for women was to improve their ability to prepare future citizens of the nation. Tarbell, restating the concept of the Republican Mother, declared that the reason for the "revolutionary change in the education of American women" was "the realization that if we were to make real democrats, we must begin with the child, and if we begin with the child, we must begin with the mother." Complaining that women had come to believe "the tools more important than the thing for which they were to use them," Tarbell chided mothers who turned their children over to others for education and women who used their education to campaign for suffrage.[37]

Contemporary views of evolution appeared to confirm what had long been believed about woman's special nature, especially their moral superiority. Darwin himself wrote, "Woman seems to differ from man in mental disposition, chiefly in her greater tenderness and selflessness." Henry Drummond declared that the human mother was the highest product of evolution. Women themselves tended to focus on their spiritual nature and ignore or rebut the message of Darwin and many other male scientists that they were intellectually inferior. Philanthropist Margaret Olivia Sage asserted that women were men's intellectual equals, adding, "God had a purpose in planting high toned and good women in American soil." It was a woman's duty, even more than her right, to help solve the crucial problems of the day.[38]

Women had other reasons for dedicating themselves to the nation's children. Well into the twentieth century it was considered inappropriate for married women to work for money. The 1890 census counted only 4.5 percent of the nation's wives and 2.5 percent of white married women as gainfully employed.[39] New labor-saving devices such as the sewing machine and improved stoves, factory production of goods formerly produced only in the home, low-cost immigrant labor available for household help and childcare, and a steady decline in family size combined to provide many upper- and middle-class urban women with more leisure and more opportunity to escape the home than ever before.[40] Historians debate the extent to which housework became easier during the nineteenth century.[41] They agree, however, that many married women welcomed the opportunity to use their education, experience, energy, and creativity outside the home in pursuit of the deeply rooted ideal of service to others. By leaving their homes to work in the public realm for the betterment of mothers and children, they were not violating but fulfilling a traditional sacred responsibility of American womanhood.

Soon after the Civil War, women's organizations, stronger and more formally structured than ever before, began to proliferate. Most excluded men. The number of church-affiliated organizations continued to grow, but most of the new organizations were secular.[42] Participation in women's clubs, especially those dedicated to child study, parent education, and welfare reform, helped women gain experience and a sense of autonomy in a secure setting as well as a sense of community provided by the pursuit of shared interests. The new women's clubs solicited members by offering them the satisfaction of serving a good cause, learning, and enjoying themselves at the same time.[43] Through the activities of their clubs, women could "regenerate the race and have their own lives enlarged and fructified," contended Andrea Hofer-Proudfoot at the annual meeting of the National Mothers' Congress in 1900.[44]

THE WOMAN'S CHRISTIAN
TEMPERANCE UNION

The Woman's Christian Temperance Union (WCTU) was "the major vehicle through which women developed a changing role for themselves in American society."[45] Since alcoholism was perceived as a threat to the home, female participation in temperance reform was accepted by men as well as women. Established in 1874, the WCTU became the largest and most powerful women's organization the country had yet known. By the 1880s branches existed in all major cities and thousands of smaller communities throughout the Northeast and Midwest, and by the turn of the century, the organization claimed 176,000 members.[46] A nonsectarian organization controlled entirely by women, the WCTU gave significant encouragement to social feminism and reached more women than the suffrage movement during the last quarter of the century.

Regarding alcoholism as a result as well as a cause of social problems, the WCTU embarked on a program of social and political reform of amazing breadth. Its charismatic leader, Frances Willard, suggested the slogan, "Do everything."[47] Following her advice, the organization sought to deal with a wide variety of social problems through charitable work and campaigns for social legislation. By 1896 two-thirds of the WCTU's thirty-seven departments dealt wholly or in major part with non-temperance issues.[48]

The early-nineteenth-century belief in mothers' responsibility for the future of the nation was often expressed in WCTU rhetoric. Describing itself as "organized mother-care," the union promoted its popular slogan "Save the child today and you have saved the nation tomorrow."[49] This maxim foreshadowed the theme of preventing social ills by improving the lives of children that dominated the Progressive Era and the 1920s. The WCTU demonstrated that basing reform on a role traditionally assigned to women made it possible to persuade large numbers of traditional women to engage in radical activities and legitimized these activities to many.

WCTU reform efforts on behalf of children included sponsorship of kindergartens, model facilities for neglected and dependent children, foster and permanent homes for orphans and dependent children, shelters for the care of children of working mothers, and federal aid to education. Regarding kindergartens as an important service for working-class mothers and their children, the WCTU founded its first free kindergarten in 1880 in San Francisco, and, by the 1890s, it was advocating kindergartens as part of the public school system. Willard called the establishment of kindergartens "the greatest theme, next to salvation by faith, which can engage a woman's heart and brain." The WCTU shared with the settlement house movement the belief that poverty was the underlying cause of most social problems, and anticipated by a decade many of the services and reform activities of that movement.[50]

The WCTU was more radical than most women's organizations, including the General Federation of Women's Clubs, which it surpassed in size and power until 1910. It endorsed the ballot for women as a "weapon for the protection of the home" more than a quarter-century before the General Federation did so in 1914. Yet, in some respects, the WCTU was the epitome of Victorian culture. Members wore a white ribbon to symbolize the organization's dedication to social purity and preached reform through moral regeneration. The WCTU failed to recognize how scientific reform in the mantle of science could advance its cause.[51]

THE AMERICAN SOCIAL SCIENCE ASSOCIATION, 1865–1909

The American Social Science Association (ASSA) provided a link between women reformers and empirical investigation. Established in 1865 by a group of Boston reformers, one of them a woman, the association flourished during the 1870s and 1880s and became the most important forerunner of professional social science in the United States. It is described by William Brock as an organization that "attempted to draw together the theoretical, moral, and practical aspects of social policy" and "a monument to the nineteenth-century hope that accumulated knowledge scientifically recorded would provide answers to the most pressing problems of the age."[52] Bureaus of labor statistics, factory inspectors, and railroad commissioners imitated its methods.

At the time of the ASSA's prominence, the term "social science" had a meaning very different from the one it has today. Reform-minded ASSA members identified moral progress with advances in objective knowledge, but their devotion to social reform took precedence over their dedication to science.[53] With few exceptions, however, the new generation of professional social scientists ranked science ahead of reform. By the first decade of the twentieth century, academic "social science" had become transfigured as the social sciences, including political science, economics, and sociology.[54]

ASSA members were particularly interested in inquiry tied to improvement of sanitation, prevention of crime, reform of prisons, treatment of the insane, and employment of the poor. They strongly believed that the results of investigations should be communicated to ordinary people in everyday language, so that they would not "have to hunt social issues" in the colleges. Social science "should come to people where they are, through public lectures, cheap tracts, press, pulpit, popular library, museum, and forum."[55] The subjects investigated by the ASSA harmonized with women reformers' concern with moral issues. The ASSA's conviction that scientific findings should be widely disseminated in simple language was echoed and acted upon by Jane Addams, Julia Lathrop, and other settlement workers.

Thomas Haskell argues that the ASSA and social reformers of the Progressive Era operated from different moral systems based on very different beliefs about the cause of social problems. ASSA members saw a world composed of autonomous individuals, masters of their own fates. Progressive reformers, on the other hand, impressed by the complexities of city life, saw social interdependence and argued that vice and corruption were effects, not causes, of poverty. Instead of trying to change individuals by inculcating habits of thrift, prudence, and self-mastery, Progressives set out to alter the social circumstances that harmed them. This reorientation of social thought, focusing on the power of society rather than the independence of the individual, took place during the watershed decade of the 1890s, and was reflected in professional social science as well as Progressive reform movements.[56]

From its inception, the ASSA demonstrated a strong feminist bias.[57] By 1874 six of the thirteen members of its governing board were women, and the male members tended to promote women's causes, particularly female higher education. During the 1880s women dominated the state affiliates, which had far more members than the national organization, and women were also forming their own social science organizations. Leach argues that "Social Science perspectives colored every facet of the feminist movement and tended to unify the vast array of organizations that appeared after the Civil War."[58]

Both Leach and Haskell comment on the feminist bias of Franklin Sanborn, a founder of the association and its permanent secretary after 1873. "The work of social science is literally women's work," Sanborn wrote.[59] Sanborn's own province was the department of social economy, established in 1873 when he was appointed ASSA's permanent secretary. He characterized social economy as the "feminine gender of political economy" and interpreted it as "synonymous with the cause of the poor."[60] According to feminist May Wright Sewall, women outnumbered men ten to one in the "study of the conditions of the poor and unfortunate."[61] The ASSA provided an institutional setting in which women could undertake empirical investigation, sometimes cooperating with male colleagues, sometimes working independently. Women reformers, who participated in the efforts to establish child study, continued this tradition.[62]

The ASSA sponsored so many new professional organizations that it was often called the "mother of associations." Before long, many of them became more important than their parent and contributed to the rise of academic social science. In decline by 1890, the ASSA held its last meeting in 1909.[63]

CHARITY ORGANIZATION SOCIETIES
AND SCIENTIFIC PHILANTHROPY

During the same years in which the ASSA flourished, charity organization societies became the dominant force in American philanthropy. Modeled on the London Charity Organization, American charity organization societies were first established in the late 1870s and multiplied rapidly during the 1880s and 1890s. By 1904 there were about 150 societies, most in large or medium-sized cities.[64] Members of charity organization societies generally held beliefs similar to those of the ASSA about the causes of poverty, the value of voluntarism, and the importance of the scientific method. The ASSA supported the societies and worked closely with their umbrella organization, the National Conference of Charities and Corrections, established in 1879.[65] Like the ASSA, charity societies focused on reforming individuals rather than society. In 1910 they began to decline. Private charity remained important, however, until the Great Depression created a vast expansion of public relief programs.[66]

Charity organization societies did not grant relief themselves but practiced "scientific philanthropy," which sought to promote cooperation among charity agencies; eliminate fraud, inefficiency, and duplication; and encourage constructive ways of treating poverty.[67] Both the ASSA and the charity organization societies were designed to invigorate and systematize the collection and dissemination of factual information. They assumed that once the facts were known, solutions to problems would follow.[68]

Charitable agencies usually had three components: the board of directors, mostly businessmen; charity workers, usually female (and called social workers after 1910); and "friendly visitors," upper- and middle-class female volunteers who "exemplified the ideals of social feminists." "Friendly visiting" with the poor in their homes, in order to convey sympathy and improve and uplift them, was the core of the movement. When "friendly visitors" shifted their interests to civic reform, suffrage, or other causes, charities were left without a source of volunteers.[69]

Josephine Shaw Lowell, founder of the New York Charity Organization Society, declared that its true aim was to build character, rather than to relieve need. Although scientific philanthropy reflected late-nineteenth-century reverence for efficiency and scientific methodology, it shared with the ASSA the traditional view that poverty is caused by human frailty—weakness of character, body, or intellect. Investigation was considered the keystone of treatment, but, in the long run, investigations by caseworkers undermined traditional assumptions about the poor, as they forced the recognition that such problems as ill health, unemployment, and low wages were caused more by social and economic conditions than by personal inadequacy.[70] Beginning in the late 1880s, the rapid growth of the settlement house movement hastened widespread acceptance of the new view of poverty and a new approach to reform. It also provided women with unique opportunities to gain proficiency in social research.

THE SETTLEMENT HOUSE MOVEMENT:
FROM CHARITY TO SOCIAL JUSTICE

"Redefining womanhood by . . . extension rather than by . . . rejection of the female sphere," Estelle Freedman has suggested, "may be best illustrated by the settlement house movement."[71] The first settlement was Toynbee Hall, established in a London slum in 1884. Five years later Americans had founded six settlement houses, including Chicago's Hull House. Its founder, Jane Addams, soon became the most famous woman in America. By 1900 one hundred settlement houses had been established; by 1910, four hundred.[72]

The American settlement movement differed significantly from its British counterpart. Most British settlements were church-related, whereas most American settlements were nonsectarian. The majority of both British and American settlement workers were college-trained, but British workers were mostly men, while three-fifths of American settlement residents, between 1889 and 1914, were women. American men who joined settlements seldom stayed more than a few years, but women seldom left, and they played a far more important role than men. The American setting was an urban population dominated by immigrants. In 1890, 80 percent of the Chicago population were immigrants or children of immigrants.[73] By 1900 international leadership of the settlement movement had passed to Americans.[74]

Of those enrolled in colleges in 1890, 36 percent were female, and the percentage continued to grow between 1889 and 1914.[75] Nine-tenths of settlement women had been to college.[76] These educated, idealistic women, eager to use their education in a worthy cause, found that settlements gave them experience with the urban poor, fellowship with other women, training in social research and social policy, and opportunities to use their education in the service of reform. Unlike charity workers, many settlement women were motivated by political goals and tended to be "more neighborly than charitable . . . more democratic and fraternalistic."[77]

Addams defined a settlement as "an institution attempting to learn from life itself."[78] Most settlement workers lived among immigrants in over-crowded cities, observing at first hand the effects on children's lives of slums, child labor, poor sanitation, and other adverse conditions associated with poverty. Because their experiences were very different from those of charity workers, they reached very different conclusions about how to reform society. They demanded concrete efforts by public agencies to improve the social and economic environments in which children lived.[79]

After 1900 the term "social work" began to replace "scientific philanthropy."[80] The settlement point of view penetrated the charity movement by around 1902, and eight years later it was dominant.[81] Addams, elected president of the National Conference of Charities and Corrections (NCCC) in 1909, remarked in her presidential address, "Charity and Social Justice," that reform had benefited enormously from the recent union of charity workers, moved to action by "pity for the poor, " and settlement workers, "fired by a hatred of injustice."[82] She insisted, however, that efforts to reform individuals and help from private charities would not solve the problems of poverty. Benevolence was "totally inadequate"; positive government action, essential.[83]

Settlement workers provoked a radical rethinking of the role of philanthropy, which had fostered a double goal: social service and social action. By 1905 social action began to seem more important than social service, and the goal of reform became prevention rather than cure.[84] This new approach to reform initiated a new approach to investigation, the social survey, which soon enjoyed widespread use by settlement workers and other urban reformers.[85]

THE SOCIAL SURVEY

The social survey became the most important new technique for documenting causal connections between the urban industrial environment and poverty, child labor, crime, and other urban problems. It built upon methods of investigation used by the ASSA and others during the last part of the nineteenth century, but with important differences. Unwilling to rely on broad statistical aggregates developed by others, survey researchers collected first-hand data through field work, thereby obtaining detailed information about individuals, families, and households within limited geographic areas. Interviewing residents in their homes, they recorded information about household composition, occupations, incomes, expenditures, school attendance, living conditions, diets, health, sanitation, and special problems.[86] The American social survey owed much to the British model, particularly to Charles Booth's seventeen-volume study of poverty, *The Life and Labour of the People in London* (1889–1903), the first great empirical study in the social survey tradition.[87] Three outstanding early examples of the social survey in America were the pathbreaking *Hull-House Maps and Papers: A Presentation of Nationalities and Wages in a Congested District of Chicago* (1896), a collaborative effort by residents of Hull House; W. E. B. Du Bois's *The Philadelphia Negro* (1899); and the six-volume *Pittsburgh Survey* (1909–11) sponsored by the Russell Sage Foundation, an agency founded and directed by a woman.[88] By 1927 the Russell Sage had completed 2,775 surveys.[89] In 1922 the sponsors of the Pittsburgh Survey changed the name of the magazine with which they had been affiliated since 1909 from *Charities and the Commons* to the *Survey*.

The social survey was distinguished from former methods of social investigation by purpose as well as by method. Its intention, always made explicit, was to inform, in order to promote social action and change public policy.[90] The Chicago sociologist Robert Park considered the survey a method of publicity rather than of research, a higher form of journalism.[91] Most academic social scientists, however, valued objectivity over reform and thought the two were incompatible. To them, the social survey was not real science.

Social surveys, nevertheless, gave settlement women a way to acquire training and professional status in social science before such opportunities existed in universities. The University of Chicago, which established the first department of sociology, was founded three years after Hull House.[92] Furthermore, most social science departments hired no women, or gave the few who were hired little chance for advancement.[93] Settlements functioned as a kind of graduate school in which women wishing to practice social science were able to gain experience and acquire skill. Katherine Sklar suggests that the masterful execution of surveys, beginning with *Hull-House Maps and Papers,* put Hull House residents on an equal footing with male academic scientists. Leading male scholars, including John Dewey, George Herbert Mead, Henry Demarest Lloyd, and Richard Ely, welcomed them as allies.[94]

Social surveys also offered women unique opportunities to pursue their own reform agendas. Sklar quotes Florence Kelley to show how female social scientists promulgated the view that women's unique qualities were essential to the new social sciences. Kelley declared in 1882, "While the science of man was a science of wealth . . . and self-interest, there was slight inducement for women to touch it. The new social science has humane interest, and can never be complete without help from women. . . . Any attempt by the part of the race to explain phenomena produced by complementary beings must be inadequate."[95] Female social scientists who worked in settlements and other reform organizations distinguished themselves by pursuing topics of special interest to women and issues related to their moral vision of social change. Julia Lathrop and Grace Abbott, first and second chiefs of the Children's Bureau, used survey techniques to correlate children's problems with poverty and, in Abbott's case, to document the effects of the Great Depression on family and children. The social survey offered more to women than to men, Sklar suggests, because it "enabled a generation of college-trained women to forge life-long commitments to social science–based reform organizations that were independent of the political climate in universities that sometimes interfered with the freedom of academic male social scientists."[96]

THE OVERLAPPING WORLDS OF FEMALE
SOCIAL REFORMERS AND MALE SCIENTISTS

The social survey movement, like the ASSA, illustrates cooperation between women and men in advocating and using social science research as an essential basis for reform. In their work together, professional men ratified the credentials of female social scientists while women reformers endorsed the service claims of men.[97]

The social sciences and the behavioral sciences, psychology and psychiatry, had very different origins, but the social reformers who helped to establish child study drew upon both traditions. The new science of psychology was the only "social science," as it was then labeled, to receive full professional recognition before the 1890s.[98] During that decade, Hall placed the child at the center of psychology, launched the popular phase of his child study movement, and sought to use science in the service of reform, all of which made him a natural ally of women child welfare reformers, and newly organized mothers. The support Hall and these women gave to each other, discussed in the next chapters, marked the beginning of joint efforts by women reformers and the first generation of male behavioral scientists to establish scientific child study.[99]

Chapter 2 G. Stanley Hall and

the Child Study Movement

THE BABY BIOGRAPHY

A new scientific psychology, modeled on the physical sciences, emerged in Europe in the 1860s, flourished in Germany, and reached America in the 1870s. It was the product of evolutionary biology, the empirical tradition in philosophy, and experimental studies of the physiology of perception and sensation. Now called early experimental psychology, it was based in the laboratory, where researchers studied conscious reactions to touch, sights, and sounds. Since subjects had to be aware of and able to articulate their inner experience, animals, illiterate or abnormal persons, and children were excluded. Wilhelm Wundt, who founded the first psychological laboratory in Leipzig in 1879, warned that the results of experiments on very young children were "wholly untrustworthy." The belief that the mental life of adults can be understood only through the analysis of children's minds, Wundt declared, is an "error," the exact opposite of the "true position."[1]

Many parents and some scientists ignored Wundt's advice and recorded observations of children in "baby biographies."[2] Charles

Darwin provided a scientific model by studying his first child, born in 1839, but he did not publish the study until 1877. He recorded observations on the emergence of vision, winking, anger, fear, pleasure, affection, shyness, language, and sympathy. "I had not the smallest conception that there was so much in a five month old baby," he declared. He also observed his nine subsequent children "at every opportunity" as well as other children.[3] Concentrating on instinctive and emotional behavior, he compared European children with children from primitive societies and with the infants of orangutans, chimpanzees, and other primates. These comparative studies were included in his *Expression of the Emotions in Man and Animals*.[4]

In his time, Darwin's work stimulated the study of animals far more than the study of children. Objecting to this trend, Emily Talbot, secretary of the Boston chapter of the American Social Science Association (ASSA), announced in 1881 that the association's Education Department had issued a register to encourage parents to record observations of their very young children, in the hope that such observations would be of value to educators and psychologists. This was the first of several initiatives by women for the study of children on a broad scale. Darwin wrote Talbot, approving the project, and suggesting the kinds of inquiries that might "elicit information useful to science." Other scientists reacted with indifference or ridicule. The register was dropped, but not before it was widely covered by the press.[5]

Wilhelm Preyer, a German physiologist and a pioneer in the study of behavioral embryology, was also drawn to the study of children by the birth of his first child. His three-year study of his son, published as *Die Seele des Kindes,* was the first full-scale baby biography by a scientist to receive wide acclaim. Translated into English by G. Stanley Hall, Preyer's book was published in the United States as *The Mind of the Child.*[6] Even before Darwin, many parents had kept records of children's development. Now it appeared that such records might be of scientific value. Preyer's book inspired Millicent Shinn, a member of the Association of Collegiate Alumnae (later the American Association of University Women), to undertake careful study of her niece for her master's thesis.[7] Published as "Notes on the Development of a Child," it stimulated others throughout the country to keep diary records of infants and young children.[8]

G. STANLEY HALL'S EARLY CAREER

G. Stanley Hall was among those who struggled to free American psychology from philosophy and religion and to establish experimental psychology in the newly emerging universities. At Harvard he studied under William James and physiologist Henry Bowditch, who pioneered in measuring the physical growth of children.[9] In 1878 Hall received the first Ph.D. in psychology awarded in the United States. Like many other American scholars and physicians, he went abroad for two years of additional training, studying mainly under leading German philosophers, physiologists, and psychologists.[10] Hall returned to the United States in 1880, determined to become the leader of American experimental psychology. For a time he considered medicine as a profession, but in 1881 he was appointed to a lectureship at Harvard in philosophy and pedagogy. In Europe J. F. Herbart, later known to Americans as a leader of the kindergarten movement, was urging the establishment of scientific pedagogy. The enthusiastic response to Hall's Harvard lectures suggested that scientific pedagogy might be a way to earn his living while awaiting an opportunity in psychology. Unlike scientific psychology, scientific pedagogy could hardly ignore children, and was already studying them empirically in Germany.[11]

Hall's conversion to the cause of scientific pedagogy coincided with a groundswell of support for school reform in the United States. Education traditionally had been the chief route through which Americans hoped to realize the promise of democracy. By the late nineteenth century, the schools had become increasingly inadequate to the task of preparing a heterogeneous population of children to function in the complex and fluid urban industrial society that was emerging. Immigration from peasant cultures in Southern and Eastern Europe surged in the 1890s. The assimilation and acculturation of children of the new immigrants, with their diverse languages, religions, and customs, and little or no experience with democracy, was a complicated and difficult task for the public schools. The passage of compulsory school laws between 1870 and 1890 made the schools responsible for educating children who previously would have been working for pay. The schools were also charged with helping to realize the American promise of equal opportunity to rise in the social hierarchy.[12]

Hall's conviction that social progress could not be achieved through education placed him well outside the mainstream of late-nineteenth-century reform. A social Darwinist, he believed that helping the poor, the mentally or physically handicapped, or other "unfit" persons to survive would interfere with progress through natural selection. He argued that social reform programs were not only unavailing but could retard social progress.[13]

The antireform bias of Hall's social Darwinism was mitigated, however, by his belief that evolutionary progress could be encouraged by modifying institutions to foster the expression of individual talents and interests and by his neo-Lamarckian faith in the heritability of educational benefits. Hall shared the views of romantic educators, a small but active reform group within the National Education Association (NEA). During the 1870s American disciples of J. H. Pestalozzi, Friedrich Froebel, and other European romantic educators established kindergartens and attempted to reform educational practice in all grades.[14] Education, they said, should be adapted to children's capability, curiosity, and spontaneity because such methods were more apt to succeed than those that tried to impose society's goals. Trusting and following the child's natural impulses and interests automatically produces the good citizen.[15] When Hall began his efforts to promote scientific pedagogy, romantic concepts of childhood had influenced American child-rearing practices but had made little headway in the schools, which often continued to reflect Calvinist doctrine in their formality, rigidity, authoritarianism, and moralism. The accepted function of the schools was to impose a fixed body of knowledge and moral principles on the child through exhortation and discipline. Francis Parker, the leading American exponent of European romantic educational practice, had introduced its methods into the school system of Quincy, Massachusetts, but the experiment was terminated in 1880 after a five-year trial.[16]

THE CONTENTS OF CHILDREN'S MINDS

Unlike earlier romantic educators, who thought they already understood the nature of children, Hall was convinced that empirical knowledge of what children believed, knew, and felt was essential. He therefore decided to undertake a study, modeled on German precedents, of four hundred children entering public schools. He adopted both the German questionnaire method and the German goal of finding out how much information city-raised children had acquired before they entered school. Interviewers asked the children 134 questions about topics including plants and animals, numbers and geometric concepts, astronomy, and local geography. Hall's questionnaires, covering a broader range of subjects than the German studies, were designed to discover what children felt as well as what they knew. They included questions on children's beliefs, imagery, and concepts of right and wrong, and elicited samples of children's drawings and stories. Hall took pains to make the methodology as rigorous as possible by pre-testing the questions, training four kindergarten teachers in interviewing techniques, and dividing his data into subsets in order to test their reliability. The results showed that, like children in Germany, American children were generally ignorant about the subjects dealt with by the questionnaire and that city children were more ignorant than country children.[17]

Hall's article based on this study, "The Contents of Children's Minds Upon Entering School," launched the American child study movement.[18] Along with Preyer's *Mind of the Child,* it is often cited as the beginning of the scientific study of children. Although not the first empirical studies of children, these two works were vastly superior to earlier research. They stimulated and served as models for similar studies by both scientists and lay persons. Following the publication of his study, Hall discussed scientific pedagogy before receptive audiences at NEA meetings. He also issued a thirteen-page pamphlet for teachers with instructions on how to obtain and record information about school children through direct observation and questions addressed to the children, their mothers, or their nurses. The pamphlet proposed the creation of a scientific foundation to encourage educators and teachers to study children and to promote educational reforms. American enthusiasm for educational reform, the rising status of the new scientific psychology, and the professional status scientific pedagogy could bestow on teachers made Hall's message highly appealing.[19]

Hall himself, however, soon lost interest in educational reform. In 1882 a three-year appointment as lecturer in psychology and pedagogy at Johns Hopkins University seemed to bring leadership in experimental psychology within his reach. At Hopkins he founded one of America's first psychological laboratories in 1883 and was appointed to the first American chair in psychology in 1884.[20] Child study, scientific pedagogy, and educational reform quickly became peripheral interests. He did not attend meetings of the NEA in 1889 and 1890, published only two brief articles on the mass of data collected by his disciples, and continuously made no pronouncements about child study that might alienate the positivist scientists among whom he was then making his career. The first issue of *Pedagogical Seminary,* an educational journal he founded in 1891, contained no articles on child study.[21]

Hall's career as a scientific psychologist did not go well. Failing to establish a psychology department at Johns Hopkins, he left in 1888 to become president of newly established Clark University, in order to create a university dedicated to pure science. Pedagogy was omitted from the curriculum, and his attempt to make Clark the leading center for experimental psychology also ended in failure. Three years after its founding, two-thirds of its faculty and three-fourths of its students left, most of them for the newly founded University of Chicago.[22]

In spite of these disappointments, Hall achieved much eminence as an organizer, founding the *American Journal of Psychology* in 1887, and organizing the American Psychological Association and becoming its first president in 1892. Resuming his attendance at NEA meetings in 1891 and 1892, Hall found that during his absence child study and educational reform had gained in popularity, in large part because of his lingering influence. The enthusiastic reception he received encouraged him to return to the child study movement in pursuit of the success that continued to elude him in experimental psychology. In 1893 he threw himself wholeheartedly into leadership of the movement, apparently motivated at least as much by the hope of bolstering his faltering career as by dedication to the scientific study of children.[23]

NEW GOALS, 1893–1898

"Hall's child study movement" is the conventional label for a series of efforts under Hall's leadership that spanned more than a quarter century. The movement embraced a shifting coalition of individuals and organizations with diverse, often conflicting goals, held together by the common interest of the participants in the empirical study of children for practical ends. Hall himself most vividly described it: "It is a nondescript, and in some sense, an unparalleled movement—partly psychology, partly anthropology, partly medico-hygiene. It is closely related at every step to the study of instincts in animals, and to the rites and beliefs of primitive peoples; and it has a distinct ethico-philosophical aspect—partly what a recent writer classed as the higher biology—with a spice of folk-lore and of religious evolution, sometimes with an alloy of gossip and nursery tradition, but possessing a broad practical side in the pedagogy of all stages. It has all the advantages and the less grave disadvantages of its many-sidedness."[24]

The Hall who led the new movement was not the aspiring experimental psychologist of the 1880s, who had preached a different message. Child study was now the center of his interest and career. His new goals and extravagant claims contrasted sharply with his formerly cautious utterances. Child study's chief purpose, Hall declared, was not scientific pedagogy but the reconstruction of psychology in order to encompass the study of children of all ages; its model was evolutionary biology rather than physical science. Eventually, Hall hoped, his version of genetic psychology (not fully articulated until 1896) would relegate much of existing adult psychology to history's "ash heap."[25]

Hall also proposed a bold new reform goal: knowledge emerging from the scientific study of children should not be used to transform schools alone, but all institutions affecting children, in ways that would encourage free expression of their natural tendencies and interests.[26] The movement was "not only an educational renaissance but a scientific reconstruction that aims at the top and is the salvation and ultimate . . . aim of creation and of history." Hall no longer limited himself to experimental methods but used any method that could help to realize his purpose. He would lead the movement as scientist and also, according to Dorothy Ross, as prophet, preacher, poet, and humanist.[27]

To Hall, the methods of experimental psychology were restrictive and tedious. He had done "much patient experimental work . . . in Germany and . . . at Johns Hopkins . . . under the stimulation of circumstances rather than the impulses of his own nature," Thorndike observed.[28] William James agreed with Hall's view of experimental methodology, pointing out that "the method takes patience to the utmost and could hardly have been born in a country whose natives could be bored." Experimental psychology's insistence on a neutral, objective, value-free approach was even less compatible than its methods with Hall's expansive, exuberant temperament and his need to pursue religious and ethical goals.[29]

EVOLUTIONARY THEORY

In Darwinian evolutionary theory, as it was then understood and misunderstood, Hall found both a theoretical framework and a methodology that suited his own nature and goals. Although Darwin shared with introspective psychologists an interest in the contents of the mind, he did not equate consciousness with mind. In contrast to those who, like Wundt, believed that the contents of the mind could be discovered only through the description of inner experience by articulate human adults, Darwin wrote at length on the origins of intelligence in plants and earthworms.[30] He believed that the emotional states and cognitive processes of animals and children could be inferred from careful observation of their behavior.[31] Darwin's claim that all of life—animal and human, mind as well as body—was the product of the same process of evolution by natural selection meant that human behavior could be studied by the methods of natural science.[32] His focus on how things came to be as they are through gradual change, as well as his specific interest in the study of infants, gave legitimacy to research on the development of the human mind from birth to death.

Darwin's interest in the study of the emotions was particularly important to Hall. As we have seen, Hall's "Contents of Children's Minds" included observations on children's feelings as well as their knowledge.[33] He had subsequently come to believe that adult psychology as well as child psychology should concentrate on the study of instincts, feelings, emotions, and unconscious processes. His child study questionnaires between 1894 and 1898 covered a great variety of emotional topics, including crying, laughing, pity, anger, envy, and jealousy.[34]

Hall wanted to reconcile the concepts of romantic poets, philosophers, and educators with evolutionary theory.[35] As a farm lad, he had learned to love nature; as a schoolboy, he had been attracted to romantic literature. In Germany he had responded to German neo-idealist philosophers, and in both Germany and America, he had been influenced by romantic educators. William James said of experimental psychologists, "They mean business, not chivalry."[36] However, Hall made a place for chivalry in his interpretation of evolution. What appealed was not so much Darwin's own works as their interpretation by writers such as George John Romanes and Henry Drummond, who elaborated the role of emotions in a way that was closer to romanticism than to Darwinism.[37] In 1894, for example, Drummond declared that "altruistic love" was more important than natural selection in the struggle for survival. He extolled the human mother as the highest product of evolution.[38]

HALL'S GENETIC PSYCHOLOGY

Hall's career is a particularly clear and vivid example of the interaction among the cultural climate, the scientist's personality, and scientific practice. Hall declared that a psychologist should love life. (Some of his critics thought he loved life more than science.) He rarely allowed the lack of solid evidence to keep him from proclaiming as new scientific discoveries his revisions of familiar philosophic and religious concepts. Since Hall believed that science revealed God's design, perhaps he also believed that he was not violating the requirements of science but merely anticipating its discoveries.[39]

The genetic psychology Hall presented in 1896 was based not on Darwin's ideas about adaptation and evolution through natural selection, but on the theory of German scientist Ernst Haeckel. Haeckel insisted that individual development recapitulates the evolutionary path of the species.[40] Hall's genetic psychology appealed to an analogy between ontogeny and phylogeny; understanding one would provide the key to understanding the other. He believed that human behavior is largely determined by unconscious impulses, inherited from distant ancestors, that make their appearance throughout childhood, recreating at different stages of development feelings and behaviors experienced by primitive man during corresponding epochs of the primordial past. To encourage rather than suppress children's expression of these vestiges of the past was necessary for the healthy development of the child and, therefore, for the survival of the species.[41] The study of children, Hall explained, would enhance understanding of phyletic change. The study of animals, living primitive peoples, and prehistoric remains, would, in turn, provide insights into the child's nature.

To Hall, all stages of childhood were equally worthy of study, but since his efforts had failed to establish a home for child study outside the NEA, his main focus continued to be the school child.[42] The high school was firmly established as part of the public school system in the late nineteenth and early twentieth centuries, a time of considerable interest in youth as a stage of development. Partly for these reasons, and partly because Hall found adolescence to be "the most interesting and the most important phase of childhood," he began a ten-year study of adolescence in 1894.[43] His two-volume work *Adolescence: Its Psychology and Its Relation to Physiology, Anthropology, Sociology, Sex, Crime, Religion, and Education* (1904) presented a complete synthesis of his genetic psychology.[44]

During the mid-1880s Hall sent fifteen to twenty thousand questionnaires a year to more than eight hundred teachers, school superintendents, and principals, who in turn administered them to twenty thousand children in 1894–85 and to eighty thousand the following year.[45] Although the responses yielded interesting and suggestive data about children, most psychologists believed them to be unreliable, and the data from thousands of unqualified observers could not be quantified. Hall, now careless about his methodology, was criticized for his sloppy procedures and loss of control over his lay researchers.

Not until 1902 did Hall try to use his questionnaire data to test his hypotheses about the relationship between stages in the evolution of the species and the development of the child. In doing so, he only demonstrated the weakness of his theory, his method, and his ability to conceptualize.[46] Through observational studies, however, Hall and his followers were able to show some age-related patterns. Studies of rates of physical growth, development of muscles, and other aspects of physical development proved fruitful because fairly accurate measurement was possible in these areas.[47] Although Hall and his colleagues observed many children, they studied only twelve children systematically.[48] Hall failed to employ the experimental method even in circumstances in which it would have been highly appropriate. He never tested children in a learning situation, as John Dewey did in his experimental laboratory school at the University of Chicago, and as Thorndike later did with older students at Teachers College at Columbia University.

In addition to Hall and Dewey, the eminent psychologist James Mark Baldwin was also studying children. Baldwin, who articulated his genetic psychology in *Mental Development in the Child and the Race* and *Social and Ethical Interpretations of Mental Development*, undoubtedly would have had a strong influence on early developmental psychology in the United States (as he has had on later developmental psychology) if a personal scandal had not forced him to abandon American academic life in 1909.[49] Baldwin's theoretical work anticipated much of Jean Piaget's theory of cognitive and moral development and influenced Russian child developmentalist Lev Vygotsky.[50]

HALL'S GENETIC PSYCHOLOGY REPUDIATED

When Hall resumed leadership of the child study movement in 1893, he still had the aura of a great scientist. During the 1880s he had applied recapitulation theory to only one subject, children's religious development. During the mid-1890s, however, he threw caution to the winds. At a time when recapitulation theory was losing favor and other scientists were struggling to make psychology more quantitative, reliable, and professional, Hall made recapitulation the cornerstone of his philosophy, even encouraging nonscientists to participate in scientific investigations. While other scientists were cloistered in their laboratories and academic departments, he traveled to forty states and gave more than 2,500 public lectures.[51] At a time when the study of children was out of favor among most psychologists, he dared to propose that it become psychology's chief task. And while the application of psychology to social problems was still untested and generally regarded as unprofessional, Hall made grandiose claims for the potential achievements of reform based on knowledge of children. By 1898 even colleagues like Thorndike, who had been sympathetic to or at least tolerant of the child study movement, had lost patience with Hall.

Hugo Munsterberg, a German-born and -educated experimental psychologist at Harvard, led the attack. He summed up his distaste for child study in one terse sentence: he himself "would love his children but never study them."[52] The most disturbing aspect of child study research for most psychologists was the use of untrained lay persons to administer the questionnaires, a "travesty of science, according to Thorndike."[53] Baldwin and James joined Munsterberg in criticizing Hall's child study in the popular press and at teachers' meetings, asserting that it was not only bad science but harmful to educational reform.[54] After these attacks Hall's child studies waned, and by the turn of the century, they were no longer consequential.

Hall replied to psychologists like Munsterberg, who believed scientific knowledge could be obtained only through systematic experimentation, by arguing that the naturalistic, comparative methods of evolutionary biology were particularly suited to the study of the diversity and complexity of childhood, a point of view increasingly endorsed by developmentalists today. If psychological acts have meaning and value "only when . . . sharply demarcated within water-tight compartments from art, history, physiology, and life itself," Hall argued, the result would be a "psychology devitalized or versus life." His own conception of psychology was "as different from all this as science is from epistemology or metaphysics." Admitting that the popularity of child study had attracted a "crowd of camp followers" whose enthusiasm prompted them "to attempt things beyond their power," Hall suggested that "perhaps the wheat and the tares might best grow together a while longer, lest modest merit be discouraged; and I even fail to see why it is more absurd to show a baby to a class in psychology than to one of medical students."[55]

Both James and Thorndike valued naturalistic methods and lay participation. Psychiatrist Adolph Meyer used attendants in mental hospitals to gather information, just as Hall had used parents and teachers. It was not Hall's naturalistic method nor his use of lay informants that these scientists objected to but his carelessness and excesses.[56] His interpretation of recapitulation was, one scholar notes, "so absurd as to make satire unnecessary."[57]

OPPOSITION TO CHILD STUDY

In the closing years of the nineteenth century, scientists and nonscientists alike derided the very idea that children could and should be studied scientifically. When the ASSA announced its register of parents' observations of children, a lecturer at Yale University's Sheffield School of Science scornfully remarked: "The registers will go like la grippe into every house. Mothers, sisters, aunts, grandfathers, of course, possibly even fathers, will engage in the scientific study of infant intelligence and the merits of the newly born generation will be rolled into the fold of a permanent record with as much precision and certainty as we used to operate last year's puzzle of the little-pigs-in-the-clover. Every properly constituted university will have its cradle of science and its baby chair of philosophy."[58]

Many opposed child study of any kind, even during the peak of its popularity. In the 1890s Hall encountered objections to the weighing and measuring of school children.[59] A "public furor" was raised by Franz Boas's psychometric measurements of school children in 1891. Thorndike, working under James in 1896, was denied access to the orphans he hoped to study, even though he had planned only to ask questions and reward correct answers with candy. He substituted chickens for children.[60] Hall often commented on what he considered exaggerated fears of harming children by studying them, ridiculing a prominent New York daily that had "accused a leading professor of Columbia of subjecting his own children to research as if it were a new and diabolical species of torture."[61]

Public antipathy to child study before 1920 is not easily explained. During this period, almost all research on children was observational. "Experimental" research usually meant something similar to that proposed by Thorndike, rather than the laboratory experiments of John Watson and other psychologists after World War I. In his famous experiments on "Little Albert," Watson, the first psychologist to use children as "experimental subjects," inflicted painful stimuli on the baby in order to demonstrate his theory of conditioning.[62] Why these experiments aroused so little criticism is puzzling in view of the hostile reactions to observational studies. Numerous letters from parents and physicians protested the 1918 campaign of the Children's Bureau to weigh and measure babies and preschool children. Parents may have been less concerned with the inhumane treatment of a few unknown children than with research they thought might somehow threaten their control over the upbringing of their own children.[63]

NEW APPROACHES IN EXPERIMENTAL PSYCHOLOGY: EDUCATIONAL PSYCHOLOGY, MENTAL TESTING, AND FUNCTIONALISM

During the 1880s and most of the 1890s, Hall was regarded as a bold innovator, the apostle of scientific psychology, pedagogy, and child study, the esteemed founder of a psychological laboratory, professional journals, and new institutions. He cleared a new path that attracted diverse followers: psychologists, psychiatrists, physicians, physical anthropologists, educators, social workers, and parents. By 1900, however, Hall seemed mired in the past, unable or unwilling to adapt to new developments in experimental psychology.

In the 1880s experimental psychology was an infant science in the United

States. By 1895 twenty-four psychological laboratories had been established in the United States, more than in all of Europe, making American psychology primarily a laboratory science. By 1900 experimental psychology had more followers in America than in Germany.[64] Between 1885 and 1918 more than half the doctoral degrees granted in the sciences in the United States were in psychology.[65] The American Psychological Association had thirty-one members at its founding in 1892. By 1910 it had 222.[66] New laboratory methods used to study children of high school and college age were not widely applied to babies and young children until the 1920s.

The transformation of psychology into a quantitative laboratory science was especially rapid in educational psychology. In spite of disagreements with Hall, Thorndike, who founded this field, remained an active and sympathetic participant in the child study movement for many years. He declared that although "child study has few exact statements as yet, [this] is due to the incompetence or thoughtlessness of its students and not to the nature of the subject."[67]

Thorndike studied first with James and later with James McKeen Cattell, who was testing the mental capacities of Columbia students in the 1890s. When Thorndike joined Teachers College in 1901, he sought to measure and account for differences in learning achievement rather than learning capacity.[68] Hall and other psychologists were asking the right questions but getting the wrong answers, he thought.[69] Thorndike looked for better answers through experimental work on animal learning, applying statistical methods developed by Darwin's cousin Francis Galton and his colleagues Karl Pearson and Charles Spearman.[70] His *Educational Psychology* departed from Hall's work in important ways.[71]

To Hall the basis of learning was repetition. Thorndike's "law of effect" stressed the importance of success and failure, reward and punishment, satisfaction and annoyance.[72] According to Thorndike, his law of effect refuted both Hall's recapitulation theory and faith in genetic determinism. What has occurred in phylogeny need not be repeated in ontogeny, Thorndike said, and genetic differences could be overcome by social engineering.[73]

In some ways, John Dewey's ideas were more compatible with Hall's than with Thorndike's.[74] Like Hall, under whom he had studied for two years at Johns Hopkins, Dewey recognized the limitations of laboratory science.[75] He shared Hall's romantic views of the importance of discovering and liberating the natural, uncorrupted child but differed strongly on the goal of education and its potential for reform.[76] Hall believed that the liberation of the natural child would foster individual expression; Dewey, that "education is the fundamental method of social progress and reform."[77] Dewey's *The School and Soci-*

ety (1901), an account of his experiences in his experimental school in Chicago, was a plea for education to take account of the changing environment and shape it for the better. According to historian Henry May, "The book glows with the excitement of the new century and its possibilities."[78]

Dewey believed that schools should motivate children to pursue social goals and develop the sense of community necessary to the proper functioning of a democracy. By 1910 most progressive educational reformers agreed with Dewey's view, rather than with Hall's position that good citizens are produced by helping the young to express and fulfill their individuality. By then Dewey had moved from Chicago to Columbia, which, under his and Thorndike's influence, produced more educators and educational psychologists than Clark University. According to Ross, "this shift of educational power sealed the death of the child study movement."[79]

The French psychologist Alfred Binet published more than two hundred studies in experimental, developmental, educational, and social psychology between 1890 and 1911, but most of his work was neglected or misunderstood by Americans, who knew him primarily as the father of the IQ test.[80] The intelligence scale supplanted the mental tests developed by Galton and Cattell.[81] Henry H. Goddard translated the scale and used it to test mentally retarded children in 1910, and William Healy also began using it that year in his research on juvenile delinquents. Terman's 1916 adaptation of the scale for American use launched the American mental testing movement. Mental testing was highly unusual in that it was applied to children first, adults later. Its use to classify army recruits during World War I seemed to demonstrate psychology's practical value and played a crucial role in gaining acceptance for the study of children, as well as for applied psychology, after the war.[82] Hall had reluctantly permitted Goddard and Terman to experiment with its methods. But his distaste for mental testing persisted. Due to its use, he declared, "Child study has increased in accuracy, method, and definiteness of result but has, at the same time, greatly narrowed its field."[83]

FUNCTIONALISM: THE TRANSFORMATION
OF EXPERIMENTAL PSYCHOLOGY INTO
AN AMERICAN SCIENCE

Experimental psychology began as a science well suited to the intellectual climate of Germany—"abstract, authoritarian and philosophical," but Hall was able to accommodate it to nineteenth-century American romanticism by drawing on the recapitulation version of evolutionary theory.[84] James and Dewey found another way to make both psychology and evolution consistent with American values. They drew upon Darwin's central concept—adaptation by natural selection—to transform the structural school of Wundtian psychology into a distinctly American "functional psychology" that served democratic purposes and became a sharp spur to twentieth-century Progressivism.[85]

The American version of structural psychology, whose chief apostle was Edward B. Titchener of Cornell University, sought to analyze the mind by distinguishing and describing its basic elements.[86] Functionalism derived its name from its emphasis on the functions of the mind in enabling humans to adapt to their environments. James's and Dewey's view of adaptation turned Social Darwinism on its head and undermined the fatalism of many Social Darwinists. Because human beings are endowed with mind, they argued, they are not merely passive victims of the inexorable forces of evolution, but are capable of dealing with their environment actively and creatively and of changing it to their own benefit. For James, good "was not something to be contemplated but something to be brought to pass."[87]

Hall's genetic psychology legitimized the concepts of romantic philosophy and Social Darwinism, but functional psychology restated, in scientific terms, the beliefs and attitudes of the eighteenth-century American Enlightenment. Derived in part from the concepts of John Locke, the American Enlightenment embraced the idea that human nature is plastic at birth, that human institutions as well as human nature are shaped by the physical and social environment, and that human beings are capable of reforming human nature and human institutions by changing their environment. Merle Curti has suggested that Locke's environmentalism became an essential ingredient of American democratic philosophy partly because it was consonant with the American experience: "The conquest of the physical environment seemed to be evidence of the human ability to arrange institutions."[88] Functional psychology developed at a time when Americans were ripe for a psychology and a philosophy that justified vigorous action to reconstruct society and restored faith in the possibility of social progress. They were also glad to be told that science could solve practical problems.

PRAGMATISM, PROGRESSIVE REFORM, AND CHILD STUDY

For James and Dewey, philosophy and psychology were intertwined; functionalism merged with their philosophical theories to become pragmatism, which maintained that the worth of ideas was measured by their usefulness in solving human problems. James and Dewey differed, however, in their interpretation of pragmatism. James was primarily interested not in a philosophy of social reform but in "an empirical, experimental psychology which acknowledged human effort in the bettering of life."[89] To James, pragmatism was a philosophy of individualism, of "purpose, hope and will." Dewey's instrumentalism transformed pragmatism from a philosophy of individualism into one of social consciousness. Instrumentalism proclaimed that ideas could be an effective instrument for changing the world.

Pragmatism became the philosophical underpinning of the Progressive Era and by 1914 had become a popular doctrine with profound effects on education, science, philosophy, politics, and American society as a whole.[90] Functionalism, instrumentalism, and pragmatism transformed Darwinism into a "gospel of social reform."[91] Historians of early child study tend to focus on scientists who specialized in studying children and to ignore or neglect philosopher-scientists and generalists, such as James and Dewey, whose influence was indirect but profound. Psychological functionalism and philosophical pragmatism provided an important impetus to child welfare reform. The pragmatists' belief that investigation is a necessary prelude to action also encouraged scientific child study. Pragmatists proposed research on children that emphasized the impact of the environment and the beneficial results that could be brought about by the combined efforts of many individuals.

HALL'S FINAL YEARS AND HIS LEGACY

By 1909 Hall was no longer in the mainstream of experimental psychology, but he confounded those who thought him outmoded. In a daring move that looked toward the future, he introduced Freud to America, using Clark University's twentieth anniversary to sponsor a conference featuring Freud and other renowned scholars from Europe and America.[92]

Hall's romantic view of the child conflicted with Freud's view of him as a "little savage," and his emphasis on the child's inheritance of instincts from distant ancestors differed significantly from Freud's focus on interfamily psychodynamics. But they agreed on the importance of emotions and on psychopathology. Hall conceded that evolutionary theory could not explain everything, and he accepted psychoanalytic theories as viable alternatives, declaring that "realizing the limitations and qualifications of the recapitulation theory in the biological field, I am now convinced that its psychogenetic applications have a method of their own."[93]

By providing a hospitable climate for Freud's first lectures to Americans, and by continuing to interpret and popularize psychoanalytic theory, Hall powerfully influenced the future scientific study of children in the United States.[94] Although Hall was the only American psychologist of his time to be strongly affected by psychoanalysis, several American psychiatrists, including Adolph Meyer, William Alanson White, and William Healy, were influenced by Freud, as were the psychiatric social workers in the child guidance clinics.

From 1910 until his death in 1924, Hall continued to speak and write on child study, but it was no longer his chief interest. His autobiography, *Life and Confessions of a Scientist* contained little about his child study movement.[95] New leaders had taken the scientific study of children in directions Hall was neither willing nor able to follow. In 1919 members of the new Division of Anthropology and Psychology of the National Research Council ignored Hall's advice on a proposed child welfare committee and appointed other psychologists to the committee. Planning an ambitious program in child development research and parent education in 1923, administrators of the Laura Spelman Rockefeller Memorial avoided any association with Hall and his child study movement. In 1924 the NEA changed the name of its Child Study Department to the Department of Health and Physical Education. The organization that had served as the main institutional base for Hall's child study movement was henceforth concerned with only a narrow part of its original program.[96]

"Inspiration" may be the best one-word summary of Hall's scientific influence. Terman wrote, "If I had suffered some disillusionment about Hall as a scientist this was more than made up by the burning enthusiasm which he inspired."[97] Many graduate students at Clark, including Terman and Arnold Gesell, chose to study under other faculty members and selected research topics that Hall barely tolerated. Even so, Hall, and the free atmosphere he encouraged at Clark, influenced them all. Pioneer child developmentalists Florence Goodenough and John Anderson wrote that one "cannot measure Hall in terms of his own accomplishments but by what he inspired in others."[98]

Many echoed these sentiments, but Thorndike may have captured Hall's essence better than anyone. Five years after Hall's death, he wrote, "He had the passion to be interesting and the passion to convince. He was not content with a victory over nature but must have an interesting, not to say exciting result. . . . He was not content with discovery alone, nor with the approbation of a small body of experts whose verdict would decide whether his work was without flaw. . . . The truth he sought was preferably important, bearing directly upon great issues pregnant with the possibilities of evolution and revolution."[99] Hall supported professionals who studied children outside as well as inside psychology, most importantly, Adolph Meyer and Franz Boas, who dared to try unconventional approaches.

Before Hall's child study movement ended in 1910, it had spread to twenty-three states, Europe, Asia, and Latin America; had motivated and influenced efforts to improve schools, juvenile justice, playgrounds, recreation, and child-rearing methods; had gained powerful allies among organized mothers and welfare reformers; and had left a legacy that affected subsequent endeavors to study children. Hall's influence is obscure because so many of his contemporaries replaced his methods and refuted his conclusions. Outstanding examples are Thorndike's educational psychology, Terman's contributions to mental testing, and Dewey's instrumentalism. Margaret Mead, the first cultural anthropologist to study children in a primitive society, was motivated in part by a desire to show that Hall's "storm and stress" view of adolescence was not universally valid. Undertakings such as these, Thorndike claimed, were nonetheless Hall's "true offspring." Many today agree with William Kessen's conclusion that "Hall's contribution far outruns his present reputation."[100]

Hall successfully challenged early introspective psychology's objection to child study and persuaded many Americans that better child rearing and schooling depend on applied scientific knowledge of the child. As we have seen, new directions in experimental psychology contributed both to Hall's loss of esteem among scientists and to new ways of studying children. The next chapter discusses another transition. During the 1880s the emergence of pediatrics as an independent specialty drew attention to new knowledge about the physical care of children, especially infant feeding. The new psychology and the new pediatrics stimulated the organization of mothers' clubs throughout the nation for the purpose of acquiring and applying scientific knowledge of children. Members of the National Congress of Mothers became Hall's staunchest and most enduring supporters. But just as new methods and theories in experimental psychology undermined Hall's status among scientists, so "scientific" pediatricians opposed his child-rearing advice. By the second decade of the twentieth century, their view had triumphed.

Chapter 3 Scientific Child Rearing, Organized Motherhood, and Parent Education

SCIENTIFIC CHILD REARING

In the decades just before and after 1900, scientists and physicians offered American parents new versions of the nature of childhood and new advice on how children should be reared. For the first time in U.S. history, ostensibly scientific views of childhood challenged traditional wisdom. Parents, of course, were not aware that the new ideas and the data on which they were based were questionable. Mothers formed clubs throughout the nation to acquire the new "scientific" child-rearing information and to share experiences. Scientific advice on children was also disseminated through mothers' clubs, kindergarten and child study movements, milk stations, well-baby clinics, child health centers, lectures, and magazine articles.[1]

The phrases "scientific child rearing" and "scientific motherhood" were common parlance among well-educated women. Scientific child rearing was expected to transform motherhood into a true profession. According to Swaim, Cora Bussey Hillis traveled throughout Iowa telling women to pay more attention to their children than to household chores. Such advice from Hillis and other members of the National Congress of Mothers inspired a spate of editorials and letters to newspaper editors from irate men warning women not to neglect cooking and other wifely duties for childcare.[2]

The Progressive period saw a decline in the authority of religion, doubt about whether traditional ways could meet the challenges of a transformed society, and dramatic examples of successful application of science and technology. Mothers and women social reformers, impressed by the fruitful use of science in agriculture, conservation, and public health, fervently believed that science could and should be used to bestow comparable benefits on children.[3]

Psychologist G. Stanley Hall and pediatrician Dr. L. Emmett Holt, the Dr. Spock of his time, assured mothers of the importance of scientific child rearing. Holt's *Care and Feeding of Children,* which went through six editions by 1912, advised his readers that, just as farmers should not plant crops before consulting the latest scientific reports from the Department of Agriculture, so parents should not try to rear children without the help of specialists. Many parents looked to the new disciplines of child psychology and pediatrics for what they believed was the best and latest scientific information on children.[4]

HALL'S CHILD

As we have seen, Hall's advice to parents was well received partly because it was in tune with the romantic views of childhood popular during the late nineteenth century. "Childhood as it comes fresh from God is not corrupt," he told parents. It "illustrates the survival of the most consummate thing in the world."[5] The goal of child rearing, as he and other romantics saw it, was to preserve as much as possible of the divine in the child. Parents should not attempt to implant ideas in children but to draw out what is already there. Hall idealized childhood and motherhood, but contrary to the views of many Americans, insisted that childhood be valued for its own sake. Recognize, respect, and encourage the expression of individuality, he advised, and be aware of the superiority of instinct over reason.

Hall's "scientific" re-formation of romantic concepts of childhood, together with his assurances that science was man's instrument for discovering God's design, reconciled religion and science. He believed that "the spirit of research is to the new era what the Holy Ghost was to the early church" and claimed that child study was accomplishing for children what the Protestant Reformation had accomplished centuries earlier for the religious life of many adults.[6]

Hall's child-rearing advice required a radical reconsideration of child nature.

Drawing on recapitulation theory, he rejected child-rearing principles based on both Calvinism and the Enlightenment. He introduced the notion that childhood is not an entity, but a series of developmental sequences, each with its own moral, psychological, and social characteristics produced by unconscious impulses inherited from distant ancestors. According to Ross, recapitulation theory "allowed Hall to use the biological and anthropological record as a limitless store of analogies with which to thicken his text."[7]

Hall explained that emotions that usually are attributed to the child's experience, such as morbid fears, are actually evoked by ancient influences. It is "convenient" but a "fallacy" to explain emotions by the nearest cause. Childhood emotions are not indication of childhood depravity, as Calvinists had claimed, nor ominous signs of potential adult disorders, as many child guidance psychiatrists would later warn, but are transitory, like physical "growing pains," and, if allowed proper expression, will disappear.[8]

Before Hall, the Reverend Horace Bushnell had stressed the powerful influence of the unconscious on the formation of the child's character.[9] His views were closer to Freud's than to Hall's, because he believed that family members, rather than ancient ancestors, are the major source of unconscious emotions in the child. Bushnell and Freud stressed the overwhelming importance of early childhood, while Hall advised that healthy development depended on successful passage through each stage. Hall's view was both a reflection and a cause of the shift, during the second half of the nineteenth century, from interest in the very young to interest in the school-age child, especially the adolescent.

Discipline, Hall stressed, should be adapted to the child's stage of development, his temperament, and the circumstances surrounding the offense. He saw the expression of anger as a natural part of development,[10] and many children's lies as the product of imagination rather than willful misrepresentation.[11] The adolescent's "belonging" instinct was a recapitulation of ancient psychological and social impulses that gave primacy to the rights and welfare of the group. He urged society not to destroy adolescent gangs but to try to channel their activities through supervised play and thus "transform an otherwise evanescent tribalism into a habitual lifelong moral posture."[12] The Enlightenment's emphasis on rationality was mistaken because instinct and emotion are superior to reason and "regulate conduct in the interest of the species."[13]

Hall conceded that strict parental control of children, even corporal punishment, might sometimes be necessary. Nevertheless, the general temper of his child-rearing advice was gentle, based on respect for children. Approving the advice offered by Alice Birney, president of the National Congress of Mothers,

Hall wrote the introduction to her book *Childhood*. "Sympathy," Birney wrote, "is the golden key which unlocks the realm of childhood to all who would enter." Parents are children's guardians, not their owners; children should be allowed freedom of choice rather than "managed."[14]

Hall's stage theory of child development challenged the veneration of the untutored mother typical of the pre–Civil War period and supported the movement for educated motherhood. To judge a child's behavior intelligently, mothers need to understand the unique characteristics of each developmental stage and each child. Hall urged mothers to acquire scientific information and to keep daily records that would enable them to understand their children's development. Possibly, more than any scientist before or since, Hall gave status to the educated mother.[15]

Hall's emphasis on the mother's need for knowledge of children and of the uniqueness of each child affirmed the mother's autonomy. Although scientific knowledge is necessary, he warned, it should not displace maternal intuition and sensitivity. Stage theory dictated different prescriptions for different age groups, but Hall's emphasis on individual differences and maternal wisdom provided considerable leeway for the mother to determine what was best for her child. She was not to be merely a passive recipient of expert advice, but the ultimate authority. In this view Hall was directly opposed to Holt and other "scientific experts" who triumphed after World War I.

HOLT'S CHILD

The first American attempt to apply laboratory science to childcare came from pediatrics, rather than experimental psychology. Pediatrics had become a specialty during the 1880s because of new developments in bacteriology and chemistry that led to experimental approaches to childhood pathology and a preoccupation with infant feeding. The 1890s were the heyday of "percentage feeding," when doctors carried slide rules to calculate the appropriate formula for the individual needs of each baby. Scientific feeding was based primarily on untested assumptions.[16] Many pediatricians insisted on strict infant feeding schedules because diarrhea diseases were the chief cause of infant morbidity and mortality, and they believed that loose schedules cause loose bowels.[17]

L. Emmett Holt was elected president of the American Pediatric Society in 1895. More than one hundred pages of the first edition of his *Care and Feeding of Children* (1894) presented a popular version of scientific feeding. The fifth edition (1909) devoted more than 100 of its 188 pages to feeding. Fewer than forty pages dealt with other aspects of physical care, such as airing, clothing, and care of eyes and skin. Twenty-four pages discussed the care of the older child. Psychological aspects of childcare, such as crying, nervousness, and play, occupied less than thirty pages, and only one page discussed thumb sucking, head banging, masturbation, and other behaviors so worrisome to many parents.[18]

Holt advocated infant formulas based on scientific calculations and strict regularity in feeding. On sleep, toilet training, and modes of discipline he offered authoritarian advice. Although Calvinism was not the source of Holt's authoritarianism, the tone and even some of the content of his advice bear striking resemblance to that offered by ministers during the colonial and early national periods of American history.[19]

Holt's book was written in the form of hypothetical questions about child rearing to which he gave short, precise answers that allowed the mother little leeway. Mothers should not permit a baby to suck on a thumb or a pacifier or to sleep on the mother's breast while nursing. He forbade rocking a baby to sleep. Holt's response to the question, "Why do babies cry?" was a list of possible causes, such as hunger, pain, and temper, and instructions on how to use the nature of the cry to determine the actual cause. What should one do if the cause could not be determined? Let the baby "cry it out." What is the most certain way of causing a child to develop the crying habit? "Giving him everything he cries for." How is such a habit broken? "By never giving a child what he cries for." He insisted that babies were made more nervous and irritable by play. If the mother insists on playing with her baby, it should be in the morning or after a nap, but never before bedtime. Babies of less than six months "should never be played with . . . and the less of it at any time, the better for the infant."[20]

Holt dismissed maternal instinct and the accumulated lore of generations as obsolete in a technological society. In 1926 he abandoned the farming analogy he had used in 1899, declaring that a baby, like an automobile, is a "very delicate piece of machinery," and the "blunders" even "highly intelligent parents" make with their first baby are much worse than the blunders of untrained owners who try to repair their own cars. The "worst sinners," however, are the grandparents, especially the grandmother, whose influence is "particularly pernicious as she is supposed by her previous experience to know everything about babies." He strongly advised parents to seek the best medical care available and to "turn a deaf ear to all suggestions from other quarters."[21]

Like Hall, Holt often addressed the National Congress of Mothers and other child study organizations and wrote popular articles. His advice, with its aura of the laboratory and prestige of mathematics, must have been irresistible to educated mothers who had been taught to respect science. A 1914 magazine article illustrates the spread of attitudes reflecting the importance of scientific child rearing. It opens with the heartrending story of a devoted mother whose baby died because she had relied on "instinct" and failed to sterilize the baby's bottles. She was the "amateur mother of yesterday instead of the professional mother of tomorrow." Maternal instinct is as "scientific as the classic statement that an upstanding fork means a caller, or that the moon is made of green cheese." The author characterized rich mothers as "poor-rich" because poor and immigrant mothers were receiving instruction not available to prosperous families, through well-baby clinics or through daughters who attended "Little Mothers' League." Anticipating John Watson's disapproval of maternal affection, the author cited a pediatrician who argued that babies of well-to-do mothers are victims of "over-care" and that it would be better if such mothers could have twins so as to ensure some "wholesome neglect." Educated women, the article concluded, realize that they need expert training in motherhood more than in "Greek verbs" or the "fauna of South Africa."[22]

Two studies of child-rearing advice in women's magazines found, however, that most articles from 1890 to 1910 continued to reflect the "sweet permissiveness" of Hall and the romantics rather than the regimentation of Holt. The exaltation of motherhood and the assumption that the child learns by imitating the virtuous mother continued to be dominant themes. Most of the prescriptive literature paid scant heed to infant feeding except to recommend loose scheduling. By 1920, however, a striking change had occurred: 77 percent of articles in that year recommended strict feeding schedules and a generally rigid, severe approach to child nurture.[23]

Historians warn that child-rearing practices do not necessarily coincide with child-rearing advice.[24] Some evidence suggests, however, that a shift from permissive to authoritarian practices did indeed occur before World War I, was reinforced by the advice of Watson and other behaviorists during the 1920s, and was perpetuated by other experts as late as World War II.[25] The shift may have occurred first among upper- and middle-class urban mothers.[26]

ORGANIZED MOTHERHOOD
AND PARENT EDUCATION

In no country other than the United States, Max Lerner declared, "has there been so pervasive a cultural anxiety about rearing children."[27] During the Progressive period this anxiety was expressed in an unprecedented organization of mothers for the purpose of acquiring and applying scientific information about children. By the early twentieth century, organized motherhood had become a mass enterprise that embraced parent education campaigns and a variety of reform activities. President Theodore Roosevelt, who joined the National Congress of Mothers, declared, "You cannot really be a good mother if you are not a wise mother."[28]

The Society for the Study of Child Nature was the nation's first formal child study organization. During the 1920s it would become the prestigious Child Study Association of America. Organized in New York City in 1888 by Dr. Felix Adler and his wife with only three members, by 1908 it had gained so many chapters that it changed its name to the Federation for Child Study. Its purpose was to collect, tabulate, and distribute information about child study findings and their practical application and to undertake original research. An upper-middle-class scholarly organization, it sought to gain knowledge directly from experts trained in child study rather than from popular writers. Its members studied Locke and Rousseau as well as the latest psychological and medical findings about children.[29]

In 1890 the Association of Collegiate Alumnae (later the American Association of University Women) established a section for the study of children, which published record sheets designed by Millicent Shinn to facilitate documentation of a baby's development. Following Shinn's example, many members wrote baby biographies. After 1910 the association shifted from child study to action programs, but it reinstated child study as one of its chief concerns in 1923.

Owing in part to Hall's influence, the kindergarten movement also stimulated parent education during the early Progressive period. The number of kindergartens in the United States increased from 348 in 1880 to 1,131 in 1890, and to five thousand by 1900. Kindergarten enthusiasts, motivated primarily by the reform impulse, endeavored to rescue slum children, to help assimilate immigrant children, and to aid working mothers. Strongly influenced by Hall and other romantic educators, they organized mothers' clubs, counseled parents in their homes, lectured, published journals, and wrote books and articles for the popular press. Elizabeth Harrison's *Study of Child Nature from the Kindergarten Standpoint* went through fifty printings and was translated into eight foreign languages.[30]

The establishment and rapid growth of state child study associations during the mid-1890s encouraged Americans to learn more about children. Mothers, some fathers, and teachers were all participants in these organizations. Established in 1894, the Illinois Society for Child Study, the largest of twenty-three state associations, was national in scope and influence, published a journal, and held summer workshops in 1895 and 1896 that attracted about three thousand participants.[31] The large and active Iowa Child Study Organization sent Cora Bussey Hillis as its delegate to the 1899 convention of the National Congress of Mothers, with significant consequences for the founding of scientific child study.

THE NATIONAL CONGRESS OF MOTHERS

The National Congress of Mothers was the largest, most active, and most influential organization of mothers. The first congress was organized in 1897 by Alice Birney, a child welfare reformer who was inspired by the kindergarten movement and influenced by Hall.[32] Phoebe Hearst (mother of William Randolph) provided financial support.[33] By 1910 the National Congress had fifty thousand members and local chapters in twenty-one states. In 1914 it sponsored the third international meeting on child welfare. It advocated the formation of local mothers' clubs in schools rather than churches to promote secularization and to bring mothers and teachers closer together. It became the Parent Teacher's Association of America in 1924.

The National Congress sought to bring to parents of all races and social classes the latest scientific information on children, and enable them to compare and discuss their own child-rearing experiences. It also undertook ambitious reform programs for the benefit of mothers and children, including lobbying for better child welfare laws, housing codes, pure food and drug regulations, mothers' pensions, better sanitation, and penal reform.[34] "'The mother in the home,'" one spokesman said, "merges into the broader term 'the mother for the home.'"[35]

Parent education and child welfare reform, the two great grassroots movements that encouraged the establishment of scientific child study, were intertwined in the Progressive period. Before World War I leaders in parent education were drawn from diverse fields and were deeply involved in child welfare reform. After World War I they usually were specialists in early childhood education, psychology, or home economics. Felix Adler, a professor of culture and political ethics at Columbia University, founded the organization that became the influential Child Study Association of America. When the National Child Labor Committee was organized in 1904, he became chairman of its trustees.

Hillis and the first two presidents of the National Congress of Mothers were very active in child welfare reform.[36]

Hall was the chief scientific authority for the National Congress of Mothers. His research, unlike Holt's, was concerned with psychological topics of compelling interest to parents. When Hall shifted his interest from the schoolchild to the adolescent, the National Congress did so also.[37] After *Adolescence* was published in 1904, the National Congress stepped up its efforts for penal reform, and the establishment of juvenile courts, and probation systems. When Hall left child study, the congress sought leadership from Hall's disciple, Michael Vincent O'Shea.[38]

National Congress policy reflected a cautious redefinition and limited extension of the pre–Civil War precepts of the Republican Mother and domestic ideology. "This is the time known pre-eminently . . . as the 'woman's era,'" Birney declared. "Much has been said and written . . . about women's higher education and her extended opportunities, so much that we have failed to hear the small voice appealing to us in behalf of childhood. Yet, how, I ask, can we divorce the woman question from the child question?"[39]

Leaders of the National Congress clung tenaciously to the early-nineteenth-century ideology of domesticity. Believing in the importance of fellowship and unity among women of all races and classes, they welcomed all mothers to their ranks. Any mother could organize a mother's club, Birney insisted; no special skills or training were necessary. National Congress members were deeply involved in helping poor mothers, not only through social reform but also in concrete ways, such as providing food and clothing to families in their communities.[40] Schlossman suggests that the "endorsement of political activity on behalf of the poor . . . best distinguishes the goals and methods of parent education in the Progressive period from what follows." The National Congress's emphasis on unity among women was reflected in its repeated refusal to endorse women's suffrage. Birney asked, "Could we afford to champion a cause which all the mothers of the land do not advocate?"[41]

Birney believed that the primary purpose of higher education for women was training for motherhood and hoped that the congress would "eventually turn back into the home the tide of femininity which is now straining outward in search of a career." The National Congress urged mothers to engage in volunteer activity for social justice, not to pursue careers, and to organize special clubs for mothers whose children had left the nest. Single professional women, who were leaders of child welfare reform, were frequent speakers at congress meetings.[42]

"SO, YOU SEE, THERE ARE SEVERAL THINGS THAT WOULD INTEREST YOU, AND I'M SURE YOULD ENJOY YOURSELF VERY MUCH. NOW, CAN'T I PERSUADE YOU TO COME TO OUR N: IOTHERS' MEETING?"

"WELL, YER LEDDYSHIP, YOU'RE VERY KIND. BUT I WAS NEVER A SOCIETY WOMAN!—(P:

The National Congress of Mothers was deeply engaged in helping and involving poor mothers in child welfare and parent education. From the Cora Bussey Hillis Scrapbook Inventory, Iowa State Historical Society, Iowa City. Courtesy of the State Historical Society of Iowa, Iowa City.

At the fourth annual convention of the National Congress in Des Moines in 1900, three thousand delegates overflowed the civic auditorium. Newspapers throughout the state reported activities at the congress on their front pages and discussed them in feature stories, letters to the editor, and editorials. The male consensus was that the meeting was silly but harmless. These mothers, one writer observed, were not "ancient maiden ladies," "women with double chins," the "disappointed in love," or the "new woman who has invaded every occupation except breaking prairie," but wives and mothers who were tending their homes and "leaving politics and mercantile affairs to their husbands and sons." Another writer calculated that six women on the executive board had twenty-seven children among them and were therefore entitled to their "tea party" even though it was a "useless expenditure of money and lavender perfume." Some women speakers appeared to be placating the men. Mothers must train a daughter "to understand the lives and work of men so that she may not be a deadweight but may lead, inspire, cooperate and idealize," preached sociologist Mary Roberts Smith. "Moderation is the wise handmaiden of impulse."[43]

The conservative rhetoric contrasts sharply with the radical accomplishments of the women who attended the congress. Two years after the convention, Hillis, addressing the Iowa legislature, served notice that women would soon be presenting bills on behalf of children. The legislature enacted a juvenile court act in 1904, the first of many child welfare laws passed in Iowa during the next dozen years.[44]

The blending of the private and public roles of motherhood was an outstanding characteristic of the Progressive period. Not only the leaders of parent education and child welfare organizations, but also thousands of their supporters, attest to the dedication of Progressive women to other people's children. Upon her withdrawal from the affairs of the Iowa Child Welfare Research Station shortly after she had helped to found it, Hillis declared that the station was second only to her own children in her affection. Now that her mission had been fulfilled, she compared her feelings to those she had had when she put away her own children's clothes and toys when they had left home. This statement is especially poignant since three of Hillis' five children had "left" when they died at ages two, eight, and nine. In giving the station "over forever out of my constant care," Hillis said, "I have only done what every mother must do to the child of her love."[45]

Carroll Smith-Rosenberg points out that professional women of the Progressive era, even though they were usually unmarried, also assumed the role of "public mothers." Most of them chose nurturing professions or led others in campaigns for educational and child welfare reform. "Women teachers and reformers," she writes, " felt the same devotion to their children that biological mothers did." She quotes Mrs. Horace Mann who argued in 1870 that "the maternal feeling is as intense and pure in many unmarried women as in their married sisters." Women, whether mothers or single women, were generally believed to be morally superior to men, and, as Sheila Rothman perceptively observed, in the Progressive period "social problems were finally moral ones."[46]

THREE TRANSITIONS TO THE TWENTIETH CENTURY

The 1893 World's Columbian Exhibition marked three significant turning points on the road to scientific child study. One was the launching by the fair's child study sessions of the popular phase of G. Stanley Hall's child study movement. Its decline by 1900 marked the end of the nineteenth-century approach to child study.[47] On the other hand, settlement house exhibits that dramatically contrasted sordid, industrial Chicago with the gleaming "White City" of the fair foreshadowed twentieth-century approaches. Press and public interest in the settlement house movement suggested its future influence, although not its crucial role in promoting and shaping scientific study of children. The third turning point was the display at the Woman's Pavilion of women's growing independence and activism.[48]

While members of the National Congress urged a conservative approach to reform that would not divide women,[49] settlement workers and other "new women" groped their way toward a new definition of women's rights and responsibilities. They recognized that if substantial improvements were to be made in the lives of women and children, female reformers would need to employ more aggressive tactics to gain entry to the male-dominated political arena. The greatest achievement of the new women may have been to enlist members of the rapidly growing women's organizations in campaigns for child welfare reform and child study. Chapter 4 begins by tracing how this was accomplished. It goes on to describe the alliance between social welfare reformers and the first generation of male behavioral scientists, including Hall and his followers, in two major child welfare reform efforts, the play and recreation movement and the quest for juvenile justice. Hall and the women social reformers reached their shared faith in the importance of scientific child study by different paths. To Hall, the child was the center of psychology; to women, the center of reform. Starting with different goals, Hall and the women reformers arrived at a friendly and productive community of interest that persisted until the first few years of the twentieth century. Before 1910 arrived, however, Hall and the social justice reformers advocated different strategies as well as different goals. The ascendance of social justice reformers helped bring an end to Hall's child study movement in 1910 and cleared the way for the establishment of the federal Children's Bureau in 1912.

Chapter 4 Social Welfare
Reformers and Reform-Minded
Scientists

FROM TRUE WOMANHOOD
TO THE NEW WOMAN

The New Woman first appeared on the stage and in magazines in the mid-1890s. According to Rosalind Rosenberg, "Her distinguishing characteristics were her independent spirit and her athletic zeal. She rode a bicycle, played tennis or golf, showed six inches of stocking beneath her skirts, and loosened her corsets. She expected to marry but she wanted a life beyond her home—perhaps even a career."[1] Rheta Childe Dorr described the New Woman as one who wanted "to belong to the human race, not to the ladies' aid society."[2]

Settlement workers were conspicuously new women of a different type. Mostly single, highly educated, and economically autonomous, they challenged existing gender and power relationships, but they also drew on the concepts of "true womanhood" and women's separate sphere to gain entry into politics.[3] Only women, they believed, were capable of bringing about a new order in which American democracy would find social as well as political expression; women alone possessed the moral insight, nurturing temperament, experience and skills needed to counteract the influence of businessmen and male politicians. Their ideas were based on the prevailing view that evolution had made men more combative and exploitative, women more concerned with social morality. Although women's political activism during the Progressive period was a real departure, according to Jill Ker Conway, "the controlling stereotype of the female temperament . . . remained dominant from the 1870s until the 1930s."[4]

Jane Addams used her skills as consummate storyteller and propagandist to dramatize conditions in city slums and move women, and even many men, to political action. Especially adept at using analogies to justify women's entry into the public sphere, Addams portrayed women's participation in municipal reform as "civic housekeeping." Women were "knowledgeable about and attentive" to the needs of modern cities while men were "carelessly indifferent."[5]

WOMEN'S ORGANIZATIONS IN THE 1900S:
FROM CULTURAL PURSUITS
TO SOCIAL REFORM

Settlement workers understood the importance of enlisting the help of women's organizations to achieve reform goals. As a member of the Illinois State Board of Charities during the 1890s, Julia Lathrop gained the assistance of women's clubs to improve state institutions.[6] Addams perceived women's clubs as "an instrument through which many were led from a sense of isolation to one of civic responsibility" through club activities that made visible the urban conditions that needed correcting.[7]

The 1890s witnessed a tremendous spurt in the growth of women's clubs organized on the basis of patriotism, race, religion, professional affiliation, culture, or other defining characteristics. Most were created not to promote social action but to provide opportunities for fellowship and the pursuit of cultural interests.[8] The General Federation of Women's Clubs, organized in 1890, had 495 affiliates and 100,000 members. "The federalism of those local, unrelated groups," Breckinridge said "into a general affiliation for no particular reason other than that of mutual conferences about problems not yet enunciated or apparent, was a significant introduction to the nineties." Between 1896 and 1900, the federation doubled its membership. Within a few more years, it had gained more members and wielded more influence than the Woman's Christian Temperance Union, the most important nineteenth- century women's organization.

By 1905 "problems not yet enunciated or apparent" in 1890 had transformed the activities of the federation into effective reform programs on behalf of women and children. Women soon learned that their clubs gave them great influence. An important first step in the transition from fellowship and culture to social activism occurred in 1898, when Addams and British socialist Beatrice Webb addressed the General Federation on "the industrial program as it affects women and children." The convention adopted resolutions proposing labor standards for women and children in industry. After Addams addressed the 1902 biennial convention on "The Social Waste of Child Labor," the General Federation urged members to work for improved child labor laws.[9]

The 1904 convention is often cited as the crucial turning point in the General Federation's transition from the pursuit of culture to social activism. Sarah Platt Decker, its newly elected president, declared, "Ladies, you have chosen me your leader. I have an important piece of news for you. Dante is dead . . . I think that it is time that we dropped the study of his *Inferno* and turned our attention to our own." Decker identified and discussed numerous urgent social problems and urged federation members "to get into the struggle for a better civilization."[10] Two years later Helen Winslow reiterated Decker's sentiments: "We prefer Doing to Dante, Being to Browning. We've soaked in literary effort long enough; today nothing but an organization of philanthropy will satisfy us." By "philanthropy," Winslow meant not charity but Addams's concept of social justice.[11]

The shift from culture to reform was achieved with amazing speed. As early as 1905 the Maine federation had to make a special point of retaining a place for literature and art in its program.[12] By 1910 the General Federation had 800,000 members, five times as many as it had had in 1900. Referring to the progress in child welfare reform, Judge Richard Tuthill declared that "women's clubs . . . have taught the state how to be a parent."[13] Several newly established women's organizations joined the General Federation to support humanitarian causes that focused on women and children.[14] The National Association of Colored Women's Clubs, the National Consumers' League, the National Women's Trade Union League, the Young Women's Christian Association, and the American Home Economics Association were founded between 1896 and 1908. The movements spearheaded by the "new women" raised an implicit but basic question, according to Robert Wiebe: "What public tasks would women seek and which would men allow them to fill?"[15] Carroll Smith-Rosenberg suggests that the answer lay in "using the loving world of female bonding and traditional familial concepts" to "forge a web of interlocking social justice organizations that became a singularly effective political machine."[16] A poem by a Sorosis clubwoman expresses the transformation of the earlier concept of the Republican Mother into the early-twentieth-century concept of social feminism:

> The Woman of the Future if I read the stars aright
> Will love her club at Breakfast but she'll love her Home at night.
> The Woman of the Future will cast an honest vote;
> She'll seize the erring lobbyist by a metaphoric throat;
> She'll dust the halls of Congress and she'll sweep the civic stair;
> And ventilate the corridor with some unpolluted air.[17]

SCIENTISTS AND REFORMERS UNITE ON "CONSTRUCTIVE" CHILD WELFARE REFORM

Early Progressive child saving focused on rescuing children from slum life, child labor, and adult criminal justice systems. Addams and G. Stanley Hall shared an intense dissatisfaction with this negative approach. To save children from misery, they said, it was necessary to enhance and enrich the lives of *all* children, "normal" as well as disadvantaged, to help *all* to happy childhoods. Addams insisted that the welfare field promote constructive programs such as playgrounds, recreational activities, prevention of juvenile delinquency, mothers' pensions, kindergartens, and better public education.[18]

The "constructive" approach to child welfare enlisted the support of both welfare reformers and many first-generation professional social scientists. According to John Burnham, this was possible because American progressivism, unlike British progressivism, was not limited to politics nor to economic or social philosophies, but permeated the thinking of many psychologists, psychiatrists, and social scientists.[19] Scientists and nonscientist reformers, united by common assumptions emanating from pragmatism, welcomed the opportunity to work together to achieve social reform. Social justice reformers and social scientists alike wanted to abandon assumptions from medicine and academe that were based on speculation, logic, or the study of man as a species. They preferred hypotheses generated and tested by concrete evidence gained from experience, whether derived from the fact-finding surveys of urban reformers or from individual life histories reported by psychiatrists. Social reformers and "progressive" scientists also found common cause in the need to educate the public about scientific discoveries. Two notable examples of such collaboration were the movement to establish playgrounds and improve recreation and the campaign to improve the juvenile justice system.[20]

PLAYGROUNDS AND RECREATION

During the Enlightenment, John Locke recommended that poor children between three and thirteen years of age be sent to working schools where they could "contribute substantially to their own upkeep" and their tendency to pauperism could be partially overcome.[21] Most early-nineteenth-century Americans, influenced by the Protestant work ethic, approved of labor as a normal, desirable function of childhood. Idleness in children was associated with delinquency; work was considered an important means of rehabilitating wayward youth.[22] Attitudes toward the value of play in children's development changed significantly toward the end of the nineteenth century. The first movement to establish public playgrounds and recreational opportunities for children and youth came in the 1880s. During the next four decades it swept the nation. Between 1880 and 1920 municipal governments spent over one hundred million dollars for the construction and staffing of playgrounds. The renaissance of play stemmed from two sources: the sorry plight of children who had only city streets for playgrounds and new psychological theories asserting that play was neither frivolous nor harmful but rather was essential to healthy development. Joseph Lee, a founder of the Playground Association of America, argued that "the boy without a playground is father to the man without a job."[23] Lillian Wald, director of the Henry Street Settlement, declared that "young offenders' presence in the court" might "be traced to a play impulse for which there is no safe outlet."[24]

In 1890 the urban population of the United States was only about half as large as the rural population, but by 1910 the two were almost equal in size. Between 1900 and 1915 nearly fifteen million immigrants came to America. Most settled in cities. Settlement workers needed only their own eyes to see the bleakness of slum children's lives and to conclude that city children urgently needed better play and recreational opportunities. Neighborhood playgrounds, Davis claims, were but one component in the overall strategy that "dared to dream that American cities could be safe and stimulating for all citizens."[25] Residents of Hull House and the Henry Street Settlement established public playgrounds in Chicago and New York City in 1893. The Playground Association of America was established in 1906, and by 1915 150 cities had established public playgrounds.[26] Settlement workers, agreeing with Hall that country life was better for children than city life, arranged country vacations for many city children.

The playground movement is a striking example of the interaction of cultural trends and scientific and educational developments. Psychologists and educators advanced theories about the value of play that supported the activities of play organizers. Romantic educators drew upon Friedrich Froebel's concepts of creative play. In spite of the diversity of their psychological theories, Hall, James Mark Baldwin, William James, John Dewey, and Edward Thorndike agreed on the importance of play. [27]Between 1890 and 1910 the playground movement meshed with, was influenced by, and mimicked the style of Hall's child study movement. Arnold and Beatrice Gesell perceived it as an integral part of the child study movement, an illustration of "the unique character and spirit of the child-study movement as a whole—a focalization of thought upon the nature and needs of the child; a union in understanding and helpfulness of experts, laymen, academic investigators, and practical workers."[28]

Addams used Hall's theories to argue for more parks and playgrounds.[29] Play organizers such as Lillian Wald, a settlement worker; Henry Curtis, a founder of the Playground Association of America; and Luther Gulick, the association's first president; drew their ideas on the importance of play explicitly from Hall's recapitulation theory. It postulated that children's play at different stages of development was a reenactment of evolution, a "rehearsing of racial history," indispensable to healthy development. Hall's theory also stimulated much psychological research on play and games.[30]

In his aptly titled *Muscles and Morals,* Dominick Cavallo presents Hall's "physicalism" as a "radical departure" from traditional approaches to child nature. Hall argued that "there is a sense in which all good conduct and morality might be defined as right muscle habits." Mind and body were not distinct but "separate faculties . . . interpenetrating each other."[31] Muscular conditioning, primarily through play, was the key to mental and moral development. Although the child's intellect could be trained in part in school, moral instruction could be controlled only through play.[32]

Leaders of the playground movement disliked both the "home as haven" concept and the cult of moral and economic individualism. They encouraged a shift from a private to a public orientation and believed that the playground experience would teach the importance of cooperation, social order, and unity. Understanding of the physical, social, and intellectual stages of childhood was crucial. Consequently, the study of child development became more important to playground directors than training in physical education.[33]

Addams was sympathetic to Hall's view of adolescence. To her, adolescent behavior was the "natural expression of an impulse too old and too powerful to be easily and wisely controlled." She perceived the deviant behavior of youth as a "blundering effort to find adventure and self-expression in a society which provided few opportunities for either."[34] *The Spirit of Youth and the City Streets,* her favorite of her books, was a major contribution to urban sociology. Hall's two-volume *Adolescence* attracted much attention among welfare professionals and helped to foster more sympathetic attitudes toward youthful rebelliousness and misbehavior. It also encouraged a variety of new efforts to transform deviant adolescent behavior through proper recreation.[35] Steven Schlossman believes that historians have underestimated the significance of Hall's influence on the Young Men's Christian Association, the Boy Scouts, and boys' clubs sponsored by churches and missionary societies. Hall was their "guiding light."[36]

Although Hall exerted the most influence, other psychologists also contributed important ideas to play organizers. James Mark Baldwin's theory of imitation indirectly influenced Joseph Lee. After 1900 Dewey's ideas on the need to foster cooperation and social democracy in children tended to supplant Hall's individualistic beliefs in play programs. James's and Thorndike's belief that habit training could instill and sustain important moral and intellectual functions was incorporated into various play and recreational programs.[37] Play leaders also experimented with ways of using play and games to instill in boys the feminine traits that Addams believed were essential for humanizing industry and socializing democracy.[38]

THE MOVEMENTS FOR JUVENILE JUSTICE
AND THE SCIENTIFIC INVESTIGATION
OF DELINQUENCY

During the first decade of the new century Hall, Thorndike, and Dewey, along with other psychologists and social justice reformers, showed a growing interest in using psychology to achieve practical goals. Their solidarity was based on their conviction that science is essential to the solution of the most vital problems of life.[39]

Hall, lukewarm about campaigns to reduce child labor, clear slums, and establish a federal children's bureau, was enthusiastic about both juvenile justice reform and playgrounds because of the importance he attached to adolescent development.[40] His reservations about many efforts to help poor children, on the other hand, reflected his belief that pauperism was inherited and that mankind would be damaged by encouraging the reproduction of the unfit.[41]

Yet Hall also identified many environmental causes of juvenile delinquency, such as bad homes, unhealthy infancy, and crowded slums.[42] His suggestions for the elimination of social conditions that could lead children into trouble with the law, according to David Rothman, were a "reformer's checklist."[43] Hall pointed out that children and youth were often the victims of "circumstances or of immaturity" and consequently deserved not condemnation, but "pity and hope." Since they inhabited different moral worlds from adults, they should not be judged by adult standards.[44] Ben Lindsey, the most renowned of the juvenile court judges, told Hall that his genetic psychology had been a "lamp to his feet."[45] Settlement workers and other practical-minded reformers initiated the movements for the better treatment of juvenile delinquents, but scientists helped to ensure the rapid growth of the juvenile justice system.

Campaigns to improve recreation and juvenile justice found social reformers and social scientists in fundamental agreement on theory and tactics. As reformers became more concerned with the reduction of child labor, pensions for mothers of dependent children, and the establishment of a federal children's bureau, Hall's Social Darwinism kept him from endorsing and participating in these campaigns. Social justice reformers began to withdraw support from Hall and to work out their own approaches to child study.

THE CHILDREN'S INSTITUTE: AN ALTERNATIVE
TO THE CHILDREN'S BUREAU

As Hall lost the allegiance of scientists and educators, he was gratified to discover that many social workers responded favorably to some of the ideas in *Adolescence*.[46] Here was a group that had recently achieved professional status and won the support of some of the new foundations, most notably the Russell Sage Foundation, established in 1907. Hall thought that welfare professionals and philanthropists might be persuaded to provide much-needed support for a permanent child study institute at Clark University if he could unite them with scientists who studied children.[47] Seven months after the 1909 White House Conference for Dependent Children, Hall organized a child welfare conference at Clark University. Its announced purpose was to coordinate the work of academic scholars studying children with that of welfare professionals and child-care practitioners, but its real purpose was to gain support for Hall's proposed children's institute.[48] With Hall as president, the conference held eighteen sessions with a distinguished group of speakers and included a broad representation of welfare professionals. Although a second conference was held in 1910, it did not become the annual event Hall expected.[49]

The Children's Institute was established in 1909 with a modest $5,000 grant from Clark University and had two purposes. The first was "to collect, diffuse, and increase scientific knowledge of children." This purpose appeared to be very similar to that of the federal children's bureau proposed in the same period, but the plans for the institute reflected familiar Hall objectives. The ten departments that Hall hoped would constitute the institute reflected a potpourri of approaches to the study of children that included both educational and welfare goals, with emphasis on the former. One department was to be a library of published information on childhood from all over the world, including literature on legislation relating to children and on the legal status of children, the latter of obvious interest to welfare reformers. Scientific pedagogy was the subject of four departments. Another department was titled "eugenics," although the subjects to be studied did not reflect the extremes of the eugenics movement, but included, for example, infectious diseases, milk purification, and infant mortality, all subjects of intense interest to social justice reformers.[50] A department of anthropology and sociology was to study children's growth and development and to establish norms of physical and mental development.[51]

The second and more important goal of the children's institute, Hall said, was to end the separation of research on children from child welfare activities. "We must have a new and vital bond between knowing and doing," Hall declared.[52] The proposed children's bureau would be a wholesome step in this direction, he conceded, but Congress appeared reluctant to affirm the idea, and should the bureau be established, his institute still would be needed to coordinate research and welfare programs. To support this view, he drew attention to the distressing lack of contact between the Federal Bureau of Ethnology, which studied Indians, and the Bureau of Indian Affairs, which cared for Indians.[53]

Hall was unrealistic in expecting welfare workers to endorse his children's institute. His Social Darwinism limited his support for reforms that they cherished. He continued to be popular with organized mothers, but his antagonism to feminism alienated women reformers, and his relationship with the "new women" was ambivalent.[54] Hall believed that women should not engage in scholarly pursuits, not because they were intellectually incapable but because such activities would interfere with their primary duty: to bear and rear children. He expressed contempt for feminists' "man-aping fashion" and urged women to restrict their new power to their special sphere of public morals. He favored separate education for boys and girls after puberty and a curriculum for girls that would prepare them for motherhood. For single women who insisted upon careers, he favored the nurturing professions: teaching, nursing, and social work.[55]

Hall's and Lathrop's diametrically opposed views on the role of pity in social reform vividly illustrate the chasm separating Hall and other Social Darwinists from social justice reformers. Hall wrote: "The mission of pity is to minister to the needs of elite youth, youth at the stage of later adolescence . . . to add to human euphoria so that the plateau of the best half of the race will be high, so that the summits of human possibility may be easier attained." He added: "There is considerable difference . . . between different social classes, and . . . what would really seem hardship to one may be luxury to another. . . . The children of the poor . . . thrive well under a certain degree of neglect."[56] Providing aid for the economically disadvantaged, "moribund sick," and defective children; educating children beyond their capacity; mounting aggressive campaigns to eliminate child labor—all of these measures represented to Hall "pity misdirected," pity that would reverse evolutionary progress.[57]

Soon after the Children's Bureau was established, Lathrop declared "The justice of today is born of yesterday's pity; and so I take it this bureau . . . is an expression of the nation's sense of justice. It will need, as perhaps no other government agency will need, the continuance of the popular pity which demanded and secured it; but sure of that it will become . . . the nation's greatest aid in making effective the constantly richer terms in which the sense of justice toward all children is expressed." "Appeal to pity could be misdirected," she wrote "only if it were based on sentimentality rather than on truth secured through scientific inquiry."[58]

Hall decided that the failure of his "experiment" to bring scholars and welfare professionals together was due to their "basic incompatibility." Given the hereditarian assumptions and conservative versions of Social Darwinism that permeated Hall's writings and the thinking of most of his followers, he was right. Lathrop undoubtedly had in mind academic child psychology as it had developed under Hall when she declared, in her first address as Chief of the Children's Bureau: "We must make a constant effort . . . to avoid the faults of academic methods and aims." She refused to include in the bureau the department of child study that Hall had proposed.

Two years after the founding of the bureau, a memorandum composed by a group of unidentified psychologists and doctors presented other reasons for their hostility to the welfare reformers who staffed and supported the bureau.[59] The memorandum was written to justify an amendment to a bill introduced in the House of Representatives on May 15, 1914. The amendment provided "that the chief and assistant [chief of the bureau] shall be experts in child study . . . and that the supervisory officers and all other persons now or hereafter employed in the bureau, in investigations . . . of a medical nature, shall have medical training." It criticized Lathrop and her assistant as unmarried women who "had no training or experience in the study of children." Although Children's Bureau personnel might "read up on child study, it was hardly intended that the Bureau should become a training school at public expense." When the bureau was established, "the question as to whether anyone KNEW anything about children was never asked." The memorandum concluded that child study is "scientific," but "collecting statistics about children is sociological research. . . . Only those trained in the scientific study of children are capable of classifying and interpreting statistics on children." The most important purpose of the amendment, it asserted was to "cause the Bureau to take up some of the basal work first: that is the study of children themselves, as well as their environment."

The criticism that the sociological investigations conducted by the bureau were not "real science" was repeated often during the next two decades. Sociologists and developmentalists eventually agreed that both approaches to child study were valuable and that it was unfortunate that early leaders of child study saw them as alternatives. The two approaches imposed different choices about how to study children, which children to study, and who should sponsor the studies. Hall's reform goal, to match institutions to the changing needs of developing children, dictated the study of children's development at every stage and emphasized the study of "normal" children. Lewis Terman, who was sympathetic to Hall's elitist goals, studied gifted children. Social justice reformers, who championed the cause of disadvantaged children, focused on social surveys of environmental conditions that harmed children's development. Hall was opposed to paternalistic government and wanted a private university to sponsor child study. Social justice reformers demanded government sponsorship.

By 1910 settlement workers and their allies had focused the nation's attention on the problems of dependent children, proposed and mustered support for a federal children's bureau, and launched a national movement to prohibit the exploitation of child labor. The child welfare reform campaigns they initiated dominated the Progressive reform movement during the years just before World War I. Sustained by grassroots support from women's organizations, these campaigns gained momentum in the 1920s and stimulated and supported that decade's expanding efforts to establish scientific child study. Clark-trained psychologists continued to study children within academic departments, but social justice reformers shifted the institutional settings of their new child study programs to locations outside the academic and medical establishments.

A PROPOSAL FOR A FEDERAL AGENCY
FOR CHILDREN

In 1903 Lillian Wald and Florence Kelley, two of the most eminent early settlement leaders, suggested that the federal government should assume responsibility for the nation's children by establishing an agency devoted exclusively to their needs. Their proposal led to campaigns that culminated in the founding of the Children's Bureau in 1912.

The idea for a federal agency devoted to children came to Wald and Kelley as they read through the mail at the Henry Street Settlement, heavily weighted with questions about how to help parents and communities do well by their children. Turning to the morning newspapers, they noticed a news story reporting a cabinet meeting to deal with problem of the cotton boll weevil. They could not imagine any catastrophe related to children that would evoke a similar governmental response.[60]

Wald and Kelley discussed their plan for a federal agency for children with Edward Devine, editor of *Charities and Corrections,* who volunteered to send the proposal to President Theodore Roosevelt. Roosevelt wired back, "It's a bully idea. Come to Washington and let's see." At their meeting in 1905 he agreed to support a bill for a children's bureau in the next congressional session.[61]

Wald and Kelley had become interested in children's problems very early in their careers. Exposed to the deplorable conditions in tenement houses as a young medical student in New York City, Wald decided to withdraw from medical school and devote herself to helping slum families. She led the movement to found the profession of public health nursing and established the "Nurses' Settlement" on Henry Street in Manhattan in 1895. Wald and her nurses assumed responsibility for helping families with a wide variety of social as well as medical problems, and the house on Henry Street soon became a full-scale settlement. She worked primarily for reforms that would improve the health, recreation, and education of children and for the eradication of poverty, which she considered the underlying cause of most family problems.[62]

Kelley, more than any other settlement worker with the possible exception of Lathrop, was committed to research as the foundation for reform. She wrote the description of the Children's Bureau's investigatory functions in the statute establishing the agency. She had expressed strong interest in children even as an undergraduate at Cornell University. Her senior thesis, "On Some Changes in the Legal Status of the Child since Blackstone," was published in 1882. She later earned a law degree from Northwestern University. Kelley, who published her first research on working children in 1889, was one of the earliest advocates of government's responsibility to eliminate child labor. Largely through her influence, the Illinois legislature passed a factory act in 1893 limiting hours of work for women and prohibiting child labor. Appointed Illinois' first chief factory inspector in 1894, she investigated violations of the new law and, through her annual reports, focused public attention on the plight of child workers and the need to enforce the factory laws.[63] Efforts to reduce and regulate child labor were to became one of the major goals of the Children's Bureau.

A resident of Hull House during most of the 1890s, Kelley directed an investigation of Chicago slums that led to the publication in 1895 of *Hull-House Maps and Papers: A Presentation of Nationalities and Wages in a Congested Neighborhood of Chicago, by the Residents of Hull House* (*HHMP*), a pathbreaking social study that stimulated other settlements to undertake surveys. Kelley contributed chapters entitled "The Sweating System" and "Wage-Earning Children." Her most significant contribution to the survey, however, was to instruct agents from the U.S. Department of Labor in the collection of data on every tenement house and every individual resident in Chicago's nineteenth ward. Hull House residents used the data from the 1895 survey to construct maps of the ward. These thematic maps, unique in contemporary American social science, were *HHMP*'s chief claim to fame.[64] According to Sklar, Kelley's biographer, *HHMP* represented the "state of the art of social science analyses of working-class urban life in the United States" until the publication of the multivolume *Pittsburgh Survey* between 1909 and 1911.[65]

Kelley, while dedicated to research, believed that its findings must be interpreted and publicized in order to arouse the public to corrective action. She declared: "Figures never impress. It is boys and girls and not percentages that are maimed." The statute establishing the Children's Bureau reflected Kelley's faith in the importance of both investigation and reporting.[66]

A change in administration in Illinois lost Kelley her position as chief factory inspector in 1897. She accepted an offer to become general secretary of the National Consumers' League and left Chicago for New York. She became a resident of the Henry Street Settlement, where Wald supported her efforts for child welfare and child labor reform. Commenting on the significance of Kelley's career, Sklar declares that she exemplified the ways in which women social scientists worked in reform-oriented organizations independent of universities, challenged laissez-faire public policies, addressed gender-specific issues, and continued early "humane" social science traditions.[67] With President Roosevelt's endorsement of their proposal, Kelley, Wald, and Devine asked the National Child Labor Committee (NCLC) to draft a bill for a children's bureau and to muster congressional support.[68] Bills were introduced in the Senate in January 1906 and in the House that May. Although the NCLC had united many important organizations in support of the bills, neither was reported out of committee, in part because of the opposition of private charities and in part because of resistance to child labor reform.[69]

The bills were based on a plan for a children's commission that Kelley had proposed earlier in lectures published in 1905. The function of the bureau, she wrote, should be to correlate, interpret, and disseminate the essential facts concerning the condition and prospects of children in the United States. Its purpose, reflecting the Progressive emphasis on utilitarianism, should be to promote the "social efficiency" of the future citizens of America. Kelley proposed seven subjects that urgently required investigation: infant mortality, birth registration, orphanages, child labor, desertion, illegitimacy, and degeneracy.

Bureau supporters believed that the nation needed a federal agency concerned exclusively with children. Information about children gathered by several government agencies was not being coordinated, was too technical to be of practical use, was too difficult to obtain, and often was released too late for appropriate action. Kelley complained that private agencies were forced to do research that was properly the responsibility of government. She observed that a "feeble volunteer society" (the National Consumers' League) was compelled to raise a few hundred dollars each year to collect and publish new statutes relating to child labor since the bureaus of labor and education both failed to do so. This was a "standing reproach to the federal government."[70] The models for the Children's Bureau were not local or state agencies for children but the Department of Agriculture and the Bureau of Mines in the Department of the Interior, because the research of these organizations led to regulation and legislation. Proponents of the bureau never tired of calling attention to the disparity between the large sums the government spent on research on agriculture and natural resources and the meager sums devoted to investigating child life. The first Children's Bureau bill called for a staff of fourteen and an annual appropriation of $59,000.[71]

THE *DELINEATOR'S* CHILD RESCUE CAMPAIGN

The 1909 White House Conference for the Protection of Dependent Children was a critical turning point in the campaign for the Children's Bureau. The appeal to President Roosevelt to call the conference came from James West, an editorial consultant to the *Delineator* magazine. West was a lawyer, active in child welfare reform, and a close friend of President Roosevelt. Orphaned at age six, he had spent most of his childhood in institutions.[72]

The *Delineator,* founded in 1873 as a ladies' fashion magazine, retained its emphasis on fashion, but after 1900 it introduced articles on social issues of special interest to women. Inspiration for its Child Rescue Campaign came from George Wilder, the magazine's publisher, who was moved to action by the homeless waifs he saw on the streets near his office. The young novelist Theodore Dreiser had joined the magazine as editor in 1907, just before it launched the crusade.[73] The cover of the first issue on the campaign announced that two million American children needed homes. In response to dramatic stories of four orphans who needed adoption, the *Delineator* received five hundred applications. In the next four years it sent thousands of letters to clergymen asking them to awaken the "mother-consciousness" of the nation and awarded prizes to those who preached the best sermons on the subject.[74] The Child Rescue Campaign appealed to the nation's patriotism more than to its charitable impulses: its chief goal was to help dependent children to become good citizens. A few years after the campaign, Theodore Roosevelt, in a statement called "The Conservation of Childhood," declared that developing the right kind of citizen was more important than developing the mine, the factory, or the railroad. "How far would you get in a stock farm if you ploughed with your colts?" he asked, adding "if you do not have the right kind of citizens in the future, you cannot make any use of natural resources."[75]

West and Dreiser visited President Roosevelt on October 10, 1908, to ask him to call a conference to stimulate a national movement on behalf of dependent and destitute children. Roosevelt agreed, provided that social welfare leader Homer Folks endorsed the idea.[76]

THE 1909 WHITE HOUSE CONFERENCE FOR THE
PROTECTION OF DEPENDENT CHILDREN

With the help of Folks and other prominent child welfare leaders, West drew up a formal plan to submit to the president. At the same time, Dreiser strengthened and expanded the *Delineator*'s effort, primarily by establishing the National Child Rescue League with West as its secretary. On December 22, 1908 West sent President Roosevelt a formal request for a national conference and suggested nine propositions that it should consider. The President issued the call for the conference on Christmas Day 1908. One month later, 216 participants of diverse races, ethnic backgrounds, and political views assembled at the White House.[77]

At that time, institutional versus foster care and public relief versus private charity for dependent children were controversial issues among social workers. The conference reflected these conflicts, but its participants resolved enough of their differences to make thirteen recommendations to the President. They included a strong declaration in support of the care of children in their own homes, with no child to be removed from his or her family solely because of poverty; a statement of preference for home or foster care over institutional care for dependent children; and support for private over public financing. Although many participants favored the establishment of a national private agency for children, the final recommendation of the conference called forcefully for the establishment of a federal children's bureau. Nearing the end of his term, Roosevelt sent a message to Congress on February 2, 1909, outlining the resolutions of the conference, urging their implementation, and recommending prompt legislative action to establish the Children's Bureau.[78]

Although Congress failed to act, the conference successfully promoted improved care for dependent children and support for child welfare reform at the state level. Its support for keeping normal children in their own homes provided the impetus for laws in most states to provide pensions for widowed and dependent mothers. The conference also encouraged the passage of additional child labor laws.[79]

Addams thought that linking the campaign for the bureau to an appeal for a national effort to protect and provide for homeless children was a masterstroke.[80] The issue of dependent children, much less controversial than child labor, evoked deep feelings about the importance of the family and appealed to American sentimentality and patriotism.[81] By focusing the nation's attention on dependent children, the conference marshaled support for government planning and protection for *all* children. Through its discussions and its statement to the president it showed the need to deal with the underlying causes of dependency and other childcare problems, and it served as a symbol of the federal government's new commitment to the nation's children. This symbol was renewed by each of the decennial White House Conferences for children that followed.[82]

AN ENDING AND SEVERAL BEGINNINGS

The years just before, during, and after 1910 saw a profound change in attitudes toward child welfare reform and the related movements to establish the scientific study of children as a basis for reform. They were marked by one important ending and several beginnings.

The important ending was that of Hall's child study movement, with all that it implied about the decline of nineteenth-century views about social reform and of how and why children should be studied. In 1909 psychologist James Mark Baldwin, who had made an important contribution to the study of children through his biological, evolutionary approach, left the United States permanently for Europe and thereby ended his involvement in American efforts to institutionalize child study. William James, whose functional psychology and pragmatic philosophy profoundly influenced both child welfare reform and child study, died in 1910.

The two important beginnings were made by the first White House Conference for Children and Freud's visit to the United States, both in 1909.[83] The next chapter discusses another beginning, the first clinical study of juvenile delinquents and the establishment of the National Committee for Mental Hygiene, in 1909. The end of the decade also witnessed the triumph of scientific pediatrics over traditional views of child nurture, the evolution of courses in "applied philanthropy" into schools of social work, and the first application of the Binet-Simon intelligence scale to American children. By 1909 Cora Bussey Hillis had reached the halfway mark in her campaign for the Iowa Child Welfare Research Station. Two years later Arnold Gesell established his small "psycho-clinic" at Yale, which in 1926 became the Yale Clinic of Child Development. In 1912 the Children's Bureau was founded. All of these beginnings, most of them inconspicuous at the time, took root in important ways during the years up to and including World War I and prepared the way for the breakthrough in the institutionalization and professionalization of scientific child study soon after the war.

Part 2 Creating the Models, 1910–1921

Chapter 5 The Children's Bureau under Julia Lathrop: Government at Its Best

Although many diverse groups supported the campaign to establish a federal agency for children, no bill reached the floor of Congress during President Theodore Roosevelt's administration. And, in spite of President William Howard Taft's support in 1910, no bill reached the floor of either house that year or the next.[1] Opponents argued that a children's bureau would be unconstitutional, because it would give the federal government jurisdiction over state and local agencies concerned with child welfare. Moreover, they maintained, a children's bureau would duplicate the work of other government agencies, particularly the Bureau of Education and the Census Bureau, which could carry out legitimate federal responsibilities more effectively. Such a bureau, they argued, would also interfere with the functions and privacy of the family. Senator Weldon Heyburn of Idaho warned "we have sometimes an oversupply of sympathy . . . for the children whose condition in life is not as favorable as that of some other children. Our sympathies are human; you cannot avoid them; but those clothed with the responsibility of government must be on guard against being swept away on unsafe seas of legislation. This is not a proper subject for legislation. It is a police measure."[2]

Congressman William Joad of Mississippi complained about potential invasion of privacy: "A nine hundred dollar clerk, drest [sic] in a little brief authority, inflated with self-importance, and puffed with impertinence, can knock on the door of an American family and demand admission, and if denied, force his way in." The bill, he said, was "most unregardful of the rights of American citizens." Senator William Borah of Idaho declared, on the other hand, that the federal government's interest in nurseries would be no more unconstitutional than its interest in pigsties, again using an analogy to agriculture.[3]

In later years, many concluded that the close alliance between advocates of the bill and the National Child Labor Committee hurt the bill's chances; its most powerful opponents were southern senators and others who objected to the regulation of child labor. Fearing that the bureau would hinder its work, the New York Society for the Prevention of Cruelty to Children led a vigorous campaign against the bill in 1912. The Commissioner of Education testified against the bill the same year, but officials of the Census Bureau pointed out that the bureau did not have the power to investigate the causes of the unfortunate conditions the data disclosed.[4]

Advocates of a federal children's bureau worked mainly behind the scenes. To reassure critics, they accepted limitations on the proposed bureau's activities: it would have no administrative, executive, or legislative functions and would not investigate physical degeneracy, illegitimacy, or juvenile delinquency. An argument over where to place the bureau was settled by an agreement assigning it to the Department of Commerce and Labor.[5]

President Taft signed the act establishing the bureau on April 9, 1912, nine years after Lillian Wald and Florence Kelley had proposed a federal agency for children to President Roosevelt. The U.S. Children's Bureau was the first government agency in the world to assume responsibility for improving the welfare of a nation's children and until the Great Depression the only federal agency in the United States with a social welfare mission. Although a truly radical agenda had propelled the movement for the Bureau, no newspaper considered its founding worthy of mention.

The statute gave the bureau a broad mandate to "investigate and report . . . on all matters pertaining to the welfare of children and child life among all classes of our people." It instructed the bureau to examine especially "infant mortality, the birthrate, orphanage, juvenile courts, desertion, dangerous occupations, accidents and diseases of children, employment, legislation affecting children in the several states and territories." These subjects were identical to those Florence Kelley had proposed for a U.S. Commission on Children and clearly reflect the Progressive preference for serving the needs of disadvantaged children. Other provisions of the act prohibited the bureau from lobbying members of Congress and specified that its representatives "shall not, over the objection of the head of the family, enter any house used exclusively as a family residence."[6]

In view of the bureau's broad mandate, the funds appropriated seem ludicrously small. Congress cut the bureau's proposed annual budget of $59,000 to $25,640 and prohibited larger appropriations in later years unless authorized by amendment to the establishing law. The bureau therefore had to cope with recurring appropriation crises during its early years.[7] Since authorization of the staff was delayed until March 3, 1913, the bureau had to accomplish the work of the first year with a staff working only two-thirds of a year.

Congress allowed the bureau only fifteen employees, nine of them clerks. Children's advocates were quick to contrast the bureau's minuscule budget and staff with those of the Bureau of Animal Studies, with its annual appropriation of $1,427,800 and a research staff approaching one thousand.[8] They also pointed to the amount of money private foundations and voluntary organizations spent on research on children: the Russell Sage Foundation, $100,000; the Children's Bureau of Philadelphia, $250,000; and the National Child Labor Committee, $50,000.[9]

Handicapped by its small budget and staff, the bureau also encountered continued opposition from congressmen, rival government bureaus, state and local health departments, citizens who objected to what they saw as threats to family privacy, and others who had opposed the bureau's founding. Social justice reformers had hoped that the establishment of a federal bureau would permit them to consolidate and extend their outstanding achievements for child welfare, but even fervent supporters of the bureau now doubted that it could long survive or that it would achieve anything important.[10]

The doubters had not counted on the outstanding leadership of the bureau's first chief, Julia Lathrop, or on the steadfast support she received from her professional networks and the grassroots constituencies for child welfare reform created by women's organizations over the previous two decades. Jane Addams and other social justice reformers had persuaded President Taft to appoint Lathrop, whom Congress quickly confirmed. She thus became, at a time before women could vote, the first woman to hold an important federal office. Progressive women reformers could not have been better represented.[11] President Woodrow Wilson reappointed her in 1918, setting the precedent that bureau chief was not a partisan position.

Lathrop's twenty-two-year experience as a settlement worker prepared her well for her new post. At Chicago's Hull House she had participated in a wide variety of social reform efforts, including the campaign to establish the first juvenile court in the country in 1899. Ten years later, she helped to found the first child guidance clinic. Appointed to the Illinois Board of Charities in 1893, she served until 1901 and again from 1905 to 1909. As a member of the board, she fought vigorously for enforcement of the Illinois civil service law. (On becoming chief of the Children's Bureau, she refused to accept President Taft's recommendations for its staff until he agreed to appoint only persons qualified by federal civil service standards). In Illinois, Lathrop tried to improve conditions for the insane and became a charter member of the National Committee for Mental Hygiene and a leader in the mental hygiene movement. With Sophonisba Breckinridge and Edith Abbott, she helped to establish the research department of the Chicago School of Civics and Philanthropy in 1907, lectured at the school, and remained a trustee until it became the School of Social Service Administration of the University of Chicago in 1920. The school became a professional setting in which social justice reformers continued the research and social activism initiated by Hull House residents. Lathrop often hired its graduates. Starting in 1917 she contracted with the school to undertake research programs for the Children's Bureau.[12]

Possibly the most important consequence of Lathrop's experience as a settlement worker and social justice reformer was her membership in a vast network of Progressive social reformers, including social welfare experts, philanthropists, scholars, physicians, politicians, and eminent clubwomen. Lathrop's skill in tapping this network and transforming it into a constituency for her agency enabled her to overcome the limits of the bureau's budget and staff.[13]

Lathrop approached her new job with a sense of adventure. She wrote to an employee, "Those of us who began four years ago have a special sense of having started out together in a small way on a great undertaking needing almost an explorer's courage."[14] Believing that "a fruitful fact needs no compulsory legislation nor military sanction, nothing but a chance to be used," she appeared undaunted by her meager budget and the ban on lobbying.[15] Lathrop knew that she could count on the support of large numbers of women on issues relating to mothers and children. She had been one of those who helped women's organizations move from cultural and charitable pursuits to welfare reform goals.[16] The clubwomen, many of whom were well educated and informed, had gained valuable experience in social action during the two decades before the bureau's establishment. They were determined to help the bureau do its job.

Recognizing them as a great resource not available to foundations or other government agencies, Lathrop planned to use them not only as a constituency for the bureau but also as a source of volunteer labor.[17]

Since more than a million members of the General Federation of Women's Clubs had campaigned for the bureau's establishment, Lathrop chose the federation's biennial meeting in August 1912 for her first major talk on the bureau's goals. She began by reminding her audience that the Children's Bureau was first urged by "women who have lived long in settlements and who by that experience have learned to know . . . certain aspects of dumb misery which they desired through some governmental agency to make articulate and intelligible."

Jane Addams once remarked that Americans believe local government is the only true self-government.[18] Early in her talk, Lathrop tried to reassure skeptics about the "danger repeatedly mentioned" that a federal bureau would relieve local governments and volunteer associations of responsibility for children. The bureau, she insisted, wished "to arouse rather than to dull" the sense of personal responsibility, "stimulate rather than usurp" the functions of states, cities, counties, and volunteer associations.[19] This turned out to be not mere rhetoric but one of Lathrop's consistent goals. In her conclusion, she reassured her audience that the bureau's work would be carried forward "in a way to respect and to express the spirit of parenthood. . . . There will then be no risk of undue interference, no danger of overbearing agents forcing their way into homes over parental protest, as has been feared."[20]

The bureau was "ready to accept the function of popularizing the wisdom of others." Lathrop told the General Federation that the bureau's first endeavor would be to survey what various private and public agencies and foundations had already found out about child life, and make this information available to the general public in brief, readable monographs.[21] Like Addams, Lillian Wald, and Florence Kelley, Lathrop believed that the bureau could arouse the public to corrective action by giving it clear, objective, vivid information about the harmful social conditions under which many children lived.

Infant mortality, she announced, would be the subject of the bureau's first study. Lathrop knew that this topic appealed to women and was less controversial than child labor. She cited an unnamed authority who claimed that half of the babies who died could be saved by methods within the reach of every community. But the infant death rate could not be known until one knew how many babies were born, and "not a single state, not a single city, has complete registration of births."[22] Lathrop then served notice of the important role she expected clubwomen to play in assisting the bureau. "Within twelve months," she told her listeners, "the members of this great organization could secure for this country effective birth and death records. The federal government cannot do this but the women could."[23]

INVESTIGATION OF ALL MATTERS
PERTAINING TO CHILDREN

The bureau's research continued the pattern of Progressive fact-finding social surveys. Lathrop believed that the bureau should justify, objectively and scientifically, all recommendations it made for the improvement of child life. Child welfare research was therefore its "primary duty." In her view, investigation of social conditions affecting children was "the basic safeguard which the government of the United States seeks to throw about its children."[24] Responding to complaints that the Children's Bureau was taking over functions of the Public Health Service, she argued that child welfare research should be assigned to an agency responsible for the "whole child," rather than partitioned among the sciences. And since medical and social problems were often connected, the bureau had to study both.[25]

Reflecting on the broad mandate Congress had given the bureau, Lathrop decided that it could aim for change only by "small increments," trying to improve rather than to transform life for children.[26] "All we can do to save our faces with posterity," she wrote, "is to go on experimentally in the slowly increasing knowledge of our day, doing what the caveman did—trying to improve things."[27] As we shall see, Lathrop's realistic melioristic approach was in sharp contrast to that of the Laura Spelman Rockefeller Memorial and the Commonwealth Fund, which shortly after World War I launched child study programs with grandiose goals that were soon trimmed or abandoned. Lathrop created less ambitious programs, which her successors were able to carry out. Infant mortality, she pointed out, for instance, was a problem that could be studied piece by piece with quick results.[28]

The bureau's investigation of infant mortality is a good example of its use of social survey research. Its purpose was to find social and economic as well as medical correlates of infant death; its approach was sociological as well as medical, and statistical rather than clinical. The bureau reversed the usual method of studying infant mortality from death records by beginning with birth and following each infant in its sample through its first year or until death, whichever came first.

In response to pressure primarily from women's organizations, Congress in

April 1914 amended the Children's Bureau Act to increase the bureau's authorized appropriation of $25,640 to $139,000. This permitted a staff increase
from 12 to 76 and the initiation of infant mortality research. The bureau's effort
to find out why babies die was a first for any nation.[29]

RESEARCH ON INFANT MORTALITY

Investigation of infant mortality absorbed most of the bureau's energies from
1913 to 1915. Johnstown, Pennsylvania, was the first of eight industrial cities selected for study. Through a house-to-house canvass, female agents identified
and interviewed every family to which an infant had been born during a specified period. They recorded a history of each baby's growth and illnesses and a
description of its home environment, with special attention to feeding practices, hygiene, sanitation, housing conditions, mother's employment, and family income. In each of the eight cities they also gathered data on social, industrial, economic, and sanitary conditions, as well as public health and infant
welfare activity.[30]

Before beginning each study, the bureau won the cooperation of municipal
officers, women's organizations, and local elites and created public interest in
the study through the press and local clergy. Interviewers were instructed not to
ask questions about such sensitive subjects as alcohol use, venereal disease, illegitimacy, and income from boarders or private charities. The bureau's careful
preparations and tactful approach paid off. In every case, the "whole city became interested," local women increased their activities to promote infant welfare, and the result was a lower rate of infant mortality.[31]

The bureau's studies of infant mortality proved to be more comprehensive
and sophisticated than anything previously undertaken. "The combined studies provided a detailed picture of infant mortality in America that both confirmed and challenged prevailing opinion."[32] They confirmed the basic accuracy of census reports and the suspicions of public health officials that in most
mid-sized American cities, public health and infant welfare activity was minimal, and that in cities where such activity was more prevalent, infant mortality
was significantly lower. The most significant findings, however, were derived
from the family interviews because they identified critical factors influencing
the survival of infants. Their greatest impact, Meckel continued, was "in their
demonstration of and insistence on the overwhelming causal significance of
family economic status."[33] An "infant thermometer" showing the inverse relationship between infant mortality and father's income was one of the most

popular devices the bureau developed, according to Katherine Lenroot, "more effective in reaching the public than any report on the study."[34]

Meckel declared, "With their constant reiteration of the influence of family income," the Children's Bureau studies "helped reinvest the American discourse on infant mortality with a substantive economic dimension."[35] The studies showed that the causes of infant mortality "would not be sufficiently countered simply by eradicating maternal ignorance in regard to prenatal and infant hygiene."[36] Although the bureau made enormous contributions to maternal education under Lathrop and Abbott, it never ceased to emphasize that poverty was the fundamental cause of children's problems.

INVESTIGATION OF MATERNAL MORTALITY

The bureau studies on why babies die led directly to the question of why mothers die. After 1914 the focus of infant welfare work shifted from postnatal perils to prenatal care. The Children's Bureau followed this trend by publishing the first of its advice manuals, *Prenatal Care*, in 1913 and by investigating maternal mortality three years later.[37] Beginning with the maternal mortality studies, the bureau turned its attention increasingly to the problems of parents and children in rural areas, especially in the South and pioneer West. Since settlement work had originated in city slums, and the infant mortality investigation had been limited to industrial cities, Lathrop and most of her colleagues had had limited experience with such problems. However, as most families lived on farms, letters to the bureau spelled out the harrowing circumstances in which farm mothers often experienced pregnancy and childbirth and cared for their young children.[38]

A letter from Alice Cutting Phelps, who lived on a ranch in southwestern Wyoming, is a vivid example of the detailed, moving information the bureau received and of the personal relationship that often developed between the agents of the bureau and the mothers who sought its help. As a result of Phelps's letter, Lathrop sent investigators to look into conditions in Wyoming and Montana and to take more direct steps to help mothers there. Phelps wrote to Lathrop in October 1916:

> I should very much like all the publications on the care of my self, who am now pregnant, also on the care of a baby, both No. 1 and No. 2 of the Infant Care series. I live sixty-five miles from a Dr. and my other babies (two) were very large at birth, one 12 lbs., the other 10½ lbs. I have been very badly torn each time through the rectum the last time. My youngest child is 7½ and when I am delivered this time it will be

past 8¼ years. I am 37 years old and I am worried and filled with perfect horror at the prospects ahead. So many of my neighbors die giving birth to their children. I have a baby 11 months old in my keeping now, whose mother died. When I reached their cabin last Nov. it was 22 below zero, and I had to ride 7 miles horse back. She was nearly dead when I got there and died after giving birth to a 14 lb. boy. It seems awful to me to think of giving up all my work and leaving my little ones two of whom are adopted—a girl of 10 and this baby. Will you please send me all the information for the care of myself before and after and at the time of delivery. I am far from a doctor, and we have no means, only what we get on this rented ranch. I also want all the information on baby care, especially right young, newborn ones. If there is anything I can do to escape being torn again won't you let me know. I am just four months along now, but haven't quickened yet.[39]

Lathrop replied:

Your letter of October 19th came in my absence and I have just read it with most earnest attention and sympathy. It is not the only letter of that kind the Bureau has received—it makes very urgent the great question of protecting motherhood. The Bureau is trying to find a plan by which mothers living in remote places can secure the nursing and medical care to which they are certainly entitled. It is an old need, but a new practical question, and it will not be solved until many people can be made to see that a way to provide the required care is possible in every part of our country. May I have the privilege of publishing your letter? Every reference by which it could be identified will, of course, be eliminated. I am sure it will help.

In the past, Lathrop and her staff had often sent clothes or money of their own to mothers in need. Turning to her friend Chicago philanthropist Ethel Dummer, Lathrop asked, "Do you wish to take a flier at old-fashioned practical neighborliness at long range? . . . We have just made a statistical study of maternal mortality which will be sent to you as it issues from the press, and this strange human confirmation of our abstract figures is particularly touching, because the government has no way at present of really helping people such as the writer." Would Dummer, Lathrop asked, like to contribute fifty dollars, half the cost for Phelps to have her baby at the state hospital? Lathrop would personally meet the remaining cost.[40] Dummer immediately sent a check for fifty dollars and later contributed additional funds.[41] The Phelps's baby was delivered safely in the state hospital at Rock Springs in June 1917.[42]

Physician Grace Meigs, who had been appointed director of the bureau's Division of Hygiene in 1914, had initiated investigations of maternal mortality.[43] She wrote to Dummer that a personal visit to Wyoming had "deeply convinced" her that "the demonstration made by Mrs. Phelps's care was a very valuable one" because it showed how impossible it was for a woman to obtain adequate confinement care in isolated districts like those in Wyoming and Montana.[44] In both regions, she added, there was great local interest in having a public health nurse. Lathrop then wrote to Dummer that Mrs. Katherine Morton (president of the State Federation of Women's Clubs, executive secretary of the Wyoming Public Health Association, and president of the State Defense Committee) "is convinced of the importance of a public health nurse and may persuade the Wyoming Public Health Association to pay part of the costs of an 'experimental nurse.'" "Since a new law might be necessary before the county could help pay for a nurse," Lathrop wrote, "this would cause an unfortunate delay . " Estimating that the nurse's salary, a Ford and its upkeep, and an "indispensable margin for emergencies" would cost $3,000 a year, Lathrop asked, "Would you like to contribute something toward the first public health nurse?" Dummer replied, "I will mail you a check for $3,000 whenever you are ready to begin."[45]

Lathrop wrote Morton that the bureau had been offered funds for experiments in the Northwest and she saw no reason why the money could not be turned over to the Wyoming Public Health Association for a prompt demonstration of the benefits of employing a public health nurse.[46] Morton replied, "Your letter astonished me. It is something so new in my experience to have such generous help offered that it is a distinct shock."[47] She explained that she would have to convince the county commissioners of the value of the experiment and would do her best. What plans did the bureau have for the use of the money, she asked? "That is entirely a matter to be decided in Wyoming," Lathrop replied, adding, "Personally, I find it a little embarrassing and exceedingly difficult to separate myself as a government employee from my personal relation to this project."[48]

In February 1918 Morton wrote to both Lathrop and Dummer that the commissioners of Sweetwater County (where Phelps lived) had accepted the money for the nurse, but "never have I talked more earnestly in my life than I did to those two men." She prepared for her meeting with them by obtaining numerous letters from county voters, estimating costs, outlining in detail the duties of such a nurse, and bringing with her a couple who represented "perhaps the most influential family in that county."

This incident and hundreds of others during the bureau's first decade show how it learned about local conditions and problems from the public it served, as well as from its formal studies, and how it then sought solutions. Lathrop's response to Phelps shows her deep sympathy for mothers and children in trouble, her strong personal involvement in the bureau's work, and her ability to draw on her professional and personal network to stimulate local action, always taking great care not to impose the bureau's will. Katherine Lenroot, who became third chief of the bureau in 1934, summed up Lathrop's approach when she declared that the emphasis of the bureau was not only on programs but on getting people involved and finding new ways to utilize human and material resources.[49] Through a series of small steps like the experiment in Sweetwater County, the bureau gained the knowledge and experience to suggest legislation for the protection of mothers and infants that led to the passage of the Sheppard-Towner Act in November 1921. Letters to the bureau and the actions of civic leaders like Dummer and Morton are a few of many examples of the important role women played in creating the welfare system.

During the first decade of the bureau's existence and for several years after Lathrop's resignation in 1921, Dummer helped the bureau in large and small ways. When the United States entered World War I, she offered to become a volunteer staff member of the bureau. That was not possible, Lathrop replied, because bureau staff had to be civil service appointments, but Dummer could become a "roving reporter" on the subject of maternal and child health in rural areas. Dummer helped the bureau for over a decade with its investigations of the effects of illegitimacy on children and what to do about them. Intensely involved in the plight of prostitutes and unwed mothers during the war, she shared her experience and the research she sponsored with the bureau.[50]

OTHER INVESTIGATIONS

Although the bureau focused mainly on infant and maternal health during its first ten years, it also studied such traditional concerns of child welfare reformers as child labor, dependency, and delinquency. It studied child labor in anthracite coal mining, home manufacturing, and farm labor, with particular attention to the effects of farm work on school attendance. It studied the causes and extent of juvenile delinquency, how it was being handled in the courts, and what improvements had been made.[51] It analyzed the results of laws on child labor, juvenile courts, illegitimacy, and mothers' pensions in the United States and abroad. It investigated the effects on children of dangerous occupations and accidents, child neglect, desertion, and physical and sexual abuse. Drawing on the knowledge of experts in child development, pediatrics, and public health, it initiated studies of the health problems of preschool children, their physical status, mental habits, nutrition, and community methods used to improve their care. It pioneered in the study of children abroad, including the effects of World War I on children in allied countries.[52]

The bureau's studies of state regulation of child labor led the Secretary of Labor to ask the bureau to administer the federal child labor law, passed in 1916. Congress appropriated $50,000 for this purpose. The bureau set up a new division to handle this responsibility, directed by Grace Abbott until June 1918, when the law was declared unconstitutional.[53]

During the campaign to establish the Children's Bureau, some congressmen tried unsuccessfully to limit its reporting function to providing information to a few specified government agencies.[54] Had they succeeded, the character of the bureau would have been very different. Lathrop interpreted the reporting function to mean that the bureau should provide as much information about child life as possible directly to the American people, so as to help parents to care for their own children and inform citizens about the needs of "other people's children." Demonstrations such as Baby Week and Children's Year, special exhibits, answers to letters, and publications, radio spots, and pioneering motion pictures for parents on childcare were designed to help prosperous native-born parents as well as immigrants and the poor.[55]

LETTERS TO THE BUREAU

The bureau received more than 8,000 letters in 1913, 90,000 in 1919, and in subsequent years as many as 125,000.[56] Most were from native-born white women in rural areas who did not have access to the health and welfare resources of large communities. Letters also came, however, from women working in industry and urban homemakers.[57] People from all walks of life and all regions of the country wrote for all kinds of reasons. Parents' letters carried an unmistakable message: they wanted, often urgently needed, their government's help with child rearing. Lathrop and other members of the bureau answered every letter, often at length. Answers sometimes required research to locate authorities on particular problems or to identify local agencies that could help. Many letters were addressed "Dear Friend," and the bureau's responses, often handwritten, were appropriately warm and personal.[58] Letters to the bureau showed how difficult it was for most parents to obtain trustworthy, up-to-date child-rearing advice and how many needed help. Parent education literature was scarce before 1925, and no government agency had published childcare advice addressed to parents.[59] Even in communities served by physicians, the professionals often were too busy caring for the very sick to have time for parents' questions about the everyday care of well children or even of children with minor illnesses. L. Emmett Holt's manual on infant care, as we have seen, was impersonal, authoritarian, and provided little help with matters other than feeding.[60]

Letters also showed in striking detail just how difficult and primitive conditions of life were for many American families just before and after World War I. Most homes lacked indoor plumbing, gas, electricity, and central heating. Mothers washed diapers and laundry by hand, and cooked the family's meals and heated water on wood or coal stoves. Some had to pasteurize milk at home and cool it in well water or a cellar. Most travel was on foot, horseback, or horse-drawn vehicle. Outside cities, roads were unpaved and often impassable. Parents were more troubled, however, by frequent childhood illness, often leading to early death, than by everyday hardships. No one knew the cause of infant diarrhea or why so many babies died of it each summer. Parents feared recurrent outbreaks of diphtheria, scarlet fever, whooping cough, measles, typhoid fever, and other childhood diseases. Smallpox was the only disease against which a child could be protected.[61] The letters vividly convey a picture of overburdened, anxious mothers struggling to do their best.[62] Concern for the problems of the poor diminished during the prosperous 1920s, but Lathrop and her successor, Grace Abbott, continued to focus on service to poor families. The bureau's investigations and the letters it received from poor mothers reinforced their convictions that poverty was the main cause of children's problems.

Middle- and upper-class mothers and even some fathers also sought the bureau's help. The new "scientific pediatrics" or the "new psychology" stimulated many of these requests. Patients asked for reassurance when their children did not live up to the norms set by height and weight charts, for advice about left-handed or ambidextrous children, and for help with infant formulas. They also requested clarification of advice in *Infant Care* and literature to distribute to mothers less fortunate than themselves.[63]

CHILDCARE LITERATURE

Lathrop decided very early that the bureau should provide advice on prenatal care and child rearing, beginning with "questions affecting the youngest lives of the nation."[64] The content of both *Prenatal Care* (1913) and *Infant Care* (1914) was influenced by the infant mortality studies. Lathrop chose as author for the bureau's advice manuals Mrs. Max West, a published writer, widow, and mother of five. Since the pamphlets were to be primarily for mothers, Lathrop believed a mother should write them, rejecting the Progressive tendency to rely on experts. The manuals reflected Lathrop's conviction that infant health and welfare depended on much more than medicine and that doctors and mothers should be partners.[65]

West prepared for writing *Infant Care* by undertaking an exhaustive study of the standard literature. She found little that was nontechnical and much that was controversial. Like most bureau staff, she became personally involved with the difficulties mothers faced. In a quest for better material for diapers, for example, she wrote to people throughout the country. West also consulted with physicians, nurses, and other childcare specialists. A particularly difficult problem was to determine under what circumstances parents should seek treatment of a sick child by a physician.[66]

In June 1919 Lathrop asked several leading medical organizations to name representatives to serve on an advisory medical committee to review all its childcare publications. The new committee immediately asked that West's name be removed from the title page of *Infant Care* because she was not a physician. Thereafter no author's name appeared with the title.[67] West was solely responsible for writing *Infant Care* until 1921, when she collaborated with bureau staff member Dr. Dorothy Mendenhall. After 1921 Dr. Martha Eliot and other medical specialists wrote the bureau's childcare literature.[68]

The first edition of *Infant Care*, eighty-five pages in length, selling for five cents or sometimes given away, was an instant success, soon surpassing the Department of Agriculture's *Care of the House* as the most popular government publication. So many congressmen sought the booklet for their constituents that a quota system had to be established. By 1921 almost 1.5 million copies of *Infant Care* had been distributed; the revised 1921 edition sold 2.8 million. By 1922 fifty-two congressmen were receiving copies.[69]

Letters demonstrate that *Infant Care* circulated among the poor. Translated into several foreign languages, it was accessible to immigrants as well as to foreign readers. Some historians have criticized it for reflecting middle-class values and customs.[70] The manual certainly was more middle-class in character than the bureau's typical research report, but it also provided much advice that middle-class mothers would not have needed, such as how to make an icebox. Since Holt made major contributions to the manual, much of what seems middle-class to current scholars may be a reflection of "scientific pediatrics." For example, *Infant Care* endorsed strict scheduling as a way of serving the mother's needs as well as the baby's.[71]

THE CHILDREN'S BUREAU IN WARTIME

World War I had a profound effect on the Children's Bureau by creating a climate favorable to the interests of mothers and children. Familiar admonitions to conserve the nation's children assumed new meaning when almost one-third of potential draftees were deemed unfit for military service, mainly because of unhealthy conditions and inadequate medical care in early childhood. Lathrop's skill in exploiting the new concern for children benefited child welfare reform well into the 1920s.

Once the United States entered the war, Lathrop instructed the bureau to study maternal and child health and welfare in the warring European countries to "see how they were moving to protect children." The studies found that, in spite of the war, several countries had maintained and even strengthened their efforts on behalf of mothers and children. In 1915 England reduced infant mortality to the lowest rate in its history. Meigs used Britain's 1916 "Report on Maternal Mortality in Connection to Child Bearing and Its Relation to Infant Mortality" as a model and source of information for her own important report on maternal health, published by the bureau in 1917.[72]

Lathrop was quick to use the war to dramatize the high rate of infant mortality in the United States. Life in the trenches, she said, was not as dangerous as being a baby in parts of the United States.[73] Josephine Baker, director of the New York Bureau of Child Hygiene, pointed out that more American children than American servicemen died during the war.[74] The bureau's main goal during the war was to accelerate the effort to improve maternal and child health. Lathrop repeatedly linked child-saving to patriotism. President Wilson reinforced her message by announcing, that "next to the duty of doing everything possible for the soldiers at the front, there could be, it seems to me, no more patriotic duty than that of protecting the children who constitute one-third of our population."[75]

Wilson also proclaimed 1918 Children's Year and announced that its purpose was to save the lives of 100,000 American children under five years of age who would otherwise die during the year. Inspired by the successful Baby Week campaigns sponsored by the bureau since 1916, Children's Year was to begin on April 6, the second anniversary of America's entry into the war.[76] President

Wilson gave the bureau $150,000 from his special war emergency fund to carry it out.[77] This enabled the bureau to continue Children's Year for six months after the Armistice, while other agencies were dismantling programs.[78]

Children's Year expanded the bureau's work in birth registration and its efforts to establish prenatal and well baby clinics and increase the number of visiting nurses and public health agencies. The bureau set two significant new goals. First, it focused for the first time on the health care of preschool children. Before World War I almost all public health work had been directed toward babies or school children. The discovery that many of the defects of draftees were caused by rickets and other early-childhood diseases led the bureau to direct its attention to children between the ages of two and five, the ages of most of the 6,500,000 youngsters who were measured during Children's Year. The bureau also expanded its health and welfare services in rural areas. Contrary to the general assumption that country children were universally healthy, Lathrop wrote, the bureau's studies showed the great prevalence of defects among rural children that were "mainly remediable if not preventable." Adapting "creative innovations" developed by local communities, the bureau devised "dramatic ways" to take child welfare into rural areas.[79] This experience led to the special provisions for rural children in the Social Security Act of 1935.

The creation of the Woman's Committee of the Advisory Committee of the Council of National Defense helped Lathrop to consolidate and expand the bureau's work during and after the war. The committee's purpose was to coordinate women's voluntary associations in support of the nation's defense. It represented 7,000,000 women in local units in 17,000 communities. Like the General Federation and other women's organizations, the women's committee agreed to help the bureau carry out Children's Year. Lathrop appointed each state chair an agent of the bureau. The woman's committee helped the bureau to strengthen the relationship with clubwomen it had established during the earlier birth registration and Baby Week campaigns.[80] An estimated 8,000,000 women assisted the bureau during the year.

By the end of the war, Robyn Muncy points out, Lathrop's bureau stood at the head of a consolidated female dominion devoted to child welfare. After the war, the bureau formed a permanent advisory committee consisting of the chairs of the state committees. "As middle-class women emerged from the war better organized than ever," Muncy continues, "they carried the clearest agenda for child welfare reform." They demonstrated their power in 1921 by successfully lobbying for the passage of the Sheppard-Towner Act.[81]

THE SECOND WHITE HOUSE CONFERENCE
FOR CHILDREN AND YOUTH

Lathrop drew on the success of Children's Year to persuade President Wilson to convene a second White House conference in May 1919, thus setting a precedent for decennial conferences on children that continued through 1970. The conference convened some two hundred experts to recommend and publicize "irreducible minimum" standards of child welfare.[82]

Lathrop expected the standards only to set a "goal to work for," the eventual achievement of a "minimum uniformity" among diverse state laws and between the conflicting standards of public and private agencies.[83] Always aware of the importance of interpretation and promotion, she used the conference to define and publicize the bureau's basic philosophy, which she perceived as the extension of democracy to children. The child was entitled to public protection and access to the opportunities democracy promised through the provision of conditions favorable to health, growth, and education proportionate to individual ability. Children were not solely the possession of parents. No less than adults, they had inalienable rights that society was obliged to recognize.[84]

The conference, which included black speakers, made the radical demand that racial discrimination be abolished. In her 1919 presidential address to the National Conference of Social Work, Lathrop referred to the large number of rural child laborers and adult illiterates "who are colored." This population, she reported, "grown three or four fold in the last 50 years, now spreading over the country, north, east and west, is demonstrating that the welfare of colored children is a nation-wide problem which no section can ignore with prudence or honor."[85]

In the same address Lathrop warned, "The public protection of childhood . . . is costly. The standards we are willing to accept and carry forward are a test of democracy because they are a test of whether it is the popular will to pay the cost of what we agree is . . . the wise and safe bringing up of children. . . . Are we willing to spend the money? Can we make ourselves spend the money . . . necessary to give every child a fair chance in life?" she asked. "Let us not deceive ourselves," Lathrop cautioned as she delivered a message that Abbott would repeat during the prosperous twenties to a less receptive public, "Children are not safe and happy if their parents are miserable, and parents must be miserable if they cannot protect a home against poverty. . . . The power to maintain a decent family living standard is the primary essential of child welfare. . . . Society can afford no less and can afford no exceptions."[86]

The minimum standards agreed to at the 1919 conference were meant to apply to all children, Lathrop explained, "not alone the care of special classes, the
poor or sick or orphaned or wayward or helpless—but the essential needs of all
childhood."[87] In her emphasis on *all* children, including preschool children,
Lathrop moved away from the dominant concern of Progressive social reformers with the disadvantaged child, especially the schoolchild, to the "everyday
child" and the preschool child.

The attempt to set standards reflected the desire to replace traditional views
of childhood, based on long-held moral and religious concepts, with views
based on democratic principles and scientific findings. Many immigrant families assessed the child's value in terms of its economic contribution. (The
mother of a thirteen-year-old girl who had died in 1914 responded to Katherine
Lenroot's expression of sympathy with the statement, "Yes, and this child was
almost ready to go to work."[88]) The conference standards with respect to child
labor and compulsory education were part of an effort to persuade parents that
education was more important than the wages children could earn. Agents of
the bureau were on firmer ground when they based their advice on democratic
principles rather than new scientific theories or findings.[89] Alice Hamilton acknowledged how mistaken she had been to trust the recommendations of the
new "scientific pediatrics" and advise mothers to stop feeding babies foods that
nutritionists later recommended.[90]

"What Do Growing Children Need?" a modest four-page pamphlet for parents the bureau issued in 1919, listed the basic requirements for every child under the headings shelter, food, clothing, health and personal habits, recreation
and companionship, education and work, and religious and moral training. In
conclusion it asked, "Is your child getting a square deal? If not what are you going to do about it?" The needs included three square meals a day, a regular bed
hour, at least two hours of outdoor play every day, and a pure water supply. The
bureau received complaints from those who found the standards too high or
too low. One correspondent believed the pamphlet to be "an exceptionally
clever idea" but advised that it could be used with only a minority of the families her agency served.[91] She explained, "We have to be exceptionally careful to
put nothing in their hands which has the appearance of suggesting that they
can afford things beyond their means. We know that a majority of the families
with which we come in contact could not have a separate bed for every child,
and at this time of the year it is practically impossible to have green vegetables,
especially leafy vegetables, every day. And under the conditions in which these
people find themselves a bath every day is almost impossible. While we wish

every child might have all these conveniences and perhaps necessities we cannot hold up such standards before them with their present wages and these few suggestions on a folder on which there are so many valuable suggestions would only tend to make them more reserved with us."[92]

PROTECTION OF MOTHERS AND INFANTS:
THE SHEPPARD-TOWNER ACT

As it entered its fourth year, the bureau gave the first indication that it wanted its studies of maternal and child health to lead to legislation: it recommended the adoption of a nationwide plan for the public protection of infant and maternal health. Again using an analogy to agriculture, the bureau cited the Smith-Lever Act of 1914 as a precedent for such legislation. Smith-Lever gave money to the states for cooperative extension programs involving agricultural colleges and the U.S. Department of Agriculture. The bureau now proposed federal funding for a similar cooperative arrangement between the federal government and state boards of health with child hygiene divisions.[93] In 1917 the bureau proposed a broader plan that included aid for maternal as well as child health. Also in 1917 the bureau began to publish a series of studies that showed the urgent need for maternal and infant health services in rural areas. New Zealand, which had maintained the lowest infant mortality rate in the world for several years, was especially worth emulating because, like the United States, it had large rural areas and a scattered, diverse population.[94]

Members of the bureau believed that advances in child and maternal health would not come primarily from new hospitals, medical research, the training of medical specialists, or even from new cures. Rather, they would be promoted by the better education of mothers in maternal and child hygiene, and the extension of basic medical services to the rural regions of the country. Although the bureau's studies of infant mortality had emphasized poverty as the main cause of infant deaths, its investigations of maternal mortality downplayed economic causes and stressed the lack of obstetrical services outside of large cities.[95]

The New York City Bureau of Child Hygiene served as a model for the maternal and infant health centers that the bureau proposed to establish. Under Baker's direction, it emphasized prevention rather than treatment of illness, relying on public health nurses and well-baby clinics as "educational preventoria." According to Sheila Rothman, this was consistent with the belief during the Progressive era that "maintaining health and preventing illness was a woman's task."[96] The bureau was not proposing anything new or radical but rather asking to expand woman's role in health care by setting up a national network of centers in which women trained in maternal and infant hygiene would teach other women how to maintain good health.

The new health centers that the states were to establish were meant neither to offer remedial services nor to replace services offered by private physicians. Medical schools did not then train physicians to offer preventive health examinations. Obstetricians did not offer prenatal care but restricted their practice to treating complications of pregnancy and delivering babies. General practitioners and pediatricians treated the sick, not the well child. As it turned out, Sheppard-Towner led to a measurable increase in the private practice of pediatricians.[97]

Congress took no action on the first maternal and infant health bill, which was introduced to the House in 1918 by the first woman elected to Congress, Jeannette Rankin of Montana. Congress remained indifferent to a similar bill introduced in 1919 by Senator Morris Sheppard and Representative Horace Towner that included services for preschool children as well as for babies and mothers. Since the bureau had not supported the movement for maternity insurance, its proposals to create more local health centers did not include any provision for financial assistance to mothers. Undoubtedly congressional approval seemed unlikely at that time. Given the hard fight for the passage of the Sheppard-Towner Act and the refusal of Congress to renew it in 1929, this assumption was correct.

Sheppard and Towner reintroduced their bill in 1921, and after a campaign distinguished by the passion of both supporters and opponents, it won by a landslide. Arguments against the bill included attacks on feminism, defense of state's rights, charges that it would impose socialized medicine and lay control over medicine, and the familiar claim that such federal programs would allow government to intrude into the private realm of the family. Opposition was overcome by a powerful lobby of women, the fruit of long effort by Jane Addams, Florence Kelley, Lillian Wald, and especially Julia Lathrop. The opponents were too afraid of the unknown power of the women's vote to reject the first bill that enfranchised women strongly supported.[98]

The passage of Sheppard-Towner was hailed as a great victory for the woman's movement for child welfare reform. Kelley declared that the campaign was the most important effort she had shared in her forty years of working for social reform. But it was not a complete victory. Congress reduced the proposed annual appropriation of $4,000,000 to $1,240,000. The states could not receive grants unless they passed enabling legislation. Then they had absolute control over how the money was to be spent. The most important change from the original bill was the provision that the program could be funded for only five years, after which it had to be evaluated and reproved by Congress. The statute included a clause almost identical to one in the Children's Bureau Act, forbidding government employees to enter a home without the consent of the head of the family. Congress designated the Children's Bureau to administer the act.[99] The Sheppard-Towner Act was a stunning verification of Lathrop's belief that proper action would follow "truth made public." Historians have viewed the act as a continuation of Progressivism into the 1920s, the first venture of the federal government into the area of social legislation, and the most important social legislation before the New Deal.[100]

LATHROP'S LEGACY

Assured that President Warren G. Harding would appoint Grace Abbott to succeed her, Lathrop resigned in August 1921, three months before Sheppard-Towner became law.[101] In 1921 the bureau had an appropriation of $164,640 and a staff of 76. In 1922, partly because of its administration of Sheppard-Towner, its appropriation increased to $355,213 and its staff to 132.

After retiring from the bureau, Lathrop served as president of the Illinois League of Women Voters from 1922 to 1924. Deeply concerned about the findings of a survey of the postwar conditions of European children, she happily accepted an appointment to the Child Welfare Committee of the League of Nations in 1925, where she served for six years. She decided not to run for Congress because she thought she could accomplish more in the private sphere. She believed her major achievement as Children's Bureau chief was that she kept it from becoming politicized. She died in 1932 at the age of seventy-three.[102]

While chief of the bureau, Lathrop was ridiculed as a "maiden lady" unqualified because of her "spinsterhood" to advise the nation about its children. During the Red Scare and the outbreak of patriotic fervor after the war, she was attacked as a socialist or a Bolshevik plotting to overthrow democratic institutions.[103] Historians generally speak well of her, except for the middle-class assumptions reflected in *Infant Care* and for what some consider her outmoded unemancipated views on feminist issues.[104] Scholars, however, have neglected her. Addams, Wald, Kelley, and Grace and Edith Abbott have all been subjects of at least one full-length biography, but the closest approximation to a biography of Lathrop is a memoir by Jane Addams that omits Lathrop's years at the

Children's Bureau. Historian Mary Beard, Lathrop's contemporary, thought it unfortunate that Lathrop's biography had been left to her old friend Addams because she took Lathrop "more for granted than others remote from the friendship might be inclined to do." Beard commented, "We have the record of the woman—a thing of infinite value, of course—but not the drama of the woman battling against vested interests, social indifference and emotional lethargy."[105]

Beard eloquently expressed her own view of Lathrop: "Julia Lathrop's calm, rational thesis that poverty underlies social problems was put forth as her mature interpretation of history, even from the center of government while she was Chief of the Children's Bureau. . . . This was a valiant as well as an intellectual performance. It called for both insight and courage to the highest degree. The conviction animated Miss Lathrop's action all along the line of social endeavor. . . . There it stood, while she lived—her clear analysis of social struggle expressed in terms unveiled and unmistakable. . . . Her life and action were throughout her days a challenge to thought and action by her fellow citizens."[106]

Lathrop's most striking achievement may have been the relationship she created between the bureau and the nation's mothers. One wonders if there has been any other government bureaucracy so trusted and loved. Affection for and gratitude to the bureau are documented in correspondence and by the ways in which women, and many men, rallied to its support.

Two anecdotes told by Katherine Lenroot, the third bureau chief, convey how much the bureau meant to mothers who sought its help. Riding on a bus, Lenroot overheard a woman giving information about childcare to a fellow passenger, who asked the former how she knew so much. "Oh, I'm a state mother. I receive mother's aid and have to know about these things," she proudly replied. The bureau was determined to remove the stigma of the poor law from aid to mothers and children. Its success is in sharp contrast to today's attitudes toward welfare mothers. Lenroot's second story is about a mother who bore a healthy baby boy after receiving prenatal care from a state health department funded under the Sheppard-Towner program. She was so grateful that she named the baby State Board of Health, calling him State for short. To many who are familiar with its story, the early Children's Bureau still represents, in the words of Margaret Mahoney, "government at its best."[107]

The Children's Bureau was one of three new institutions created by women welfare reformers in their quest to find out what children really need. Another, the child guidance clinic, also created with important help from both Dummer and Lathrop, is the subject of the next chapter.

Chapter 6 From Juvenile

Delinquency Research

to Child Guidance

No Progressive Era reform movement provides a better example of the interaction of clubwomen, settlement workers, male welfare reformers, psychologists, psychiatrists, and sociologists than the effort to improve juvenile justice. The main goals of this conglomerate were to help young offenders to discover and eliminate the causes of their misconduct, instead of punishing them as adult criminals. "We all felt," Jane Addams wrote, "that in addition to the study of conditions responsible for the delinquency of the child there should be added the study of the child himself, not only that a scientific estimate of his abnormality might be placed at the disposal of the judge, but also that the child's full cooperation might be secured in the task of his own rehabilitation."[1] Cooperation among these diverse reformers was made possible by shared assumptions drawn from functional psychology, instrumentalism, and pragmatism.[2]

Hull House residents and Chicago clubwomen led the campaign to establish the first juvenile court in the nation in 1899. Ten years later they arranged for an investigation into the causes of juvenile delinquency by neurologist William Healy, who conducted a five-year clinical study of 823 children and youth referred to the Chicago court. Healy's research, supported by Chicago philanthropist Ethel Dummer, was published as *The Individual Delinquent.*[3] As David Rothman has commented, it is hard to imagine a title more expressive of progressive thinking.[4] A classic in its own time, *The Individual Delinquent* helped launch the child guidance movement of the 1920s, which led ultimately to the emergence of a unique American child psychiatry.

ETHEL STURGES DUMMER

The activities of Healy's sponsor, Ethel Dummer (whose collaboration with the early Children's Bureau has been described in Chapter 5) illustrate the dominance of beliefs and values associated with Progressivism in the thought of early-twentieth-century reformers. In 1909 Dummer was a forty-year-old mother of four. Her father, a banker, had left more than $300 million to his widow and three daughters. Dummer used much of her share to help support reform programs and scientific investigations, to which her husband, mother, and one of her sisters also contributed.[5] Her work with the National Child Labor Committee and the Juvenile Court Committee of the Chicago Woman's Club earned her an appointment to the Juvenile Protective Association, established in 1906 to investigate social conditions contributing to juvenile delinquency.

Dummer's reaction to the children she observed through her work with the association illustrates Addams's conviction that club work released middle-class women from sheltered lives, exposed them to the effects of urban poverty on children and families, and incited them to action. Exposure to "poverty and perversion" caused Dummer "months of acute suffering" and "confusion" and forced her to rethink her values. Her first year of work with the association "brought many a shock as case after case taught me the realities of life. I would return to my husband, saying, 'Any one of the cases reported today would break the heart, but when thirty are heard, it stirs the brain. Those people are not to blame. It is the fault of conditions. We who have time to think must alter them.'"[6] She found herself unable "to condemn that which I had always been taught abstractly was evil." Evil was "an anachronism."[7] Echoing Addams, she asserted that "not charity but justice" was the goal.

Along with other Progressive social reformers, Dummer believed that science should be the foundation of reform.[8] Therefore, she supported scientific investigation of social problems, rather than charitable enterprises. Her initiative in discovering social problems in need of research and arranging for their investigation distinguished her from other woman philanthropists of her time.[9] Her customary procedure was to identify experts, bring them together in a conference, and arrange for and finance publication of the conference proceedings. A founder and trustee of the Chicago School of Civics and Philanthropy, she corresponded with eminent scholars in the United States and abroad (including Freud), whom she often tried to influence as well as learn from. Like Hall, Dummer believed that science and religion led to the same truths. "What wonderful psychologists the old Hebrews were," she wrote to Healy. "We seem to be rediscovering through science what they knew by intuition."[10]

Dummer financed Healy's postgraduate studies abroad two years before his selection as director of the five-year juvenile delinquency study and continued to support his research even after he left Chicago to direct a new guidance clinic in Boston. Her support of Healy's research anticipated by about a dozen years the funding of clinical study of children by the Commonwealth Fund. Dummer also supported the work of sociologist William I. Thomas, psychologist Miriam Van Waters, and others. Dummer was the only woman leader who participated in all three major efforts to study children: the child guidance and child development movements and the work of the Children's Bureau.

Directly after her appointment to the Juvenile Protective Association, Dummer invited scholars and settlement workers to meet at her home to consider how the association should proceed with its investigation of juvenile delinquency.[11] In 1908, after an unsuccessful attempt to persuade a judge that "a wise physician rather than a man trained in the law would be of value in a juvenile court," Merritt W. Pinkney, a juvenile court judge, appointed the Research Committee on Delinquency, Its Cause and Prevention.[12] Lathrop was named its chair, and Dummer a member. The committee invited scholars throughout the country to suggest a specialist to undertake the research. Dummer's assignment was to consult psychologists, and Healy was among those invited to present a plan of study. His response, plus an endorsement by William James and Adolph Meyer, made him the committee's choice.[13] Dummer donated $25,000, which permitted the Illinois Juvenile Psychopathic Institute to begin its five-year study in April 1909.

Historians of child study have emphasized the role of settlement workers in launching Healy's juvenile delinquency study and have failed to give Dummer sufficient credit for her part in these events. They also have given insufficient attention to important developments between 1915 and 1922 that prepared the way for the Commonwealth Fund's decision to sponsor its influential child guidance and mental hygiene programs of the 1920s.

WILLIAM HEALY AND THE JUVENILE
PSYCHOPATHIC INSTITUTE

William Healy was nine when his family came to America from England in 1878. He dropped out of elementary school to help support his family but continued to educate himself. His participation in the Chicago Ethical Culture Society attracted the attention of the Reverend William M. Salter, William James's brother-in-law, who helped Healy enter Harvard as a "special student" at age twenty-four. At Harvard he studied under and enjoyed a personal relationship with James and was influenced by psychiatrist Elmer E. Southard, a staunch advocate of social involvement by psychiatrists. Seven years after entering Harvard, Healy had earned his B.A. and an M.D. from Rush Medical College of the University of Chicago. He attributed his zest for scientific knowledge to his faith that science would lead him to a truth superior to religion, a "better truth" than that of his fundamentalist father, who "never read a nonreligious book."[14] As an instructor in neurology at the Chicago Polyclinic in 1903, his perceptive comments on troubled children attracted the attention of Hull House residents. Healy joined the Hull House circle and through it met the woman he soon married. He later emphasized that the idea for the study of juvenile delinquents came from settlement workers, not physicians or psychiatrists. "They were a glorious set of women," he declared, "a most remarkable set of women."[15]

During postgraduate studies in Europe, Healy had found no research, either on children or criminology, that would be useful to his investigation, nor did he find any useful information in the United States. He located two psychological clinics engaged in research on children, the Lightner Witmer clinic at the University of Pennsylvania, founded in 1896, and the research clinic at the Training School for the Feebleminded at Vineland, New Jersey, established in 1906.[16] Both were more interested in measuring mental capacity and discovering mental deficiency than in psychopathology. "Not even physiological norms were available," he wrote. "Standardized mental tests had to be developed, . . . the importance of family attitudes and conditioning was barely realized. As for any scientific studies of the bases of children's behavior tendencies, it was said that we in Chicago would have to blaze a new trail."[17]

Healy began his research without preconceptions about the causes of juvenile delinquency and devoted himself entirely to fact-finding. "I had never studied children before," he said. "I had no theories about them." Like other pragmatists, he kept an open mind about "ardently espoused, widely accepted, and curiously disparate determinist theories about human behavior." Some alleged causes were "enlarged tonsils and adenoids, infections in tonsils and teeth or elsewhere, impacted teeth, uncorrected refractive errors, cigarette smoking," and "degeneracy," or defective genes.[18]

Although he acknowledged that inherited traits and organic disorders often contributed to delinquency, Healy believed that his most important discovery was the complexity and multiplicity of factors involved in causing, preventing, and treating delinquency. The multiple causes of children's deviant behavior could be understood, he emphasized, only through careful study of individual life histories: "We called our institute the Juvenile Psychopathic Institute. . . . That just goes to show how much at that time I was under the influence of everybody else. . . . There was something the matter with the kid mentally or he wouldn't be an offender."[19] After 1921 no clinic used "psychopathic" in its title, and child guidance began to shift its focus from the abnormal to the normal.[20]

Dummer also believed that the maintenance of health and a good environment were more important than treating problem children.[21] After 1915 she worked to improve elementary school education and for programs to enrich the lives of normal children. In 1934 she resigned from the board of the National Probation Association, explaining, "More and more I am impressed with the danger of giving children court records." Mental hygiene work for children "should be carried on in schools rather than through courts and probation."[22]

Healy's case histories focused on the extent and causes of individual variation among children with emphasis on the settings in which differences arise. Each history was based on interviews with the child's family and other relevant persons, but most important was the "child's own story."[23] Healy's approach differed not only from that of clinical psychologists but also from that of most institutional psychiatrists, who were satisfied with asking their patients a few pointed questions. To Healy and his followers, with a few exceptions—notably Adolph Meyer and Thomas Kirkbride—psychiatrists were more concerned with classification of mental disease and custodial care than with the treatment of patients. Healy's case studies, according to Lawson Lowrey, were "practically revolutionary."[24]

Healy believed that delinquency and other conduct disorders were usually caused by underlying, usually unconscious, emotional conflicts. Most significantly, he defined delinquency as "learned behavior" that could be unlearned or kept from being learned in the first place. This was a dramatic departure from the prevailing pessimism about the possibility of preventing or treating delinquents. Acknowledging the influence of the social environment on behavior and strongly endorsing the efforts of social justice reformers, Healy nevertheless emphasized that poverty and other adverse conditions did not, by themselves, produce criminals. It was, rather, the unique effect of the particular environment on the particular psyche.

British readers of *The Individual Delinquent* were "astonished," according to Cyril Burt, by Healy's lack of emphasis on poverty. He cited poverty as a major cause of delinquency in only 0.5 percent of the cases and as a minor cause in only 7.1 percent. In a volume of 830 pages, the only paragraph on poverty occupied seventeen lines. Healy gave more attention to "extreme love of adventure," "marked sensual type," "excess masturbation," and "defective vision" than to poverty as a cause of delinquency.[25] He emphasized the selective influence of the environment on behavior, believing that it was "necessary to adjust man's inner nature and inner disposition to social change as well as to modify man's physical and social environment."[26] His intention was not to undermine reform of the physical and social environment but to suggest that social action alone was not enough to enable individuals to overcome emotional problems. Indeed, he showed his impatience with the slow progress of social action in a letter to Dummer written three days before the Armistice from a hospital where he was recovering from an illness. He wrote, "There are blocks of houses right here by this hospital and dram shops and other vile holes which ought to be destroyed on the spot. . . . You can work at your ameliorations as long as you please but decent citizens on the average are not going to be forthcoming from such conditions. I am mighty glad that this government has taken up the housing question and I pray for the success of prohibition."[27]

The Individual Delinquent played a crucial role in changing traditional assumptions about the causes of delinquency and other childhood disorders, promoted well-rounded studies of individual children, and caused a decisive break in the United States from European approaches to the study and treatment of criminals. Healy and most other scholars considered it his most important book, but by 1930 he had published eight additional works, including collections of case studies and books on pathological lying, honesty, the mental conflicts of delinquent children, and the structure and meaning of psychoanalysis.[28] Within another decade Healy had published an additional five books and numerous articles. He dedicated the 1929 edition of *The Individual Delinquent* to Dummer.

The detailed factual information in *The Individual Delinquent* was primarily responsible for its success in challenging previous assumptions about the causes of juvenile delinquency. As Healy put it, "the mass of ascertained facts overwhelmed theory."[29] Psychologist Augusta Bronner, who participated in Healy's research in Chicago in 1917, became co-director with Healy of the Judge Baker Foundation in Boston. She observed that, unlike some researchers, who accompany a page of facts with a page and a half of interpretation, "we give a paragraph of interpretation to several pages of facts."[30] Healy endorsed many psychoanalytic views of the child that were beginning to find expression in American literature, but, like his mentor Adolph Meyer and unlike Freud, he was strongly empirical and pluralistic in his thinking. He disregarded theoretical consistency and deliberately used the term "mental analysis" rather than "psychoanalysis." He discovered that, as a child told his or her story, unconscious motivations often became apparent, not only to the therapist but to the child as well, who would exclaim that he or she now knew the reason for stealing, or running away, or some other problem.[31]

ADOLPH MEYER AND THE MENTAL HYGIENE MOVEMENT

Adolph Meyer's important contribution to the beginnings of child guidance was less direct than Healy's and is less recognized.[32] Meyer was the most eminent psychiatrist in the United States between 1895 and 1940. His "psychobiology," rather than Freud's psychoanalysis, was chiefly responsible for the transition in the United States from a passive and descriptive to a dynamic and biological psychiatry. Meyer, rather than Freud, influenced the psychiatrists who directed the early guidance clinics. He gave American psychiatry its distinctive character by incorporating pragmatism, instrumentalism, and pluralism. His works refer repeatedly to the important influence on his development of James, John Dewey, Charles Peirce, and other pragmatists.[33]

Meyer emigrated from Switzerland in 1892, when he was twenty-six. During his years in Illinois he became a close friend of Dewey and also came to know Addams, Lathrop, George Mead, Charles Cooley, and others associated with Hull House and the University of Chicago. He was active in the Illinois Child Study Society, the largest and most influential of the state child study organizations. Like G. Stanley Hall, Meyer called attention to the importance of childhood. He emphasized the need to recognize and treat childhood disorders in order to prevent adult mental illness, and the potential contribution of schools as therapeutic agencies.[34]

When Meyer became chief pathologist at Worcester State Hospital in Massachusetts in 1895, Hall immediately appointed him docent in biology and psychiatry for graduate students at nearby Clark University.[35] He became chief of the Pathological Institute of New York State Hospitals in 1902, professor of psychiatry at Johns Hopkins in 1908, and, in 1913, founding director of the Henry Phipps Psychiatric Clinic at Johns Hopkins, where he spent the rest of his life.[36]

Meyer's influence on child guidance clinics stemmed primarily from his important role in American psychiatry and the mental hygiene movement. Several years before Healy sought the "child's own story," Meyer insisted on obtaining a complete personal history of each patient. Spurning the separation of body and mind, constitution and environment, he was interested in the interaction of genetic and social factors that made each person, in Meyer's phrase, a "unique experiment of nature."[37] Life histories of Meyer's patients "seemed to clarify why they were disturbed and suggested ways of helping them," and he would therefore "cease looking for 'something else' to explain their mental disorders."[38] For Meyer, as for Addams and other settlement workers, learning from concrete experience was all-important. Like Healy, he began his clinical studies without preconceptions.[39] The generalizations of psychoanalysis, of hereditary determinists, and of other schools, he suggested, should be appraised on a pragmatic basis. He would "try to make more and more convincing and attractive the study of the accessible facts and their use in contrast to that of the exotic and largely dogmatic."[40] He tried to ascertain what worked and what did not and spent much of his life overcoming philosophical systems that he believed blocked constructive thinking. Although he believed that a patient's life could be changed by modifying both his environment and his habit patterns, he eschewed the extreme optimism of some reformers, and his meliorism made him critical of those who saw in child guidance clinics a panacea for the nation's ills.

Inspiration for the American mental hygiene movement, as for the study of delinquents, came from a lay person, Clifford Beers, a former inmate of a mental institution who was determined to arouse the public to the need for better treatment of the insane. Meyer saw in Beers "the voice of the sensitized layman destined to bring physician, patient and the public together."[41] James, Meyer, and other psychiatrists and social justice reformers quickly offered help. Meyer played a leading role in the emergence of the mental hygiene movement be-tween 1907 and 1909.[42] He convinced Beers to revise the concluding chapters of his book *The Mind That Found Itself* and suggested that Beers substitute "mental hygiene" for "insanity" in the title of a new organization he was pro-posing.[43]

James wrote Meyer, "I find that 'mental hygiene' doesn't bite."[44] Meyer replied, "We have to outgrow the term insanity and the connotation of the nar-rower psychotherapy" and should use a "constructive term."[45] "Mental hy-giene," Meyer believed, would suggest that the organization would be compa-rable to public health agencies, which had been so successful in reducing morbidity and mortality. James responded, "scourges fix attention more than ideals," but Meyer prevailed, and the name of the new organization, founded in 1909, was the National Committee for Mental Hygiene (NCMH). Meyer per-suaded Beers to broaden his therapeutic goal to include positive and preventive measures that would enable the committee to serve as an agency for reform and education.[46]

THOMAS SALMON AND THE NATIONAL
COMMITTEE FOR MENTAL HYGIENE

Thomas Salmon was the most influential proponent of psychiatric clinics for children during the years immediately before and after World War I. He be-came medical director of the National Committee for Mental Hygiene in 1912, a staff member of the Rockefeller Foundation the following year, and from 1915 to 1921 was an influential member of its board of directors. At the Common-wealth Fund's request, he wrote the 1920 report that became the basis for its first five-year child guidance program. Endowed with enormous ability and great personal charm, Salmon nevertheless seems an unlikely ambassador for child guidance. His biographer described Salmon's inability to support his fam-ily properly and declared him a better husband than father.[47] Salmon was fond of telling how he entertained his children by shooting rats that ventured out of their holes into the living room of the family's Staten Island home.[48]

Through Salmon's influence, and with the financial support of the Rocke-feller Foundation, the NCMH initiated a series of important surveys and stud-ies of criminals and the mentally retarded. One of the most influential was a study of the psychopathology of crime conducted at the psychiatric clinic of New York's Sing Sing Prison by psychiatrist Bernard Glueck.[49] By tracing crim-inal behavior to childhood disorders, Glueck supported the argument that psychiatric intervention to prevent delinquency must be made available to children younger than those brought before the juvenile court. Salmon regarded the Sing Sing study as a "prelude to the child guidance movement."[50]

Another influential NCMH study showed that mental retardation was responsible for a far smaller proportion of prison inmates than Henry Goddard, author of *The Kallikak Family: A Study in the Heredity of Feeblemindedness,* had suggested.[51] By this time Goddard himself had changed his mind about the connection between mental retardation and delinquency. Appointed director of the Bureau of Juvenile Research in Ohio in 1918, Goddard undertook research showing that psychopathology was present at all intelligence levels.[52] Convinced that emotional disorders were responsible for criminal behavior and that these disorders were often acquired rather than inherited, Goddard abandoned his fatalistic attitude toward juvenile delinquency and joined the child guidance movement.[53]

Salmon argued that Healy's research and the NCMH studies showed that treatable emotional disorders were responsible for criminal behavior and that adult disorders could often be traced to childhood experience.[54] Admitting that some mental diseases are "beyond control with present knowledge," Salmon predicted that "not less than 50 percent of the enormous toll which mental disease takes from the youth of this country can be prevented by the application, largely in childhood, of information and practical resources that are now available."[55]

THE EFFECTS OF WORLD WAR I

World War I was an important influence on the evolution of psychiatric clinics for children. Juvenile delinquency increased during the war, drawing additional attention to an already well-known social problem. Psychiatry gained prestige because of its wartime affiliation with the military and because publicity about widespread mental disorders among soldiers increased public awareness of mental illness.[56]

In 1916 the NCMH asked Salmon to investigate mental disease among soldiers. When the United States entered the war, Salmon became chief of the Section of Neurology and Psychiatry in the Office of the Surgeon General and quickly established a screening process to detect recruits with mental disorders. The careful selection of recruits, followed by the rehabilitation of soldiers who broke down during the war, led psychiatry to recognize the importance of mental deviation in everyday life.[57] As director of psychiatry for the American Expeditionary Force, Salmon emphasized that "shell-shock" was not correlated to shelling, had no apparent physical cause, and should be attributed to prior environmental influences.[58] His overseas experience also reinforced his belief that emotional disorders originated in early childhood. "There is no essential difference between the mechanisms shown in much of the 'nervousness' of children," Salmon claimed, "and those of the war neuroses, for even at a very early age a flight from the facts of life into the fancied security of 'nervousness' is possible."[59] After treating soldiers in combat, neuropsychiatrist Douglas Thom also turned to preventive psychiatric work with children after the war.[60] Freed of its responsibilities to the military, the NCMH decided to focus on children and prevention, all but forgetting its original goal, better care of the mentally ill.

The war influenced the development of psychiatric clinics for children as well as adult psychiatry and social work. The apparent military usefulness of mental testing contributed to its high repute after the war, and psychologists versed in mental testing became an integral part of the child guidance team. They were used mainly to administer and interpret a variety of new tests to measure intelligence, special abilities and disabilities, educational achievement, and personality traits. Healy's colleague Augusta Bronner observed that her mentor, educational psychologist Edward Thorndike, had used mental tests to accumulate statistical findings that would allow him to formulate general principles. Thorndike, she added, "didn't care a hoot about" helping individuals. Healy used mental tests to learn how to understand and help the child.[61] Healy's approach to mental testing became the model for the child guidance clinics.

The shortage of psychiatrists during the war prompted Smith College to establish a training school for psychiatric social workers that provided the guidance clinics of the 1920s with well-trained workers. The New York School of Social Work, strongly influenced by Glueck's study at Sing Sing, offered its first course in mental hygiene in 1917. The school helped the NCMH and the Commonwealth Fund to plan their first five-year program for the prevention of juvenile delinquency, begun in 1922.[62]

THE REVOLUTION IN SOCIAL CASEWORK

Healy's view of poverty as an indirect rather than a direct cause of children's problems and the related shift from a predominantly sociological to a more psychological outlook were significant departures from the views of the settlement workers who had prompted his study of juvenile delinquents.[63] Even though Mary Richmond's classic *Social Diagnosis* insisted that social casework and social action must proceed together, caseworkers joined Healy in shifting emphasis from economics to emotions, from poverty to personality, as they sought to understand the different consequences of experience for different individuals.[64] Independently of Healy, they reached many of the same conclusions about the need to recognize and analyze the complexity of the interaction between the outer world and social reality and the value of detailed information about families. They focused less on physical home conditions and more on the family and its relationships.[65] Instead of trying to reform the nation, they concentrated on ways to help their clients adjust to the circumstances in which they found themselves. This shift in focus was to have a profound influence on child guidance clinics.[66]

The shift was readily apparent at the 1919 convention of the National Conference of Social Work (NCSW). The conferences had always included mental hygiene and psychiatry in their convention programs, but these topics dominated the 1919 meeting. Historian Kathleen Woodroofe concludes that the shift from social reform to children's emotions had swung too far, that too little attention was being paid to the context in which the personality was formed. Psychiatrist C. Macfie Campbell's comment that "delinquency may be delinquency not of the individual but of society," Woodroofe added, was "an environmentalist voice crying in a wilderness of individualism." Salmon, she wrote, "emphasized the fact that attention must be directed first, last, and at all times to the individual, but how the individual was affected by the structure and functioning of the social order was never considered, nor were ways in which his mental processes were influenced by the prejudices and predilections of society."[67] Psychiatric social worker Jesse Taft observed a "new note" at the 1919 conference, "prophetic of the next step, the new focus of psychiatry and caseworker interest on the mental health of the child, the maladjusted school child, the delinquent child, the placed-out child." Nevertheless, according to Taft, social caseworkers were on the whole focused on parents and still unfamiliar with children.[68]

INNOVATIONS OF THE JUDGE BAKER
FOUNDATION

Healy left the Chicago Juvenile Psychopathic Institute in 1917 to direct a new psychiatric clinic for children, the Judge Baker Foundation in Boston. Judge Harvey H. Baker had decided to establish a clinic modeled on the one in Chicago when an adolescent girl brought before the Boston juvenile court told him, "I know that you can do what you like with me but you don't understand me in the least." Her response made him want to understand more about the children whose futures he decided.[69] Within two years of Baker's death in 1915, his friends had raised enough money to establish a clinic, guarantee its operation for ten years, and persuade Healy and Bronner to become its directors.[70]

They accepted mainly because Boston's social welfare agencies were superior to those in Chicago.[71] The quality of local agencies and schools was crucial because the Judge Baker clinic and other early clinics did not themselves administer therapy but relied on local agencies and schools to carry out their recommendations. Their focus was on neither large-scale social reform nor individual psychotherapy but on "environmental manipulation," including educating teachers about a child's problem, offering special tutoring, arranging for medical care, transferring a child to a military academy or another school, sending him to the country or to a summer camp, placing him in a foster home, providing better recreation, or counseling parents on better child rearing methods.[72]

Healy and Bronner introduced several important innovations at Judge Baker that reflected changing attitudes toward the treatment of troubled children, most of which were adopted during the 1920s and early 1930s by the Commonwealth Fund's demonstration clinics and other new clinics inspired by its program. The Judge Baker clinic accepted referrals not only from courts but also from social agencies, schools, and even parents. Within ten years, fewer than half of its referrals came from courts. The clinic's need to deal with many social agencies led to the introduction of the "child guidance team."[73] The team, always composed of psychiatrists, psychologists, and social workers, became so ubiquitous that Leo Kanner dubbed it the "holy trinity."[74] Pediatricians were on the staffs of some clinics but were never part of the team.

An important consequence of the team innovation was a change in the relationship between psychiatrist and social worker. Previously, they had collaborated in hospitals, where the social worker was very much the subordinate. Unlike hospital psychiatrists, guidance clinic psychiatrists worked with relatively normal children in the context of home, school, and community. In this unfamiliar setting, they were highly dependent on the knowledge and experience social workers had gained from working with families and community agencies. As they learned from social workers and psychologists, psychiatrists changed their own views and lost some of the superior status they had enjoyed in the hospital.[75]

Healy introduced the team because he believed that the knowledge and skills of different specialists were required to understand the multiple conditions contributing to each child's problems. Each team member assessed the child and his situation from a different perspective and then joined other team members in regular staff conferences to integrate their evaluations before making a diagnosis.[76] In 1930 the fund declared that the staff conference was "the most important contribution of child guidance to the emergence of a unique American child psychiatry."[77]

The Judge Baker Clinic differed from its Chicago predecessor in attributing interpersonal relations, and the social rather than the economic environment, as the crucial cause of children's problems. This shift in emphasis was explicitly expressed in educational literature and particularly in its twenty-year report, which contained many statements like the following: "the physical features of the home are not nearly so important as the attitudes and feelings of members of the family toward each other"; "neighborhood conditions are not so important as the effects of school and other social contacts upon the child"; "those who advance the 'economic pressure theory' . . . disregard the fact that children in the same families, or living under similar conditions elsewhere, are not troublesome."[78] Judge Baker's outstanding contribution, Healy believed, was "selling the idea of that type of clinic."[79]

Research on juvenile delinquents and the mental hygiene movement paralleled each other for a dozen years. They came together in 1922, when the NCMH and the Commonwealth Fund cosponsored a five-year program for the prevention of juvenile delinquency, described below in chapters 13 and 14.

THREE APPROACHES TO CHILD STUDY

Child guidance clinics' initial purpose was to study juvenile delinquents and children with serious emotional or behavioral problems. Children's Bureau research was primarily concerned with disadvantaged children, those who were physically or economically handicapped or were living in rural areas with few medical or social service resources.

By the mid-1930s, the third new approach to child study, the field of child development research, had been institutionalized and professionalized. Unlike the guidance clinics and the bureau, however, this field's primary purpose was to study "normal children." The next chapter discusses events leading to the founding of the Iowa Child Welfare Research Station in 1917, the essential model for the child development research institutes of the 1920s.

Chapter 7 Better Crops, Better Pigs, Better Children: The Iowa Child Welfare Research Station

Early in 1915 a group of Iowa women led by Cora Bussey Hillis asked the state legislature to establish a child welfare research organization to study the development of normal children. Their slogan was "Better Normal Children for Iowa," a radical suggestion.

The study of disadvantaged and "defective" children at the State University of Iowa during the eight preceding years had been justified by the hope that research would find ways to eliminate children's suffering, prevent child dependency and juvenile delinquency, and replace charitable and public funds devoted to remedial efforts. For those involved, disadvantaged children were, of course, other people's children. To most Americans, efforts to improve children like their own would have been a meddlesome intrusion into family affairs. The prevailing attitude in Iowa, psychologist Carl Emil Seashore said, was "Improve anything and everything that you wish but you shall not improve our children."[1]

Public opposition was overcome by two statewide campaigns beginning in 1915. On April 2, 1917, the state legislature passed an act establishing the first organization in the world to study the development of normal children, a crucial turning point in the history of scientific child study. The Laura Spelman Rockefeller Memorial drew heavily on the Iowa model for the child study and parent education programs it established and financed in the 1920s. These programs created the new field of child development and set in motion a series of events that had a profound impact on child-rearing advice and on social policies for children.[2]

WHY IOWA?

Of all the places in the world that could have led a movement for scientific study of normal children, why Iowa? First, the urgent social problems confronting most American cities were less urgent in Iowa's prosperous rural economy. Iowa was proud of the healthy environment it provided for its children, and its clubwomen were active in child welfare reform activities that promised to make this happy state of affairs even better. Second, Iowa did not have to cope with a flood of immigrants from southern and eastern Europe and had relatively few children living in deep poverty. Free of the concerns that motivated settlement house workers and big-city clubwomen to concentrate on social welfare reform, it could afford the luxury of investing in a program intended to make life even better for the fortunate majority of its children.[3] Finally, the land-grant colleges and their affiliated institutions, the agricultural experiment station and the extension service, had demonstrated to Iowa citizens the enormous benefits of applied science.[4]

The land-grant colleges were based on belief in the utility of science in a great many endeavors. Vermont representative (later senator) Justin S. Morrill, who backed the legislation that established and ensured the continuation of the land-grant colleges, intended them to emphasize the "useful sciences," a significant departure from the pursuit of basic science and the classics in Eastern universities. They were to be the "people's colleges" or "democracy's colleges," where useful knowledge could be discovered and transformed into practical benefits.[5]

Applied science had produced spectacular results in agriculture. By the mid-1870s the states began to set up agricultural experiment stations to provide land-grant colleges with research facilities. Experimental research by the stations on animal breeding, nutrition and pathology, soil analysis, crop improvement, and every phase of the dairy industry brought revolutionary changes in American agriculture and enormous benefits to farmers.[6]

Farmers' initial indifference to these institutions was overcome by presentations of research findings at farmers' institutes, fairs, and other rural gatherings and by demonstrations of the advantages of scientific farming. These early efforts to disseminate the practical results of academic research, especially in agriculture, were the beginning of state extension work. The Smith-Lever Act of 1914 provided for an agricultural extension service based on cooperation between land-grant colleges and the U.S. Department of Agriculture.[7] The Smith-Hughes Act of 1917 required federal grants-in-aid to be matched by state contributions for promoting instruction in agriculture and other vocations. Defining home economics as a vocation opened the way for government support for the dissemination of child development research and for parent education. The number of rural women enrolled in extension programs increased rapidly after the passage of these two acts.[8]

From the beginning, agricultural experiment station research encompassed the home and the family, and extension work offered practical instruction in nutrition, clothing, home management, health, and safety. Although the service's chief responsibility was to farm families, it also served urban residents. All extension education emphasized the normal child and family. The extension service provided an established network that could be used to disseminate research findings on children.[9]

CORA BUSSEY HILLIS CAMPAIGNS
FOR THE STUDY OF NORMAL CHILDREN

If agricultural research could help farmers grow better crops and livestock, was it not possible that research on children's development and optimal child-rearing methods could help farmers and their wives grow better sons and daughters? After all, were not children Iowa's most important crop? Cora Bussey Hillis began asking her fellow Iowans these questions as early as 1901. She crusaded for the next sixteen years to accomplish her goal, a "child study laboratory."[10]

Cora Bussey was born in Bloomfield, Iowa, in 1858, the descendant of a long line of doctors, lawyers, teachers, preachers, and other professionals, many of whom had dedicated their lives to public service. Cora spent most of her childhood in New Orleans, an only child for ten years until a sister, Laura, was born. At age two, Laura was stricken with a spinal disease. Physicians predicted that she would not survive childhood and would never attend school, yet she lived to be thirty-four.[11] Both Laura's invalidism and the discovery that doctors often gave bad advice profoundly affected Cora's childhood. Long before she had children of her own, she began to wonder why so little reliable knowledge of children was available.[12]

Cora's diary, written between the ages of seventeen and eighteen, shows her confidence that she was destined to accomplish important things. She considered herself "worthy of a great, good man. I feel within myself a power undeveloped which in future years shall command homage for me." After a long engagement, she married Isaac Hillis, a lawyer, in 1880. Shortly thereafter her mother died, and Hillis, a bride of twenty-two, assumed sole care of her invalid twelve-year-old sister. Between 1883 and 1896 Hillis bore five children, three of whom died in childhood. Especially poignant, in retrospect, are descriptions of Hillis's eight-year-old daughter's involvement in the 1906 meeting of the National Congress of Mothers, where members were so taken with the youngster that they presented her with a doll. The child died on the first day of the next year. Hillis could not resume work for a year. She often referred to the research station as "another child." Possibly, her devotion to this "other child" assuaged her grief and enabled her to persist in her long quest. The loss of her children made it difficult to carry on, but she continued because she hoped that science applied to children might help prevent the kinds of problems and losses that she had faced.[13]

Hillis sought information that would help her to be a better mother. "I got books and magazines; I read everything I could find that wise men had written; I listened to doctors and educators; I waded through oceans of stale textbook theory, written largely, I fancy, by bachelor professors or elderly teachers with no actual contact with youth." She discovered that "all knowledge of the child was theoretical and most advice experimental." She had to solve her "mother" problems as best she could alone.[14]

STANDARDS FOR SCIENTIFIC CHILD REARING

Settlement house workers, most of whom had no children of their own, lived in slums where they observed the terrible effects of poverty on children. Consequently, they emphasized reforms that would improve the physical and social environment of poor children. Hillis, preoccupied with the problems of motherhood in a prosperous midwestern state, was struck by the disparity between the quality and amount of knowledge available to farmers and to parents. Her goal was to promote research that would provide a scientific basis for better child rearing. Standards existed by which chickens, calves, trees, and shrubs could be judged, she noted, but there was no similar knowledge of child development, no reliable norms to help parents know whether or not their children were as healthy—physically, mentally, and emotionally—as they could be. Why not "give the normal child the same scientific study by research methods that we give to crops and cattle ?" she asked. "Learn how the normal child develops in body, mind, and spirit and gradually evolve a science of child rearing." Convinced of the soundness of her idea, she nonetheless did not see how a mother like herself, untrained in science or education or for any public role, could achieve the dream of founding a laboratory for scientific child study. Her spirits revived when she realized that she had a "calling," comparable to the call to preach. She would accomplish her mission; God would help her.[15]

Hillis had become involved in women's club activities while still in her twenties and had helped found the Des Moines Women's Club in 1887. She delivered the traditional lecture on a literary figure (her choice was Browning), sold short stories to a midwestern magazine, and wrote a regular column for the *Iowa Homestead.* She discovered that charitable work on behalf of children was especially fulfilling. A significant turning point came in 1899, when, at her father's suggestion, she attended the second annual conference of the National Congress of Mothers and became friends with congress president Alice Birney. Learning that the site of the next annual meeting had not been determined, she decided that it must be Des Moines. She wired the congress an invitation from the mayor of Des Moines and then wired the mayor to tell him what she had done. Upon returning home, she persuaded prominent Iowans to express to officials of the National Congress of Mothers their hope that Des Moines would be chosen for its next meeting and to extol the city's advantages as a convention center. Sixteen other cities also sent invitations, but the National Congress chose Des Moines.[16]

HILLIS BEGINS HER CAMPAIGN

By 1901 Hillis knew that her ultimate goal was to found a child study laboratory. Unlike urban reformers, Hillis could not find support from diverse women's organizations. Some Iowa town and city women belonged to clubs but most of the state's rural women were unorganized. Hillis realized that she would have to organize them herself. As one means of doing so, she called on the secretary of the State Agricultural Association to offer to help him establish women's departments in Farmers' Institutes.[17]

To have more time for "planting the seeds" for a future child study campaign, Hillis resigned the presidency of the Iowa chapter of the National Congress of Mothers in 1906. Appointed a member of President Roosevelt's Country Life Commission in 1908, she was offered the opportunity to enlist one capable woman in each county of Iowa to help the president in his campaign to "conserve the child." She organized the women she selected as the Iowa County Committee on Home Life in Rural Communities and kept them busy in child welfare reform for seven years, until the first campaign for the Iowa station needed their leadership.[18]

Hillis had taken the first step to secure acceptance of her idea of a laboratory for scientific child study in 1901 by presenting it to President Weir Beardsheer of the Iowa State College of Agriculture and Mechanic Arts at Ames. It would be logical, she suggested, for the state agricultural college to undertake the study of the human animal as an advanced step in human husbandry. Beardsheer found the plan premature. His successor decided that any such proposal must come from educators. Another successor dismissed her idea but proposed a "great work" she could do: "Get us a set of chimes in a campanile." Of all the college and university presidents she approached over thirteen years, only George F. MacLean of the State University of Iowa was interested. He offered to speak publicly on behalf of a child study laboratory in 1908. Unfortunately for Hillis, he left the university shortly thereafter.[19]

Undeterred by lack of academic support, Hillis tried to persuade women's club leaders and other influential Iowans. She spoke before a variety of clubs and Farmers' Institutes on such subjects as "Corn Culture Versus Child Culture," "A Seed Worth Sowing," and "A Field Worth Cultivating," always reflecting an agricultural analogy. In addition to promoting her special cause, she urged that mothers should have more leisure time and boys more time for play.[20] Her talks were prominently reported in Iowa newspapers, which commented on her charm and her appeal to audiences. Hillis had the typical Progressive faith in the power of an aroused public opinion. Between 1901 and 1903 she spoke in forty-four Iowa counties.[21]

Exhibits and baby health contests at county and state fairs were among the most effective venues Hillis found through which to impress rural audiences and call attention to the need for better child rearing. Her proposal for a "children's palace" for the World's Fair in St. Louis in 1904 to show American parents how to "grow" better sons and daughters was not adopted, but she helped to organize the first "scientific baby show" in the world at the Iowa State Exposition in 1908. The baby health contest in 1912 brought a complimentary letter from Julia Lathrop, who later came to Iowa to observe the contest.[22] In 1913 a children's building was established at the State Fair for the use of the Iowa Congress of Mothers.

HILLIS WINS COOPERATION
FROM THE STATE UNIVERSITY

Hillis's fifth attempt to interest a university president in her plan for a child study laboratory succeeded in 1914. Thomas H. MacBride of the State University of Iowa endorsed her idea and chose Carl Emil Seashore, chair of the psychology department and dean of the graduate college, to carry it out. The laboratory became Seashore's "favorite child" for the remaining thirty-two years of his life, and others regarded it as his most significant administrative achievement."[23] Seashore admired Hillis and helped her with her various projects until her death in 1924. "It was interesting," he recalled in 1942, "to see how a woman with such warm inspirations and towering aspirations and a cold-blooded professor and administrator could work together in complete harmony on a radically new project."[24]

CARL EMIL SEASHORE

Born in 1866, Seashore was eight years younger than Hillis. When he was three, his family had migrated from Sweden to Iowa. He spent fourteen years on a farm and often compared pioneering on "the frontier of experimental psychology" to pioneering on the farming frontier in Iowa. He receiving a Yale Ph.D. in experimental psychology in 1895 and in 1897 joined the faculty of the State University of Iowa. He founded the university's psychological laboratory and the second psychological clinic in the United States. In 1908 he became dean of the graduate college. His three main interests were the advancement of psychology, education, and the fine arts. His interest in music and art led to research at the Iowa Station on the development of the aesthetic sense in children. Starting in 1902, he fathered four sons at two-and-a-half-year intervals, making, he pointed out, "a fine series for psychological studies.[25]

Seashore did not immediately accept Hillis's proposal for a child study laboratory but kept her waiting and "suffering" while he considered it. She believed he had misunderstood her. "Your plans are advanced plans over previous methods in Iowa," she wrote to him, "but not such as will develop a dependable science of child rearing. I do not want and would not work 'to establish a branch orphan asylum in Iowa city.' I am unfortunate in somehow having given you that impression. The point I make is this: if children are to be thoroughly studied, there must be a selected group of children to study in an environment absolutely under the control of the station. As we are so handicapped for money, it might help solve the problem to secure the cooperation of the Board of Control of State Institutions to let some of its wards be used for experimental purposes."[26] It was the mother, not the scientist, who kept the focus on research rather than welfare.

Seashore agreed that Hillis was right "in insisting that this work shall be primarily research."[27] Hillis's letter to Seashore demonstrates her concern at this early date with the problem of obtaining children as research subjects. Against Seashore's wishes, she and her supporters later pushed through a plan for a nursery school laboratory that used children between the ages of two and five as subjects of experimental psychology.[28] Seashore, who favored studying children in their homes, later decided that he had been wrong.[29] The Iowa nursery school served as a model for twenty other nursery school laboratories established before 1931.[30]

THE CHILD WELFARE RESEARCH STATION COMMITTEE

Members of the State University of Iowa committee to consider plans for the Iowa Child Welfare Research Station included President MacBride, Seashore as chairman, representatives of the extension division and the colleges of medicine, dentistry, and education, and, by special invitation, Florence Brown Sherbon from the Extension Division of the State University of Iowa at Colfax. At a meeting on December 7, 1914, the university committee decided that a statewide committee made up of presidents or representatives of the chief women's organizations of Iowa should be organized to promote and support the establishment of the station, with Dr. Sherbon representing the university. It was agreed that the station should focus on study of the normal preschool child, specializing in six areas: psychology, education, sociology, preventive medicine, dentistry, and home economics. Although research was to be its primary goal, it was also to disseminate information to the public and train students and professionals.[31]

Most of the faculty opposed establishment of the station because there was no precedent for such an institution and because they believed it would divert university funds from established needs. The faculty's opposition and the refusal of the State Board of Education to ask the legislature to appropriate funds for the station made it necessary to provide the station with an independent charter. The university decided that the request for such a charter must come from the women of Iowa. Although an autonomous unit with its own budget, the station was to use existing facilities and equipment at the State University of Iowa and was to be controlled by the president of the university and the State Board of Education.[32] An initial appropriation of $50,000 and an annual appropriation of the same amount were to be requested from the legislature.[33]

PROBLEMS OF NOMENCLATURE

The name given to the proposed organization for research on children was the Iowa Child Welfare Research Station. Although Hillis always compared research on children to agricultural research, the term she used was "child study laboratory." Seashore substituted "research station" in order to emphasize the analogy to agricultural experiment stations. He also wanted to distinguish the study of normal children at the station from the study of defective and delinquent children at the university's Psychological Laboratory. The appeal of suffering children, he said, led to neglect of the study of normal children. It was imperative to present the station as a new and separate entity.[34]

The inclusion of the words "child welfare" in the title of the station, Seashore wrote, was a "concession." He would have preferred "euthenics," which referred to being well cared for, because it was "parallel" to "eugenics," which referred to being well born. Although euthenics carried more scientific connotations than child welfare, "a new name of such a high brow character," Seashore decided, "would have defeated our purpose."[35] It should be noted that, at that time, "child welfare" did not refer to aid to poor children, as it does today, but to social services that could improve the well-being of all children.

PREPARATIONS FOR THE CAMPAIGN

A conference chaired by Seashore, held at the Hillis home on December 23, 1914, made final decisions. Conference participants agreed that a bill to establish the station should be submitted to the state legislature in February 1915. Hillis and Sherbon were instructed to form a new organization of women to conduct a campaign to win the support of legislators. Some members worried that influential clubwomen might not join the campaign and that Hillis might not have the experience and the talent to lead it. They feared that it would be regarded as a one-woman Des Moines crusade rather than a united movement of all Iowa women.

Seashore and Sherbon warned Hillis of potential problems, urged her to "disarm opposition before launching," and expressed discouragement about prospects for success. Hillis confidently advised them not to worry, assuring them that she was accustomed to the "petty jealousies" and "self-interest" of women club leaders and the fear of suffragists that other causes would detract from their own. She had years of experience working with Iowa clubwomen and knew what she was doing. All would be well, because individual differences soon would be subordinated to the great cause of working for the station. She offered to step aside to let someone else run the campaign, but she wondered if anyone else could provide the necessary "ginger."

The doubts of some committee members were soon resolved. The president of the Iowa Federation of Women's Clubs, who had firmly refused to join the new organization five days earlier, was among those present when the Child Welfare Association to Promote the Establishment of the Iowa Child Welfare Research Station was organized on January 5, 1915. It immediately elected Hillis president.[36] A newspaper headline on January 6, 1915, announced, "Iowa Child Welfare Association Begins Monster Task."

CAMPAIGN THEMES

"Nobody knows what constitutes a normal child," Seashore admitted early in 1915. A major goal was to solve this mystery. Until scientific research established norms of child development and a range of deviations from these norms, parents had no way of judging the well-being or progress of their children. Seashore cautioned that the norm should not be the goal of improved child rearing. "The normal is merely the average. . . . We should seek our standard from among those who have achieved superior excellence."

The call for prevention was familiar to Progressive reformers everywhere. Progressives contrasted the high cost of maintaining hospitals, detention homes, jails, and other remedial and custodial institutions with the lesser cost of preventive measures based on research on disadvantaged and "problem" children. Advocates of the station cited statistics on the expense of remedial care in letters to legislators and farmers and in numerous newspaper stories, but they proposed an unconventional alternative. Although they did not want to eliminate the customary Progressive investigations into the causes of children's problems, they gave precedence to studies designed to discover the conditions favoring optimal child growth and development. This proposal anticipated a shift that would occur in the 1920s, when studies of abnormality were replaced by studies of the normal child. They were justified by the belief that the abnormal could be identified and prevented only through better knowledge of the normal.[37]

Another novel feature of the proposed station was its intention to study very young children. G. Stanley Hall had wanted to include younger children in his child study movement, but cultural pressures had kept the focus on the school-age child and the adolescent. Yet, Seashore contended, "the child learns more in the first five years of its life than in any other equal period of his life; and at the age of five the child's character is well set." Education begins in the home, where the child's character is formed. Sounding very much like Hall, Seashore asserted that common conditions of home life "interfere with Nature's ways and prevent a reasonable development of the human mind." The time had come to divert research from educational reform to research that would allow the "light of science . . . to penetrate into home life."[38]

In both campaigns the analogy to agriculture was pervasive, elaborated and repeated in letters, pamphlets, speeches, and the press. Its appropriateness was debated in the legislature. One senator declared that he regarded scientific study of plants and animals as necessary but that he preferred to trust Mother Nature when it came to children. Another senator, thrusting his fist in the face of the first retorted, "You wouldn't trust Mother Nature for your cows, or pigs, or mare."[39] The Iowa chapter of the National Mothers' Congress had been asserting for fifteen years that mother love without enlightenment was insufficient to meet children's needs. This message permeated the campaign literature, but now with emphasis on the fruits of research on baby animals.

One legislative debate centered on the value of research compared to service. A representative hauled in wheelbarrows full of books to make his point. Plenty of published research about the child was available. Needed were more welfare workers, not more scientists.[40] Seashore and other spokesmen for the university also assured parents that research on children would be undertaken by qualified specialists, and only with parental consent. "Facts, facts, facts about the child," should be the campaign slogan, Seashore suggested.[41] Although specialized and scientific, research would focus on the practical rather than the theoretical and the results brought to parents through university publications and extension service agents, just as the results of agricultural research were brought to farmers.

News stories supporting the station sometimes promised too much. One headline declared, "You can make your child what you want when Iowa gets her new research station." If and when the research station was established, it promised, "all you will have to do is to send him to the research laboratory for a stay of a few weeks or months and at the end of that time he will come back to you a much brighter, more robust youngster than when he went away."[42] Behaviorist John B. Watson used this very message during the 1920s, when he argued for the superiority of scientific child rearing. Hillis later said that the association founded to promote the station did everything possible to control excessive claims for its potential but did not always succeed.[43]

One variation on the agricultural theme in the campaign for the station was an appeal to state pride. Hillis pointed out that Iowa had taken 285 out of a possible 289 prizes for farm products at the Pan American Exposition. If Iowa were to invest in its children as it had in its farms, she predicted, it could become the "best place on earth for the child" and the "Mecca of the world for those seeking knowledge of the child."[44] Moreover, she argued, improving the normal child was the best way to improve the nation.

Advocates of the station used the analogy with conservation as well as with agriculture. "The problem of child conservation," Seashore declared, "is quite analogous to the problem of conservation of the forest. The first move is to get the facts about the sources of devastation and positive procedures which may foster and favor natural conditions of growth."[45] To charges that it was not possible to apply science to children, he replied, "The time has passed for intelligent people to regard mental forces, individual or environmental, as unknowable."[46]

EUGENICS

The campaigns for the station coincided with the peak of the eugenics movement. Eugenics was a British invention, but it assumed unique American characteristics that would cause profound social and political consequences. Darwin's cousin, Francis Galton, who pioneered the mathematical treatment of heredity, coined the word *eugenics*. By the mid-1880s the term had become commonplace. The sentiment for a eugenics movement gained greater strength when the beginnings of the modern science of genetics coincided with certain profound social changes occurring around the turn of the century.[47]

The birth of modern genetics stemmed mainly from three important developments in European biology: the rediscovery of Mendel's laws, which explained how traits were transmitted and distributed from generation to generation; August Weissmann's decisive rejection of the inheritance of acquired characteristics; and Hugh de Vries's elaboration of mutation theory.[48] In themselves, the new theories did not justify hereditarian interpretations of social pathology, but their focus on inheritance seemed to some to imply that heredity was decisive in determining human capacities and behavior.[49]

A few years before the opening of the campaign for the Iowa station the publication of several works on the feebleminded attracted popular attention, particularly Henry H. Goddard's *Kallikak Family* (1912), a description of the social pathology of one family. The new studies suggested that temperament, intelligence, and behavior, as well as physical characteristics, were determined by heredity. The American mental testing movement, which began around 1910, enabled psychologists to correlate what appeared to be accurate measurements of low mental age with social pathology. Goddard, for example, linked feeblemindedness with crime, prostitution, and pauperism. Many social scientists regarded the mentally retarded as a serious menace to American society. Growing public concern was reflected in an increase in institutional care for the feebleminded in the United States, which more than doubled between 1910 and 1923.[50]

The results of agricultural research were used to argue both sides of the nature-nurture controversy. Improvements in both the breeding and the care of livestock and crops raised hopes that "positive eugenics" could achieve similar improvements in the human stock. Positive eugenics encompassed efforts to increase desirable traits in the population by encouraging careful selection of marriage partners, persuading the "better classes" to produce more children, and holding "fitter family" and baby health contests at state fairs. "Fitter family" competitions were held in the "human stock" sections of fairs, and contest brochures urged that human husbandry be developed on the principles pioneered by scientific agriculture.[51] During the baby contests, which originated in Iowa, "terrified infants were judged as if they were prize cattle."[52] Sponsors of baby contests advocated scientific manipulation of hygiene and parenting as well as of breeding.[53] A cytogeneticist at the Connecticut Agricultural College declared that "in the garden of human life as in the garden of corn, success is the resultant complex of the two factors, environment and heredity." He concluded that society could be improved by non-genetic means and warned against intemperate campaigns by proponents of "negative eugenics" to restrict immigration and sterilize the unfit."[54] Yet such campaigns had considerable success. Sixteen states enacted sterilization laws between 1907 and 1917. Iowa enacted the most wide-ranging of these in 1911.

THE ENVIRONMENTAL BIAS OF HILLIS
AND SEASHORE

Since the eugenics movement was an integral part of the American social scene in 1915, it is not surprising that the nature-nurture controversy was reflected in the program proposed for the Iowa station. What is surprising, in view of the dominance of hereditarian interpretations of human behavior at this time, is the environmental bias of the program.[55] Hillis and Seashore both assigned a primary role to environmental influences on human behavior.[56]

Hillis's purpose in founding the station was to initiate research that would lead to a "dependable science of child rearing." At a time when "childhood was viewed in a fatalistic way," Seashore pointed out, Hillis was "far-sighted" and "optimistic" about what could be accomplished through research.[57] Although Hillis's interests and the station's purposes included research on the effects of heredity, her main goal was to provide better childcare. Her understanding of the nature-nurture controversy was naive. Both her naivete and her environmental bias were reflected in her proposals for exhibits in the Children's Palace at the 1904 St. Louis World's Fair designed to show that physical differences among the peoples of different nations were the result of habits acquired during the first ten years of life. "Human nature is much alike the world over," she declared, "sweet and sound at the core."[58] One of her illustrations attributed the short stature of Japanese adults to their habit of sitting cross-legged in school. During the campaign for the station, she claimed that most mental retardation and juvenile delinquency could be prevented.

While acknowledging that hereditary diseases could produce "illborn children," Seashore asserted that much inborn weakness was due to ignorance and neglect by parents. There were countless opportunities for improving the human child, he declared, not by destroying the unfit or selecting the most desirable, but rather by discovering and popularizing information about improving conditions for children.[59] "Modern eugenics is hopeful and aggressive and not satisfied with warding off evil."[60] Seashore's desire to use the term *euthenics* in the title of the station is another example of his environmentalism.[61]

THE FIRST CAMPAIGN, 1915

The association sent letters, telegrams, petitions, and appeals to an estimated 300,000 influential leaders and ordinary citizens during the six weeks of the first campaign.[62] That most Iowa newspapers were extremely favorable to the station seems surprising in view of the scorn and contempt expressed in their coverage of the meeting of the National Congress of Mothers in 1900 (see chap. 3). Particularly effective in creating support for the station was a series of cartoons by future Pulitzer prizewinner Jay Norwood ("Ding") Darling in the *Des Moines Register and Leader* that contrasted Iowa's investment in agricultural research with its indifference to children. One cartoon illustrated how much the state did for the pig family, how little for the human family.[63]

Before the bill to create the research station came to a vote, the proposed appropriation was cut in half, to $25,000. Two weeks before the vote in the house, Hillis was called to Washington, D.C., to attend her dying father. The vote on April 12 was seven short of a majority. Newspaper editorials and stories contrasted the defeat of the bill with the passage of an appropriation of $25,000 for a sheep barn at the next state fair.[64] "The denial of the bill," Hillis asserted, "makes the women want it all the more." She and Seashore immediately began planning the next campaign.[65]

THE SECOND CAMPAIGN, 1916–1917

Thirty state organizations representing half a million people were involved in the second campaign, launched early in 1916.[66] Toward the end of the year, Hillis was injured in a fall and was confined to bed for five weeks. Undaunted, she moved her bed to the parlor of her home, installed a telephone next to it, and hired a full-time stenographer. When the bill was held up in a House committee, she hobbled to the Capitol on crutches to help get it out. It passed the House by a vote of seventy-nine to six, but a majority of senators were opposed. Hillis did everything possible to change the minds of the eleven senators who, according to a knowledgeable friend, were the most vehemently opposed. Because of her efforts, they received calls from a bishop, doctors, members of the Board of Control of State Institutions, and other influential Iowans. One senator was visited by a mother of eight children, who persuaded him to vote for the bill, but a majority of senators remained opposed.

The United States declared war on Germany on April 6, 1917. Preoccupied by the conflict in Europe, Iowa legislators forgot about the campaign for the station. When a morning edition of the *Des Moines Register* headlined the announcement that only 41 out of 250 Iowa men had passed the military physical, Hillis seized the moment. "By nine o'clock," she wrote, "I had dictated and multigraphed an open letter, which before noon, was placed on the desk of every member of both houses." The letter suggested that the rejected young men had been reared by mothers who relied on "inherited tradition" and "instinct" and concluded with an appeal for the station as a "far seeing and patriotic service to the Nation."[67] The bill was promptly reported out of committee and passed the senate by a vote of thirty-eight to five on April 15, 1917. After signing the bill Governor William L. Harding wired Hillis, "I am saving the pen for you."

A MILESTONE IN THE SCIENTIFIC STUDY
OF CHILDREN AND AN EXAMPLE OF RURAL
WOMEN'S ROLE IN PROGRESSIVE REFORM

Historians have perceived the founding of the Iowa station as a prelude to its later role in controversy over the constancy of the IQ. They should see it as a milestone in the founding of child study and an example of women's role in Progressive reform.[68] The campaign for the Iowa station, as Seashore pointed out, was one of the first and most significant movements of Iowa women in public welfare and in politics. It may also be the most important example of a Progressive reform movement led entirely by rural women with a goal other than suffrage or prohibition. Cora Bussey Hillis is well known in Iowa. An elementary school bears her name, and she is second only to Carrie Chapman Catt in Iowa's Women's Hall of Fame. Yet she is not included in *Notable American Women,* nor has she been the subject of a scholarly article.

Women would have been the principal leaders of the campaign for the Iowa station even if the university had not insisted that they assume the entire responsibility. Seashore's description of his own role as that of a "sort of technical advisor whose duty it was to muster the forces of science in the university for action" is too modest. With the exception, however, of Seashore, a few other university faculty members, and two officers of the Iowa Child Welfare Association to Promote the Establishment of the Iowa Child Welfare Research Station, all the leaders of the campaign and most of its participants were women. Only two of the twenty-nine officers of the Child Welfare Association were men.[69]

The tradition of equality of the sexes associated with the land-grant colleges may have contributed to the daring of the women in initiating their unusual campaign, their tenacity in campaigning until they achieved their goal, and the willingness of farm women to support them. Even before the Civil War, agricultural reformers had urged that farmers' wives be educated not only in household duties but also in the underlying principles of farm organization and operation so that they might be true partners of their husbands.[70] Iowa State

Agricultural College was the first of the land-grant colleges to enroll women. The women argued that the addition of child development research to the research programs of the University of Iowa was a natural extension of many ongoing programs to help Iowa women.[71]

Seashore described his association with the women as "one of the happiest experiences of my public career." He emphasized the influence of their altruism on the attitude of Iowa men.[72] A campaign led by women who were devoid of self-interest and concerned only with improving the welfare of children and the state was precisely the image Hillis wished to convey.[73]

Hillis's background and many of her ideas were very different from those of the settlement house workers and other "new women." Refusing to engage in lobbying or other forms of "button-hole politics," she influenced legislators by cultivating the friendship of their wives and converting them to her cause.[74] Many women expressed preference for her methods over those of suffragists and temperance workers. She regarded the latter as competitors for the time and energy of the women she needed to help her cause. She avoided the suffrage issue because it was a "red rag to many people" and maintained cordial relations with the Iowa Woman's Christian Temperance Union. Hillis portrayed herself as a self-effacing, devoted wife and mother with a spiritual mission, a woman who did not wish to infringe upon male prerogatives. She was eager only to help men see that establishing the study of normal children was a noble cause that served their self-interest as parents and citizens.[75]

Seashore frequently alluded to Hillis's "superb charm." She could "appeal to men and women, cultured and uncultured, with a feeling that she voiced the spirit of the womanhood of America. It was the heart of a woman, with complete presence and self-command on the platform . . . that swayed emotions and carried profound conviction."[76]

Hillis was a talented organizer. Her promotional materials, instructions to her co-workers, and frequent progress reports were carefully prepared and promptly delivered. She hoped that this "prompt attention to detail would encourage workers, 'as the boys say,' to get a move on."[77] Participants in the campaign were not always united in sisterly feeling. Some officers of women's organizations were unhappy to be led by a "non-professional"; others were eager to claim the station as the child of their own organization. Hillis managed to retain their loyalty by keeping a low profile and making accomplishment of her goal more important than personal recognition, and she succeeded in her determination to reach the "masses."[78]

Historians of Progressive reform have focused primarily on the leadership of professional career women, women who insisted on their right to vote and to participate in the public sphere on equal terms with men. Since most of these women were not mothers, contemporaries often accused them of being incapable of understanding children.[79] Hillis, not handicapped by the prejudice against childless women working for children's programs, demonstrated that a mother could be a successful reformer. Neither lobbying nor demanding the vote, she used methods of persuasion that did not threaten men. Her methods appeared compatible with the ends she sought and surely contributed to their realization.

THE EARLY YEARS OF THE IOWA STATION

Seashore announced that his first task was to find a director "who can take an inventory of the child as a whole, his mental and physical aspects from an intensive point of view, for the purpose of organizing and guiding research on the best proved lines," and concluded: "I, therefore, have to look for a psychologist."[80] He could have added that the director must also be a practical man who could retain the support of the station's constituency.[81] Bird Baldwin was appointed director in August 1917 and remained until his death in May 1928. While Baldwin was director, he carried forward the goals of the station's charter and became one of the nation's most influential psychologists in the new field of child development.[82] His pioneering studies of the physical and psychological development of preschool children and rural children became classics in the field.[83]

Baldwin was away from the station from March 5, 1918, to August 1, 1919, serving as a major in the U.S. Army. Seashore found the shortage of qualified personnel a severe hindrance to the new station's progress. Hillis, however, was undaunted. Elated by her success in establishing the station, believing that even the most ambitious programs to help children were now possible, she became impatient, demanding, and broke her promise not to interfere in station affairs. Her husband's death in March 1918 may have made her more eager than ever to advance her life's work. She expressed her dissatisfaction with the station's program by mail and in person. Fearful that the station would lose popular support if it did not quickly demonstrate accomplishments, she proposed that it undertake child welfare and parent education activities until it could pursue its primary goal of research. This time it was Seashore who insisted that the station adhere to its goal of research.[84]

"I am anxious for the work to be underway that we may serve not only the children of Iowa but the whole stricken world," Hillis wrote in June 1917. Convinced that European children would be too damaged by the war to participate effectively in the prolonged postwar reconstruction of their countries, she thought it more important than ever to conserve American children who could then save the world. These sentiments were expressed in a 1917 proposal, "Conservation of Young America: A War Necessity," a plan for a nationwide survey of child life in the United States that included suggestions for the enrichment of child life after the survey's completion. She asked Baldwin to see President Woodrow Wilson and to ask Herbert Hoover to "offer that your Station Administrator be appointed whose duty would parallel that of the Food Administration."[85] Seashore and Baldwin helped her revise and limit her proposals, so that they might have a chance of at least partial acceptance. Baldwin, like Seashore, had a close friendly relationship with Hillis. Instead of a nationwide survey, he proposed a comprehensive survey of Iowa children. Almost a year later, Hillis sent a two-page proposal on child conservation to President Wilson, but nothing came of it.[86]

Hillis persuaded the Woman's Christian Temperance Union to give the station $10,000 in 1919 to be used for a department of eugenics.[87] This solicitation may seem to contradict her environmental position, but, as Martin Pernick has shown, at that time the meaning of heredity was expansive enough for eugenics to claim for study the entire range of human imperfections. Many eugenicists believed that inherited traits could be altered by a person's life and that they could pass these alterations on to the next generation, an interpretation of heredity that encouraged a version of eugenics that emphasized improvement of the environment. WCTU suggestions for research on the effects on children's development of the elimination of alcohol, tobacco, and coffee, reflected this view.[88]

Hillis's death in an automobile accident in 1924 ended her career with the station. It also prevented the erection of a children's building at the Philadelphia Sesquitennial comparable to the women's building at the Chicago Fair in 1893, a proposal she had sold to the National Research Council Committee on Child Development.

The Iowa station occupied one floor of a university building during the war years, but it had access to facilities throughout the university. Its work during the war included mental testing of school children, research on speech development disorders in normal children, and measurements of the physical development of babies in connection with the Children's Bureau program for Children's Year. To fulfill its training obligations, it offered a seminar on the normal child to graduate students at the university. The first staff appointment was Amy L. Daniels in July 1918 as research professor in charge of nutrition. By 1920, at Seashore's initiative, the station was studying the gifted child in a five-year study sponsored by the National Research Council. Seashore also persuaded it to study the aesthetic development of children and their musical abilities.[89] The station's pioneering research on preschool children began when its preschool nursery laboratory was founded in October 1921.[90]

Part 3 Breaking Through, 1922–1940

Chapter 8 The Children's Decade

No one could have predicted before World War I that the 1920s would be hailed as the Children's Decade, a time when children would assume unprecedented importance. Signs of children's enhanced status were reflected soon after the Armistice in the strength and exuberance of grassroots child welfare and parent education movements, and in the rhetoric of leaders in government, philanthropy, and social reform.[1]

Following the lead of prewar social justice reformers and the founders of the Iowa Child Welfare Research Station, many Americans began to demand prevention rather than amelioration. They asked for positive new measures to create a better life for *all* children, average "normal" children as well as those who were physically, mentally, or economically disadvantaged.[2] Reflecting this shift, the name of the *Child Welfare Bulletin* was changed in 1919 to *The American Child*.[3]

The child as the key to the national future became a paramount theme of the 1920s. While other Progressive reform campaigns faltered or ceased after the war, social welfare reform, including especially the "crusade for children," gained momentum.[4] President Woodrow Wilson anticipated the Children's Decade when he proclaimed 1918 as Children's Year.[5] President Warren Harding supported the Maternal and Child Health Act of 1921, and Secretary of Commerce Herbert Hoover led the movement to improve children's physical health.[6] Soon after his inauguration, President Hoover secured funding and took other steps to ensure that the third decennial White House Conference for Children and Youth would be much more ambitious than its predecessors. In his opening address to the 1930 conference, he declared, "These questions of child health and protection are a complicated problem requiring much learning and much action. And we need have great concern over this matter. Let no one believe that these are questions that should not stir a nation; that they are below the dignity of statesmen or governments. If we could have but one generation of properly born, trained, educated, and healthy children, a thousand other problems of government would vanish."[7] This was not empty rhetoric but a reflection of Hoover's and other prominent Americans' new attitudes about the importance of children. Cora Bussey Hillis had preached this message for nearly a quarter century, but her words were often dismissed as the sentimental excesses of a mere mother.[8]

The least anticipated development of the "children's decade" was the rapid professionalization and institutionalization of scientific child study. Although child welfare movements had been the center of Progressive reform, prewar efforts to provide a scientific basis for child welfare reform had not fared well. The establishment before the war of the first child guidance clinic in Chicago, the United States Children's Bureau, and the Iowa Child Welfare Research Station marked the institutional beginning of three new approaches to child study, but the new organizations had little money, small staffs, and limited influence. None had an initial budget of more than $25,600. There was no indication at the end of the war that philanthropists would soon invest millions in child study and parent education programs modeled on the child guidance clinic and the Iowa station, nor that the federal government would vastly increase its commitment to child study. Yet, by the end of the decade, more than three hundred psychiatric clinics for children had been founded, and the Iowa station, with an annual budget of $160,000, had become one of seven major child development research institutes in the United States. The Children's Bureau had undertaken more than one hundred and fifty studies of children, and the organizers of the 1930 White House Conference had spent a half-million dollars to seek out and summarize existing knowledge of children.

Without the achievements of reformers and scientists during the Progressive era, the institutionalization of scientific child study only fifteen years after the Armistice would not have been possible. It is equally true, however, that without dramatic changes stimulated by America's wartime experience and by the unique social climate of the 1920s, the new child study organizations founded during the Progressive era could not have thrived and indeed might not have survived. If American philanthropy had not decided that social reform must come through the application of the new social sciences to the child, if it had not modeled its programs on the prewar child study institutions, the child sciences would have evolved slowly within academic departments. Furthermore, they would not have been shaped by the reform motive.

WORLD WAR I AND THE "NEW ERA" OF THE 1920S

The revelation that almost one-third of the young men examined for military service had physical defects caused by unwholesome childhood conditions shocked the nation and reinforced the message of Progressive reformers that if the nation were to thrive, it must attend to its children. Julia Lathrop and Cora Bussey Hillis had used information on the unfitness of potential military recruits to muster support during the war for the Children's Bureau and the Iowa station. Social reformers continued to use the same information after the war to agitate for broader, more ambitious child welfare reform goals based on broader, more ambitious research programs.

In addition to calling attention to the nation's urgent need to help its children to become better citizens, the war also helped to define what should be done for children and what means should be employed. Winning the war created a new sense of national confidence and pride and proved to be a major turning point for faith in progress and in the social sciences as a vehicle of progress.[9] Early in the 1920s the conviction spread that the nation was entering a "new era" of major social change for the better. The "new reformers" challenged the assumption of Progressive social justice reformers that the most compelling tasks were to eliminate poverty and improve institutions. Many Americans accepted President Hoover's assurance that poverty could be abolished from their land. To those enjoying the "prosperous twenties," flaws in the economy no longer appeared to be a significant source of social ills.[10] A 1924 report by Vassar College asserted, for example, that comparative studies of the wealthy and the poor showed that "poverty is a smaller factor than ignorance in the causation of malnutrition, and the same is probably true of psychological maladjustment."[11]

THE NEW PRESTIGE OF SOCIAL SCIENCE

Psychological maladjustment soon took the place of poverty as the main target of child welfare reformers. Before the war, there was little confidence in applied social science, including psychology. Recall, for example, Carl Seashore's remark that the benefits of applying science to children would have to be taken on faith. Psychology's usefulness in military manpower selection and training, especially its apparently successful use of mental tests to screen 1,700,000 men for the armed forces, enormously enhanced its prestige.[12] Even before the United States entered the war, G. Stanley Hall commented on the contributions of psychology to the French and German war efforts. He founded the *Journal of Applied Psychology* in 1917, and by 1920 more than half of the psychologists in the United States were engaged in applied research.[13] Behavioral psychology and Freudian psychiatry became more familiar to the American public as a result of wartime exposure.[14] Their emphasis on the influence of early childhood experience on adult behavior persuaded many social reformers that preschool children must have better care.[15] Following the war, the "new psychology," including both psychology and psychiatry, became "one of the characteristic fads of the age," and "both symptom and cause of critical social change."[16] It not only focused attention on the needs of young children but also fostered hope of solving all social problems through psychological knowledge.

In response to wartime needs, the National Research Council (NRC) was created in 1918 as part of the National Academy of Sciences. Its Division of Anthropology and Psychology was a sign of the new prestige of the social sciences.[17] Another sign was President Hoover's appointment in 1929 of a group of social scientists to undertake research on recent social trends in the United States. Hoover was motivated by the belief that knowledge derived from the social sciences could provide a basis for reformulating national policy.[18] Influential leaders from various fields, including the eminent political commentators Walter Lippman and Herbert Croly, extolled the potential of applied social science. Many Americans came to believe that science could do almost anything, even cure social ills.[19]

Although academic social scientists were eager to establish their emerging fields as branches of pure science uncontaminated by utilitarian goals, some psychologists, in particular, were confident that advances in knowledge would inevitably bring large practical benefits. Behaviorist John B. Watson defined psychology's aims as prediction and control.[20] James McKeen Cattell, then psychology's most eminent spokesman, asserted that "scientific men should take the place that is theirs as members of the modern world. . . . The order of science should be the chief concern of a nation that would conserve and increase the welfare of its people."[21] Even G. Stanley Hall ignored his previous views on the difficulty of changing the course of human evolution and declared, "Science in its largest sense is from this time forth to rule the world. The age of laissez-faire is ended and research, discovery, investigation and invention . . . must now take the helm."[22] Faith in the potential of the social sciences to achieve reform encouraged faith in progress. To believe in progress was to insist that far better ways of life were still to be discovered and translated into practice through science.[23]

Related to faith in science and progress was the concept of cultural lag, which referred to the belief that a major source of America's ills was the gulf between traditional social practices and institutions and the nation's brilliant scientific and technological achievements. The proposed remedy was to replace outworn tradition as quickly as possible with better ways derived from science. Disdain for tradition was widespread during the 1920s.[24] "For different reasons," Henry May explained, "spokesmen of business, social science and literary revolt all wanted to get clear away from the past, to discard history." Out of the postwar civilization was emerging, in this view, a new civilization, "conveyed by the phrase New Era." The Fords and the Edisons, who scorned history, were as revolutionary as the writers and artists, and "most revolutionary of all perhaps were the prophets of psychology and social science."[25]

PHILANTHROPY IN THE "NEW ERA"

During the first two decades of the twentieth century wealthy entrepreneurs had established a series of great foundations, unprecedented in the size of the fortunes they dispersed, the efficiency and skill of their management, and the expectations of what they could accomplish.[26] World War I transformed this unique new American philanthropy in unexpected ways. Philanthropists profited from their experience with relief efforts in Europe and from active involvement in the organization and support of science to further the war effort.[27] Unprecedented response to the appeals of the American Red Cross and other philanthropies demonstrated the power of voluntarism.[28]

The "new era" of the 1920s meant for foundations a new social-scientific utopianism and the possibility of developing nongovernmental systems for achieving social progress through science.[29] Although a movement to create a private endowment for scientific research failed to win support from the great philanthropies before the war, philanthropy rather than government became the chief patron of science soon after the war.[30] The number of foundations increased substantially during the 1920s as they shifted their activities from beneficence to pioneering ventures in education, health, and welfare. Simultaneously they shifted support from adults' to children's programs. Between 1920 and 1930 grants for child-related programs nearly doubled, while grants for adult programs increased by less than one-third.[31]

THE LAURA SPELMAN ROCKEFELLER MEMORIAL

Belief in the importance of children, the rising prestige of applied social science, and confidence in the possibility of progress through science converged soon after the Armistice in ambitious efforts by two new foundations to promote and institutionalize child study.[32]

The Laura Spelman Rockefeller Memorial was John D. Rockefeller's fourth and last great benevolent trust, established in memory of his wife, who died in 1915, and endowed with $74 million to continue her work for the welfare of women and children. The Memorial's charter specified that it could not support social legislation or organizations involved in social action, a defensive reaction to charges, investigated in 1914 by the United States Commission on Industrial Relations, that the Rockefeller Foundation was "merely a vehicle" for the family's private business interests."[33] To further protect itself from public scrutiny, the Memorial asked that grant recipients restrict announcement of their grants to mention in their regular reports. It was a policy of anonymity with regard to its grants that "stopped just short of secrecy."[34]

Like many other foundations at that time, the Memorial, instead of relying on its trustees, selected a paid professional to manage its affairs.[35] Twenty-seven-year-old Beardsley Ruml, a University of Chicago experimental psychologist experienced in mental testing, was appointed director late in 1921. Ruml was responsible for a radical change in the policies of the Memorial and the Rockefeller Foundation, approved by the foundation's directors in 1923.[36] Before the war the Rockefeller philanthropies had shied away from economic and social research, focusing on health, education, and charitable services.[37] Instead of continuing to invest in the charities Laura Spelman Rockefeller had supported, the Memorial promoted the advancement of the social sciences.[38]

Ruml argued that the social sciences could provide a new base for the betterment of mankind.[39] Philanthropic support for social science research before the war had been limited mainly to the Russell Sage Foundation's funding of social surveys. Now, in the postwar decade, the Memorial invested millions in all of the social sciences in order to test their ability to solve social problems. From 1923 until the dissolution of the Memorial in 1929, Ruml's reasoning guided its strategy.[40]

To perpetuate Laura Spelman Rockefeller's support of child welfare reform, Ruml committed one-fifth of the Memorial's resources to child study programs. In 1923 he invited Lawrence K. Frank, aged thirty-three, to become his assistant and a program officer of the Memorial, with responsibility for designing and administering programs for children that would accord with the Memorial's general program for the social sciences. Frank had majored in economics at Columbia University but was knowledgeable about psychology and euphoric about the potential of the social sciences to reconstruct society. "The next great achievement of man," he predicted, would be the creation of a social science as "different from contemporary science as modern chemistry from the old alchemy and yet capable of achieving for man the same kind of power over himself as natural science has given over the rest of the world."[41]

Frank's keen interest in children had been stimulated by John Dewey's ideas about progressive education, Lucy Sprague Mitchell's leadership of the nursery school movement, and behaviorist John Watson's pioneering use of children as subjects of experimental psychology.[42] Another "profound influence" was Frances Perkins, with whom Frank had worked on a study of infant mortality.[43] Frank's third wife (he was twice widowed) said that her husband's interest in child development stemmed from problems in his own childhood, particularly desertion by his father when he was a young child.[44]

Even before Ruml and Frank joined the Memorial, the Rockefeller Foundation expressed a keen interest in the Iowa Child Welfare Research Station.[45] In 1920 Hillis wrote to the Rockefeller Foundation, the Commonwealth Fund, and other philanthropic organizations and individuals in an effort to obtain an "adequate, permanent endowment for the station." The endowment, she insisted, must never be "less than three to five million to start," plus enough funds for the "erection of nine to fourteen buildings."[46] Vincent Rockefeller, president of the Rockefeller Foundation and an old friend of Hillis, responded to her letter by inviting her to meet with him.[47] Following the meeting, Rockefeller sent foundation representatives to inspect the station. One sees little trace of the humble mother in the Hillis of the postwar years. Instructing Seashore about a program she wanted him to get Hoover to approve, she wrote, "I want to be appointed superintendent in whatever they call it."[48]

Baldwin's grant proposal requesting a million dollars to enable the Iowa station to become a national agency was rejected by Ruml and Frank because they had decided that the size and diversity of the United States required a national network of child development institutes at strategic locations. Recognizing, however, that the Iowa station could serve as a useful prototype for their plans for a national network of child study and parent education programs, they gave the station a modest grant in 1923, followed in 1925 by a grant of $100,000 for a five-year program expansion.[49]

The Iowa station became a model for the child development institutes that the Memorial founded during the 1920s because it represented so many of Ruml's and Frank's ideas about what such an institute should be. It was an autonomous entity with an interdisciplinary approach. However, it was also affiliated with a state university and had access to agricultural extension service networks, an excellent mechanism already in place for carrying out Ruml's goal of diffusing and applying research findings.[50] All the institutes founded during the 1920s adopted Iowa's emphasis on the normal preschool child; Iowa's three goals: research, parent education, and training of developmental specialists; and Iowa's and Merrill-Palmer's nursery school laboratories.

While establishing the new child development institutes, Ruml and Frank avoided association with Hall's child study movement and never considered Clark University as a possible site for an institute. Nevertheless, the institutes founded in the 1920s showed Hall's influence. Their purpose, like Hall's, was to produce useful knowledge of the normal child. Both Hall's child study movement and the institutes operated outside mainstream academic psychology for many of the same reasons. Both had a more humanistic orientation than academic psychology. Both tried to capture the "whole" child, rather than a "fragmented" child (Hall's term) divided among disciplines. Many developmentalists at the new institutes shared Hall's reservations about laboratory research and his preference for natural settings. Summing up the legacy of pioneers such as Hall and J. Mark Baldwin, the editors of *A Century of Developmental Psychology* declare that the "agenda of contemporary psychology has more in common with the field's agenda near the turn of the century than with the agenda of more recent times of the 1950s and 1960s." They criticize the "narrow emphasis on experimental psychology and social learning theory" that was "a sharp break from the origins of the field."[51]

THE LAURA SPELMAN ROCKEFELLER MEMORIAL CHILD DEVELOPMENT INSTITUTES

Between 1924 and 1927 the Memorial financed a nationwide network of child development institutes consisting of the Iowa station and four new centers, which received a total of a million and a half dollars.[52] Reflecting their Progressive heritage, three of the five institutes used "child welfare" rather than "child development" in their names.

The first institute was established in 1924 at Teachers College, Columbia University; its primary purpose was to train parent educators and nursery school teachers.[53] Another institute was established in 1925 at the University of Minnesota as a "friendly competitor to Iowa."[54] Their staff members were expected to act as counterparts of agricultural extension agents, disseminating the new findings to parents instead of to farmers.[55] In 1925 the Memorial also founded St. George's School for Child Study at the University of Toronto, which maintained a close alliance with the institutes in the United States. In 1926 the Memorial awarded a five-year grant to the Yale Psycho-clinic, later the Yale Clinic of Child Development. It sponsored its last major institute at the University of California at Berkeley in 1927.[56] In addition to the major institutes, the Memorial also created and supported numerous smaller child study and parent education programs in colleges, universities, and other organizations throughout the country.[57] The Memorial's grants to child study and parent education programs between 1923 and 1929 totaled more than five million dollars.

In addition to the Laura Spelman Rockefeller Memorial institutes, two other major child development institutes were founded in the 1920s. Lizzie Merrill-Palmer, childless widow of a Michigan senator, died in 1918, leaving four million dollars for the founding and maintenance of a Detroit school to train young women for motherhood and homemaking. Home economist Edna Noble White transformed the school into what was later named the Merrill-Palmer Institute, the second major child development center and the only one unaffiliated with a college or university. Merrill-Palmer opened officially in 1921 and established its nursery school laboratory only three months after the Iowa station had founded the first such school laboratory.[58] White helped to attract home economists to the field of child development and influenced Frank in many ways.[59]

To support science that would contribute to "human betterment," Samuel Fels, a Philadelphia financier, founded The Fels Research Institute for Human Development, affiliated with Antioch College, in 1929. Lester Sontag, a physician, directed the Fels Institute until 1970. He initiated a major longitudinal study of child development and focused research on the psychological problems of children and on their socialization.[60]

PARENT EDUCATION: A BRAVE NEW WORLD
THROUGH BRAND-NEW HUMAN BEINGS

The stated purposes of the Memorial's child development centers were research, training, and dissemination. As we have seen, the Iowa station subordinated dissemination and application to research. Frank and Ruml declared research and parent education to be of equal importance because they wanted to narrow the gap between discovery and application. "Our whole interest in social science is merely to provide something that can be diffused," Ruml said.[61] Frank explained that the Memorial's activities in social science were conceived not as ends in themselves but as "an advancement of scientific principles and scientific bases that might be relevant to our developing society."[62] Parent education was to be the institutes' main mechanism of social policy. The Commonwealth Fund also stressed parent education in its first child guidance program from 1922 to 1927.

Even at their peak, Hall's parent education programs could not match the enthusiasm or the utopian expectations of the programs in the 1920s.[63] Asserting that parent education would save the world, one leader declared that it had accounted for more profound changes than anything "since mankind emerged from the cave."[64] The rampant character of the revived postwar parent education movement and Ruml's and Frank's interest in it reflected important changes in attitudes on how to achieve social reform.[65]

To the innovative, overconfident reformers of the 1920s, amelioration of social problems was too modest a goal. They sought prevention and believed that the best way to prevent problems was not to reshape institutions but to use the new psychology to reconstruct individuals. According to social psychologist and former Hall student Miriam Van Waters, "the true springs of action are in the internal nature of man, hence the uselessness of programs dependent on state action or force."[66] To prevent problems one must go to the source, which, of course, was the child.[67]

Following the war, many social reformers and scientists rejected hereditarian determinism and contended that children are plastic creatures, capable of being molded to conform to adult desires and goals. Watson claimed that the technique of conditioning could reshape human nature. "Children are made, not born," he asserted.[68] It followed that the best way to create a brave new world was to create brand-new human beings. He suggested that the ideal way to prevent social ills would be for people to stop having children for about twenty years, until experimental laboratory research on child subjects could discover optimum child rearing methods.[69] But even Watson recognized that people could not be stopped from having children until science discovered perfect ways to rear them. The only feasible way to change the child was to change parents first. Frank agreed.[70]

Watson lost his faculty appointment at Johns Hopkins in 1919 because of a sexual scandal. Never readmitted to academe, he became an advertising executive and lectured and wrote popular articles on child rearing throughout the twenties. In 1928 he published the first child-rearing manual to offer psychological advice, modeling the book on L. Emmett Holt's bestseller on the physical care of the child. Watson's tone was as authoritarian as Holt's, and his book also became a bestseller. Frank applied Watson's child-rearing advice to his children by his first wife. Helen Lynd claimed that theories on child development in America could be traced by observing the changing methods Frank used in rearing the children by each of his three wives.[71]

Optimism about continued economic prosperity and assumptions about the importance of proper child rearing led to a widespread conviction that parent error was then, and would remain, the chief source of children's difficulties. President Hoover told the 1930 White House Conference that "the ill-nourished child in our country is not the product of poverty, it is largely the product of ill-instructed children and ignorant parents," a conclusion Frank had reached six years earlier.[72] "By far the largest number of the physical effects and mental handicaps of the child which are remediable," he asserted, " may be attributed to parents who, through ignorance, misunderstanding, timidity, and neglect have failed to give their children that wholesome regime, the lack of which makes necessary these many child welfare programs."[73]

The menace of cultural lag was a fundamental assumption underlying the focus on postwar parent education. "A better rearing of children," the authors of *Recent Social Trends* speculated, "may lead to a healthier psychological adjustment of man to civilization through the refusal to accept irrational and unhealthy customs that exist all around us."[74] Social welfare leader Eduard Lindeman cautioned, "The midwife's lore and the grandmother's mysterious formulas have no place in a society which is committed to science and technology."[75] Sociologist Ernest Groves went even further, declaring that parents who rely on tradition "socially menace their children."[76]

Frank, a fanatic on the subject of cultural lag, saw the lack of scientific child-rearing practices in the home as the "most tangible obstacle to rapid progress in child care." The "crux of the problem," he declared, was how to "persuade or compel adults to give up traditional beliefs and established habits for procedures established by science." During the Progressive era parent education was only one important aspect of child welfare reform; in the 1920s it became the panacea. Ultimately, all child welfare reform was to be achieved by changing parents' behavior. Remedial child welfare activities were to be continued until perfectly reared children would render them unnecessary. The "basic child welfare agency is the home," Frank asserted; "parent education is the ultimate solution."[77]

PARENT EDUCATION: A CENTURY
OF CONTINUITY AND CHANGE

New and radical as it seemed, the parent education movement of the 1920s reflected early- and mid-nineteenth century beliefs about the power of the mother's influence and the importance of early childhood in determining adult character and behavior. New England social reformers had been motivated by these beliefs to seek social reform through "domestic education," which like "parent education" a century later, meant the education of mothers in approved ways of rearing children.[78] The focus on the school child from the end of the Civil War through World War I dimmed the national memory of this earlier focus on early childhood. Social reformers of the 1920s, who believed that they could change society by changing child-rearing practices, thought that they were advocating a revolutionary new approach. None of the psychologists and psychiatrists who emphasized the importance of early childhood seemed aware that they were restating, in scientific terms, beliefs espoused by early-nineteenth-century clergy, educators, and civic reformers.

The content of the lessons mothers were taught in the 1920s was, however, *very* different. Advocates of domestic education a century earlier believed that the survival of the nation depended on the restoration of the democratic and Christian values that seemed to them responsible for the founding and early success of the American republic. The principal duty of mothers then was to serve as exemplars of traditional moral and spiritual values. Reformers in the

1920s wanted to overcome "cultural lag" and stood the early-nineteenth-century program on its head. Frank preached that religion and patriotism were the two major obstacles to progress because they caused people to cling to outmoded ways. "Religion and patriotism through their preoccupation with the past serve more frequently to block cultural diffusion than to promote it," he wrote, a message that no one in Frank's position would dare to deliver today.[79]

Earlier proponents of domestic education also differed sharply from 1920s social reformers in their attitude toward mothers. The former revered maternal instinct, especially the clergy, who saw mothers as their allies. Reformers and child specialists in the 1920s often regarded mothers as subjects to be "persuaded," "cajoled," or "coerced" into using scientifically approved child-rearing methods. Frank even suggested that allowances to dependent and foster mothers be conditioned on their acceptance of instruction.[80] Even before the war, social feminists, many professional women, and members of the National Congress of Mothers all believed that one of the most important functions of higher education for women was to prepare them for motherhood. In 1915 Julia Lathrop asserted that research on children and the conduct of a household were the subjects most neglected by science, "a neglect long hidden behind tradition and sentimentality." She called upon college-educated women to "put an end to this neglect" and defined higher education for women as "training in original research applied to the life and interests of the family."[81]

Paradoxically, however, as the postwar parent education movement gained momentum, many administrators and faculty members of elite women's colleges rejected the creation of an "educated motherhood" as a valid function of women's higher education.[82] They wanted instead a curriculum identical to that of men's colleges. The president of Vassar, Lathrop's alma mater, rejected Frank's attempts to persuade her to support courses in child development or to establish preschool laboratories.[83] Many presidents of women's colleges also opposed the parent education program of the American Association of University Women.[84] Frank perceived the study of child development as "scientific study of human behavior," but they saw it as preparation for homemaking and wanted no part of it.[85]

Professional home economists also tended to be contemptuous of or indifferent to child study, preferring chemical analyses of foods and textiles or other laboratory tasks to the study of child development, a "second-class, unscientific field."[86] Edna Noble White, Louise Stanley, Lydia Roberts, and the few other home economists who defended the value of scientific child study met stiff resistance from their colleagues.[87] The prevailing attitude, according to psychologist and developmentalist Myrtle McGraw, was that studying children in life rather than in the laboratory was not science.[88] Academe had not changed much since Hall said that it would be considered absurd to show a baby to a class in psychology.

Although Frank had tried to interest professional women in child development research, and Rockefeller had founded the Memorial to continue his wife's work, not a single woman was ever a Memorial trustee, and the only female member of its professional staff was responsible for its social work program. This was an irony often noted by trustee Leonard Outhwaite, who told Ruml that he was asked repeatedly, "Where are the women who should be guiding the programs for families and children."[89] Nothing, however, was done to change this state of affairs within the Memorial, and, as we have seen, the only woman director of a child development institute was Helen Woolley at Teachers College.

THE CART BEFORE THE HORSE:
PARENT EDUCATION IN THE INSTITUTES

Postwar social reformers disagreed significantly with Progressive reformers about the ease and speed with which social ills could be overcome. Although they were environmentalists (favoring the influence of nurture over nature), founders of the Iowa station recognized that what could be accomplished was limited by children's inherited characteristics and the paucity and untested nature of scientific knowledge of children. Hillis, as described earlier, became upset when newspapers promised Iowans more than she and Seashore believed the station could deliver. They expected only to improve children, not to remake them. The rhetoric of Watson and Frank, on the other hand, often gave the impression that a child's Utopia was just around the corner.[90]

Believing that parent education and child development research were linked goals, the Memorial rushed to promote a variety of parent education programs even before the research programs of the new institutes were well underway. Before the Memorial would support a research institute, it insisted on commitment to an active parent education program. [91] The Memorial founded and funded the National Council of Parent Education to organize and professionalize the parent education movement. It gave support and guidance to the Federation for Child Study, which became the Child Study Association of America, the most prestigious organization in the field of parent education.[92] It persuaded the American Association of University Women to transform its social action program into a parent education program.[93] It worked out an arrangement with four of the institutes to provide financial support for *Parents Magazine,* a mass-circulation periodical founded by George J. Hecht, in a failed attempt to enable developmentalists to exercise some control over the magazine's contents.[94]

Ruml and Frank soon began to regret their headlong rush into parent education. A primary reason for supporting the parent education movement was to keep it under control, but Ruml soon realized it was "out-of-control." He found the situation to have "all the dangers of boom-over-enthusiasm and probable disillusioned deflation because it is impossible to meet the public demand for knowledge and instruction. . . . The public is "rapidly taking matters into its own hands."[95]

Memorial trustee L. B. Day was particularly critical of the parent education programs. Disseminating information to parents from an infant specialty such as child development, he wrote to Ruml, was "putting demonstration ahead of research . . . the cart before the horse."[96] He wanted to know whether the Memorial's primary aim was "development of research or development of the parent."[97] Memorial president Colonel Arthur Woods approved of the parent education programs but said of the research programs, "I find myself wondering whether we are not thinking that the scientific method will carry us further than it can. The wisdom of the human instinct must be given proper play."[98] Many of the child development professionals Milton J. E. Senn interviewed in the 1960s and 1970s complained about the unfortunate consequences for parents and children of uncritical acceptance of early research on children and the premature dissemination of new findings.[99] Harold Stevenson, deploring the vogue for Watsonian behaviorism, pointed out that Watson relied on "one study, one subject . . . to validate his theory that the conditioned response was the key to understanding the development of human behavior. . . . We are aghast today to see the uncritical acceptance this study received." Stevenson continued, "Not only was the evidence minimal but the question has been raised recently whether conditioning was indeed demonstrated in this single case."[100]

Only a few years after the decision to make parent education and research equal goals, the Memorial decided to devote most of its child study funds to research. This decision was motivated by more than the deficiencies of the parent education programs and the desire to expand research: its principal purpose was to institutionalize and professionalize the new field of child development, to have it recognized as a science by university scientists.

The Memorial had two apparently irreconcilable goals. Following the passion of the times to rely on science to solve social problems, it insisted on social science research that would be useful to society. In practice, this meant diffusion of "scientific" child-rearing advice to parents rather than reform of institutions. Within the universities, however, social scientists demanded basic research that would satisfy the requirements of scientific objectivity, and this meant divorcing research from social reform goals.

Another formidable obstacle in establishing child development research as a valid scientific field was the disdain of most academic social scientists for research on children. During the 1920s and 1930s, child psychology, which became the primary focus of child development research, was an insignificant part of academic psychology, unrecognized as a specialty by the American Psychological Association. The index of the first edition of E. G. Boring's *History of Experimental Psychology* (1929), which covered developments up to 1940, has only two references to child psychology. Academic contempt for research on children also stemmed from its reputation as a woman's field. The next chapter discusses some of the ingenious ways in which the Memorial tried to overcome these obstacles.

Chapter 9 Child Development
Research: Preventive Politics

The National Research Council (NRC) Division of Anthropology and Psychology established a Committee on Child Welfare and Parent Education in 1920. It appointed Bird Baldwin, director of the Iowa Child Welfare Research Station, its chair. Carl Seashore discouraged Baldwin from involving the new committee in any significant activities, however, and it remained unfunded and almost totally inactive during its first four years.[1]

When Robert Woodworth, an eminent Columbia University psychologist, became chair of the NRC Division of Anthropology and Psychology in 1924, Lawrence K. Frank and Beardsley Ruml seized the opportunity to use the moribund child welfare committee to achieve the Laura Spelman Rockefeller Memorial's goal of professionalizing and legitimizing the new field of child development. Although Woodworth did not himself engage in research on children, he strongly endorsed it; one of his first activities as division chair was to ask 1200 social scientists if they studied children. Only 124 answered yes.[2]

A first step in disassociating the committee from welfare activities was to rename it the Committee on Child Development in May 1925.

A conference in 1925 confirmed the need for the committee and determined its functions. Thirty scholars, carefully selected by Woodworth and Frank, attended the conference. Wholeheartedly approving the new committee, conference participants defined its purpose as demonstrating that child development research is both possible and necessary. They proposed a four-year committee program with three components: the holding of biennial conferences, the publication of bibliographies and research surveys, and the administration of an award program to support the training of child development researchers.[3]

Baldwin continued as chair of the committee, which received a grant of $40,000 from the Memorial in January 1926.[4] Woodworth and John Anderson, director of the Minnesota institute, were its other members. In accordance with its new name, the committee soon eliminated the parent education and welfare functions of its predecessor. Its primary strategy for transforming child development into a legitimate academic discipline was to confine itself to activities related to research and to minimize its association with child welfare reform or parent education, both regarded as scientifically inferior women's fields.[5] Training fellowships in parent education, administered by the institute at Teachers College, were limited to women. In 1926 the committee recommended that training fellowships administered by the committee itself be limited to research and that every effort be made to induce qualified men to apply. Frank wanted child study programs to provide employment for college-educated women but reluctantly agreed, in October 1926, to open committee-administered fellowships to men. Parent education fellowships were still restricted to women.[6] But by 1928 the Memorial had established an autonomous parent education organization, the National Council on Parent Education, separated physically from the Committee on Child Development by its location in New York City.[7]

At the committee's 1925 conference, Baldwin clarified its purpose, declaring, "We are concerned with a scientific analysis of the fundamental problems underlying childhood, rather than formulating remedial measures or outlining methods of training."[8] Frank and Ruml were having it both ways: keeping parent education alive in the child development institutes to fulfill the Memorial's commitment to dissemination of research findings, and trying to making child development research scientifically respectable through the Committee on Child Development.

Reflecting the tension between those who were interested in research in order to help children and those who were primarily interested in scientific understanding, a major objective of the committee's 1925 conference was to work out the proper relationship between research and practice. Woodworth reassured those who complained that current knowledge was an inadequate guide for the thriving child welfare movement. Agreeing that fundamental research must be supported, he pointed out that "practical endeavor is certain to go on without waiting for a thorough scientific grounding." Even if it were possible, he advised, "we should not halt all practical endeavor until we have the necessary knowledge. . . . Our inevitable blunders will be valuable and even necessary as clues to the investigator. Research and practice will react upon each other."[9]

In 1927 the committee's membership was enlarged to encourage the evolution of child development research into an interdisciplinary endeavor. Pediatrician Martha Eliot of the Children's Bureau, E. V. McCollum, a Johns Hopkins biochemist interested in nutrition, and T. Wingate Todd, an anatomist at Western Reserve University, were the new members. Anderson succeeded Baldwin as chair after Baldwin's death in 1928.[10]

The Committee on Child Development sponsored four important conferences and published *Child Development Abstracts,* a summary of relevant research reported in professional journals. It also administered training fellowships for scientists wishing to acquire experience in child development research. In spite of these accomplishments, the committee's survival was threatened by the dissolution of the Memorial in 1929, by the rival 1930 White House Conference committee, by the expiration of its grant in 1930, by dim prospects for future support, and by the destructive nine-month chairmanship in 1932 of Wingate Todd. Todd attempted to restore the parent education function of the committee and made no progress toward its goal of establishing a professional society. In order to oust him, the committee dissolved and recreated itself.[11] Woodworth became chair and, against what seemed insuperable odds, succeeded in organizing the Society for Research in Child Development (SRCD) in June 1933. One hundred professionals attended its first meeting.[12]

The new society assumed the most important function of the NRC committee, enlisting the cooperation of researchers from many fields in the effort to stimulate and support child development research. At its first meeting, it settled the continuing controversy over whether or not to limit the society's function to the support of research by passing a motion to restore the service functions that the committee had eliminated in 1925. Although the society's constitution, adopted in 1934, committed it to promote both research and application, for several decades most of its energies were confined to research.

EARLY RESEARCH IN THE CHILD DEVELOPMENT
INSTITUTES, 1924–1929

Frank wanted child development research to be a new venture, not a stand-in for child psychology. Scientists in the institutes were not to use the child as one more source of data, as academic researchers have used rats or fruit flies "to pursue their own narrow interests . . . only rarely concerned with further information." The primary aim of child development researchers, Frank believed, should be to contribute to the understanding of children through cooperation with colleagues in other disciplines.[13]

Frank decided that autonomous organizations like the Iowa Child Welfare Research Station, attached to a university and benefiting from university faculty and facilities but with their own independent charter, would be able to recruit scholars from diverse disciplines, encourage the coordination and integration of these findings, and come closer to understanding the "whole child." Frank recruited multidisciplinary staffs that included psychologists, pediatricians, physiologists, anatomists, biochemists, nutritionists, nurses, dentists, sociologists, physical anthropologists, social workers, and educators. He preferred, however, that the directors of the major institutes be psychologists, as were all but one.[14]

Reflecting the emphasis of the 1920s on the importance of early childhood and the goal of improving the lives of all children, Frank wanted child development research to focus on normal preschool children. He refused to support a proposed study of children in "uncontrolled environments and unenlightened homes," because he believed that there were already too many studies of disadvantaged children. He also believed that knowledge of how physically and emotionally healthy children were reared could provide valuable insights about effective child-rearing practices. Unlike Seashore, Frank did not attempt to define "normal."[15] Emphasis on the average child meant that most research subjects were middle-class children. The ease with which the children of faculty could be recruited to nursery school laboratories also contributed to the popularity of middle-class children as research subjects. Some in the field of early education, still motivated by the Progressive era's impulse to help the disadvantaged, protested that they had not entered the field to help a lot of middle-class children.[16]

John Watson insisted that experimental research on babies was crucial, and Frank defined child development research as the investigation of the growth of children from conception to maturity. Nevertheless, the overwhelming majority of subjects during the 1920s and early 1930s were between the ages of two and six. The 1937 *Directory of Research in Child Development,* for example, listed only research on children who were at least two years old but under seven years. One scholar attributed the delay in research on infants to the prevailing belief that the formation of personality did not begin until a child was two. For whatever reason, few developmentalists studied babies during the 1920s. Arnold Gesell was a notable exception (see chapter 10).[17]

Since nursery schools were the first readily available source of research subjects younger than six, the Memorial supported the establishment of nursery school laboratories in child development institutes, and in nursery schools in other settings, to provide faculty and students with the opportunity to study preschool children. According to Barbara Beatty (1995), nursery school research was concerned primarily with how nursery schools could enhance young children's growth and development. A 1935 bibliography documented 840 items of nursery school research.[18]

Frank encouraged the research orientation of the American nursery school movement because he wanted to avoid the separation of research and practice that had occurred in the kindergarten movement. He also wanted to tie nursery school education to parent education and to other family services no longer offered by kindergarten programs.[19] He believed that "the only hope of checking the increasing cost of diagnosis, therapy, and custodial care for stunted, distorted and socially maladjusted children and adults is through the development of pre-school education programs for children and their parents."[20]

Margaret MacMillan established the first nursery school in London in 1908 to provide better food and care for slum children. Ten years later the British government made nursery schools a part of the national school system. The nursery school movement in the United States, sponsored by mothers rather than government, began only after World War I. It should not be confused with the day nurseries provided for working-class parents before the war. The number of nursery schools in the United States increased from three in 1920 to 262 in 1930, twenty-one of which were laboratory schools.[21]

In contrast to the British nursery schools, which had been established in order to help poor children, American mothers, with few exceptions, established nursery schools for the benefit of privileged children. They wanted to provide companionship for their children, to meet and share experiences with other mothers, and to learn how to use new scientific findings in their child rearing. Mary Cover Jones, who observed nursery schools in both countries, found the British schools much more authoritarian than those in the United States.[22]

WHAT DID CHILD DEVELOPMENTALISTS
STUDY?

Researchers in the institutes were concerned primarily with investigating the normal developmental process. "With a developing organism," John Anderson wrote, "norms are an essential base upon which psychology must be built. Without them one is never sure whether the particular phenomena studied are the results of development . . . or of the artificial conditions so essential to experiment. . . . The study of developmental psychology is more complex than adult psychology and the normative approach, far from being a pseudo-scientific psychology, is, in the very nature of the case, the basic methodological structure upon which an experimental psychology of the child must be constructed."[23] Investigators relied on objective measurements to discover norms in children's development, and variations related mainly to sex and age differences.

Early studies focused on children's physical development and physiological functioning. Even simple norms, such as those for weight and height, were not easy to establish. Since a Children's Bureau committee of experts could not reach agreement in 1923, the norms were published without the committee's formal endorsement.[24] Nevertheless, investigators in the institutes quickly established many norms of physical development and soon began to explore children's mental and emotional development. Before the end of the 1920s, Baldwin and some of his colleagues at the Iowa station, Gesell and his associates at the Yale clinic, and Lewis Terman at Stanford University had begun to correlate physical and mental growth.[25]

It may have been useful for child development research to begin by focusing on average, "normal" developmental outcomes for children of each sex and age when reared in favorable circumstances. It was not, however, a strategy that could support the Memorial's reform goals or its hopes for parent education. To discover and teach better child-rearing practices required study not only of normal outcomes in uniform circumstances, but also of better or worse results in different circumstances and with different practices. As research became more sophisticated, scholars paid more attention to multiple factors affecting children rather than focusing on age and sex variables divorced from social context. "Cross-sectional" research continued, but by far the most important innovation was the introduction of longitudinal studies before the end of the 1920s. Frank and most investigators agreed that only long-term studies of individual children would yield the kind of information necessary to understand the developmental process and do justice to the uniqueness of every child. The use and refinement of longitudinal methods were what most helped to distinguish child development from academic child psychology.[26]

With the notable exception of the nature versus nurture framework, early research on children was essentially atheoretical because it seemed sensible in a new field to observe children without preconceived assumptions. Harold Jones called it "dragnet research," asking, "Must we at all times specify just what fish we are after, or is it permissible to cast a net in fishing waters for anything we can get? We may waste a lot of time fishing for a fish that isn't there when a more random procedure may be more productive."[27]

The best description of the character, diversity, and growth of early child development research, preschool and parent education, and child guidance clinics during the first postwar decade is presented in *The Twenty-Eighth Yearbook of the National Society for Education: Preschool and Parent Education*. Three years in preparation, with twenty-nine contributors, the *Yearbook* filled 864 pages with reports of new developments.[28] Lois Meek (Stolz), chair of the committee that organized the *Yearbook*, pointed out that its publication before professional journals or associations in most of these new fields had been established made it a "spearhead of information."[29] The ferment in the field and the diversity of the issues are vividly reflected in the proceedings of the four conferences sponsored by the NRC Committee on Child Development (NRCCD) between 1925 and 1933. Conference participants seem to have raised every conceivable question relevant to a new field struggling to become a science; these questions are often strikingly similar to those developmentalists still ponder. Conference topics included reservations about applying the findings of an underdeveloped science, the measurement and prediction of mental growth and the controversy over the constancy of the IQ, the relative value of naturalistic and experimental methods, theoretical and methodological problems related to the nature-nurture controversy, ethical problems related to research on children, the relevance of psychoanalysis, the place of clinical methods in child development research, and how to draw more pediatricians, mathematicians, sociologists, and other specialists into the field.

At the 1929 Toronto conference, the best-attended and most important of the NRCCD conferences, Harold Jones questioned the insinuation of values into what was supposedly an objective science. He objected particularly to the concept of "adjustment," presented in a paper by William Blatz, director of the Toronto institute. Blatz observed: "We are getting here dangerously close to the ethical field, and this may be a good point for a mere psychologist to pause."[30] Psychologist George Stratton, chair of the Division of Anthropology and Psychology, responded: "In the end human beings themselves are going to be interested in these aims—in what we are going to do with our science and what direction we should give to a child's traits. And yet these aims, I feel, cannot be determined as yet by scientific methods. I am still a believer in intuition and in morals, and I feel that something outside of our actual scientific techniques is needed." The words "as yet" suggest that Stratton may have agreed with G. Stanley Hall that, in time, science would furnish a moral guide.[31]

The first *Handbook of Child Psychology* in 1931, containing twenty-two chapters, was followed in 1933 by a revised and expanded edition. Like the papers delivered at the NRCCD conferences, the two handbooks demonstrate the enormous breadth and variety of research undertaken during the 1920s and early 1930s. Their subjects included methods in child development research, the effects of environmental forces on child growth and development; the developmental psychology of twins and the light it sheds on the nature-nurture controversy; the effects of birth order on child development; physical growth and motor development in relation to mental development, maturation and the patterning of behavior; emotional development; social behavior; the measurement of mental growth; the origin and prenatal development of behavior, eating, sleeping, elimination, language, learning, morals, drawing, play and games, dreams, and philosophies; gifted and mentally retarded children; and "primitive" children.[32] Many of the topics investigated by developmentalists in the 1920s, including seeing and hearing defects; small muscle development; emotional reactions; and children's language, sounds, and vocabularies at different ages were studied by Hall and his colleagues in the 1890s.

The astonishing vitality of early child development research in America stands in sharp contrast to its status in Europe. Ruml and Frank found few European researchers who were interested in the kinds of child study and parent education programs the Memorial wished to promote and few cooperative studies. European research tended to focus on the study of disadvantaged children or the search for better educational methods rather than on children's growth and development.[33] For these reasons the Memorial decided not to fund child study in Europe, with the exception of a modest grant to the Rousseau Institute in Geneva, where Jean Piaget was working.

"GOALS NOT ACHIEVED"

Frank's public rhetoric about the promise of the Memorial's child study and parent education programs concealed misgivings he expressed to Memorial staff and trustees in 1927. In spite of approval of the child study programs three months earlier by the Trustee Committee on Review, Frank confessed to a profound "let down" and "disillusionment" about what they could accomplish. With the programs only three years old, Frank doubted that "stereotyped ideas and patterns of the several branches of science" could be broken down in order to unify the life sciences into an integrated scheme of developmental studies.[34] He was distressed that psychologists dominated child development research and that most pediatricians were too preoccupied with helping sick children to study the development of well children. Pediatricians remained on the fringes of both the child development and child guidance movements. The first pediatric panel discussion of child development did not occur until 1941.[35]

Frank was discouraged by the rejection of his efforts to establish preschool laboratories and courses in child development in most elite women's colleges. He was also deeply disappointed when Grace Abbott, chief of the Children's Bureau, refused to participate in the Washington Child Research Center, the organization the Memorial had sponsored to encourage cooperative research by developmentalists and government agencies concerned with children.[36] The Memorial's effort to establish a child development center in the South in order to make its network of institutes truly national and provide an opportunity to study the development of black children also failed.[37]

Frank may have been troubled by a disheartening lack of progress in enhancing the academic status of child development research. On the whole, both academic scholars and physicians were condescending. For example, Emil Seashore would not permit Nancy Bayley to do her doctoral research on children at the Iowa Child Welfare Research Station. Bayley had chosen the State University of Iowa because she believed that the station offered a unique opportunity to study children. At Seashore's insistence, she researched new galvanic equipment acquired by the psychology department.[38] In the preface to the first edition of the *Handbook of Child Psychology* (1931), its editor complained about experimental psychologists who "continue to look upon the field of child psychology as a proper field of research for women and for men whose masculinity is not of the maximum."[39]

THE INSTITUTES DURING THE DEPRESSION

A reorganization of the Rockefeller Foundation during 1927–28 led to the dissolution of the Memorial in January 1929. Before closing, the Memorial gave new grants to the major institutes to help keep them alive until they could find other means of support and ways to reduce their costs. The Spelman Fund of New York, a Rockefeller subsidiary, was assigned temporary responsibility for overseeing the administration of these grants.[40] Frank joined the Spelman Fund but left almost immediately to become part of President Hoover's research team for *Recent Social Trends.*

The Memorial had warned its beneficiaries that grants were awarded for a limited period, but its termination of support could hardly have come at a worse time. With the exception of the Iowa station, the research institutes had had no more than five years to look for other sponsors, and the Depression made it extremely difficult to obtain new funds. Nevertheless, the Fels and Merrill-Palmer institutes and all but one of the Rockefeller institutes managed to endure for another four decades. The institute at Teachers College, Columbia, closed in 1936, but the others survived by curtailing programs, reducing emphasis on multidisciplinary research, and focusing on subjects preferred by the academic departments with which they affiliated. Many of the child developmentalists who participated in the Senn oral histories discussed the harm done to research in the field by the termination of the Memorial's grants.[41]

Throughout the lean years of the Depression, the belief persisted that social problems could be prevented by applying findings from developmental and clinical studies of young children. Not only did most of the original child research institutes and the child guidance clinics survive but many new ones were established. As mentioned previously, the Children's Fund of Michigan was established in 1929. The Moosehead Institute was established in Illinois in 1930 for the care and education of orphaned children of Moose Lodge members. Its child study laboratory used these children, who ranged in age from infancy to eighteen years, as subjects of longitudinal studies.[42] Founded in 1936, the William T. Grant Foundation, today one of the most active institutions in the field of child development, was charged with the prevention of social ills through research on children.[43] The Rockefeller Foundation's General Education Board also established several new child development research institutes during the 1930s.

CHILD DEVELOPMENT RESEARCH UNDER THE
GENERAL EDUCATION BOARD, 1933–1940

Between 1930 and 1940, Rockefeller philanthropies invested an estimated $2.4 million in child study programs.[44] In 1933 responsibility for continuing or terminating the Memorial's child study programs was assigned not to the newly established Social Science Division under the direction of former memorial trustee Edmund E. Day, but to the General Education Board (GEB). Since the GEB had been founded in 1903 for the purpose of assisting education in the United States, its support for child study programs depended on their potential contribution to education rather than to social science, a major change in policy.[45] Frank joined the GEB in 1933 as an associate director and for the next three and a half years continued to guide the child study programs to the extent that GEB trustees permitted. He resigned to become vice-president of the Josiah Macy, Jr., Foundation.

Except for its short-term transitional grants to some of the institutes, the GEB decided to stop support for research on preschool children.[46] The child study programs focusing on the preschool child had proven so fruitful, the GEB announced with seeming illogic, that it would now shift its support to research on prenatal, infant, and adolescent development.[47] The GEB allocated $630,000 for prenatal and infant research.[48] It sponsored programs at Yale, Columbia, Harvard, Cornell, and the State University of Iowa, the most important of which were the Normal Child Development Study at Columbia and the longitudinal study of prenatal, infant, and child growth and development at Harvard under the direction of Harold Stuart. Responsibility for infant research was soon assigned, "for administrative purposes" to the GEB's director of medical sciences.[49] In June 1937 about a third of the money intended for infant research, more than $200,000, was still uncommitted.

According to the GEB, research on adolescence was allotted $1,340,000, but by 1938 only slightly more than half of this sum had been committed. The GEB's focus on adolescence was, in part, a reaction to the almost exclusive ties of previous adolescent research to the prevention and treatment of juvenile delinquency.[50] It was also motivated by the plight of unemployed youth, a subject of much sympathetic discussion at staff meetings. The focus of developmental studies on normal adolescents often was combined with an aversion to new studies of deviant youth. A chapter on the delinquent child was omitted from the second edition of the *Handbook of Child Psychology* because its editor viewed delinquency as a "purely social" rather than a "psychological" problem.[51] The Memorial had refrained from psychiatric study of children because this was the essence of the Commonwealth Fund's child guidance programs.

Recognizing the need for basic research on normal youth, in 1927 Frank and Ruml reviewed a proposal for a longitudinal study of adolescents with staffs of the Berkeley institute and the Oakland public schools.[52] The Oakland Growth Study, funded by the Spelman Fund of New York, was launched in 1931 and was so highly valued by the GEB that in 1938 it was extended until 1950.[53] In 1981 the surviving original subjects, sixty-one years old, collaborated with Berkeley institute staff members to bring their life histories up to date. The GEB initiated important long-term studies of adolescent development at Harvard and Western Reserve and also funded studies of specific aspects of adolescence, such as those on hormone production at Yale.[54]

The Memorial had tried but failed to initiate a study in a southern university of the "development of Negro children." The GEB considered trying again, at Atlanta University, but soon abandoned the plan, because, like the Memorial, it found the personnel "second-rate."[55] In addition to its grants to research institutions, the GEB allocated $200,000 for child study fellowships, $25,000 for conferences and committee meetings, and approximately $15,000 for publications of the Committee on Child Development.[56]

GEB staff and trustees criticized the Memorial's child study programs in a 1934 memorandum while Frank was still a GEB officer. The critics are not identified in the memorandum, and some of the criticisms may have come from Frank himself. His plan for autonomous institutes to carry on interdisciplinary research had failed because they "suffered from isolation within the university." Their autonomy freed the institutes from control by academic departments but also discouraged their participation in cooperative research. Numerous research projects that had no relationship to each other beyond the similar ages of their subjects were cited as another hindrance to coordinated research. With few exceptions, staff from the institutes had been unable to find employment in the academic departments of their host universities.[57]

A 1938 GEB memorandum found that even though the Memorial's child study programs had provided an immense amount of first-hand knowledge about different aspects of childhood, they had failed to illuminate the developmental process in individual children and had permitted psychological interests and techniques to dominate. Too much attention had been paid to motor development, learning, and habit formation; too little to the development of personality. Longitudinal studies were judged significant, however, especially the Guidance Study and the Oakland Growth Study at the Berkeley institute. Inadequate analysis of data was attributed to "poorly developed" statistical techniques. Longitudinal researchers were praised for their efforts to develop new methods as they accumulated data, methods that "would benefit later and more significant studies."[58]

Shortly after Frank left the GEB in 1936, its Committee on Child Growth and Development (CCGD) announced that it was "under no obligation" to continue Frank's programs and that future decisions about their fate "should be made solely on the basis of whether or not they are germane to the field of general education."[59] Six months later the committee voted itself out of existence. Late in 1937 the GEB decided that child study programs stimulated and responded to "enormous demands for therapy, correction, guidance, and advice," which rendered them ineligible for the basic research grants that were now the GEB's principal interest.[60]

In 1939 the GEB reserved $250,000 "at the most" for its future obligations to child study programs, announcing their termination in 1943 "at the latest." It made two exceptions, awarding the Yale Clinic of Child Development $85,000 for 1939 through 1944 and the Institute of Child Welfare at Berkeley $190,000 for 1938 through 1950, most of the sum left from the earlier allocation for adolescent study and now intended primarily for the institute's longitudinal studies.[61]

EARLY CONSEQUENCES OF PHILANTHROPIC CHILD STUDY PROGRAMS

American child psychology emerged between the two World Wars as the product of child development research supported by philanthropy, rather than by academic child psychology departments. Most of the articles in the first two editions of the *Handbook of Child Psychology* were written by researchers at the child development institutes.[62] *Child Development* was the only journal publishing more than occasional reports of research on children. Seventy-one first authors of the articles it published between 1930 and 1940 worked in the institutes, only ten in psychology departments and ten in medical schools. Thirty-seven of the first authors came from the Iowa station.[63]

Philanthropic child study programs provided the first significant opportunities for training and employment in research on children. A 1918 survey found only three psychologists and two psychiatrists who were primarily interested in studying children.[64] Looking for people to direct and staff the institutes, Frank found few scholars with relevant experience.[65] Child study had not been the first interest of most institute personnel. Helen Woolley, first director of the Teachers College institute, could not find a job that would enable her to pursue her initial interest in the mental differences between men and women. She began to study children because she was offered employment by Cincinnati women social welfare reformers.[66] Before psychologist John Anderson was appointed director of the Minnesota institute, he had studied the effect of nutritional changes on rats.[67]

Philanthropic child study programs eased the way during the early 1920s for aspiring female scientists who were eager to study children and to rectify what they perceived as the dullness of child psychology.[68] Women more than held their own in the new field. Even though Woolley was the only female director of a Rockefeller child development institute, all the editors of *Child Development* were men, and women found it more difficult than men to gain faculty appointments. Between 1930 and 1934 female authors outnumbered male authors by more than three to one in *Child Development*. The Committee on Child Development obviously did not succeed in its efforts to maximize the participation of men in child research.[69]

NRC surveys found that the number of scholars who reported that they were studying children rose from 124 in 1924 to 621 in 1931, a five-fold increase within seven years.[70] Also noteworthy was the extent to which child development research had attracted scholars from diverse backgrounds. The new field was already influencing cultural anthropologists, sociologists, biologists, psychiatrists, pediatricians, and other scientists employed in universities and medical institutions. Many of these were elected to the Governing Council of the SRCD, a few to its presidency.[71]

The child development viewpoint, Frank declared, was a "very large and significant break with the past." It was "preventive politics" because it offered "the most effective instrument for translating democratic aspirations and faith into practice." He predicted that it would be perceived as one of the "more significant developments of the Twentieth Century for here concretely and practically is being shown how at last man may take charge of his own destiny."[72]

The failure of child study programs between the two World Wars to fulfill Frank's utopian expectations should not obscure their remarkable transformation of scientific child study. The institutionalization and professionalization of child development research within fifteen years of the Armistice was a dramatic breakthrough that led, even while it was happening, to profound scientific and social consequences. Without the programs sponsored by philanthropy, child development research undoubtedly would have remained a feeble enterprise for decades. Most new specialties within universities and medical schools evolve slowly; the rapid founding of child development research was an atypical, if not revolutionary, occurrence.

Today, child development research is an established field, studied in universities and sponsored by federal institutes. Its further consequences are, of course, unknowable, but are potentially enormous, and its importance became apparent very early. The unprecedented amount of research on children resulted in the first substantial accumulation of scientific information about children's physical, mental, and emotional development. The study of normal children provided a much larger and far more representative sample of children than any previous studies. The establishment of developmental norms and the range of variations provided fundamental knowledge of great practical value in assessing the development of normal children and in identifying and interpreting childhood mental illness and deviant behavior.[73] Parent participants in child study and parent education programs supplied new and valuable information on the nature and importance of parent-child interactions, as G. Stanley Hall had predicted they would. Robert Woodworth was also correct when he said that research and practice would interact, enabling researchers to learn from their blunders. In spite of some unfortunate consequences for parents and children, the premature application of findings made possible the refinement and improvement of both theory and method.[74]

Child development research became an important addition to the sociological approaches to child study introduced by the Children's Bureau and other urban reformers, to the clinical study of children begun in the guidance clinics, and to academic child psychology. Sociological surveys had produced important information about the average effects on development of variation in the social environments in which children grew up, but none of the direct knowledge of individual child development that was yielded by longitudinal studies. The developmental approach was an important corrective to psychological research, which had hitherto studied children at points in time rather than investigating development over time.[75] Harold Stevenson points out that the three theories of learning that had the greatest impact on early academic child psychology, those of John Watson, Edmund Thorndike, and B. F. Skinner, were "theories of learning applied to children, not learning theories of development." The research motivated by these theories did not "offer insight into the ways in which learning might differ at successive developmental levels." Conditioned response experiments were conducted in the same manner, whether the subject was a newborn or a six-year-old.[76] Cross-sectional studies of children contributed to the establishment of norms but, unlike longitudinal studies, failed to demonstrate the uniqueness of individual development.[77] Clinical study researched individual histories, but mainly those of children with emotional or behavioral problems, and contributed little to understanding the developmental process.

Developmental studies of children in natural settings of home, nursery school, and community demonstrated that the findings of laboratory studies were often biased by laboratory circumstances. Repeating Watson's famous experiment on conditioning a child to experience fear, Mary Cover Jones used her own child in her own home and got a very different result from Watson's. By the 1930s developmentalists such as Kurt Lewin at the Iowa station were devising experimental studies to be carried out in a "natural" context.[78]

THE INCREASE AND CHANGE
IN NURSERY SCHOOLS

An important early consequence of the child development and early education movements was their influence on federal nursery schools established during the depression and World War II. What had started in the early 1920s as a relatively modest movement serving privileged children expanded during the depression years to include children from lower-class backgrounds. By 1936, 1,913 emergency nursery schools had been established, sponsored jointly by the federal government and local groups, in which seventy-five thousand children were enrolled.[79] According to Lois Meek Stolz and George Stoddard, the experimental nursery schools founded by the Memorial's child study programs inspired the establishment of the emergency nursery schools.[80] In 1933, Jacob Baker, associate director of the Federal Emergency Relief Administration (FERA), asked Lois Meek Stolz, director of the child development institute at Teachers College, to educate him about nursery schools because he believed that supporting nursery schools would be a good way to provide employment and, even more important, to help poor children. FERA director Harry Hopkins agreed and appointed leading experts in early childhood education and child development to an Advisory Committee on Emergency Nursery School Education.[81] The FERA program and the advisory committee were later continued by the Works Project Administration (WPA).[82]

Members of the Advisory Committee, according to Stolz, "were more than advisory. . . . We were planners and educators and told them what to do."[83] Developmentalists and early educators throughout the country helped to develop the program. The child development institutes released staff to help organize the nursery schools. Four of them offered training courses for nursery school teachers and administrators. Stoddard, then director of the Iowa Child Welfare Research Station, pointed out that although the emergency schools were a response to the Depression, they were based on what research and experience had previously discovered about the fundamental needs of children and about child development. Their emphasis was on nutrition, parent education, community relations, and educational programs. Federal support for nursery schools was continued during World War II under the Lanham Act (1943).[84]

In the sixteen years between liquidation of the Lanham Act childcare program in 1950 and the launch of Project Head Start in 1965, the federal government gave no serious consideration to the possibility that organized childcare could provide important benefits for preschool children.[85] The number of private nursery schools continued to increase, however, and the developmental approach first practiced in nursery schools began to influence teaching and policy in elementary and secondary schools.

CHILD-REARING LITERATURE

Child study and related parent education programs led to an enormous increase in prescriptive literature for parents at the end of the 1920s and throughout the 1930s. In 1925 only a few dozen pamphlets for parents on psychological childcare were available, and they were of poor quality. Parents were a receptive audience for the new child-rearing literature, which by 1930 was published in at least fifty-eight popular periodicals as well as in many technical and scholarly journals.[86] Analysis of a 1935 bibliography of child-rearing literature showed that 75 percent of 840 items had been published after 1928.[87] *Parents Magazine* became the most popular educational periodical in the world during the 1930s and 1940s and the "only commercial periodical whose circulation and advertising revenues climbed steadily during the Great Depression."[88]

The proliferation of prescriptive literature has been documented, but the extent to which this literature actually affected parental behavior cannot be determined. One generally accepted measure of the effectiveness of new ideas is the marketplace, and there is some evidence that the new scientific theories and findings were having a commercial effect. In 1931 a five-part article in *Fortune*, "Merchants to the Child," described substantial changes in the manufacturing and retailing of children's food, clothing, furniture, and toys that had been prompted by the new scientific findings on children. The article referred to the influence of research by the Rockefeller child development institutes. It also mentioned a new product, "me-do" clothing, without buttons for the self-reliant Watsonian child. The article concluded that "the great new problem for the merchant to the child is whether to cater to science or tradition. He who once pondered old wives' tales now ponders vitamins and behaviorism and the mothers to whom he sells are divided in allegiance." *Fortune* was perspicacious in sensing that a major turning point had occurred in the long transition from a traditional view of childhood based on folk wisdom and the pronouncements of preachers, philosophers, and poets to one based on the "expert" advice of psychologists, psychiatrists, pediatricians, and child developmentalists.[89]

Chapter 10 Out of Step with His Times: Arnold Gesell and the Yale Clinic

Although each of the seven major child development institutes supported by philanthropy in the 1920s made important contributions to the new field of child development, their unique histories remain largely untold. Only one, the Iowa Child Welfare Research Station, has received book-length attention and, as far as I know, the history of only one other, the Berkeley Institute of Human Relations, has been traced in a scholarly article. Of the remaining five, the Yale Clinic of Child Development, directed by Arnold Gesell, most urgently demands attention.[1]

The Yale Clinic began as the one-room Yale Juvenile Psycho-Clinic that Gesell founded in 1911, six years before the Iowa station opened its doors. The high praise bestowed on Gesell's *Mental Growth of the Preschool Child* convinced the Laura Spelman Rockefeller Memorial (LSRM) to sponsor the psycho-clinic as a major child development institute in 1926. Renamed the Yale Clinic of Child Development in 1930, it continued under Gesell's direction until he reached Yale's mandatory retirement age in 1948. Plans for a smooth transition from Gesell to his successor, Milton J. E. Senn, did not work out. Senn was chosen because he was a pediatrician with psychiatric and psychoanalytic training and orientation. According to Louise Bates Ames, when Senn sought to broaden what he and others at Yale saw as Gesell's too narrow focus on maturation, Gesell's principal investigators resigned, or, as they saw it, were forced out. In 1950 these colleagues established the independent Gesell Institute of Human Development in New Haven, which carries on his work to this day. Gesell was an active participant until his death in 1960. The Yale Child Development Clinic, under Senn, became the Yale Child Study Center, which has become a part of Yale's department of psychiatry.[2]

Gesell's half-century-long career brought worldwide renown to the Yale clinic and made Gesell a household word in the United States. His books were translated into twenty languages, including French, German, Italian, Spanish, Swedish, Russian, Greek, Chinese, and Japanese.[3]

At a time when normative research was the characteristic activity in the new field of child development, Gesell carried it further than anyone else, studying the sequential development of infants and children from the age of four weeks to sixteen years. He also constructed a system of "developmental diagnosis," which was and still is widely used by clinicians. He invented the co-twin control technique, the developmental study of identical twins, pioneered the use of photography in child development research and parent education, was among the first to research and advocate self-regulatory schedules for infants, and proposed and promoted the establishment of a new specialty, developmental pediatrics. According to Dr. Walter Miles, "the widening of the horizon for a responsible department of pediatrics may be considered the crown of Dr. Gesell's life work." Beginning in the early 1920s, Gesell led efforts to improve understanding and treatment of preschool children, promoted parent education, and influenced the curricula of nursery schools. He suggested programs to enhance the development of preschool children that anticipated by four decades the Head Start programs of the 1960s. Perhaps most important was Gesell's impact on parents. According to Miles, Gesell began to write and make films for parents more than a decade and a half before Benjamin Spock published his famous *Baby and Child Care* and, more than anyone, interpreted and popularized child development norms.[4]

The Yale clinic was the main link between G. Stanley Hall's child study movement and the child development movement of the 1920s. It adopted a clinical rather than experimental approach to child development research. Like Hall, Gesell viewed child development as a biological science; and antagonized many psychologists by insisting that pediatrics was its most appropriate home.[5] The clinic fell out of favor with the Laura Spelman Rockefeller Memorial because, according to Lawrence K. Frank, Gesell refused to allow others "to collaborate in what he considered to be his own developmental studies."[6] In contrast to the Iowa station's environmental focus, the Yale clinic represented the hereditarian position among the institutes. At a time when environmentalism was rampant, Gesell insisted upon the primacy of genetically coded maturational sequences. He was, however, much more concerned than is generally recognized about the harmful effects a noxious environment could have on development. Firm in his opposition to both Watsonian behaviorism and psychoanalysis, Gesell called them authoritarian philosophies unsuitable for a democracy.[7] He has often been perceived as a man out of step with his times.

Yet, in important ways, Gesell was a supreme representative of his times, particularly in his dedication to the twin goals of science and service. In the past, hereditarian views have often been associated with fascism, racial and ethnic intolerance, and laissez-faire policies. Gesell, however, was an ardent champion of democracy and tolerance and an eloquent spokesman for social welfare programs for poor and mentally handicapped children. He concluded his autobiography with this statement: "A science of man under the heightening pressures of the second half of this atomic century should help to define the mechanisms and principles which underlie child and family life. This alone can enable man to act more consciously and more rationally as an agent in his own evolution." Like Cora Bussey Hillis and Lawrence K. Frank, Gesell relied on a science of child development to preserve democracy.[8]

GESELL'S BOYHOOD AND EARLY ADULTHOOD

Gesell was the eldest of five children in a family he described in his autobiography as "closely united," "affectionate," and "dedicated to education." According to Theo Buehler, Gesell's father, the photographer of Mississippi River life, inspired his son's lifelong interest in photography. Since the family spoke German, Gesell knew no English when he started school.[9] As a boy, he was responsible for the care of his sister, eight years his junior. Children, he recalled, were always a "spontaneous, natural interest."[10]

Gesell's genetically oriented philosophy of child development was rooted in his childhood experiences in Alma, Wisconsin, a two-street village on a bluff overlooking the Mississippi. He frequently commented or quoted others on "how much of a child's psychology comes through his eyes." A passage in

Gesell's autobiography describes the extent to which early experiences influenced his research:

> During my boyhood I saw the dark as well as bright facets of our microcosm. I saw death, funerals, devastating sickness, ominous quarantines, accidents and drownings at close range. Acute and chronic alcoholism were common sights open to public view. Epileptic convulsions occurred on the street and sidewalk. A muttering crazy man walked endlessly back and forth in his garden. A condemned murderer stared at us through the bars of the county prison. A watch dog was poisoned and a burglary committed in the blackness of night. Strange and sobering experiences kept happening as though they were part of the normal course of existence. None of these experiences were overpowering; but cumulatively they left a deposit of impressions, which sensitized a background for my clinical studies in later life.[11]

Gesell earned a doctorate in psychology in 1906 at Clark University, where he was profoundly influenced by G. Stanley Hall. He regarded Hall as a genius and kept in close with him touch until Hall's death in 1924.[12] After obtaining his Ph.D., Gesell taught psychology at the Los Angeles State Normal School, where he met and in 1909 married Beatrice Chandler, a teacher sympathetic to progressive education who is reputed to have had considerable influence on him. She may have helped Gesell to decide, in 1910, to devote his life to the scientific study of children.[13]

Arnold and Beatrice Gesell's *The Normal Child and Primary Education* presents their views on the importance of integrating humanitarian and scientific approaches in child study. The child, often called "the last serf of civilization," they wrote, was being emancipated by this new approach. Through science, humanitarianism "is losing some of its sentimental tears and romantic miscarriages, and changing into a more robust attitude of justice and protection—protection of the health and vigor of normal children" (27).[14] Gesell later declared that "hard headed empiricism is not enough . . . . We need to bring the creative spirit of art into the observation of children and into the experimental construction of new conditions in which these children may grow."[15] Gesell frequently included quotations from his favorite authors—Coleridge, Thoreau, Dickinson, and Lincoln—in his scientific articles. Gerhard said his father believed that science would always triumph, that however unpopular his work might be in his own time, it would endure. Gesell insisted that Yale clinic staff appearing in his motion pictures wear lab coats so that their clothing would not distract future viewers from the film's scientific content.[16]

Since Gesell believed that child development was a medical science rooted in biochemistry, anatomy, physiology, and psychology, he decided to acquire knowledge in all these fields. He studied physiology at the University of Wisconsin in 1910 and the following year accepted a part-time position at Yale as assistant professor of education while he studied medicine. During the next four years he taught, studied medicine full time, started the psycho-clinic, coauthored a book with his wife, and participated in various social welfare activities, mainly for mentally defective children. His visit in 1909 to the Vineland Training School for Defective Children, directed by Henry Goddard, gave him a lifelong interest in such children. Receiving his medical degree in 1915, Gesell decided not to enter private practice but to use his knowledge and experience to study the development of the children in his clinic and work for the establishment of developmental pediatrics.[17]

THE VILLAGE OF A THOUSAND SOULS

Gesell first made his case for the overwhelming importance of heredity in human development in "The Village of a Thousand Souls," an article published in 1913, two years before the start of the first campaign for the Iowa station in which Hillis and Carl Seashore emphasized the importance of environment in children's development.[18]

Gesell did not identify "The Village of a Thousand Souls" as his hometown but described it as a place of great beauty in a flourishing agricultural region without factories and with ample opportunities for the physical development, recreation, and education of children, a village that most people would regard as an ideal place in which to raise healthy children. By constructing a "eugenic map," Gesell set out to prove that the village was no better for children's development than a city slum. The map showed the homes of 220 families and indicated the number of family members in each home who were "feeble-minded," insane, alcoholic, epileptic, suicidal, criminal, eccentric, or tubercular. Gesell calculated that 26 percent of the families had either feeble-minded or insane members, and 16 percent of families had at least one alcoholic member. His summary of these undesirable traits presented a devastating picture of what appeared to be an ideal rural community. Since the environment was "ideal," most of the undesirable traits, he argued, should be attributed to heredity rather than environment.[19]

Gesell had spent 1907 working in a New York City settlement house.[20] Settlement house workers who portrayed poor urban children as victims of the slum may have provoked him to write the article. *Hull-House Maps and Papers,* in particular, may have suggested the mapping of every house in Alma. Contrasting the rural village with the urban slum, Gesell argued that the slum might be a symptom as well as a cause of social pathology. Incompetents from rural areas gravitated to cities, he suggested, thereby helping to create slums. Although admitting that poverty could breed social incompetence, he asserted that the reverse was also true.[21]

Discussing the improvement of animal stock through state inspection and breeding, Gesell asked, "Is it possible to raise the human stock that lives in a village?" No sane eugenicist, he conceded, would attempt to apply the methods of cattle breeding to village or urban populations, but he did approve of "negative eugenics," which Seashore repudiated.[22] The state, Gesell declared, may soon make a systematic attempt to register the unfit and prevent their mating. He wrote:

> We need not wait for the perfection of the infant science of eugenics before proceeding upon a course of supervision and segregation which will prevent the horrible renewal of this protoplasm that is contaminating the stream of village life. . . . The solemn facts of heredity must now be respected. Environment is the lesser half. . . . The banks of the racial river of life should be beautified and ennobled by all that willing hands of man can rear and contrive; but those benefactors who labor now through science and wise legislation to purify the very springs of the dying and living streams will be thrice blessed by the generations unborn.[23]

Over the years Gesell modified the extreme hereditarian position he espoused in 1913, insisting that nature and nurture not be dichotomized but regarded as "supplementary and reciprocal."[24] Although he never faltered in assigning the dominant influence on human behavior to genetically programmed maturation, his own pronouncements on heredity and environment often seemed to contradict this view.

THE YALE PSYCHO-CLINIC, 1911–1925

During the first eight years of the psycho-clinic, Gesell focused on children of school age and mentally defective children. In 1919 he turned his interest to the normal preschool child, later observing, "It was as if the preschool child had suddenly acquired some magnetic power which compels us to look in his direction."[25] Between 1921 and 1925 he published a dozen articles and two books on preschool children and their parents and on nursery school education in which he proposed programs more ambitious than those sponsored by Head Start in the 1960s, and, in their comprehensiveness, closer to the mid-1990s pilot programs that extended Head Start to children from birth through eight years.[26]

The new movement for preschool children in the 1920s, Gesell wrote, was "comparable to the democratization of elementary education."[27] It was imperative, he said, to try to "equalize the development of opportunities of earlier childhood by replacing the historic concept of education with modern biological concepts of growth and development. The nation should initiate a policy of developmental supervision, beginning with prenatal infants, and extending to the entire period of preschool childhood."[28] If developmental studies showed the same solicitude for mental as for physical growth they would "nip many mental abnormalities in the bud" and would "cut down on crime, insanity, and mental illness." [29] Sounding very unlike the man who had once advocated "negative eugenics," Gesell declared that many physical and mental handicaps take shape during the preschool period and some could be prevented if treated early.[30]

Since he believed that the fortunes of preschool children depended on their parents, Gesell thought some social control of the home was necessary but must be achieved indirectly through an approach that stimulates rather than weakens the parents' responsibility.[31] There is "no short-cut solution," he warned. Asserting that parents should be assisted rather than displaced, he said, "We cannot congregate preschool children into state nurseries."[32] Gesell was responding to proposals such as one urged by William Blatz, director of the LSRM child development institute in Toronto, that schools assume responsibility for child rearing and that parents' access to children be limited to an hour and a half a day. Help for preschool children and their parents, Gesell believed, should be provided by extending nursery school education. Good nursery schools, he said, "make concessions to immaturity and individuality and in this way become a nursery for democratic patterns of behavior."[33]

Underscoring his new interest in the environment, Gesell and a colleague made a "psychological comparison" of nursery school children from low- and high-income families. They found that children earning high scores tended to come from high-income homes. Their data suggested that "the basic growth factors which will differentiate the abilities and personalities of these twenty-two children in adult years were in operation at least as early as the age of two and three years."[34] This small study shows clearly that Gesell was then concerned with environmental as well as genetic influences on young children. A year before the study was published, he advocated better housing for poor families, citing the psychological as well as the physical effects of poor housing on children. "The mental growth of the young child is not blindly foreordained," he argued, "but will be responsive to the atmosphere and procedures of the home."[35] Although Gesell never undertook another study assessing the effects of environment on children's development, he continued to point to the wide gap separating underprivileged from privileged children, and how it could be reduced by improving social conditions, particularly family housing.[36] However, his interest in eugenics continued at least until 1932 when he was enrolled as an "active member" of the Third International Congress of Eugenics.[37]

THE MENTAL GROWTH OF THE
PRESCHOOL CHILD

The movement for the study of preschool children culminated in 1924 and 1925 in the publication of two important books, *The Psychology of the Preschool Child* by Bird Baldwin and Lorie I. Stecher of the Iowa Station, and *The Mental Growth of the Preschool Child: A Psychological Outline of Normal Development from Birth to the Sixth Year Including a System of Developmental Diagnosis* by Gesell. The Iowa study was based on 105 children between the ages of two and six years enrolled in the laboratory nursery school, with additional information on each child's home background. Addressed primarily to those interested in child study and the nursery school movement, it contained a section on physical growth and material on psychological and psychometric testing.[38]

Gesell's book was based on six years of research on 500 normal children studied at different levels of development, with primary attention to the infant. Fifty children were studied at the ages of one, four, six, nine, twelve, and eighteen months, and two, three, four, and five years to measure their progress in motor ability, language, general intelligence, and social behavior. The book presented tentative norms, an outline of stages of normal development, and a preliminary conception of what a child "ought" to be at these stages.[39] Two hundred photographs illustrated behavior norms at various ages. Addressed primarily to pediatricians, nurses, and clinical psychologists, the study avoided psychometric tests, which Gesell, like Hall, believed were too narrowly focused to capture the many facets of the child. Instead he introduced his own system of "developmental diagnosis," one he and Amatruda expanded and developed for another twenty-five years.[40]

THE YALE CLINIC OF CHILD DEVELOPMENT

When the Yale clinic became a Laura Spelman Rockefeller Memorial child development institute, Gesell continued to use the word *clinic* rather than *institute* in its title in order to emphasize his medical approach to child development research. In 1930 the clinic became part of the Yale Institute of Human Relations, occupying five floors of the institute's new building and benefiting from expensive new laboratory equipment.[41]

Gesell organized the Yale clinic for both service and research. An outpatient diagnostic service permitted examination of normal and abnormal children. Babies were referred to the diagnostic clinic for defects and deviations of early development. Soon the clinic was examining 10,000 outpatients a year, 16,000 by 1943. Sixty children aged eighteen months to four years, most of them children of Yale faculty, were then attending the nursery school. Both diagnostic service and nursery school brought the clinic staff into constant contact with parents, which Gesell deemed essential "because one learned from parents as well as children." Gesell organized the clinic to facilitate both naturalistic and experimental observations, which were "not mutually exclusive," as some believed, but "constantly combined in the clinical approach."[42] He thought the study of abnormal children a kind of substitute for experimental research.[43]

Yale clinic laboratories were designed for observing and photographing child behavior. One was equipped with a hemispherical dome, equipped to hold motion picture cameras and a clinical crib that he designed for observing infant behavior. The dome was encased in a one-way vision screen, another Gesell invention, to permit observers to view the baby without the baby seeing them. The dome cameras recorded the behavior of infants every four months during the first year, their posture, locomotion, perception, prehension, manipulation, social reactions, and spontaneous and problem-solving activities. These cinema records were then subjected to detailed study. "The psychological development of a child is so subtle that the techniques of the camera are necessary to make its progress perceptible," Gesell declared.[44] He also said, "The cinema sees with an all-seeing eye and records with an infallible memory."[45]

In 1924 Gesell undertook the first photographic survey of the behavioral development of children from early infancy to school entrance. *The Mental Growth of the Preschool Child* (1925) included two hundred action photographs. By 1948 the clinic archive contained a million feet of film. Although numerous motion pictures were made from this storehouse of film, all of the originals were kept intact for research purposes. Unfortunately, the film archive and many Gesell films were lost or destroyed after Gesell retired.[46] According to Gesell, the clinic's main research task was to discover lawful orderly patterns of individual growth, both physical and mental. A child's chronological age, the variable Gesell believed was primarily responsible for the organization of a child's behavior, was correlated with behavior and personality characteristics. Developmental research at the Yale clinic covered four major fields: motor function, adaptive behavior, language, and personal and social behavior at twelve different age levels. Among the traits studied in each child were muscle coordination, motor skills, postures, the capacity to profit from the past, language and dramatic expression, communication, comprehension, reactions to others, and adjustments to domestic life, property, and social groups. Yale clinic researchers charted normal development from birth through ten years, describing characteristic behavior for each age, but emphasizing the extent and significance of individual variations from norms. Age norms were not intended as standards to be met, Gesell cautioned, but were designed only for "orientation and interpretive purposes," a warning most people did not heed.[47]

In his pronouncements on the need for social reform, in his passionate espousal of democracy and opposition to behaviorism and Freudianism as undemocratic systems, Gesell the hereditarian frequently appears to have had more in common with progressive social justice reformers than with other child developmentalists. This may seem puzzling to those who associate hereditarian views with nativism, fascism, and intolerance toward racial and ethnic minorities. The key to both Gesell's research and his espousal of a progressive social policy may be found in his philosophy of growth, first articulated in the mid-1920s and elaborated throughout his life. He perceived growth as a unifying concept, removing distinctions between mind and body, heredity and environment, health and disease, and scientific disciplines. Leo Kanner believed that removal of the mind-body distinction was Gesell's greatest contribution to child development research.[48]

ACHIEVEMENTS, 1928–1934

Lewis Terman, Gesell's close friend and former colleague at Clark, wrote Gesell that "the old saying 'the world steps aside for the man who knows where he is going' seems to have been made for you." From 1928 to 1934 Gesell released eleven new films on child development, published four books and numerous articles, and continued to promote developmental pediatrics.[49]

Infancy and Human Growth discussed subjects of critical importance to Gesell: self regulation of infant feeding, the early appearance of individual differences, and the need to respect infants' individuality. It restated his opposition to psychometrics and extended his system of developmental diagnosis. The subject of his chapter for the first edition of the *Handbook of Psychology* was "The Developmental Psychology of Twins," a follow-up to the article that introduced Gesell's technique of co-twin control to psychologists. Gesell's contribution to the second edition of the *Handbook* was his influential "Maturation and the Patterning of Behavior."[50]

In 1934 Gesell, Thompson, and Amatruda published *Infant Behavior: Its Genesis and Growth* and the clinic's first book for parents, *An Atlas of Infant Behavior.* Within less than a decade Gesell had provided a groundwork for discussion of controversial theoretical issues, published the findings of extensive normative research, written child-rearing literature, produced films, and directed service activities. All of these activities he continued for another quarter of a century.

GESELL'S CHILD-REARING ADVICE

Beginning in the 1930s Gesell wrote a daily column on child behavior for the *Washington Post.* Between 1943 and 1956,Gesell and Frances Ilg co-authored three books that provided parents with a developmental map from infancy through adolescence: *Infant and Child in the Culture of Today, The Child from Five to Ten,* and *Youth: The Years from Ten to Sixteen.* Gesell and his colleagues were preeminent in making American parents conscious of stages of development and age-related behavior changes. Parents wanted to know what to expect of their children at different ages. Gesell told them.[51]

Like Hall, Gesell urged parents to trust in the "wisdom of nature," to rely not on authoritarian goals imposed by culture, but on forces emerging from within the child to provide clues to proper child rearing. "All child problems bear some relation to growth," he said, and "should be looked at from the standpoint of growth rather than right or wrong."[52]

Parents may have found Gesell's childcare books appealing not only because he told them what to expect but also because he offered them a welcome alternative to the authoritarian child-rearing advice of his time, derived first from Calvinism, then from Holt and other "scientific pediatricians," and later from Watson and other behaviorists. Gesell's approach to child rearing, he said, was neither "authoritarian" nor "laissez-faire," but "developmental." [53] He believed that parents and society need to exercise some controls over the child but should permit as much "self-regulation and self adjustment" as possible. "We pay vastly too much attention to mere training and instruction," he wrote.[54] Much of the child's resistance to parental guidance, he advised, would be resolved automatically when the child went on to the next phase of development. He urged parents to provide their children with continuous strong emotional support. Repeating some nineteenth-century arguments for the need for the "educated mother," Gesell asserted that children's "psychological care needs an informed developmental philosophy, based upon a sympathetic familiarity with the detailed operations of growth." Parents need not only to learn about developmental norms but also to record observations of their own children's development.[55] With obvious pleasure, he helped his own daughter chart the growth of her first child in 1938.[56]

Some parents were reassured by Gesell's norms. "I sleep with your book under my pillow," a father wrote.[57] To others, whose child appeared to fall outside the normal range, they aroused anxiety or helped them to realize that evaluation by a specialist might be needed. A mother's letter to Gesell in 1953 suggests how helpful he was to some parents. She wrote: "The child from five to eleven has brought both joy and sorrow into our home, joy because it has made possible an understanding of our seven year old during months that would have been painful or bewildering without it and sorrow because our eleven year old reached that age without having had that understanding. We look back now and realize that her behavior at six or seven was that of any child of those ages and not a behavior brought on by all the mistakes we had made as parents since the day she was born." For this mother, Gesell had achieved his purpose of alleviating the guilt that, he argued, was aroused by child-rearing advice based on Watsonian and psychoanalytic theories.

Gesell's cyclical theory of development postulated that stages of turmoil and disequilibrium inevitably were followed by stages of integration and calm. In *The Child from Five to Ten* he described age six as a period of turmoil, age seven as a period of calm. He was delighted by a trilogy of letters from a mother and her two daughters. Catherine Lowes wrote: "There has been a small amount of trouble in this family since my daughter Gillian Lowes (aged six) read *The Child From Five to Ten*. . . [You] say few children of her age bathe themselves alone—so now she won't." Twelve-year old Susan told Gesell how much she had learned about her brother and sister, ages eight and six, from reading his book and added, "Everything was fine until my sister . . . got hold of it. . . . From the time she started reading it until now . . . she has been frightfully difficult. Her explanation of all of her fretting and crying is that in your book you say something about six being a trying age and she is making the most of it . . . It's really gone to her head."[58]

Gillian, six years old, presented her side of the story: "My mother said that it is bad for me to read one of the books you made . . . because I am not behaving well. I say six is a trying age. Wait until I am seven." Gesell wrote to Mrs. Lowes that the letters had given him a "cascading series of chuckles," and promised, "we will do our best not to undermine the domestic economy and discipline." He asked twelve-year-old Susan to please tell her sister for him that "the Book does not say that the six year old should try to be 'trying.' We must not let the distinctions between SIX and SEVEN go to her head." His longest letter, written to Gillian, compared growing up to paddling a canoe down a winding stream, suggesting that she had it within her power to "steer away from choppy waves and glide into quieter waters." They exchanged additional letters, but the six year old remained resolute in her determination to make the most of her age norm. "I don't think that your letter did much good," she wrote. "I am going to say that 'nothing will help me' to anyone who speaks about this letter." [59]

Gillian's misinterpretation of Gesell's message is amusing, but many developmentalists and physicians were far from amused by parents' misuse of norms. Gesell himself was disturbed by their misunderstanding of his intention, which he tried to prevent with instructions about how developmental norms should be used and cautions to parents and childcare practitioners to exercise the same "judiciousness" in applying behavior norms as in using height and weight charts.[60] The warnings were usually as ineffective as his advice to his six-year-old correspondent. Even Gesell's own daughter, to whom he dedicated *The First Five Years of Life*,[61] ignored his message. She wrote, "You say that a two year old cannot remove his pants, just pull them down. May I remind you that at Christmas-time Sue (her daughter, then eighteen months old) was doing this well." Listing other accomplishments of Sue, now two years old, she added, "but here, I must remember that I am writing to praise you not your granddaughter."[62]

Pediatrician Joseph Brennemann asserted that infants were being "matched with Gesell, with resulting gloom or elation. . . . The psychologists, psychiatrists, behaviorists, child guiders and parent teachers can say all they may about normal variation and the rest of us can talk till the cows come home, the psychologically and psychiatrically minded mother is going to hold her child up to an ideal mental and behavioral pattern." Hilda Bruch wrote, "It has become a moral obligation to live in accordance with the average." Gesell, nevertheless, may have succeeded in preventing many parents from imposing controls advocated by authoritarian parent educators.[63]

GESELL'S PHILOSOPHY OF GROWTH

Gesell was most famous for popularizing and defending the concept of maturation at a time when many child developmentalists focused on environmental influences. The term "maturation," he wrote, had come into use "as an offset to the extravagant claims which have been made for processes of conditioning and habit formation." Growth, he explained, consisted of the interaction and interfusion of maturation and acculturation. "The heredity and environment of an organism can be completely separated only in analytic thinking, for in actual nature such separation would lead to instant death of the organism."[64] He defined maturation as the "inborn tendency toward maximum development," acculturation as "the process through which the child acquired his cultural heritage."[65] Although he argued that "the concept of maturation does not deny the importance of environment," he also insisted that "acculturation can never transcend maturation."[66] Development, he emphasized, cannot take place in a vacuum. "We need air to breathe, but the air can scarcely be called the cause of breathing. Breathing, as behavior emanates from within. We must always assume a minimum of environment, but maturation is the primary factor because the environment cannot engender the basic sequences of development."[67] Gesell quoted a favorite poet, Emily Dickinson, to underscore his meaning: "Growth of Man like growth of Nature, gravitates within. Atmosphere and sun confirm it, but it stirs alone."[68]

Gesell perceived growth as dynamic and irrepressible. According to his colleague Helen Thompson he saw it as "something like a weed pushing through the sidewalk."[69] For Gesell, growth was not only forceful but also benign, "a life tendency" that "works toward adjustment, harmony and a certain degree of completion even in the gravely handicapped child."[70] It causes a child "to benefit from what is good, and suffer less from our unenlightenment."[71] He thought it fortunate that "a high degree of inherent determination of growth . . . sets metes and bounds" to a child's conditionality.[72] To Gesell, the developmental norms his research established were the goals the maturing organism strove to achieve in spite of all environmental obstacles. His conviction that growth patterns are innately benign is hard to reconcile with his belief, first expressed in "The Village of a Thousand Souls"[73] and never withdrawn, that inherited defects were the source of the dark side of life in Alma.

Gesell's views on childcare and his conception of growth were closely related to his passionate conviction that the science of child development served democracy. Since the "spirit of liberty has its deepest roots in a child's impulsion toward optimal growth,"[74] the nourishment of democracy must begin in the home with respect for the dignity of every infant and child. Discipline is democratic, Gesell argued, only "when it is tempered to the capacity of the child and tolerant of his immaturity. Wise discipline aims not to strengthen the parent's authority but to strengthen the child's self control and responsibility."[75] Scolding and hitting are primitive and undemocratic forms of government, he declared in a particularly forceful statement, "so grossly inconsistent with the genius of democracy that they should be attacked as a public welfare problem."[76]

Respect for children, Gesell strongly believed, means respecting their individual differences. Asked what is most essential to know about human nature Gesell replied, "to know that everybody is different."[77] As children grow, their expression of individual differences needs to be encouraged rather than "ironed out."[78] Democracy benefits the individual, and respecting individual differences promotes democracy. He believed it significant that "the science of individual differences has flourished most vigorously among a democratic people."[79] Behaviorism, he argued, with its excessive emphasis on the effects of environment, inspired authoritarianism. "Such an ideology is foreign to the ideal of democracy."[80]

NATURE/NURTURE: GESELL AND HIS CRITICS

Gesell had two personalities. His voluminous correspondence includes letters to his wife by a man passionately in love, humorous and affectionate letters to his children and close friends, and charming replies to parents and children who wrote to him. "Dear Apple of My Eye," he wrote his wife soon after the birth of their first child, "I am getting tired of being so good. I shall go into 2 saloons and spit in 1. I may also go by a cigar stand." "The Daily Dirt," a mock newspaper written and illustrated by Gesell for his children is irreverent and witty. Thompson said. "You had to see him with children to really appreciate the man. . . . His feeling for the rights of children was paramount in all of his work."[81] He criticized research that hurt children,[82] such as Watson's conditioning experiment with Albert, his favorite subject.[83] He believed that Myrtle McGraw's publication of her twin research violated her subject's privacy.[84]

With colleagues, Gesell was aloof and indifferent, often to the point of rudeness.[85] Thompson said that he was not easy to work with and would never explain why he was doing things or answer criticism. He "went his own way and people didn't like that too much. He was never close to anyone."[86] McGraw, who shares with Gesell the distinction of being the most eminent student of growth in their time, was allowed only a brief visit to the Yale Clinic, and Gesell refused to discuss with her his system of developmental diagnosis.[87] Frank tried but failed to arrange for a joint research program involving Yale and Columbia universities.[88] Gerhard Gesell thought that his father's aloofness was really extreme shyness.[89] It also may have been due to his passionate and single-minded commitment to nature as the primary source of children's growth patterns at a time when most others were emphasizing nurture. Gesell was distressed by what he saw as American overemphasis on training children instead of liberating their innate potential.[90] McGraw's famous study of twins Johnny and Jimmy was an investigation of the effects of early stimulation and physical training on performance in later childhood.[91] McGraw remembered that Gesell sat silently through her motion picture and lecture on the study and then "stormed off in a huff."[92]

In his theoretical declarations Gesell emphasized the interaction of heredity and environment in the process of development. As a social reformer, he deplored living conditions that obstructed children's development. Responding to a request from Katherine Lenroot,[93] Chief of the Children's Bureau, for suggestions for the 1940 White House Conference on Children in a Democracy, he offered two subjects: "the effect of housing on infants and preschool children with special reference to psychological and developmental effects" and "psychological factors in adult-child relationships with special reference to those factors which promote or retard the development of democratic attitudes."[94] In the material he prepared for the conference, which he entitled "Democracy Begins at Home," he discussed both subjects.

And yet, after his 1927 study comparing the development of twenty-two infants from low- and high-income homes, Gesell never again investigated the relationship between environment and development. His developmental norms represented the average performance of the mainly middle-class children he studied at the Yale Clinic. Lois Stolz wrote, "The trouble is that the data have never been presented, only the theory and the generalizations. There is an assumption here that all the threads in a child's life pull in the same direction during any one year as fixed by the calendar, that irrespective of what may be happening in his life (failing or succeeding in school, moving to a new neighborhood, getting the mumps . . .) irrespective of the rate of development, irrespective of whether he is boy or girl, and irrespective of what kinds of parents he has—in spite of all these and other possible influences, the rhythm of development sweeps on."[95]

McGraw criticized Gesell for his narrow focus on the outcome rather than the process of development. To Gesell, following his mentor Hall, the essence of development is the unfolding of the child's biological heritage. To McGraw, following her mentor John Dewey, development is the process through which both the body and the mind of the child learn to cope with and adapt to the specific environment in which it finds itself. McGraw accused Gesell of creating a dichotomy between maturation and learning.[96]

In their illuminating and generally positive evaluation of Gesell's contribution to the science of child development, Thelen and Adolph ask, "How does Gesell reconcile a genetically driven maturational program with his beliefs in . . . the importance of the nursery, pre-school and school environment and with his concern for child welfare both in the home and the society at large? How can he be so aware of the dynamic interplay of multiple influences in development and yet ignore these processes in favor of biological causation? Gesell's decline as a major developmental theorist is due at least in part to these unresolved tensions in his work."[97]

Gesell may have failed to resolve these tensions, but he did not ignore them. Over his long and prolific career, he wrote many times about the interacting influence of heredity and environment on the child's development, not always consistently and always in general terms and convoluted language that left his exact meaning uncertain. It is clear, however, that he saw unfavorable family living conditions as obstacles to the fulfillment of each child's unique innate potential. This was the basis of his commitment to child welfare reform.

In his 1928 book *Infancy and Human Growth* he divided growth into two parts, one determined by heredity, the other by family environment.[98] "Tempo, trend and temperament are in large measure determined by inherent or hereditary factors," he wrote, "but personality is indeterminate until it is defined through experience."[99] He went on, in a passage remarkably congruent with Dewey's and McGraw's views, to describe personality formation as a ceaseless process of adaptation to other individuals. "The roots of the . . . infant's personality reach into other human beings. These considerations give great emphasis to the environmental or psychodynamic importance of the parent-child relationship. . . . [The] basic principles of interaction between child and parent can be fruitfully analyzed . . . . [but] in the present volume, no space will be devoted to these details."[100]

In later years, Gesell continued to devote no space to "these details." A few oblique sentences in his article "Intelligence: Its Nature and Nurture"[101] outline his reasons. After acknowledging that "we must not ignore environmental influences," he warned that "constitutional factors . . . ultimately determine the degree, and even the mode, of the reaction to the 'so-called' environment" —"so-called" because "the interaction is the crux," and therefore, "the distinction between them should not be drawn too heavily." When endogenous and exogenous factors are in balance, "the trends of mental growth . . . are likely to be most consistent. Developmental diagnosis and prognosis then come nearest to their mark. When, however, the organism is under stress . . . because of unfavorable conditions, then its ultimate adjustments, as expressed in growth characteristics, become least predictable. There are too many variables to appraise." The most important of these variables, are not the environmental ones, "which can be estimated with some shrewdness," but the "hidden reserves . . . the intrinsic insurance factors," which, because they are "hidden, cannot readily be estimated."[102]

Here, in a nutshell, is an implied reason (or excuse) for not exploring environmental effects. Gesell seems to have decided that when they matter most, they are too complex and obscure for fruitful study. The topics he suggested for consideration at the 1940 White House Conference may betray some lack of confidence in that conclusion. By 1957 he had conceded that understanding individual development must be based on analysis of a dual process, "the individual and the forces external to him in constant interaction, each at times a directive agent, each at times directed by the other."[103]

During the last decade of his life Gesell embarked on a project that united his passion for American democracy with his interest in child development, a biography of Lincoln in childhood and youth. Three years before his death at age seventy-eight, Gesell wrote to a Lincoln specialist, "I have long been occupied with getting data for a book from the standpoint of Lincoln's developmental psychology, tracing stages and ages of maturity, looking for events and experiences which influenced his formative years." The title of his preface was "A Theory of Child Biography: What It Will Become Under the Influence of Science." Gesell's copious notes and an outline of seven chapters survive, but the book was never written. He did, however, write an introduction to a book on Lincoln's youth by another author, his last publication and his only publication after 1957.[104]

Chapter 11 The Child Guidance Movement: Another Approach to Preventive Politics

Nineteenth-century literature in the field of what is now known as psychiatry was limited almost entirely to the study of "insanity" in adults.[1] What sparse comments there were on mental illness in children almost always came from Europeans. Americans contributed only four of the fifty-five titles cited in an 1883 review of the literature on childhood insanity, and none of the four dealt specifically with childhood mental illness.[2] According to psychiatrist Eli Rubenstein, this "is the story of an entire era in America prior to 1900. . . . Original research is rare . . . there is no discovery or theory of great fundamental importance to child psychiatry. No research today stems from the work of any of these early writers."[3] In Europe, Emil Kraepelin's famous classification of mental diseases (1883) was restricted to adults, and the renowned texts by Kraepelin (1904) and Eugen Bleuer (1903) included nothing on emotional disorders of childhood.[4]

Dramatic developments in the study and treatment of emotionally troubled children in the United States between 1909 and 1919 were expanded and institutionalized by the Commonwealth Fund in cooperation with the National Committee for Mental Hygiene. In 1922 they launched a five-year program to prevent juvenile delinquency. Prevention was to be achieved by establishing new psychiatric clinics for children, reflecting especially the work and beliefs of William Healy, Thomas Salmon, and Adolph Meyer. By 1934 the Commonwealth Fund had invested $6.2 million in these clinics and related mental hygiene activities.[5] Its programs inspired the child guidance movement, which swept the United States during the 1920s and 1930s, profoundly influenced American attitudes toward children, helped to reverse the influence of European psychiatry in the United States, and contributed to the emergence of a unique American child psychiatry.

THE COMMONWEALTH FUND

Anna Harkness, widow of Stephen Harkness, a major stockholder in Rockefeller's Standard Oil Company of Ohio, founded the Commonwealth Fund in 1918 with an endowment of $20 million "to do something for the welfare of mankind."[6] Like Laura Spelman Rockefeller, Anna Harkness was committed to child welfare reform.[7] So was her only surviving child, Edward, who assumed responsibility for the foundation on his mother's death in 1926 and quickly doubled its endowment. Like his mother, Edward was intent on preventing social ills through scientific research.[8]

Shortly after the Armistice, Freudian psychiatrist William A. White published *The Mental Hygiene of Childhood*,[9] hailing childhood as the "golden age of mental hygiene" and expressing many of the themes that came to dominate the child guidance movement.[10] By 1919 eleven psychiatric clinics for children had been established. The most important were the Chicago and Boston clinics founded by William Healy, the Boston Psychopathic Hospital, and the Henry Phipps Psychiatric Clinic at Johns Hopkins Hospital. Lawson Lowrey has observed that although psychiatric treatment of children was still a "fumbling, uncertain procedure without much clarity of purpose at war's end, child guidance, named and defined as such, was just around the corner."[11]

After the Commonwealth Fund had discharged its obligations for overseas war relief, it decided that the greatest opportunity for preventive work was with children rather than adults. It appointed a committee to suggest a program that would not duplicate or interfere with the research of the Rockefeller Foundation, which had supported studies of crime and mental illness by the National Committee for Mental Hygiene since 1915.[12] Thomas Salmon had already appealed to the Commonwealth Fund to support a program to prevent juvenile delinquency. He and Bernard Glueck were appointed to the new committee and together persuaded other members to adopt this proposal.

The following year, Salmon proposed that the National Committee establish a division of juvenile delinquency to conduct research and field work on the causes, prevention, and treatment of delinquency. As co-sponsor, the National Committee would "carry the whole program away from the entanglements of prison reform, general intricacies of the criminal law, and general and social relief work, putting it where it should be, in the category of preventive social hygiene undertaken with sound scientific direction."[13]

Salmon also advised the Commonwealth Fund to base its program on that of the Judge Baker Foundation clinic in Boston, directed by Healy and Augusta Bronner, possibly by expanding the Baker clinic. He suggested that the specialties represented in the Boston child guidance team—psychiatry, psychology, and social work—become the program's basic disciplines.[14] The Commonwealth Fund decided against expanding the Judge Baker clinic for several reasons: Healy worked better on his own, he wanted the clinic to remain independent, and he advised experimentation with a variety of clinics in order to meet different local conditions.[15] In addition, the Commonwealth Fund wanted control of the program to be centralized in New York City. The Judge Baker clinic did, however, become the primary model for the Commonwealth Fund's demonstration clinics.[16]

In March 1921 the Commonwealth Fund sponsored a conference of experts to help define its program. Margo Horn observed that the conference participants "were of a decidedly psychiatric-psychological bent . . . the criminologists and prisoner reformers consulted during 1920 were notably absent."[17] Conference participants reflected the postwar shift of Progressive thought from a sociological to a psychological outlook. Admitting that adverse environmental conditions contribute to delinquency, the conference report asserted nevertheless that "the relation of such conditions to the whole problem of delinquency is outside the scope of this conference except as they appear as factors in individual cases."[18]

Edith Abbott, dean of the University of Chicago Graduate School of Social Service Administration and sister of Grace Abbott, who became chief of the Children's Bureau in 1921, expressed the opposing view of Progressive social justice reformers. She criticized the conference recommendations for their bias in favor of the psychological treatment of individuals rather than efforts to improve social conditions. Ignorant of or indifferent to the Commonwealth

Fund's announcement that it would avoid involvement with social legislation or with organizations dedicated to social action, Abbott insisted that social legislation would accomplish far more than individual therapy. She also suggested that teachers should be educated about children's conduct disorders and the impact of social conditions on their lives.[19] Abbott appears to have been the only person to disagree publicly with the conference recommendations.[20]

The Commonwealth Fund's newly appointed director, Barry Smith, was trained in social work and strongly influenced by Salmon.[21] Shortly after the conference he announced a five-year project called the Program for the Prevention of Juvenile Delinquency.

THE COMMONWEALTH FUND
AND THE MEMORIAL

The child development and child guidance movements were brought to life by many of the same social and scientific developments, paralleled each other in time, and had more in common with each other than either had with the Children's Bureau. Unlike the Children's Bureau, which clung to prewar Progressive methods and goals, the Commonwealth Fund and the Laura Spelman Rockefeller Memorial emphasized the usefulness of the psychological sciences in preventing social problems and the value of studying children as individuals rather than statistical aggregates. By studying limited numbers of individual children, both foundations expected to discover how to improve the lives of all children. The Commonwealth Fund's original focus was on reducing juvenile delinquency, but it hoped that clinical data on "problem" children would yield knowledge of childhood disorders that could be applied to help children who would never need its services.[22] A primary goal of the program to prevent juvenile delinquency was to educate the community about the mental hygiene of childhood.[23]

The two foundations also shared a more ambitious and distant purpose: to improve childhood experience not for its own sake but in order to create better adults. Child guidance enthusiasts believed that early diagnosis of children's disturbances, followed by prompt treatment, would reduce the incidence of adult neurosis, psychosis, and criminal behavior. The Commonwealth Fund announced that the basis of its program to prevent delinquency was the belief that "the adult is what the child was. Whatever can control the mental, physical and moral life of the child can direct the child's future actions as an adult."[24] Lawrence K. Frank declared that the outstanding development of the 1920s was the "growing belief in the possibility of directing and controlling social life through the care and nurture of children."[25]

One optimist asked, "Can you see the ward or district organization with a district building instead of a police station, with policemen as constructive workers rather than watchdogs of their beats?"[26] Psychiatrist William A. White believed that the goal of mental hygiene was to prevent not only psychosis and neurosis but all social maladies, even unhappiness, and "to help all people live their lives at their best."[27] Sociologist Maurice P. Davie went even further, predicting that the movement would improve human efficiency, an important goal of Progressive reformers.[28] Smith, director of the child guidance program, sounded a lone note of caution by declaring that he did not expect the fund's juvenile delinquency program to reform the world.[29] But to most advocates, the program was another way of achieving what Frank called "preventive politics." Participants in both child study movements reflected the utopian aspirations of the 1920s. Until experience proved them wrong, their faith was unshakable.[30]

In spite of all they had in common, the two foundations and the child study programs they established functioned in nearly total isolation from each other. Their first encounter came in 1921 when the Laura Spelman Rockefeller Memorial made a two-year grant of $12,000 for the establishment of an experimental program in mental hygiene in rural New Jersey. The program included a psychiatric clinic as part of a general study of child health. The Memorial assigned the administration of this project to the National Committee, now formally allied with the Commonwealth Fund's program to prevent juvenile delinquency. Smith assumed that the Memorial's funding of the project would not interfere with plans for the clinic of the Commonwealth Fund and the National Committee, but he was wrong. The Memorial objected to the clinic's focus on psychopathology, asked the National Committee to withdraw, and gave the project a new purpose: the prevention of mental disorders through parent and community education.[31] This early conflict underscored the determination of each foundation to avoid the other's turf; their child study programs henceforth functioned as independent entities. The only other example of aborted interaction between them during the period in which the fund sponsored child guidance clinics occurred when Smith sent a brief note to Lawrence Frank (April 1925) inquiring about the Memorial's new child study programs. Frank promptly returned a perfunctory reply. Not until 1932, after the Commonwealth Fund had terminated its child guidance programs, did Rockefeller's General Education Board (which had taken over the Memorial's child guidance programs) sponsor a conference of child guidance psychiatrists and then support other programs in child psychiatry.[32]

Many participants in the child guidance and child development movements explicitly recognized the value of integrating clinical and developmental approaches to child study, and some engaged in fruitful cooperation on specific projects. The refusal of the two foundations to experiment with these two new approaches to child study or encourage ways of bringing them together perpetuated the traditional distance between clinicians and researchers. The histories of the two movements have been told as separate stories.[33]

THE PROGRAM FOR THE PREVENTION
OF JUVENILE DELINQUENCY, 1922–27

The Commonwealth Fund's Program for the Prevention of Juvenile Delinquency was organized into four divisions. The Division on Delinquency, administered by the National Committee, was responsible for a demonstration clinic program and a psychiatric field service to assist juvenile courts and probation officers. The Bureau of Children's Guidance, administered by the New York School of Social Work, conducted a psychiatric clinic for the treatment and study of children in New York City and also served as the chief training organization for psychiatric social workers, visiting teachers, and probation officers, but not psychiatrists. The bureau was directed by Glueck and Marion Kenworthy, a psychiatrist with psychoanalytic training. A third division, under the Public Education Association of New York City, organized and supervised visiting teacher demonstration programs in thirty communities. Based on a fifteen-year-old movement that had become a well-established part of the New York school system, the visiting teacher program reflected both the Commonwealth Fund's preference for working with the school rather than the home and its concern for "problem teachers" as well as "problem parents." The fund worked with children of school age, while the Memorial focused on preschoolers. A fourth division, the Joint Committee on Methods of Preventing Delinquency, under the supervision of the National Committee, coordinated and evaluated the different aspects of the program and interpreted it to professional and popular audiences.

From the start, the Commonwealth Fund's program was characterized by experimentation and rapid change.[34] Almost immediately after the five-year program began, reference to the prevention of juvenile delinquency was replaced by the phrase "child guidance." The new term avoided both the negative connotations suggested by "delinquency" and the association of psychiatry with insanity, and conveyed the program's broad and constructive purpose which was not just to "salvage human wrecks" but to alter the thinking and behavior of a community with reference to its children.[35]

THE DEMONSTRATION CLINICS: A HISTORY
OF CHANGE AND DISCOVERY

Between 1922 and 1926 the Commonwealth Fund sponsored and financed eight demonstration clinics, seven of which were subsequently sustained by local funds. The general purpose of demonstration programs was to awaken the community to the value of this new kind of organization. The concept of demonstration accorded with philanthropy's philosophy that it should experiment with new ventures but that others must assume responsibility for their continuance.[36] Even in their first year, the demonstration clinics introduced major innovations. By the early 1930s the function, clientele, and goal of most clinics were radically different from the Commonwealth Fund's original conception.[37] The demonstration program was a "history of continuous change and discovery."[38]

Like the initial goal of the program, "the prevention of juvenile delinquency," the first demonstration clinic, established in St. Louis in 1922, reflected views that were already outmoded. In spite of Salmon's recommendation that the clinic work with younger children, 74 percent of the cases were court-referred. The other demonstration clinics moved quickly in new directions, admitting fewer delinquent children and many younger children with mild emotional problems, referred to by a wide variety of sources. The Dallas clinic, established in 1923, had as many referrals from schools and social agencies as from courts, and the clinic established in the same year for the Twin Cities, St. Paul and Minneapolis, had no court referrals. In all the demonstration clinics established after 1923, fewer than 10 percent of the cases were referrals from courts. Even at the St. Louis clinic, court referrals were down to 25 percent by 1926.[39] The demonstration clinics and the many new clinics they inspired tended to work with families, physicians, schools, and social agencies rather than with the courts. The Twin Cities' demonstration clinic was the first to exclude mentally retarded and severely disturbed children as well as juvenile delinquents. Other clinics quickly followed, because they concluded that they were not capable of helping these children.[40]

A longitudinal study of patients in the St. Louis clinic suggests that, by reducing the number of children referred by the courts, the demonstration clinics may have excluded the children who most needed their help. Robins found that children referred for antisocial behavior were at much greater risk of psychiatric disability and sociopathic behavior as adults than were children in the control group or those referred for other kinds of problems. The prognosis for the neurotic child was much better, even if he or she were not treated.[41]

The first psychiatric clinics for children served low-income populations. Clinics sponsored by public agencies continued to accept primarily poor children, but private clinics quickly showed a preference for the middle- and even upper-class child. In part, this reflected the shift from court referrals to referrals by physicians, parents, and social agencies, but it was also a conscious effort to serve a broader public.[42] One of the "most interesting features" of the Norfolk demonstration clinic, the Commonwealth Fund pointed out, was "the apparent interest of persons of means and standing in the community, a considerable number of whom have brought their children for diagnosis and treatment."[43] The change in clientele meant that the children in the clinics came to resemble more and more the children studied in the child development institutes, except that they were older. The everyday child with everyday problems, to use Douglas Thom's label, had replaced the disadvantaged child in big trouble who had been the concern of prewar Progressive reformers.[44]

Unlike the Memorial, which supported child study organizations that could serve rural areas, the fund located all of its demonstration clinics in cities. With few exceptions, the clinics established in the 1920s were not affiliated with universities, hospitals, or medical schools.[45] Child guidance clinics had little incentive to affiliate with most hospital outpatient services, which were grossly understaffed and overburdened. Neuropsychiatrists and guidance clinic psychiatrists had little in common. Hospitals and medical schools usually were indifferent to the new clinics. Pediatricians, who were excluded from the child guidance team, were resentful.[46] As we shall later see, the location of the child development research institutes and the guidance clinics outside of academic and medical institutions profoundly influenced the character of both child development research and child psychiatry in America.

British observers of the child guidance movement were amazed that Americans perceived incipient neurosis or psychosis where Britons saw only growing pains. One British social worker told her colleagues, "I could not help feeling at times that there was a tendency to regard too many children as problem children requiring clinic treatment. Of the cases on probation under me I feel that probably 65% or 70% could be adjusted by a good probation officer but that expert advice and treatment would be helpful in the remaining 30% or 35%, whereas I think possibly in America the whole 100% would be considered definitely problem children requiring treatment at a clinic."[47] The American tendency to recommend prompt treatment for what many perceived as relatively normal problems of development was reflected in the mental hygiene movement's use of the terms "predelinquent" and "prepsychotic" and frequent references to the "fragility of childhood."[48] Americans seemed to fear that even small problems, if left untreated, might lead to social maladjustment that could have large consequences for society as well as the child.

The demonstration clinics did not ignore parents, but, unlike the child study programs of the Memorial, they focused on changing children directly rather than through their parents. During the first five years, clinic work with parents was limited to counseling by social workers and the provision of child-rearing information. Psychiatric social worker Jessie Taft recalled her naive belief in 1919 that one could change children without influencing their parents. She had reveled in "the thought of something young, unformed, unmarred, with whom mental health was as possible of attainment as physical health. What an escape from the intolerable situation of the adult with his fixed ideas and habits. Why spend one's life trying to make over a bad job when children are at hand to be ushered into the kingdom of good adjustment."[49]

In 1926 the Bureau of Children's Guidance listed problems for which it was treating children: lying, disorderly conduct in school, tantrums, quarreling, stealing, daydreaming, truancy, defiance of authority, and jealousy. These behaviors were perceived as "bad habits" that could be altered through environmental manipulation without the need for psychotherapy. Environmental manipulation sometimes involved placing the child in a new environment, such as a hospital, a correctional institution, a military academy or other special school, an orphanage or foster home, or a summer camp. It also could include treating a physical problem, offering special tutoring, providing better recreation, or counseling parents. The Commonwealth Fund agreed with Healy that a psychiatric clinic needed a network of good social agencies to carry out its recommendations for environmental manipulation and insisted upon seeing such a network before it would support the establishment of a new clinic.[50]

PERCY'S STORY: A JUDGE BAKER CLINIC
CASE RECORD

Excerpts from the case history of Percy, a thirteen-year-old boy studied at the Judge Baker Foundation Clinic in the mid-1920s, suggest how a child guidance team studied a child, drawing on a variety of social agencies to obtain boy's and mother's own stories and to conduct physical and psychological examinations.[51] The reporting agencies included Percy's school, his probation officer, the hospital where he was born, the hospital where he was twice treated for illness, and the Red Cross, because it had information on Percy's biological father's application for disability status in 1920. At regular conferences the staff discussed the findings and decided what should be done.

Percy's mother's story was prefaced by comments that she was "untidy, rather ignorant, and evidently devoted to her boy." The mother provided a family history, which was judged "reliable." It contained the significant information that Percy was illegitimate. Unknown to his mother, the father had been married when Percy was conceived and some time afterward had divorced and remarried. The mother described Percy's daily routine, his personality traits and interests, and his problems ("stealing, truancy and troublesome behavior in school") and noted that he was a great reader of adventure stories and newspapers. Percy's "own story" provides by far the longest record. It reports that Percy and a friend had been stealing as a "kind of game to see how much they could get away with before they were caught." Percy was unhappy at home because of his alcoholic uncle, who lived with the family and who called him "a word that means I don't have a father. . . . My mother says my father is dead but I wonder about it. I'd like to find out." An excerpt from Percy's diary disclosed that he and his friend had made elaborate plans to run away to Florida or South America. Some of the articles they stole were for use on the proposed trip.

After several conferences, the team listed six possible causes of Percy's problems. In accordance with Healy's emphasis on love of adventure as a cause of delinquency, Percy's need for excitement was listed first. Other causes were the unfortunate home situation and Percy's concern about his parentage. The "prognosis," which explicitly omitted psychiatric interpretations, emphasized Percy's assets, such as his intelligence, his many normal characteristics, the devotion of his mother, and, "as yet, no deep-seated criminal ideation." "Liabilities" included the mother's ignorance, the unfortunate family and neighborhood situation, especially the problems caused by the uncle, and Percy's "acquirement of dangerous interests." Recommendations for helping Percy included immediate placement in a foster home, better recreation, eye examination, posture training, tutoring in arithmetic and reading, promotion in school if possible, and, ambiguously, "frank discussion of situation about father, question of whether and when to be told truth." In addition to help for Percy, his mother was to receive counseling and information about child rearing and be urged to send the uncle away and move to a better neighborhood. The case record concluded with a report from the child-placing agency. Percy had been placed in a country home, where he was "welcomed heartily" and from which he wrote letters to the doctors he knew at Judge Baker describing his good times. When next evaluated, he had gained eleven pounds, his headaches had diminished, and he had stopped stealing. He asked to remain in the foster home, and the clinic staff decided that he could stay there until the situation in his own family changed.

By treating large numbers of relatively normal children like Percy, the guidance clinics helped to show that delinquent children were not psychopaths, as even Healy assumed in 1909. The few academic psychiatrists who were interested in children were concerned almost exclusively with severe psychopathology and therefore had little to contribute to treatment of guidance clinic patients. During the 1920s clinic practice was influenced far more by the literature on observations of normal children than by the publications of academic psychiatrists.

INTRODUCING A MORE SYMPATHETIC
APPROACH TO TROUBLED CHILDREN

Since the Judge Baker clinic was the most important model for the guidance clinics established in the 1920s, Percy's case record is a good illustration of the dramatic changes in attitudes and behavior toward troubled or delinquent children that were spread by the early child guidance movement. As late as 1950 the concept of the emotionally disturbed child was little more than a quarter-century old. "Children afflicted with what we would describe today as neurotic and psychotic illnesses," Louise Despert wrote, "were variously labeled through the ages as possessed, wicked, guilty, insubordinate, incorrigible, unstable, maladjusted, and problem children, roughly in this order." Even the last three epithets, Despert added, placed the onus of guilt on the child and accused him of having failed society.[52] Founders of the child guidance movement believed, to the contrary, that society had failed the child. Percy was treated sympathetically, not as a sinner but as a victim of circumstances. The guidance team searched for possible problems in Percy's life that might have contributed to his difficulties, and initiated changes it believed could help him. By educating the public about new perceptions of the causes of a child's problems and portraying the child as a victim of circumstances, the guidance clinics helped to dispel the harsh attitudes reflected in Despert's list.

Most psychiatrists in the United States and abroad were interested in child-hood emotional disorders only as they fit classifications devised for adults and perceived child psychiatry as a "miniature mirror image of adult psychiatry."[53] Until Melanie Klein and Anna Freud began treating children in Britain during the 1930s and 1940s, what most psychoanalysts knew about children was de-rived from the reminiscences of adult patients. Healy and his followers were the first to insist upon obtaining the "child's own story."[54]

During his training at the Philadelphia Child Guidance Clinic in the early 1930s, pediatrician Milton Senn experienced one consequence of hospital physicians' failure to question children.[55] The clinic staff met regularly with physicians from the Philadelphia Children's Hospital to discuss cases. At one conference, the physicians expressed concern about how to treat a little girl affl-icted with Sydenham's chorea who had "tried to commit suicide" by freeing herself from a straitjacket and attempting to jump from a window. Should they tie her to her bed or give her more phenobarbital? How were they to protect her? Senn asked why the child had tried to commit suicide, but no one had tried to find out. When asked, she said that she had not wanted to kill herself but only to return home. She missed her family because hospital rules permit-ted only one family visit per month. Physicians then reduced her drugs and were soon able to discharge her.[56]

Advocates of the child guidance point of view believed that the best way to educate the community about mental hygiene was to publicize what children themselves had revealed about their difficulties. Several books of case histories (with names and other events disguised) were published, and many clinics in-cluded case histories in their annual reports.

David Levy astutely observed that adult psychiatry and child psychiatry evolved in separate directions in the United States largely because of the early connection between child psychiatry and delinquency. "If the neuroses and psychoses of childhood rather than delinquency had received the same impetus and energy at the same time," he wrote, "child psychiatry would have devel-oped very differently."[57] The focus on the elimination of childhood disorders that caused delinquency and other social problems led directly to the location of child guidance work in community clinics and to investigation of the con-nections between the child's mental health and the social setting in which he lived. The development of adult psychiatry in hospitals apart from the normal life of the community led to a preoccupation with disease processes and organic disorders.[58] The guidance clinics were forced to adopt a different approach to diagnosis and treatment because after every brief visit their patients returned to parents and home, to teachers and playmates, and to interactions with a variety of other individuals. The impact of external circumstances on children came to be recognized as a major source of their problems.

THE FOUNDING OF THE AMERICAN
ORTHOPSYCHIATRY ASSOCIATION

In January 1924 at the initiative of Karl Menninger and Herman Adler, nine psychiatrists met in Chicago to consider founding a new organization representing the neuropsychiatric or medical view of crime.[59] They considered Social Psychiatry as a possible name but chose instead Orthopsychiatry. "Ortho," meaning straight, right, or correct in Greek, was intended to suggest the validity of the mental hygiene approach. "Psychiatry" was meant to emphasize the grounding of the new organization in medicine. Appointing themselves an organizing committee, the nine psychiatrists invited others active in child guidance, mental health, court clinics, or correctional institutions to the initial meeting of the American Orthopsychiatry Association (AOA) in June 1924. Twenty-six accepted.[60]

A major goal of the AOA was "to unite and provide a common meeting ground for those engaged in the study and treatment of problems of human behavior." Menninger and Healy favored admitting nonpsychiatrists to full membership, but the others decided to establish three membership classes: *fellows,* limited to psychiatrists; *associates,* open to nonpsychiatrists engaged in the study of behavior disorders; and *honorary,* open to nonprofessionals. Within two years, however, nonpsychiatrists become eligible for election as fellows. In 1927 the membership included forty-five psychiatrists, twelve psychologists, five social workers, and several lawyers By 1928, 540 individuals registered for the annual meeting. Healy was elected the first president, Ethel Dummer the first honorary member, and Augusta Bronner, later, the first psychologist president.[61]

James Plant and many other psychiatrists would have preferred to establish a child psychiatry section within the American Psychiatric Association.[62] The association refused because many members were suspicious of a close alliance with nonpsychiatrists and did not consider child guidance psychiatry to be psychiatry.[63] In 1930, the same year as the first issue of *Child Development* appeared, the AOA began publication of the *American Journal of Orthopsychiatry* (*AJO*). Lowrey, its first editor, held the post for eighteen years. Many believed that the most significant influence of the AOA was helping child and adult psychiatry to move away from organic toward dynamic interpretations of human behavior.[64]

HABIT CLINICS FOR PRESCHOOL CHILDREN

Ninety percent of the children in the guidance clinics during the 1920s were of school age, most between ten and fourteen.[65] Unlike the Memorial, which based its child study programs on assumptions about the importance of early childhood, the Commonwealth Fund believed that children's salvation would come through the schools rather than the home. Salmon asserted that there was no place for a child that was not better than the home.[66] Douglas Thom founded habit clinics for preschool children because he believed that early childhood "is not only the opportune time but the only time to initiate a program of mental health. Seeds of pugnacity, selfishness, and feelings of inferiority are sown early."[67]

Thom founded the first habit clinic in Boston in 1921. When the Massachusetts Department of Mental Diseases established a mental hygiene division in 1922 and appointed Thom director, he used his position to develop a dozen habit clinics in the state under the auspices of local community hospitals.[68] Physicians established two clinics in Missouri, and pediatrician Ira Wile founded one at Mount Sinai Hospital in New York City. Like the guidance clinics, habit clinics provided diagnostic and consultative services rather than treatment. Through experimentation in the clinics, Thom hoped to find ways to make mental hygiene of practical value to parents, teachers, nurses, physicians, social workers, and others who had daily contact with children.[69]

"Habits," Thom declared, "are the tools by which we achieve health, happiness, and efficiency . . . the term habit embraces all acquired methods of acting and thinking."[70] For example, honesty was a habit. Thom popularized but did not invent the concept of habit-training. Its scientific formulation came from William James and was adopted by Adolph Meyer and Edward Thorndike. Thom's approach was more behavioristic than that of most guidance clinic psychiatrists. He stressed the importance of rewards and punishments in habit formation and often sounded very much like the authoritarian pediatrician L. Emmett Holt.[71] John Watson later gave habit literature an even stronger behavioristic orientation.

Although small in number, the habit clinics had a significant influence. Many nursery schools and kindergartens adopted Thom's habit-training advice. The Children's Bureau published pamphlets by Thom from 1925 through 1937, and his other publications also reached a wide audience.[72]

THE END OF THE FIRST FIVE-YEAR PROGRAM

Commonwealth Fund annual reports for 1926 and 1927 discussed the results of the first five-year program and announced future plans. The demonstration clinics had evaluated and provided clinical service for four thousand children. Studies in two demonstration cities showed "partial or complete success" in 73.5 percent of the cases in one city and 62 percent in the other. The Commonwealth Fund also had provided a consultation service for cities wishing to organize a guidance clinic. Three hundred new agencies serving children with behavioral or emotional disturbances had been established. Sponsors of these clinics included individual philanthropists, foundations, community chests, juvenile courts, social welfare departments, public health authorities, private and state hospitals, and local and state governments.[73] Much clinic growth had occurred without the fund's direct influence, probably because support for the child guidance movement tapped into the same public interest that had supported the child welfare and parent education movements. By 1927, 109 full- or part-time guidance clinics were functioning, almost all following the pattern set by the demonstration clinics. In view of the rapid growth of new clinics, the Commonwealth Fund decided that the demonstration program had achieved its purpose and would not be continued.

The Bureau of Children's Guidance had trained 70 psychiatric social workers and had studied and treated 822 children. Of 196 cases selected at random, the bureau staff judged that 93 had successful outcomes, 61 were partially successful, and 42 were failures.[74]

The Visiting Teacher Program had sponsored 30 demonstrations, many in rural areas; 24 were continued at local expense. The overall program had served about 15,000 children. Between 1922 and 1927 the number of visiting teachers had doubled, and the number of cities served had grown from twenty to seventy. The Commonwealth Fund concluded that the visiting teacher demonstration program also had served its purpose and should be terminated.[75]

The Joint Committee on Methods of Preventing Delinquency had been extremely active in interpreting the child guidance viewpoint to the communities it served. Between 1922 and 1926 it sponsored several thousand talks, 120 lecture courses, and numerous articles, and it had distributed, free of charge, almost one hundred thousand books and pamphlets. It had also provided program materials to 80 schools, colleges, and universities for use in course work in education, social work, psychology, and child study.[76]

Commenting on the achievements of the first five years, Smith concluded that "the project has been somewhat more successful than had been anticipated. New methods of approach in dealing with difficult children have been worked out; much has been learned as to the technique of applying the principles of mental hygiene to the individual child; many workers have been trained; the growth in the use of the methods employed has been little short of astounding."[77] Smith had fears about the future direction of the movement similar to those of Beardsley Ruml about the parent education movement. He wrote, "There appears to be a real danger of the development in this field of a popular movement which, seized upon as a fad, and promoted without adequate scientific and technical guidance from the complementary fields of psychiatry and psychology, may well do more harm than good." The "outstanding future task" should be "careful guidance, thorough preliminary educational work, prevention of premature and ill-considered organization, . . . increase of trained personnel . . . and . . . making the scientific basis of this comparatively new field broader, more accurate, and more definitive."[78] Smith's comments explain the changes the Commonwealth Fund introduced in 1927–1928 as it began the second phase of its program, the subject of the next chapter.[79]

Chapter 12 Child Guidance
Becomes Child Psychiatry

Originally conceived as "common-sense psychiatry," child guidance became a highly technical medical specialty during the 1930s. The evolution of child guidance into a uniquely American child psychiatry began in 1927, when the Commonwealth Fund abandoned its bold effort to prevent juvenile delinquency and adult neurosis and psychosis. Its new goal was to transform child guidance clinics into psychotherapeutic centers for the treatment of limited numbers of children, and child guidance into a medical specialty.[1] It was not until 1959, however, that the American Psychiatric Association formally designated child psychiatry a subspecialty of psychiatry.[2] To accomplish its new goals the Commonwealth Fund changed its own program and encouraged the clinics to change theirs.[3] Instead of limiting its function to the diagnosis of children's problems and relying on community social agencies to use environmental manipulation to help troubled children, it urged the clinics to provide direct psychotherapy by a child guidance team.[4]

By the mid-1930s, the use of environmental manipulation and of the open case conference to teach social workers in other agencies how to treat children had almost disappeared.[5] Clinics were encouraged to retreat from the education of teachers, social workers, and other professional groups in the principles of child mental hygiene.[6] The Commonwealth Fund also decided that parent education should be the responsibility of other community agencies, halted its own activities in this area, and asked the clinics to focus on psychotherapy. As intensive therapeutic treatment became the central clinic activity, ancillary services to the wider community were neglected, and the clinics lost their position as the central coordinator of community activities related to the mental health of children and youth.[7]

Commonwealth Fund director Barry Smith declared that the fund's most urgent goal should be to provide a better scientific foundation for child guidance. Since guidance professionals were swamped by demands for service, he advocated a program that would increase the number of trained personnel, particularly psychiatrists, who had not been included in the original training program.[8]

By the end of 1927 the Commonwealth Fund and the National Committee for Mental Hygiene had established a new structure. The Institute of Child Guidance, with Lawson C. Lowrey as director and David Levy as chief of staff, replaced the Bureau of Children's Guidance. A Division of Publications replaced the Joint Committee on Methods of Preventing Delinquency. The National Committee's Division of Delinquency became the Division of Community Clinics. Still directed by George Stevenson, it halted the organizing activity of the demonstration period in favor of a conservative policy of maintaining clinic standards and controlling clinic growth. It offered consultation and field services, acted as a clearinghouse for information on child guidance programs, and administered the continuing fellowship program. After 1932 the Commonwealth Fund no longer funded child guidance clinics in the United States.[9]

FROM BEHAVIORISM TO DYNAMIC PSYCHIATRY

The program's new direction reflected the growing tendency of child guidance professionals to move away from the assumptions of behaviorism toward those of dynamic psychiatry, particularly as expressed by Adolph Meyer, Sigmund Freud, and Otto Rank. Behaviorism emphasized rationality; dynamic psychiatry, the significance of unconscious motivations. As child guidance professionals came to recognize the powerful influence of the unconscious on behavior, they shifted their focus from the social setting in which children lived, such as their neighborhoods and schools, to their emotional environment; paid more attention to children's feelings than to their behavior; and tended to define problems by internal rather than external criteria.[10] The shift from behaviorism to dynamic psychiatry was a primary cause of the abandonment of environmental manipulation (often referred to as "indirect therapy") in favor of direct treatment through psychotherapy.[11]

As psychotherapy replaced environmental manipulation, children remained in treatment longer, sometimes for more than a year, and fewer children were accepted for treatment.[12] Since clinics increased their treatment of children with mild emotional disturbances, who they believed were more likely to benefit from psychotherapy, social agencies and outpatient departments of state hospitals were left to cope with the most difficult cases.[13] Referrals to the clinics from social agencies decreased and those from private physicians and parents increased, leading to a growing proportion of patients from a more prosperous, better educated segment of society.[14]

Increasing awareness of the influence of unconscious motives in behavior, together with the frustrating failure of the first five-year program to change parents' behavior through counseling and child-rearing education, convinced guidance professionals that children could be treated successfully only if their parents also were treated.[15] Psychiatric social workers, supervised by a psychiatrist, hoped to help parents, mostly mothers, to recognize and overcome emotional conflicts that kept them from behavior helpful to their children. Sometimes the psychiatrist treated parents directly as well as supervising their treatment by psychiatric social workers. According to Stevenson and Smith, the "intensive study and treatment of the problem child had come to mean the study and treatment of parent-child relationships."[16] Observing the change in focus from the school to the home, Helen Witmer wrote that the clinics were "developing a kind of social service that seeks the origin of all the problems of child behavior somewhere along the axis where extremes are the rejection of the child by the parents at one end and overprotection at the other end. Maladjustment in school fades out of the picture, for all maladjustment . . . is home maladjustment. . . . The mental level of the child and the use he has made of his educational opportunities apparently throws no light on the problem . . . and the psychologist becomes superfluous."[17] The transformation of the parent into a patient reached a climax in David Levy's attitude therapy, the purpose of which was to help parents to discover the origins of their adverse feelings toward their children.[18] By 1933 some were arguing that child guidance treatment was rapidly becoming therapy for mothers.[19]

The change in status of the mother from receiver of advice to patient had profound consequences. First, it created considerable confusion about who was the primary patient, the mother or the child.[20] Second, clinics believed that they had to guard against parents who used a child's problems as a ticket of admission to treatment of their own problems.[21] Finally, it greatly increased the number of nonmedical personnel practicing psychotherapy.[22]

Confusion about who was the patient was compounded by confusion about who was the therapist. The original delineation of function among members of the child guidance team became blurred as all members began to practice psychotherapy. Psychologists as well as psychiatrists treated patients, psychiatric social work and psychiatry sometimes became interchangeable professions, and rivalry increased among all members of the child guidance team. Throughout this period of change, psychiatric social workers continued to bear the chief burden of child guidance work.[23] The goal of training enough psychiatrists to meet the demand for their services had not been met by 1935 or even by mid-century.[24] Between 1927 and 1933 the Institute of Child Guidance trained only thirty-two psychiatrists and fifteen psychologists, but 298 psychiatric social workers. The clinics' absorption with psychotherapy and their effort to institutionalize a new medical specialty caused them to become increasingly isolated from other community agencies.[25]

THE "BETTY ANN MEYER"
PSYCHIATRIC INTERVIEW

A condensed version of Percy's case record (discussed in chapter 11 to illustrate treatment through environmental manipulation) was printed in a four-page pamphlet. None of the case histories of children who received psychotherapy in the 1930s could have been so reduced. Descriptions of nine cases in Witmer's *Psychiatric Interviews with Children* each occupy from 21 to 73 pages.[26] Frederick Allen, trained by Adolph Meyer, appointed chief psychiatrist at the Philadelphia Child Guidance Clinic at Meyer's suggestion, and often referred to as the dean of child psychiatrists, reported and interpreted a case history that illustrates the treatment of unconscious motives through psychotherapy.[27]

Allen described Betty Ann Meyer as "an eight-year old girl whose normal development was hindered by a too close mother-child relationship and who expressed her struggle and her anxiety in willful insistence on her timidity and in physical symptoms that were without organic basis." He said that the relationship with the therapist "was used to help the child experience her anxiety as a feeling instead of a gastrointestinal reaction, and to establish herself as an independent human being who could assert her own desires and allow others to assert theirs."[28]

In twenty-two intensive weekly therapy sessions, Allen tried to help Betty Ann to differentiate herself from her mother, while the psychiatric social worker tried to help Mrs. Meyer to support her daughter's growth toward independence.[29]

Allen explained that four principles guided the therapy. The first, "participation," encouraged Betty Ann to bring into the relationship with Allen the disturbed feelings that characterized her problem. Following the second principle, "differentiation," enabled Allen to maintain his own separateness.[30] By maintaining his own integrity, not only as an individual but as part of a professional service, Allen explained, the therapist "permits the child's turmoil to revolve around him, and by providing a steady center enables the child to become himself."[31] The third principle called for joint action by therapist and social worker to bring the child's parents into therapy. Mr. Meyer, shut out of a relationship with his daughter, had grasped at the parental function through a dominating relationship with his son. After the third interview, he requested treatment for his son. Thereafter, father and mother sometimes participated in joint interviews with the social worker. The fourth principle was the necessity for the therapist to accept the changes taking place in the child without attempting to find and give a rational explanation and interpretation to all that takes place. The art of therapy, Allen emphasized, depends on "knowledge of a professional method that is designed to serve and help, but not to provide rigid schemes into which a child is fitted."[32]

Allen's report described each weekly session with Betty Ann over a period of seven months, provided summaries of three stages of the treatment, and included 155 interpretive notes. By the time Betty Ann was discharged, her physical symptoms had disappeared, Allen believed that she had achieved differentiation from her mother, and both parents were confident that they could now cope with both of their children. Mr. Meyer withdrew his request for treatment of his son, and Mrs. Meyer declared Betty Ann "ninety-five percent better. I guess I can't expect her to be perfect."[33] The case histories of Percy and Betty Ann illuminate two concepts that distinguished early from later clinic practice. Early clinics saw the child as a victim of conditions; later clinics, as an active participant in his own destiny.[34] Attention shifted from influences operating on the child to how the child utilized his social environment.[35] Most referrals to clinics during the early 1920s were by courts or social agencies that believed their function was to help children stop objectionable behavior. Percy, for example, was referred by the court to the Judge Baker Foundation for "stealing, truancy, and troublesome behavior in school." He was the passive recipient of help from those who assumed that they knew what was best for him. The outcome of Percy's treatment was judged successful because the symptoms for which he had been referred had improved. He had gained weight, his headaches were better, and, most important, he had stopped stealing.

Like many of the children referred to clinics during the 1920s, Percy was required to accept clinic treatment. Mrs. Meyer, on the other hand, voluntarily brought Betty Ann to the Philadelphia clinic. Diagnosis of Betty Ann's problems focused entirely on internal psychodynamics. There is no indication that the clinic requested help for her or her parents from the school or any other social agency. Her difficulties were interpreted primarily in terms of her conflict over wanting to remain a child but also to become more mature and gain independence from her mother. Improvement in her emotional health was expected to come primarily from inner psychological growth rather than from any changes in external circumstances. Allen's purpose was not to tell Betty Ann what to do but to help her to resolve emotional conflicts so that she could work out her own adjustment.[36]

Child guidance clinics during the early period had a social objective: to help children conform to commonly accepted social standards. By the mid-1930s, the clinics' primary purpose was to help children achieve self-determination. Clinics increasingly tried to place themselves outside the network of regulatory agencies, holding themselves responsible solely to their patients.[37]

Did the second phase of the child guidance program serve patients better than the first phase? The question has never been resolved. At least two studies indicate that replacement of environmental manipulation by psychotherapy did not increase positive outcomes. Witmer's comparison of treatments in various child guidance clinics in 1935 showed that the type of treatment did not affect success or failure.[38] Margo Horn analyzed data from the Philadelphia Child Guidance Clinic for the period 1925 through 1944 and concluded that environmental interventions were more effective than psychotherapy. She observed, however, that the psychodynamic model continued to hold out the "unsubstantiated promise of enduring personal change throughout the 1930s and 1940s."[39]

CONTROVERSY OVER OBJECTIVES

Although Adolph Meyer had steered the National Committee into preventive work with children after World War I, he believed that the goal of mental hygiene should be melioristic, not utopian.[40] He agreed with Allen that the selling of childhood as a golden age had created false hope and a great gap between expectations and achievement.[41] Although Meyer had trained eighty-three child guidance psychiatrists by 1937, he was one of child guidance's severest critics.[42]

To Meyer, a community hospital was the ideal setting for service, teaching, and research. He believed that child guidance clinics had precipitated rivalry between hospital psychiatry and independent psychiatric clinics for children. The guidance clinics, he argued, were "running ahead of rigid checking-up and could not flourish scientifically out of contact with psychiatry's mainstream." Their focus was too exclusively on the child, " at the expense of interest in the psychiatry of the adult in whose hands the fate of the younger generation lies."[43] Needed was a "little less worry about the child and a bit more concern about the world we make for children to live in." Meyer asserted that "this is a period when everyone wants to pick on and tinker with the child, although in reality we know less about the child than the adult. . . . As a basis for child guidance, character building has to begin with our own."[44] Meyer also criticized the premature invoking of Freudian concepts in child guidance work and warned that the effects of treatment could be evaluated only after the passage of twenty-five years.[45]

Many who had endorsed the first five-year child guidance program were disturbed by the changes the Commonwealth Fund initiated after 1927, especially its abandonment of the social reform goal, its shift from the educational goals of the mental hygiene movement to an emphasis on psychotherapy, and its transformation of a "common sense psychiatry" into a highly technical profession.[46] Lowrey regretted the "losses incurred in the shift of emphasis from child guidance to child psychiatry."[47] James Plant, who had worked with Healy at the Judge Baker Clinic, insisted that child psychiatry's purpose was to alter the social pressures inflicted on families and children, not to eliminate distressing conduct. He argued that matters of chief concern to therapists lie at least as much outside the child as inside.[48] Plant worked to improve the competence of teachers and others in the community who carried everyday responsibility for children, and he "tended to view each clinic patient as a random sample of community neglect."[49] Plant was distressed by the continuing decrease in the proportion of poor families the clinics served.[50] To him as to many others, the solution to children's mental disorders lay outside the clinical field.[51]

Although the prevention of crime and of adult mental illness remained a long-range objective of the child guidance movement, it receded as an immediate goal.[52] Many praised the Commonwealth Fund for its new focus because they believed that social policy for children should be geared to helping them overcome current problems, not to how useful or troublesome they would be as adults.[53] They agreed with Kanner that "prevention is practiced by maintaining health, not by agitation intended to avert disasters projected into the future."[54] Reluctantly, supporters of child guidance began to acknowledge that their hope of preventing adult crime and mental disorders by identifying and treating incipient neuroses or psychoses in young children was untenable. They came to believe that psychosis rarely can be predicted in childhood and, even if it could, that children were not likely to be cured by the kind of treatment available in most clinics.[55] Child guidance professionals also discovered that treating children often was more difficult and time-consuming than treating adults.[56]

CHANGES IN RESEARCH, 1927–1933

Part of the justification for the original child guidance program had been the hope that the clinics would facilitate valuable clinical research, but in 1929 fund officials noted the "failure of psychiatry to carry forward basic research into the origins of personality disorder and the nature and variations of normal development."[57] The paucity of clinical research was a consequence not only of the effort to transform child guidance into a medical specialty but also of the difficulty of evaluating clinical data. Stevenson and Smith explained, "The complexity of a typical syndrome in a child guidance case makes it exceedingly difficult to be dogmatic about the results of treatment, and in the absence of controlled experiment there is always the possibility that what seems to be improvement would have come about without intervention. Many of the most significant instances of clinic service relate to factors in human personality which all but elude definition; its objective is often the betterment of the patient's total adjustment to life rather than the removal of a particular symptom. In the face of these difficulties, the clinics have thus far attempted only rough clinical estimates of success or failure in particular cases."[58]

A clinic's judgment of whether a completed treatment should be rated a success, a partial success, or a failure was subjective. About three-fourths of cases were rated "successful" or, more often, "partially successful." Less than one-fourth were considered "failures." According to Stevenson and Smith, reports of the results of clinic treatment had to be viewed with skepticism until the method of evaluation was refined and standardized. They pointed out that "cold" records, accumulated by clinicians and evaluated by others, had proved to be of limited research value. Instead of focusing on treatment outcomes, they urged "more analysis of the forces that press against the child from his social environment, particularly the influences of the school, the neighborhood, and the gang."[59] In line with Arnold Gesell's insistence that development as well as disease falls within the scope of clinical medicine, they suggested coordination of pathological findings in clinic cases with longitudinal studies of normal development.[60]

Since a flair for both research and therapy is rarely present in one individual, clinics tended to employ good clinicians rather than able researchers. Even the rare clinician with research skills and interests was hindered by the pressure of clinical tasks.[61] Lowrey and Levy, both able researchers and talented clinicians, were among the few who were able to combine research and practice.[62]

Levy perceived research at the Institute of Child Guidance as the successor to Healy's research at the Chicago and Boston clinics and Herman Adler's research at the Illinois Institute for Juvenile Research, in which he had participated.[63] Levy's own research was based on his conviction that "the most important study of man as a social being is a study of his mother's influence on his early life."[64] Unlike most other researchers of his time, Levy emphasized the interaction of heredity and environment and recognized the role of the child's temperament in evoking reactions from the mother. He attempted to integrate Watsonian behaviorism with psychoanalysis because the "Freudian baby like the Watsonian baby grows up in a world determined largely by maternal love."[65]

Levy was ahead of his time in recognizing the value of integrating clinical and developmental research. He told developmental psychologists that their field needed "an infusion of psychiatrists," suggested that individual case studies could yield experimentally verifiable data, and urged statistical analysis of collections of case studies.[66]

Lowrey was interested in clinical research on the causes of human behavior, but he acknowledged that the major focus of research at the Institute of Child Guidance was the efficacy of various treatment techniques, particularly psychotherapy. Since treatment methods varied widely among clinics, he said, such research was urgently needed.[67] After leaving the institute, Lowrey investigated the effects of early institutional care on children's development.[68]

Although Stevenson and Smith believed that "specialized research into the polygenetic phenomena of child behavior" was necessary to ensure continued scientific growth and development of the guidance clinics, little provision was made for such research either inside or outside the child guidance movement.[69]

Research at the Institute of Child Guidance was the only research within the child guidance framework supported by the Commonwealth Fund after 1927. The institute gathered and analyzed information on 3,600 children, but its value was limited by the biases of an admission policy favoring children who were likely to benefit from therapy and whose case histories were judged useful for teaching psychotherapy.[70] The Commonwealth Fund supported one program in child development unrelated to child guidance, a longitudinal study of child development by the Child Research Council of Denver under the direction of pediatrician Alfred Washburn.[71]

Outside the domain of child guidance, Ethel Dummer continued to sponsor important clinical research. She was particularly interested in mothers of illegitimate children and young women who had been in trouble with the law. She commissioned *The Unadjusted Girl* (1923), a study by sociologist William I. Thomas, and wrote the preface. Throughout the 1920s she supported the work of Miriam Van Waters, referee of the juvenile court in Los Angeles and director of El Retiro, a girls' detention home (Van Waters called it a "preventorium") from 1919 to 1930.[72]

CHILD GUIDANCE AND PEDIATRICS

One of the most criticized aspects of child guidance clinics was their estrangement from physical medicine.[73] After 1927 the physical examination of clinic patients tended to become briefer and more casual.[74] Although clinics gradually increased their affiliation with medical schools and teaching hospitals, the gulf between psychiatry and pediatrics widened during the first half of the 1930s. Describing a child guidance clinic on the grounds of a large children's hospital, Leo Kanner observed, "There couldn't have been less of a working relationship between clinic staff and pediatricians than if the Atlantic Ocean rather than a few yards of dirt had separated them."[75]

Abraham Jacobi, who opened the first pediatric clinic in the United States in 1860 and later helped pediatrics to become a medical specialty, pointed out that, unlike other medical specialties, pediatrics was based entirely on age and embraced all fields of clinical medicine. He argued that it should be involved in the prevention as well as the treatment of disease and in the formulation of social policy affecting children.[76] During the Progressive era, many pediatricians engaged in child health and welfare reform activities and practiced the kind of "preventive pediatrics" Jacobi advocated but, by the 1930s, they were using the interest in well-child care created by the Children's Bureau, the child guidance movement, and other child health movements to draw middle-class patients into their private practices.[77]

Most pediatricians were preoccupied, however, with the treatment of child-hood diseases and the management of infant feeding, tasks for which they had been trained and which had yielded impressive reductions in childhood mor-bidity and mortality. They were indifferent to the well child. Lester Evans, who participated in the Commonwealth Fund's child health demonstration pro-gram in Fargo, North Dakota, as well as in its child guidance work, reported that physicians in the health program wondered why he would "mess around with well babies," and called him a "fool."[78] Milton Senn and Benjamin Spock spoke of the isolation and loneliness they experienced because they tried to in-corporate child psychiatry into their work.[79] As we have seen, Arnold Gesell struggled unsuccessfully for decades to interest pediatricians in child develop-ment.

Pediatricians agreed in principle that the child should be treated as a whole human being, not merely as the victim or potential victim of disease or poor nutrition, but few practiced this belief. Time spent mastering and applying new psychological information cut into time available for improving the child's physical health, where so much work remained to be done. A popular pediatric text published in 1927 allotted only 22 of its 922 pages to serious mental disor-ders and two and a half lines to conduct disorders, and a 1928 edition of another widely used text read as if children had no emotional problems.[80] By 1936 every accredited school of social work taught the fundamentals of child psychiatry, but only 14 of 68 medical schools and four departments of pediatrics offered such instruction.[81] Child psychiatry was taught in only five universities. Julius Richmond believes that this may be why William Healy, in spite of his fame, was never invited to join the faculty of the Harvard Medical School and never achieved academic status.[82]

Pediatricians attributed their misgivings about applying psychological infor-mation to the newness of the child sciences and to conflicting assertions, drawn from diverse schools, that confused rather than enlightened. When Spock asked his psychoanalytic friends for help with the psychological problems of his young patients, he said "they didn't have the slightest idea of how to apply their clinical insights. . . . Everything I did in those first eight years of pediatric prac-tice I did sweating. . . . I was anxious all the time [even though] I was presum-ably in a position to give superior advice to parents because I had this psychi-atric training."[83]

A 1930 White House Conference(WHC) subcommittee report, "Psychology

and Psychiatry in Pediatrics-: The Problem" (hereafter PPP), based on correspondence with two hundred pediatricians, psychologists, and psychiatrists,
expressed pediatricians' objections to the new psychological child-rearing literature.[84] It also revealed the confusion and competition among these specialists
over who should control various aspects of mental health care for children.
Subcommittee members concluded that child guidance should be a part of
medicine but could not agree on whether or not it should be a medical specialty.[85] The report reminded Johns Hopkins psychiatrist Esther L. Richards of
Margaret Fuller's comment, "I don't know where I am going. Follow me."[86]

Some members of the subcommittee asked if intervention was not doing
more harm than good. They were outraged at the declaration of another conference subcommittee that one child out of three in the United States required
treatment under psychiatric supervision.[87] Richards asserted that "childhood
can suffer as much from specialized training without common sense as it can
from common sense without specialization."[88] Another member observed that
resourceful mental hygiene is one thing, psychiatric treatment another, and
charged that overeagerness to discover hidden sources of trouble was fostering
oversolicitude.[89]

Two decades later pediatrician Milton Senn discussed the findings of longitudinal studies by developmentalists that "normal run-of-the-mill children of a
white middle-class group in our generation show many characteristics of behavior which parents consider problems, but which in themselves are not in-
dicative of mental pathology."[90]

In 1931 an article by pediatrician Joseph Brennemann, "The Menace of Psychiatry," caused a furor. Brennemann defined psychiatry as "psychology, mental hygiene, behaviorism, child study and guidance, psychoanalysis, and parent
education," declaring that the menace came not from sound psychiatry but
from extremists and charlatans who were having an unhealthy effect on the
public.[91] Psychiatrist James Plant responded in an article predicting that "The
Promise of Psychiatry" would be fulfilled because pediatricians would find children more interesting than their diseases.[92]

The number of pediatricians in the United States increased from 138 in 1914
to 689 in 1923 and 1,333 in 1929.[93] During the 1930s parents, often better informed about child psychology than their physicians were, forced pediatricians
to attend to children's mental health by demanding their help for routine child
management and training.[94] In 1930 "well children" constituted 39 percent of
Aldrich's practice, but as late as 1960, Samuel Levine, president of the American

Pediatric Society, admitted that "most of us are still more comfortable with an organically sick infant than with the anxious mother of a well child."[95]

Guidance clinics' isolation from medicine was reinforced by their growing tendency to use psychologists and psychiatric social workers as therapists. Levy argued vehemently that nonmedical therapists lacked the knowledge to recognize the organic causes of many behavioral disorders.[96] Most psychiatrists agreed with Levy, which made it difficult for them to work with psychologists and social workers.[97]

An important step in bringing pediatrics and child psychiatry closer together was the establishment in 1930 of the first psychiatric clinic in a pediatric setting, the Harriet Lane Home at Johns Hopkins Hospital.[98] Under Kanner's direction, the clinic contributed significantly to pediatricians' growing interest in child psychiatry. Kanner's *Child Psychiatry* (1935), the first English-language text on child psychiatry, was based on his experience at the clinic. Similar services were offered later at many university medical schools, including Columbia, Cornell, Yale, Stanford, Minnesota, and Toronto.

In 1934 the Commonwealth Fund supported efforts to integrate pediatrics and child psychiatry at Babies' Hospital, associated with Columbia-Presbyterian Medical Center in New York City, and at Children's Hospital of Boston, the pediatric teaching hospital of Harvard Medical School.[99] Three years later it also established fellowships in child psychiatry for qualified pediatricians, enriching psychiatry more than pediatrics because most of the fellows became psychiatrists.[100] Another attempt to improve relations between pediatricians and psychiatrists was the introduction in 1936 of a regular series of round-table conferences on child psychiatry at the annual meeting of the American Academy of Pediatrics.[101]

CHILD GUIDANCE EXPORTED
TO GREAT BRITAIN

One of the boldest innovations of the second phase of the child guidance program was the Commonwealth Fund's decision to respond favorably to a request that it organize and support child guidance clinics in Great Britain. The fund invited twelve British psychiatrists and several other interested individuals to observe the work of selected guidance clinics in the United States and offered fellowships to five British social workers for training in psychiatric social work at prominent American clinics. The London Child Guidance Council was organized in 1927, and the London Child Guidance Clinic, supported by the Commonwealth Fund, opened in 1929. The fund also sponsored several clinics in other areas of Britain and supported the London clinic until 1939, seven years after it had stopped direct support of clinics in the United States [102]Eminent British psychiatrists who trained at the London clinic during the 1930s have commented on ways in which the British child guidance movement challenged both British hospital child psychiatry and psychoanalysis. John Bowlby and William Gillespie found that their work at the clinic demonstrated the importance of parents and the family context in a child's development.[103] Michael Fordham, leader of the Jungians in Britain, said that his child guidance experience persuaded him to include children in Jungian psychiatry.[104] British psychiatrist Mildred Creak also commented on the influence of child guidance psychiatry.[105]

Psychiatric social workers trained in the London clinic distinguished themselves in providing psychological counseling to servicemen and their families during World War II. Partly because of their wartime reputation, the National Education Act of 1944 mandated the establishment of child guidance clinics throughout Britain. By 1944 ninety-five guidance clinics had been established in Britain.[106]

CHILD GUIDANCE DURING THE 1930S

By 1933 the Commonwealth Fund had decided that it was "not so easy to change the child as enthusiasts have sometimes thought" and that the limitations of child guidance had become "pretty well-defined."[107] After 1932 it halted direct funding to American clinics and terminated or drastically reduced support for those services it still offered. It closed the Institute of Child Guidance, the training and research organization that it had considered most important for achieving its goals and reduced the budget of the Division of Community Clinics to $50,000 in 1932 and to $15,000 in 1938.[108] Stevenson, director of the division, resigned in 1933. It cut total appropriations for mental health programs from more than six million dollars in 1930 and 1931 to $363,000 in 1932, and approximately two hundred thousand dollars a year from 1933 to 1938.[109] The Commonwealth Fund had decided to abandon the grandiose aspirations of its early years for the more tangible and readily attainable goals of improving medical research and education.[110] In spite of the loss of funds from the Commonwealth Fund and other sponsors during the Great Depression, the American faith that solutions to social problems could be found through the psychological sciences persisted. Psychiatric clinics for children continued to increase in number throughout the 1930s, without encouragement by the Commonwealth Fund.[111] Clinics were established under many auspices, with diverse names, and for a variety of purposes.[112] Most of the older clinics supported by other philanthropies or their local communities survived the depression.

Psychiatric services often took precedence over the dire need of huge numbers of children for food, clothing, and shelter. Stevenson argued that clinics should resist taking on relief functions in order not to undermine their professional services.[113] The Children's Fund of Michigan (CFM), established in 1929 by James Couzens, invested a considerable portion of its ten-million-dollar endowment in child guidance programs and child development research at the expense of relief for Michigan's needy children clinic.[114] The Children's Center, the CFM's guidance clinic, became the largest child guidance clinic in the nation in 1933, even though Couzens himself strongly objected to funding programs that "might properly be suspended during the crisis."[115] William Norton, the clinic's director, defended it by pointing out that the Depression had doubled the number of "problem children" seeking its services. Couzens replied, "It sticks in my crop that so much money is being spent on a few children when there are so many who need food and clothing."[116]

Although psychiatric services for children continued to grow, the Depression did affect child guidance work. Privately funded clinics fared better than those with public support.[117] Several important clinics closed, including the St. Louis clinic in 1933.[118] Economic stress changed the kinds of problems brought to the clinics, and many clinics limited their services. Social agencies with stretched budgets offered less cooperation with the clinics.[119]

More than six hundred psychiatric clinics accepted children as patients by 1935, but psychiatric services for children were very unevenly distributed.[120] Fifteen states had no clinics. Guidance clinics were concentrated in cities with a population of at least 150,000. The few clinics serving children in small towns and rural areas were state clinics which accounted for 60 percent of all psychiatric clinics for children but for less than one-fourth of the total hours of psychiatric services for children. These state clinics rarely shared the objectives of private clinics. Only one-third used the child guidance team, and most of their workers were untrained in work with children [121]The Commonwealth Fund concluded that better services for small-town children depended on extending and improving state mental health programs and incorporating the child guidance viewpoint into state-financed psychiatric services.

THE LEGACY OF CHILD GUIDANCE

"If the criterion for success of a program is that it proves its worth when it is taken over and supported by the community," Levy declared, "then the Commonwealth child guidance program was one of the most successful enterprises in the history of philanthropy."[122] After the fund withdrew its support, psychiatric clinics for children multiplied, expanded, and continued to develop new services. Yet no history of the Commonwealth Fund has attempted to assess the enduring effects of its child guidance program on adult and child psychiatry, social and public policy, or on changing attitudes toward children. Its history in both the United States and Great Britain deserves systematic study. Here, it is possible only to hint at its far-reaching legacy.

The child guidance movement began by promising to solve society's gravest problems through the clinical study and treatment of children. Failing to achieve this grandiose goal, it can still claim important accomplishments. Beginning with virtually nothing, it built a foundation for today's large public and private child mental health industry and, in the process, transformed perceptions of and attitudes toward childhood, profoundly influenced American, British, and European psychiatry, and helped to reverse the flow of psychiatric influence between Europe and America.[123]

CONTRIBUTIONS OF CHILD GUIDANCE
TO CHILD AND ADULT PSYCHIATRY

The Commonwealth Fund mental health programs made possible, for the first time, the clinical study of large numbers of "normal" children exhibiting a wide range of mild behavioral and emotional disorders. Direct observation of normal children reversed the approach of adult psychiatry, which drew conclusions about the normal from observations of the abnormal, and about children from information about adults. Experience in the clinics demonstrated that it was one thing to trace adult problems back to childhood but quite another to identify children who might become emotionally disturbed adults.

The concept of multiple causation, central to child guidance work, was incompatible with the organic view of mental illness in academic adult psychiatry. The approach of the child guidance team was a "corrective of the limitation imposed on case studies by the pursuit of the single etiological agent, like the specific organism in contagious disease."[124] No other psychiatric program in the world attempted multidisciplinary exploration of the causes of mental illness. The new child psychiatry that began to emerge in the guidance clinics was not an offshoot of adult psychiatry but a merger of many disciplines. The collaborative efforts of the clinic team profoundly changed the attitudes and approach of each of its members. The fund observed that "the psychiatrist has broken away from his previous preoccupation with mental disease. The psychologist has come out of the academic laboratory and moderated his sometimes indiscriminate enthusiasm for psychometric diagnosis. The psychiatric social worker has found a wider field than the mental hospital where her profession had its rise." [125]

The clinics' attention to intrafamily relationships yielded a tremendous amount of data on this virtually unexplored area, a contribution by parents and children as well as professionals. As Allen noted, "Child psychiatry has not developed in a vacuum of applied theory." [126] "Epoch making," Kanner wrote, was the way in which American child psychiatry forced adult psychiatry to take into account the powerful influence of interpersonal relations.[127] Through its emphasis on the external forces that shape a child's attitudes and behavior, American child psychiatry challenged, complemented, and broadened traditional British and European psychiatry and psychoanalysis.[128]

NEW WAYS OF THINKING ABOUT CHILDREN
AND THEIR PROBLEMS

The child guidance approach was rooted in the humanitarian view of children and their special needs that emerged during the Progressive era and gained momentum during the 1920s. Child guidance work, in turn, influenced, enriched, and expanded the attitudes that gave rise to it. It contributed to the discovery and documentation of the uniqueness of childhood and to the perception of children as feeling individuals, capable of sorrow, grief, depression, confusion, and a wide range of other emotions that formerly had been unrecognized or ignored. It influenced many to try to understand and help rather than to judge and punish misbehaving children. Noel Hunnybun, one of the five British social workers trained in child guidance clinics in the United States, described how a child guidance psychiatrist had caused her to change her approach to "problem children." When she complained to the psychiatrist that a little boy who lied should be rebuked, he suggested that it might be more useful to think about why the child had lied. "A very fundamental thing happened," she said, "when we in Britain were able to turn away from holy thoughts to a broader view."[129] According to Stevenson and Smith, the nonjudgmental premises of child guidance work and its methods generated genuine excitement, teaching many American families, schools, and social agencies to "substitute a flexible objectivity for moral rigidity" and look beyond children's troublesome behavior for hidden desires, emotional conflicts, cultural deprivation, or other circumstances that might have been responsible.[130]

Child guidance and related mental hygiene programs were successful in spreading a new view of children partly because they appealed to a receptive public and partly because they reached so many channels of influence. Guidance professionals worked with courts, public schools, colleges and universities, medical schools, private and state hospitals, private and public welfare agencies, public health departments, and private physicians and communicated with probation officers, judges, teachers, pediatricians and other doctors, nurses, social workers, and other child care practitioners. The child guidance point of view also was spread by many who received child guidance training but chose to work outside the clinics. The mass exodus during the 1930s of psychiatric social workers into family and children's welfare and public relief agencies was especially important in spreading the child guidance gospel.[131]

Mental hygiene movements used the popular media to call attention to children's emotional lives. Celia Stendler found that descriptions of the mental hygiene approach to child rearing first appeared in American women's magazines in the 1930s. Their authors tended to discuss emotional problems of adjustment rather than moral problems, many of them emphasizing that aberrant behavior requires investigation of its causes and understanding of children's needs.[132] Commonwealth Fund publications that provided clinic case stories in fictional form were widely used by parent educators and cited in newspapers and magazines.[133] In the 1940s Joe Musial adapted "Blondie" comic strips into a booklet to illustrate mental hygiene principles.[134]

The addition of guidance counselors to school staffs brought school systems into the mental health orbit. Research on "school phobias," beginning in 1941, contributed to an understanding of the reasons underlying children's fears of school, and helped teachers and parents to a more sympathetic view of truants and children reluctant to attend school.[135] Sol Cohen asserted: "Here in the field of developing 'consciousness' of the community as to the value of mental hygiene, especially in the public schools, is the place to look for the real significance of the Commonwealth Fund's program."[136]

Before the 1930s reports on patients in children's hospitals contained comments by parents, other relatives, and social workers, but never by the children themselves.[137] Oblivious or indifferent to the child's feelings, one physician told the mother of an eleven-year-old girl, in the child's presence, that her daughter would be blind within the year.[138] Aware of such insensitivity to children, Bernard Rosenblatt wrote in 1971: "Many adults speak to each other in the presence of children as if children could not hear or understand. Elsewhere, I wrote: 'We might find it hard to understand which has been the more important contribution: the discovery of the unconscious in the adult or the discovery of consciousness in the young child.'[139] I meant by this to convey that a great good was done for children when it became possible to attend to their mental lives. It was not only a scientific contribution, making possible a new field of study, but a charitable one which allowed the world to look upon children as fully human beings."[140]

Chapter 13 The Children's Bureau under Grace Abbott: Uphill All the Way

"Uphill all the way" was Grace Abbott's apt summary of her thirteen years as second chief of the Children's Bureau. Julia Lathrop, the first chief of the bureau, had been more fortunate. Her administration rode and skillfully exploited the high wave of Progressive social reform that lasted until shortly after the Armistice.[1]

Abbott operated in a radically different political, economic, and social environment. When she assumed office in August 1921, the bureau and its goals faced intense hostility. The bitter dispute over the proposed membership of the United States in the League of Nations, the Bolshevik revolution, and the Red Scare of 1919 reversed the impulse toward social reform that had characterized the Progressive era. As William Leuchtenberg observed, these events "reinforced the conviction that evil came from outside America and from alien sources within, and evil became identified with groups demanding change."[2] Many perceived pacifists as dangerous radicals, and Abbott was a pacifist, as were Jane Addams and many other settlement workers who had led the campaign to found the bureau. Although not a pacifist, Lathrop too was vilified as a Bolshevik, and the bureau was attacked as a communist organization.[3]

The presence of Republicans in the White House from 1921 to 1933 both reflected and encouraged the rebellion against Progressivism. The conservative belief that social problems should be solved by private rather than public agencies hampered the efforts of the Children's Bureau to expand and even to preserve the existing responsibility of the federal government for child welfare. Prosperity during the 1920s created optimism that poverty would soon be overcome by private enterprise, diverted attention from the poor, and undermined Lathrop's and Abbott's claim that poverty was the main cause of children's problems. The popularity of the "new psychology," with its emphasis on reconstruction of the individual rather than improvement of the social environment, gave credence to the argument that it was necessary to "take the poverty out of people as well as to take the people out of poverty."[4]

Children's Bureau programs based on the Sheppard-Towner Maternal and Infancy Protection Act of 1921, and the bureau's efforts to reduce child labor and protect working children, were attacked as communist-inspired. In *The Second Twenty Years at Hull-House,* Jane Addams described the decline of the fervor for social reform and how it split the social work movement during the postwar decade.[5] Many social workers, she wrote, "avoided any identification with the phraseology of reform" and turned from efforts to improve the social environment to psychological solutions to human problems.[6] Social casework replaced settlement work as the social worker's dominant activity.[7]

As we have seen, in the 1920s participants in the child development and child guidance movements shifted their attention from poor to middle-class children. Interest in social survey research declined as these two new disciplines focused on individual middle-class children rather than on populations of children and the impact of the social environment on their development.

Congress reduced the bureau's appropriations repeatedly and allowed the Sheppard-Towner Act to expire in 1929, thereby stripping the bureau of the large staff that had administered the act. The states failed to ratify a child labor amendment to the constitution that the bureau had vigorously supported. During the 1930 White House Conference for Child Health and Protection (WHC), the bureau came perilously close to having its research and reporting responsibilities for child and maternal health transferred to the United States Public Health Service. Stripped of its administrative responsibilities, the Children's Bureau was limited by the end of the decade to the investigating and reporting functions of its first five years.[8]

In spite of all the efforts to undermine the goals and methods of prewar social reform, Abbott and her staff at the Children's Bureau clung tenaciously to their Progressive heritage and strove to build on the achievements of the Lath-rop administration. Even though they were swimming against the tide until Franklin Delano Roosevelt entered the White House, they succeeded in many ways. With the deepening of the Depression and the coming of the New Deal, the bureau was in a better position to make its case for federal assistance to the poor and the unemployed. The results of its research during the 1920s and early 1930s provided a valuable basis for many New Deal programs, and the bureau's contributions to the Social Security Act of 1935 restored some of the losses it had sustained during the 1920s. The programs for mothers and children estab-lished by the Social Security Act, however, did not fulfill the original goals of the bureau, and the provisions for aid to dependent children were not at all what the bureau had recommended. Renewed attempts to diminish the bureau by transferring some of its responsibilities to other agencies continued and eventually succeeded. By 1935 the glory days of the Children's Bureau had ended.[9]

GRACE ABBOTT

Julia Lathrop and the many colleagues who supported her preference for Grace Abbott as her successor could not have made a better choice. Conditioned by both family background and professional training to support social reform, Abbott battled fiercely for the bureau's original goals. Born in Grand Island, Nebraska, in 1879, she cherished memories of her prairie childhood.[10] Both her father, a prosperous lawyer, and her mother, a fervent suffragist, pursued re-form and service activities. Throughout her life, Grace remained close to her sister Edith, two years her senior, who became a leader in the field of social work and dean of the University of Chicago School of Social Service Administration. Observing that she was "born with an interest in law and politics," Grace fol-lowed Edith to Chicago in 1907 to pursue graduate studies in political sci-ence.[11] Sophonisba Breckinridge was so impressed by Grace that she recom-mended her for a part-time position with the Immigrants' Protective League, and Abbott was appointed its director even before she had earned her master's degree. Having completed her degree requirements, Grace decided that she was more interested in improving the plight of immigrants than in continuing graduate study.[12]

Abbott had great respect for the "new immigration." She worked energeti-cally and effectively to protect foreign-born Americans, improve their working conditions, and block the use of a literacy test to restrict immigration. Her interest in social legislation to aid immigrants led her into the pioneer field of public administration, in which she demonstrated extraordinary talent. Her interest in immigrant children led her to investigations of child labor, widows' pensions, midwife training, juvenile delinquency, and juvenile courts that proved to be excellent preparation for her work in the Children's Bureau.[13]

Joining Hull House in 1908, the Abbott sisters soon became part of its inner circle and formed close friendships with Jane Addams, Julia Lathrop, and Florence Kelley. After Lathrop became chief of the Children's Bureau, she tried to persuade Grace to join its staff but was unsuccessful until 1917, when Grace became director of the bureau's new child labor division, created to administer the first federal child labor law. Abbott accepted because "this was not just research" but an opportunity to solve challenging problems in public administration.[14]

The child labor law was declared unconstitutional only nine months later, but even this short experience provided Abbott with an opportunity to pioneer in working out difficult problems in federal-state relations.[15] She remained with the bureau until 1919, directing investigations of child labor and serving as secretary of the White House Conference on Child Welfare Standards in 1919. Having returned happily to Chicago and her position at the Immigrants' Protective League in 1919, she left that post somewhat reluctantly in 1921 to become chief of the Children's Bureau at age forty-two.[16] Two years later, the National Conference of Social Work elected her president.

Abbott shared Lathrop's convictions about the causes of and remedies for children's problems, but her style was different. Lathrop was conciliatory in the face of opposition; Grace, often confrontational. She was "more outspoken" than Lathrop, sometimes even to the point of "abruptness."[17] Edith Abbott said that Grace disliked "pussyfooters" and described her as tenacious and uncompromising.[18] An exceptionally forceful leader, Grace excelled in preparing legislative remedies, pushing for their enactment, and implementing their administration. Edith was the scholar, Costin comments, but Grace "took the initiative in translating knowledge into action."[19] Supreme Court justice Felix Frankfurter declared that "the manner in which Grace Abbott translated the blueprints of social policies into effective operating institutions for the benefit of society at large made her work, in every true sense of the phrase, that of social invention."[20]

Grace Abbott departed from Lathrop in her views on the responsibility of government for the well-being of children. Lathrop was careful to reassure her audiences that the Children's Bureau had no intention of usurping the primary responsibilities of parents, private philanthropy, and local government. At a time when the bureau was under attack as a communist spearhead, Abbott boldly devoted her presidential address at the 1923 meeting of the National Conference of Social Work to the case for "Public Protection of Children," leaving no doubt that, by "public," she meant primarily state and federal government. "Local responsibility," she said, "has frequently furnished the explanation of neglect and of shameful incompetence and inefficiency."[21]

THE SHEPPARD-TOWNER ACT, 1921–1929

In order to secure passage of the Children's Bureau Act of 1912, its supporters had accepted sweeping limitations on the bureau's powers. It was to confine itself to research and reporting and to have no administrative, executive or legislative functions. These restrictions were ignored when the bureau was assigned responsibility for administering the Child Labor Act of 1916, for which it received an additional appropriation of $50,000. The Bureau had led the movement for what became the Sheppard-Towner Maternity and Infant Protection Act of 1921, which it was asked to administer. Abbott had helped Lathrop shape the programs created by the act. Now she had the satisfaction of administering a program with an initial annual appropriation of $1,240,000, and pioneering cooperative arrangements between the federal government and the states. In contrast to a brief nine months of administering the child labor law of 1917, she administered the Sheppard-Towner Act for seven years.[22]

Before receiving federal grants, the states had to pass enabling legislation, but once the grants were approved, they had full control of their use. Abbott quickly achieved her first task, securing the cooperation of the states. Forty-one states had joined the program by 1922, and, in the end, only Massachusetts, Connecticut, and Illinois refused federal aid.[23] In 1925 alone, the participating states established 561 prenatal and child health centers. Thirty-one states established midwife programs, most of which focused on training and licensing.[24] Abbott had demonstrated her interest in midwife training in Chicago as early as 1915 and had expanded the investigations of midwife training begun by Lathrop.[25]

Sheppard-Towner had passed Congress by a landslide, and the initial public response to its programs was enthusiastic. Monthly reports to the Children's Bureau and letters of appreciation from state administrators, lay participants, and hundreds of mothers all testified to the program's success. The Supreme Court dismissed two suits against the act in 1922, one brought by the Commonwealth of Massachusetts, the other by a Massachusetts woman. An estimated 3,500 lay volunteers helped the bureau carry out Sheppard-Towner's maternal and child health programs.[26] Members of local Parent Teacher's Associations assisted Sheppard-Towner agents in forty-two states. Other volunteers were drawn from women's organizations as diverse as the States' Federation of Colored Women's Clubs, the Daughters of the American Revolution, and the League of Women Voters. By 1926 state maternal and child health programs employed 50 full-time physicians and 812 nurses. An additional 2,200 physicians and 300 nurses also participated. During its seven years Sheppard-Towner workers held over 180,000 child and maternal health conferences, established almost 3,000 prenatal centers, made more than 3 million home visits, and distributed over 22 million pieces of literature. The Bureau reported that Sheppard-Towner programs served more than 400,000 babies and 7000,000 expectant mothers between 1924 and 1929.[27]

One of the main purposes of the Sheppard-Towner Act was to make health education and medical care available in rural areas, especially in the South and West. Although white farm wives received most of the benefits, Sheppard-Towner programs also succeeded in reaching African-Americans, Hispanics, and Native Americans, who previously had been virtually ignored by public health workers.[28]

Most regarded Sheppard-Towner as a permanent program, but its funding provisions were subject to renewal by July 30, 1927. When the campaign for renewal began in 1926, public opinion appeared to be less favorable to the program than it had been earlier. Those who had opposed the bill in 1921 had gained support and vigorously opposed its extension. Right-wing patriotic groups, possibly emboldened by the stalled child labor amendment, used rhetoric even more vitriolic than before to once again claim that Sheppard-Towner had been inspired by communists. As early as 1922, the American Medical Association (AMA) had tried to persuade physicians that they, rather than public agencies, should offer advisory and preventive services to mothers and children. Now it initiated a vigorous campaign to defeat renewal of the act. Some previous supporters—including many pediatricians and the Daughters of the American Revolution—joined the opposition, as did the Catholic Church, which had been neutral in 1921. Congress had an even greater number of fiscal conservatives among its members in 1927 than in 1921 and no longer feared that women would vote as a bloc.[29] President Calvin Coolidge, preaching that the least government is the best, opposed renewal. The renewal bill passed the House by a vote of 218 to 44 but was tied up in the Senate for eight months. Hoping that a more favorable attitude would emerge later, the Children's Bureau and the act's other supporters broke the stalemate in 1927 by agreeing to an amendment automatically repealing Sheppard-Towner in 1929, after a two-year extension.[30]

The hopes of Sheppard-Towner supporters were dashed. President Hoover refused to back legislation to extend the act until after the 1930 White House Conference for Child Health and Protection, and he then urged that Sheppard-Towner programs be financed as much as possible by private funds. Congress allowed the act to expire in 1929, and attempts during the early 1930s to introduce new maternal and child health legislation failed. The "stunning victory" for the women's movement, for Progressive social reformers, and for the Children's Bureau had been followed by crushing defeat.[31]

Partly because of the Depression, only sixteen states appropriated enough money to continue former Sheppard-Towner programs as they had functioned under the act, and several states dropped their programs altogether. By 1934 fourteen states each were allocating less than three thousand dollars to maternal and child health care programs.[32]

The Sheppard-Towner Act and its programs have been the subject of more scholarly literature than any other program undertaken by the early Children's Bureau. The bureau's campaigns for maternal and child health and the later Sheppard-Towner programs achieved a significant reduction of infant mortality and a slight reduction of maternal mortality between 1912 and 1929. Comprehensive data for the whole period are not available. The number of states requiring birth registration grew from twenty-seven in 1921 to forty-five in 1929, largely due to the efforts of Sheppard-Towner workers. Because many states that only began to collect data during this period had relatively high maternal and infant death rates, the available statistics undoubtedly underestimate the gains achieved by Sheppard-Towner programs. The Children's Bureau claimed that Sheppard-Towner funds saved the lives of sixty thousand babies and that infant deaths due to gastrointestinal diseases decreased by 47 percent between 1921 and 1929, due in large part to the education of mothers about the importance of pure water and milk. It is beyond dispute that Children's Bureau efforts contributed significantly to the education of mothers about prenatal, infant, and child care and succeeded in making medical care more widely available to mothers and children.[33]

The repeal of Sheppard-Towner marked a shift from the public to the private sector in maternal and child preventive health services.[34] Pediatrician Arthur H. Parmelee, Jr., has pointed out that the demand created by public health programs for the care of lower-class well children trickled up, stimulating middle-and upper-class mothers to demand preventive care from private physicians.[35] Sheppard-Towner programs gave participating physicians experience in preventive care at the very time that both parents and organized medicine were urging them to offer such services. Pediatricians were also motivated to find ways to expand their practices by fear that their specialty might not survive the Depression.[36]

The demise of Sheppard-Towner reflected and accelerated the capture by male medical specialists of the kinds of medical care that had been provided mainly by women. In 1922 all but three of the state directors of Sheppard-Towner programs were women physicians; by 1939 three-quarters of the doctors administering maternal and child health programs were men. The public health nurse lost her independence and some of her authority as she was subordinated to male physicians.[37]

Ironically, the Children's Bureau itself contributed to the shift in control of infant and maternal medical care from women physicians, public health nurses, and social workers to male physicians. From 1921 to 1929 the bureau found it necessary not only to cooperate with but often to defer to male physicians in administering Sheppard-Towner programs. State agencies frequently refused to permit a community to provide specific maternal and child health services without the endorsement of its medical society, and the bureau also had to rely on local physicians to conduct health examinations and to participate in health conferences. "Having encouraged adoption of preventive health care by private physicians and thus the expansion of medicine's own domain," Richard Meckel observed, the bureau "now faced the increasingly accurate charge that it was intruding on that domain."[38] To avoid such charges, the bureau was careful to distinguish between preventive care and medical care.[39] Perhaps unavoidably, the Children's Bureau became a victim of the prevailing trend toward denigration of the knowledge and skill of female care providers and veneration of male experts This attitude soon was reflected in the bureau's childcare publications.

REPORTING

The act founding the bureau charged it with investigating and reporting to the American people "about all matters pertaining to child life in the United States." In spite of the bureau's heavy new administrative burden, Abbott did not neglect these functions. During her administration, the bureau issued 130 new publications based on both its own and others' research. It also made effective use of exhibits and the new media of radio and motion pictures. For several years Abbott gave weekly radio talks on child welfare subjects, and the bureau was among the most active proponents of films for parent education and promotion of child health and welfare.[40]

Lathrop had interpreted the reporting function to include educating and advising parents, as well as those responsible for children's programs. Abbott continued and expanded the bureau's publications for parents but changed their character significantly. Under Lathrop, the bureau's child-rearing literature was written by Mrs. Max West, a mother. Under Abbott, the responsibility was delegated to pediatrician Martha Eliot, director of the bureau's Division of Maternal and Child Health, and a committee of medical specialists. Eliot introduced a new emphasis on physical health—particularly nutrition, prevention of rickets, posture, and the physical growth and development of preschool children. The popularity of the mental health movement was reflected in the number of publications devoted to psychological care.[41]

Eliot wrote the 1929 edition of *Infant Care*, first published in 1914. *Child Care*, first published in 1922, was superseded by *The Child from One to Six* in 1932. The view of the mother as equal partner with the doctor, insisted upon in early editions of *Prenatal Care* (1913) and *Infant Care*, was absent from the new literature, which emphasized the helplessness of even the most educated mother in the face of new scientific discoveries and technological change. Instead of encouraging the mother to rely on her own knowledge, experience, and common sense, the new literature, like the work of L. Emmett Holt, urged her to look to the experts. The 1933 edition of *Infant Care* declared, "The care of a baby is a great responsibility but it can be carried out successfully if the parents regularly seek the advice of a physician trained in the care of infants. . . . The baby should not be experimented upon with first one mode of care and then another, in accordance with various opinions offered. The doctor should be the mother's guide, and this bulletin is intended to help her carry out his orders intelligently."[42] President Hoover emphasized the same message: "Our country has a vast majority of competent mothers but what we are concerned with here are things that are beyond her power. . . . She cannot count the bacteria in the milk; she cannot detect the typhoid which comes from the faucet, or the mumps that pass around the playground. . . . The questions of child health and protection are a complicated problem requiring much learning and much action."[43]

PSYCHOLOGICAL GUIDANCE

Convinced that parents needed guidance on the psychological as well as the physical care of children, Abbott chose neuropsychiatrist Douglas Thom, founder of the preschool habit clinics, to be the sole author of the bureau's psychological childcare literature. The bureau sponsored a demonstration of one of Thom's habit clinics for the preschool child and then asked him to write a booklet on their organization and practical value.[44] It published a first edition of Thom's *Child Management* in 1925 and revised editions until 1937. Abbott wrote the introduction for Thom's *Everyday Problems of Everyday Children* and invited him to supervise the preparation of the bureau's childcare pamphlet for the 1930 White House Conference on Child Health and Protection, "*Are You Training Your Child to Be Happy? Lesson Material in Child Management.*"[45] Although Thom had established his reputation as a specialist on the preschool child, the bureau also asked him to write *Guiding the Adolescent,* a 94-page pamphlet published in 1933 and reissued in 1937. A more suitable choice could have been Leta Hollingworth, author of the highly praised *Psychology of the Adolescent.*[46]

Apparently concurring in John B. Watson's belief that "children are made not born," Thom made parents almost totally responsible for their children's behavior.[47] "The home," he declared, "is the workshop which unfortunately spoils much good material. The parents . . . control the destiny of their child."[48] Thom, like other behaviorists, viewed children as monuments to their parents' success or failure, assuming that any mistake parents made could lead to dire consequences: "The number of queer, peculiar, eccentric, unhappy, maladjusted adults in any generation that will be turned out from infants of that generation will depend to a very large extent upon the wisdom their parents have exercised."[49] The parents' "wisdom," he and other experts believed, must come from their mastery of scientific child-rearing advice.

A member of the Committee on Growth and Development of the 1930 WHC, Thom wrote the habit section of the committee's report, which included frightening examples of parents' potential for ruining a child's future. "Satisfying a baby's momentary demands," he warned, "is the foundation of bad habits." If indulgence of the child is continued, at three years of age he will "inevitably" accumulate faulty habits, develop severe eating and sleeping problems, and make unreasonable demands on his parents. By five years of age, such a child "would seem more fit for a reform school than for kindergarten."[50]

During the 1930s psychiatrists and psychologists began to add to the protests of pediatricians who had criticized psychological advice recommended at the

1930 WHC. Parent-blaming literature of the 1920s and 1930s provoked a coun-terattack in later decades from professionals dismayed by mounting evidence of parental fear, guilt and confusion, including *In Defense of Mother: How to Bring Up Children in Spite of the More Zealous Psychologists* by Leo Kanner, *Don't Be Afraid of Your Child: A Guide for Perplexed Parents* by Hilda Bruch, and, *Your Child Is a Person: An Approach to Parenthood Without Guilt* by Stella Chess et al.[51]

Child guidance psychiatrist Hilda Bruch pointed out the dilemma created for parents by experts, who told them that they were all-powerful, that even the most innocent-appearing act or carelessly spoken word might damage a child's future happiness, and who also told them not to do anything without consult-ing the experts.

The focus on parents as the most powerful influence in children's lives, to-gether with the emphasis on their need to consult experts, undermined Lath-rop's and Abbott's argument that economically secure parents, possessed of some basic information about childcare, were fully capable of rearing happy, healthy children. Continued bureau investigations of social and economic con-ditions that prevented healthy development were consistent with this view. Af-ter 1925, however, much of the bureau's child-rearing advice seemed more in ac-cord with President Hoover's belief that the major cause of children's problems was not poverty but parental ignorance.

Given the overwhelming influence of behaviorism in the 1920s and the bu-reau's close ties to the mental hygiene movement, it is easy to understand Ab-bott's choice of Thom in 1925. However, her continued reliance on him after 1939 as the exclusive spokesman for the bureau on psychological guidance of children is puzzling. By then, as we have seen, many child guidance profession-als had rejected behaviorism and its simplistic, mechanistic solutions in favor of a more dynamic approach that encouraged children to become active partici-pants in their own development. Gesell was telling this to parents as early as 1925 in *Mental Growth of the Preschool Child.* In the 1930 WHC Section on Growth and Development that included Thom's material on habit training, its chair, Kenneth D. Blackfan, offered advice that reflected the newer develop-mental approach: "Secure for each child the best environment for that child. Study each child as a lock, unique in its mechanism; and then devise the special key that will fit that lock, so will the door of opportunity be thrown open, as widely as constitution permits, for each child to develop under individual training his individual innate capacities."[52]

Between 1925 and 1934, private organizations bought more than four hun-dred thousand copies of Thom's *Child Management* for distribution to parents.

The additional number of free copies the bureau distributed is not known, nor is the extent of the distribution of other pamphlets that Thom supervised or wrote.[53] Although dynamic psychiatrists and developmentalists may have offered advice often no better than Thom's, they were more in step with new approaches to child rearing based on new research. Some of their publications could have offered alternatives to habit training to millions of parents who relied on Children's Bureau literature for help in coping with their children's emotional problems. The bureau's failure to modernize or diversify its advice on psychological guidance is difficult to understand or condone.

Under Abbott, the content of the child-rearing literature was incompatible not only with trends in child development and child guidance, but also with Lathrop's proclamation that children are entitled to all the rights that democracy promises to adults. To ensure these rights, she said, was one of the main reasons for the establishment of the Children's Bureau. Abbott agreed, and frequently quoted Lathrop on children's entitlements. The main thrust of Thom's habit training, however, was not to respect children's rights but rather to mold children to conform to parental and community standards. Lathrop declared that children were not their parents' property; Thom implied that they were.

RESEARCH, 1921–1929

Although the bureau's childcare literature changed substantially under Abbott's direction, its research program clung tenaciously to the methodology and goals of the Progressive tradition. Before joining the Children's Bureau, Abbott had expressed her impatience with "just research" because she was more interested in achieving reforms suggested by research than in the gathering of information. She nevertheless placed great value on the need for investigations disclosing social and economic conditions harmful to children and families in order to arouse the public to necessary action and provide an objective basis for social reform. Abbott set out to complete and expand the investigations Lathrop had begun and to venture into new areas. She succeeded on both counts. The bureau undertook more than one hundred investigations during her administration in forty-four states, the District of Columbia, and Puerto Rico, many of them alert responses to new problems caused by changing conditions.[54]

Unemployment

In her first year as chief, Abbott seized the opportunity presented by a brief industrial recession to investigate the effects of unemployment on families and children in two industrial cities, one in New England, the other in the Midwest. The study showed that families made up for the lost wages of the unemployed in many ways. Mothers left home and children left school in order to earn money. Families depleted their savings and accepted aid from relatives and from private and public relief agencies. Most families, however, endured great hardship during the brief recession. Over four-fifths went into debt for food, rent, fuel, medical care, and other necessities. Some lost their homes.[55]

Reporting the results of the investigation to the National Conference of Social Work in 1922, Abbott reiterated a point often made by Lathrop: "Poverty is the root of children's problems; if parents are miserable so are their children. . . . We all know that the problem of unemployment is in the last analysis a child welfare problem. A large part of the burden of this unemployment has fallen not on industry, not on the community, but on the backs of little children."[56] Along with studies of public aid to mothers with dependent children, the unemployment study helped prepare the bureau for the research it would undertake during the Great Depression of the 1930s.[57]

Maternal and Child Health

The bureau also continued to study maternal and infant mortality and published the final report of the infant mortality study in eight cities that it had begun in 1914.[58] It completed the birth registration study in 1933.[59] Probably in response to the decision to terminate the Sheppard-Towner Act, the bureau launched an important investigation of maternal and neonatal mortality in 1927.[60]

Child Labor

As important to Abbott as the fight for Sheppard-Towner were the efforts during the 1920s and early 1930s to pass a child labor amendment to the Constitution. As we have seen, the Children's Bureau was relieved of the responsibility for administering the first federal child labor law when it was declared unconstitutional in 1918. A second child labor law, which assigned administrative responsibility to the Department of the Interior, was declared unconstitutional in 1922.[61] Soon thereafter, the National Child Labor Committee, with the concurrence of the Children's Bureau, began a campaign for a child labor amendment to the constitution.[62]

Acting on her belief that research is a necessary prelude to action, Abbott launched a new series of investigations to expose the harrowing conditions in which many children worked and to determine scientifically what occupations should be forbidden for children. Between 1921 and 1933, the bureau issued thirty-one child labor reports. It also investigated poor enforcement of state child labor laws. Since most working children were employed in agriculture, in home industries in tenements, and in street trades, the bureau focused on these areas, but it also looked at children in occupations that were more likely than others to lead to accidents or disease. Abbott reported in 1923 that child labor laws in only thirteen states met standards set by the repealed federal statutes. The bureau also studied the amount and quality of vocational education.[63]

Although child labor was increasing, the campaign for the child labor amendment made little progress. Conservatives attacked the proposed amendment as communist-inspired, and by 1931 it had been ratified by only six states. Abbott wrote in 1939 that the history of the amendment, its authors, and its supporters had been so misrepresented that it seemed doomed to defeat.[64] Like adult workers, employed children were discharged in large numbers when the Depression hit, but a children's strike in a Western Pennsylvania factory in 1933 called attention to a counter-movement to replace adult workers with low-cost child labor. The resulting publicity contributed to an unexpected revival of interest in the amendment, and in 1933 President Franklin D. Roosevelt urged its ratification. By 1938 twenty-eight states had ratified the amendment, all but Kentucky in the North. Although the amendment was never ratified by enough states to be adopted, Abbott believed that the child labor campaigns "did much to convert the general public to the necessity of protecting children against premature employment and to raise the legal standard of the state laws."[65] In 1938, when the Fair Labor Standards Act was passed, the bureau was asked to administer its child labor provisions. Walter Trattner, historian of the child labor movement, concluded that, although not a substitute for the child labor amendment, the act was an important step in the right direction.[66]

Delinquency

The bureau also continued to investigate the whole range of problems connected with child dependency, neglect, and delinquency. Several of its studies dealt with juvenile courts. In cooperation with the National Probation Association (NPA), the bureau published a formal set of standards for juvenile courts in 1923 that reflected the importance of the new psychology but limited the psychologist's role to provision of diagnostic service.[67]

The bureau's research on juvenile courts led Abbott to change her view of the court as the best institution to help protect children in trouble with the law.[68] Along with Katherine Lenroot and Emma Lundberg, authors of a detailed study of ten model juvenile courts, Abbott was disappointed with the findings.[69] "In general," the report concluded, "the resources at the disposal of the court . . . did not fit together to form a complete community program for the care of delinquent children."

As we have seen, during the late 1920s child guidance professionals were beginning to move away from the belief that delinquency is caused by poor social conditions and toward the view that it is caused by psychological maladjustment that requires treatment by psychiatrists or psychiatric caseworkers. Lathrop and Lundberg had both been influenced by their service on advisory committees to the Commonwealth Fund, sponsor of the child guidance programs of the 1920s. Their beliefs about the importance of psychiatry, the new enthusiasm of social work for postwar psychiatry, and Abbott's disenchantment with the juvenile courts all influenced her to become increasingly committed to psychiatrically oriented treatment of serious behavior problems in children.[70]

As the Children's Bureau began to express a preference for psychiatric casework treatment for juvenile offenders, it also promoted the development of state and local child welfare departments. Many of these new departments supplemented and sometimes supplanted the work of the juvenile courts. By 1930 the bureau was publicizing its preference for treatment of delinquents in agencies other than the courts, such as child guidance clinics, truancy departments, and other community services.[71] "It is clear after thirty years of experience," Abbott wrote shortly before she resigned from the bureau, "that we cannot expect the juvenile courts as now organized to prevent delinquency." They are "ill-equipped to individualize and treat 90 percent of the cases coming before them."[72] Marguerite Rosenthal, who studied the bureau's changing attitudes toward juvenile courts from 1912 to 1940, concluded that "in promoting the new child welfare system while not having the authority to abolish the old court structure, the bureau set the stage for the growth of a dual and often muddled system of governmental intervention into the lives of delinquent (and dependent) children, a system which continues to this day."[73]

Legal Issues Concerning Children

Research undertaken or sponsored by the Children's Bureau reflected Abbott's eagerness to see the passage and better enforcement of laws dealing with children. The bureau investigated legal issues in a wide variety of areas related to child health and welfare, including, in addition to child labor, the indenture and interstate placement of dependent children, the administration of mother's aid, adoption, divorce and child support, child abuse, and sex offenses against children. In 1923, after a ten-year effort, it proposed a model illegitimacy statute that became the basis for legislation in several states. Abbott's goal was to continue to explore ways in which the legal system could assure that illegitimate children enjoyed the same rights as other children and were protected from the stigma of illegitimacy. The bureau also developed special services for unwed mothers.[74]

After World War I, new problems for which children required service became evident. Fewer children than in earlier decades were left without care because of the death of parents, but many more were affected by divorce, desertion, illegitimacy, and mothers' employment. Since more dependent children were being placed in foster homes rather than orphanages, the bureau conducted several studies of foster-home placement.[75] In the 1920s social agencies were just beginning to assume responsibility for arranging and supervising adoptions, but in 1924 the bureau not only published a report on adoption laws throughout the United States, but issued guidelines for state laws to protect adopted children's rights.[76] It also published a history of adoption and a pamphlet on the subject by Arnold Gesell.[77] In a two-part study, the bureau investigated the relationship between child welfare and the employment of mothers.[78] These and other studies placed the bureau in the vanguard of research on new problems affecting children.

Methodology: The Bureau and Child Development Research

During the 1920s reformers and scholars often denigrated the kinds of social survey research that had been so popular during the Progressive era and that the Children's Bureau continued to pursue. Insisting that the bureau's sociological research was as scientific and as valuable as any other type of child study, Abbott had nothing but "scorn" for certain representatives of the social science group "who tried to tell the world that social research was not scientific if its objective was to find a remedy for harmful conditions." She refused to permit the bureau to experiment with other research methods.[79]

Many social reformers tried to interest the bureau in a broader approach to child study, foremost among them Lawrence K. Frank, administrator of the Laura Spelman Rockefeller Memorial programs for child study. Frank was eager to persuade Abbott and others in federal agencies concerned with children to undertake child development research. He asked Louise Stanley, director of the Bureau of Home Economics in the Department of Agriculture, to try to interest Abbott and another federal official in collaborating on a proposal to create a nursery school laboratory in Washington, D.C., for research on child development and parent education. He promised that the memorial would provide twenty-five thousand dollars a year for three years for the research laboratory, plus five thousand dollars for equipment.[80] Abbott did not help to prepare the proposal that led the LSRM to establish the Washington Child Research Center in 1926. She did agree to serve on its board of directors, but according to board member Lois Meek Stolz, Abbott attended only a few meetings at which she "sat, never said a word unless it was to make a negative comment, then left," nor did she permit any member of her staff to participate in the center's research.[81]

Two future chiefs of the bureau offered explanations for her antagonism to the research center. Eliot reported that Abbott simply was not interested in the scientific study of human development.[82] Helen Woolley, a Children's Bureau consultant, thought Abbott's fears that children might be harmed by the research were "groundless."[83] The center was dissolved as a research laboratory within a few years, but it continued to function as a nursery school. Stanley was the only government official who published research undertaken at the center.[84]

THE 1930 WHITE HOUSE CONFERENCE
AND THE CHILDREN'S BUREAU DURING
THE DEPRESSION

"Not long after President Hoover's inauguration," Edith Abbott wrote, "Grace began to understand that he had his own plans for a child welfare conference and that he did not want any suggestions from her, the Children's Bureau, or the Labor Department in preparing the plan." President Wilson had appointed Abbott secretary of the second White House Conference for children in 1919, but her role at the 1930 White House Conference for Child Health and Protection was reduced to being one of twenty-three members of its planning committee.[85] Protests that the public expected more of the Children's Bureau led to an invitation to Abbott to serve as secretary of the executive committee of the planning committee, which turned out to be meaningless because the executive committee did not function as such.[86]

Secretary of the Interior Ray Lyman Wilbur was Hoover's choice for chair of the 1930 conference. A past president of the American Medical Association, Wilbur was an outspoken opponent of the Sheppard-Towner Act, an advocate of reducing federal involvement in social welfare programs, and an enemy of the bureau. "We want a minimum of national legislation in this field," he told the delegates. "No one should get the idea that Uncle Sam is going to rock the baby to sleep."[87] Wilbur stood for undoing much of what the first two White House Conferences for children had done to help make the federal government more responsible for children's welfare. Hoover did not mention the Children's Bureau in his opening address, nor did Wilbur in his talk.[88]

Although antagonistic to the Children's Bureau and the expansion of federal responsibility for children's welfare, both Hoover and Wilbur were intensely interested in advancing scientific knowledge of children. The 1930 "Hoover Conference," as it is often called, was an ambitious, well-funded, well-prepared effort to summarize knowledge of every phase of child life. Hoover played a crucial role in determining the conference's ambitious scope. To assure ample financial support, he diverted for its use half a million dollars from the fund that had been collected for Belgian war relief. The private sector also contributed generously.[89]

At the time of the conference, there were forty-five million children in the nation, sixteen million under six years of age.[90] Hoover drew attention to the fact that this conference, unlike its two predecessors, would be concerned with all children, "not only the dependent child or the child in need of special protection, but all children, in their total aspects, including those social and environmental factors which are influencing modern childhood."[91] The 1930 WHC for children was also the only one, before or since, that organized task forces to conduct original research.[92] Thirty-two volumes were required to publish the encyclopedia of information it gathered. The conference was the culmination and grand climax of a decade unique for its intense interest in child welfare and for unprecedented, innovative efforts to institutionalize and professionalize the scientific study of children. Hoover stated correctly that the summation of knowledge that the conference achieved had not been possible previously.[93]

Twelve hundred specialists in childcare and child study, including pediatricians, child developmentalists, child guidance psychiatrists, social workers, early childhood educators, parent educators, and childcare practitioners, prepared for the conference by meeting for sixteen months in nearly 150 committees.[94] The conference quickly became the priority for all engaged in the several branches of child study and childcare. To avoid conflict and offer full cooperation, the National Research Council Committee on Child Development canceled its proposed 1930 conference. Approximately thirty-two hundred people participated in the 1930 WHC. President Hoover called attention to the conference as the first to use radio to bring its deliberations into homes across the nation. Millions of unseen listeners, he said, were also members of the conference.[95]

The 1930 WHC reflected a transition during the preceding decade from the humanitarian impulses that had motivated child welfare and child study campaigns during the Progressive Era to a new determination to create a better world through the application of science to children. Secretary Wilbur expressed his scorn for mere beneficence, telling the delegates that "those who have developed methods without scientific preparation are often of the greatest harm in the handling of our childhood. I think that we are all more or less suspicious of those whose hearts impel them to 'do good' to children when their minds are untrained."[96] Like President Hoover, Wilbur called attention to the need for specialists because of the helplessness of parents. "It is probably true," he said, "that it is beyond the capacity of the individual parent to train her child to fit into the intricate, interwoven, and interdependent social and economic system we have developed."[97] The male scientists, physicians, and bureaucrats who displaced the women social reformers who had dominated the two previous White House conferences for children did all they could to ensure the primacy of the scientific specialist and the denigration of mere benevolence. Their efforts culminated in an attempt by public health physicians to dismember the Children's Bureau.

At an early meeting of committee chairs, from which Abbott was excluded, President Hoover announced that the Rockefeller Foundation had provided three hundred thousand dollars for maternal and child health services, to be administered by the Public Health Service. He asked the chairs what they would advise. Upon arriving in Washington, delegates received a preliminary bound report of six hundred pages, marked confidential, that contained a recommendation to transfer maternal and child health programs from the Children's Bureau to the Public Health Service. The recommendation had been included in a majority report of a subcommittee of the Committee on Public Health Service and Administration, chaired by Dr. Haven Emerson. Abbott's dissenting minority report was omitted.[98]

The recommendation of the majority report and the exclusion of Abbott's dissent caused an uproar of protest, which for a time overshadowed all other activities of the conference. President Hoover sent for Grace, Edith Abbott recalled, and asked, "What's all this about the White House and the Public Health Service trying to destroy the Children's Bureau?" Grace told Edith, "I looked him straight in the eye and said firmly, 'Well Mr. President, isn't that true?' "Abbott insisted on her right to have her dissent included in the subcommittee report, telling Hoover that he had allowed a direct attack to be made on the Children's Bureau and that many people believed that the dismantling of the bureau was the major objective of the conference. "As far as I am concerned, Mr. President," Abbott declared, "when the Children's Bureau is attacked, I shall defend the Children's Bureau."[99]

Abbott's minority report pointed out that the unity of the child, and the value of having all the techniques of the social, medical, statistical, and other related sciences of childhood in one unified system, had been approved by both President Theodore Roosevelt and Congress and still enjoyed wide support. Removing health work from the Children's Bureau, she stated, would "destroy it as a Children's Bureau."[100]

Organized womanhood came to the bureau's rescue again. When the subcommittee met to adopt the majority report, two hundred women and many eminent men who supported the bureau insisted that Abbott be allowed to read her minority report. Telegrams were read from pediatricians and other physicians objecting to the transfer. Finally, a large majority passed a motion that the minority report be included in the subcommittee report.

Objections to the attempt to suppress Abbott's report spread throughout the conference. Most vigorous in support of the bureau was Secretary of Labor James J. Davis, who praised its accomplishments, endorsed its agenda, and told the delegates, "We know from experience that we would make of the Bureau a handicapped child if we subtracted any of its functions. . . . I believe . . . with Solomon that the child should not be divided."[101] His remarks were greeted with "deafening applause." Ultimately, Surgeon General Hugh Cummings was forced to request that the recommendation to strip the bureau of its maternal and child health functions be stricken from the record and referred to the President's continuing committee along with a contrary recommendation from another section.[102] This was a momentary triumph in a war the bureau ultimately was to lose.

The conference closed by proclaiming a Children's Charter, a list of eighteen "aims for the children of America," ridiculed by many delegates and some of the press as a recital of pieties, a string of platitudes, and a disappointing result of more than a year of deliberations.[103] Since 1930 the nature off the charter and the fact that no attempt was made to translate the findings of the conference into an action program have often been cited as evidence of the ineffectiveness of the White House Conferences for Children. One significant outcome of the 1930 WHC, however, was its contribution to a great advance in pediatric practice and education that followed.[104]

The 1930 WHC also drew attention to the effect of the Depression on the nation's children and made President Hoover's declaration that not poverty but parental ignorance was at the root of children's problems seem ludicrous. Abbott used the conference to express her indignation at how little was being done to meet the desperate needs of children of the unemployed. They will be "undersized because they have been undernourished," she told the delegates. "Larger numbers will be the victims of tuberculosis. . . . None of us can be happy about what is now being done. We deserve to be unhappy about what we have not done." Children suffer more than adults from economic depression, she continued, because what they do not get in one year can never be made up to them. "We cannot feed children skimmed milk this year and make up by feeding them cream next year and there are great numbers of children all over the country who are not getting even skimmed milk this year."[105] Scorning such thoughts, Secretary Wilbur told the 1932 meeting of the National Conference of Social Work that "unless we descend to a level far beyond anything that we at present have known, our children are apt to profit rather than suffer from what is going on."[106]

RESEARCH DURING THE DEPRESSION

Abbott's staunch defense of social survey research was vindicated by the contributions of bureau studies to relief efforts during the Depression and to the social legislation of the New Deal. From 1930 to 1936, when the newly created Social Security Board began to function, the bureau was the only federal agency gathering information on the extent and adequacy of unemployment relief and the effect of unemployment on families and children.[107]

In September 1930, in response to an "urgent request" from the President's Emergency Committee for Employment, the Children's Bureau began to assemble monthly statistics on the distribution of unemployment relief in more than 120 cities with about 60 percent of the nation's population.[108] Also at the request of the committee, the bureau undertook field studies of especially depressed areas. In 1931 it cooperated with the American Friends Service Committee to extend relief to depressed coal-mining areas.[109] The monthly reports by the bureau to the President's Emergency Committee brought home to the American people the devastation caused by the Depression and the overwhelming need for federal action.[110]

The statistics collected by the bureau from 1930 through 1933 showed a continuous sharp increase in public and private relief expenditures. From 1929 to

1930 relief expenditures nearly doubled, and from September 1931 to October 1932 increased eight-fold. Bureau statistics showed that public funds provided about three-fourths of relief expenditures, including mothers' aid.[111] Since President Hoover distrusted bureau statistics consistently showing that public agencies were providing more relief than private agencies, he asked the Bureau of the Census to conduct its own investigation. Its study confirmed the Children's Bureau findings.[112]

Public relief at that time was considered to be a local function, and few states had assumed any responsibility for assistance to the indigent. Abbott cited mothers' pension legislation as a legal precedent for state-funded relief for the unemployed and urged the forty-four states that provided pensions for needy mothers to add unemployment of husbands to the list of conditions that qualified mothers to receive aid. "I hope some of them will plan to give the relief," Abbott said, "before the family has passed over into the abyss of destitution, before their last possessions and their independence are gone."[113]

As the Depression deepened, the tension between Abbott and President Hoover increased. "Month after month," Edith Abbott commented, "Grace's statistics . . . challenged the President's position with regard to the adequacy of private relief."[114] Edith added that many Americans were convinced that there were hidden dangers in public relief, and were "surprised" and "shocked" when Grace's reports showed that the major part of all the relief work of the country had been supported by public agencies even in normal times.[115]

"Get the children out of the bread lines," Grace Abbott pleaded.[116] Her insistence on the need for public protection of children and recognition of the heavy burden that unemployment placed on them could no longer be ignored. Bureau studies, especially those of extremely depressed areas, exposed the human cost of unemployment.[117] As the Depression deepened, undernourishment of children became widespread, and tuberculosis and other diseases increased among children.[118] Although it was impossible to measure the emotional disturbances children experienced because of their parents' misery, Abbott also argued that children of unemployed parents were suffering from uncertainty about what lay ahead.[119]

Information about relief activities exposed the shocking conditions in which many families and their children were living. Through a constant barrage of public pronouncements, Abbott demonstrated that large numbers of families had suffered from poverty long before 1929. In an address to the 1930 WHC, she called attention to the "degree of inequality that exists in the United States as a source of many of our social problems." She cited findings of the Federal

Trade Commission showing that "13 percent of the people own 90 percent of the wealth, . . . 87 percent of the people ten percent of the wealth," and "76 percent of the people own nothing when they die. . . . The absence of thrift and industry or poor investment are causes in some families" she added, "but the wages of large numbers of hard-working fathers leave no margin for saving."[120]

Like child developmentalists, bureau staff members had focused on the preschool child during the 1920s. Reports that unprecedented numbers of boys and some girls had taken to the road in search of work, or to escape the tension and discontent caused by the unemployment of their parents, caused the bureau to investigate the effects of the Depression on youth. Its studies of transients disclosed that 60 percent were under thirty years of age, 25 percent under twenty-one. Since transients were not legal residents, communities had no legal responsibility for their support, and, because they could not meet even the relief needs of their own residents, many communities lapsed into the practice of "passing on" transients, limiting their stay to twenty-four hours. Boys accustomed to decent standards of living, the bureau found, were going for days at a time with nothing to eat but coffee, bread, and beans. During the winter months, many became ill from exposure to cold. Others were crippled or killed while boarding moving freight trains.[121] The bureau suggested several measures to reduce youth migration and help transient youths.

By 1934 about eight million children under the age of sixteen lived in families receiving unemployment relief, but many millions of children in need were receiving no relief at all. Of great concern to the bureau as the Depression persisted was the effect on growth and development of malnutrition and illness among children.[122] In the fall of 1934 the bureau undertook a study of families in parts of five cities in order to obtain "close-up views of some of the families on relief . . . and to indicate the points of greatest stress."[123] In addition to its regular publications on childcare, the bureau published pamphlets to help families on strict budgets to buy the most nutritious food.

THE CHILDREN'S BUREAU AND THE EARLY
NEW DEAL, 1933–1935

The Children's Bureau's research and reporting functions were diminished during the New Deal years and World War II by increasing administrative responsibilities and the difficulty of getting money for either research or reporting.[124] Never again would the bureau conduct as many investigations as under its first two chiefs.

Abbott, a lifelong Republican, was pleased with the election of Franklin D. Roosevelt because she was sure he would take bold action to help families and children in ways she had long recommended. She was particularly happy with the appointment of Frances Perkins as secretary of labor, worked closely with her and became one of her most valued advisors. With Perkins's support, the bureau embarked on its own recovery program for children by holding two conferences late in 1933 and in 1934. At the 1933 Child Health Recovery Conference, one hundred forty of the Roosevelt Administration's leading officials met with federal, state, and local health officials to launch a movement "for the recovery of ground lost during the depression in conditions affecting the health and vitality of children."[125] The purpose of the second conference was to discuss the effects of the Depression on dependent children and ways to extend and improve mothers' aid provided by the states.[126]

GRACE ABBOTT'S LAST YEARS

Ill with tuberculosis during her last seven years as chief, Abbott was forced to take a nine-month leave of absence in 1928 and an eleven-month leave in 1932. During her absences, acting chief Katherine Lenroot kept in close touch with Abbott by mail and did her best to achieve Abbott's goals.[127] Abbott resigned in June 1934 and joined her sister at the University of Chicago School of Social Service Administration. Edith wrote that Grace's main reason for leaving the bureau was not poor health but her desire to have greater "freedom to speak and write freely about social or political problems."[128] She was confident that Perkins would defend the bureau against all opponents. Both Lenroot and Eliot were candidates to succeed Abbott. Lenroot was appointed chief in November 1934, and Eliot became assistant chief. Lenroot served the Children's Bureau for more than thirty-six years, seventeen of them as chief, and was succeeded by Eliot in 1951.

Abbott's resignation did not end her service to either the bureau or the nation. She spent much time in Washington during the fall and winter of 1934–1935 as a consultant to the President's Committee on Economic Security while it was assembling findings and making recommendations for President Roosevelt's social security proposals to Congress. Edwin E. Witte, director of the committee, asked Lenroot and Eliot to help with the preparations and urged Abbott, then in Colorado, to send him her recommendations. Witte wrote, "I rely on you, more than anyone else to guide our committee in its thinking on what ought to be done for children."[129] Abbott sent Witte a memo and, as a dollar-a-year consultant to the bureau, traveled to Washington to confer with Lenroot, Eliot, and Perkins about what services for children and families should be included in the proposed Social Security Bill.[130]

Bureau statistical research and its studies of laws protecting children were the basis for services to children incorporated in the Social Security Act of 1935. Three of the new programs were included in Title V of the act. A maternal and child health program, authorizing grants to the states for extending and improving health services for mothers and children, amounted to a restoration and expansion of the Sheppard-Towner Act. Part I of Title V almost exactly duplicated the Sheppard-Towner formula, but the appropriation for maternal and child health services, $3.8 million, was more than twice the annual appropriation under the Sheppard-Towner Act. In addition, there were no limitations on either the age of the children who could be served or the duration of the program.[131]

Title V also included a crippled children's services program with an appropriation of $2,750,000. Originally proposed by Abbott in a memo to the Committee on Economic Security, it authorized grants to the states for diagnosis and treatment of handicapping illnesses in children. The third program provided for "establishing, extending, and strengthening, especially in predominantly rural areas," services for the protection and care of "homeless, dependent, and neglected children and children in danger of becoming delinquents."[132]

Expected opposition to the maternal and child health proposals did not materialize, partly because the AMA hoped to fend off the more alarming possibility of national health insurance. Proposals for crippled children's services aroused no serious opposition, and opposition by Catholic groups to child welfare services was overcome largely through compromises suggested by Lenroot and Abbott. All agreed that children's services under Title V should be administered by the Children's Bureau.[133]

A fourth Children's Bureau proposal, extending mothers' pension legislation to provide for aid to dependent children made its way into Title IV of the Social Security Act. Although the Committee on Economic Security agreed that this program, too, should be administered by the Children's Bureau, Federal Emergency Relief Administration officials insisted that mothers' aid was an integral part of the general relief program. To Abbott's surprise and disappointment, they persuaded Congress to vest its administration in the Social Security Board. Abbott "feared that placing aid to dependent children in a large new administrative structure, completely outside the state's mothers' pension laws, would result in loss of standards and a program that would take on vestiges of poor relief."[134] While the Children's Bureau administered aid to dependent children, the emphasis was on service but, according to Lenroot, technical and legal questions of eligibility dominated the early phase of the program under the Social Security Board.[135]

Shortly before Abbott resigned from the bureau in 1934, she described her view of her responsibilities as its chief:

Sometimes when I get home at night in Washington I feel as though I had been in a great traffic jam . . . moving toward the Hill where Congress sits in judgement. . . . In that traffic jam there are all kinds . . . of conveyances, for example the Army's tanks, guns, carriages, trucks . . . the hayricks and the binders and the ploughs . . . of the Department of Agriculture . . . the handsome limousines in which the Department of Commerce rides . . . the barouches in which the Department of State rides in such dignity. It seems so to me as I stand on the sidewalk watching it becomes more congested and more difficult and then because the responsibility is mine and I must, I take a very firm hold on the handles of the baby carriage and I wheel it into the traffic.[136]

Abbott lived five more years. In the fall of 1937 she fell ill with multiple myeloma but continued to teach at the University of Chicago and to edit and travel until the winter of 1938. She died on June 19, 1939.[137]

By 1940 Abbott, Lathrop, Jane Addams, Lillian Wald, and Florence Kelley were all dead. Since Abbott's departure from the Children's Bureau, few representatives of children in government, with the exception of Martha May Eliot, have taken so firm a hold on the handles of the baby carriage.

Epilogue What Happened
to the Early Movements?:
The Child Development Field
after World War II

"World War I had helped bring child development alive. World War II nearly killed it," declared Robert Sears.[1] The loss of staff members to the war effort forced the child development institutes to curtail their programs significantly. The Society for Research in Child Development (SRCD), almost bankrupt, failed to meet from 1940 to 1946. The National Research Council (NRC) once again paid the society's bills and helped it to reorganize.[2]

Sheldon White recalled that in the 1950s annual reviews of psychology described the field of child development as "near death."[3] By the early 1960s massive federal funding for university research had brought the field back to life and insured its place in the academic establishment.[4] Today the main centers of child development research are in departments of psychology, but it is also represented in psychiatry, education, human development, family studies, home economics, and still other disciplines.

Once-popular investigations of physical growth and physiological functioning declined in the late 1950s, while interest in social and emotional behavior intensified.[5] The developmental psychology that emerged during the 1960s was strongly influenced by Jean Piaget, founder of the field of cognitive psychology. According to White and Phillips, it was also a continuation of the "evolutionary vision of the development of the mind" offered by James Mark Baldwin. For some, they said, "cognitive development became virtually synonymous with child development."[6]

The vast literature on child development theory and methodology that has emerged since the 1950s highlights the new directions of child development research, its enormous expansion, and the mixture of change and continuity that characterizes the field today. It includes examples of research breakthroughs and of the ways in which developmentalists continue to struggle with questions raised by their forebears.[7] Below are a few striking examples.

PRECOCITY

Jerome Bruner declared that "the importance of early childhood for the intellectual, social, and emotional growth of human beings is probably one of the most revolutionary discoveries of modern times."[8] Perhaps so. Many developmentalists have expressed their amazement at, and have confirmed new evidence of, the social, emotional, and cognitive precocity of very young children.[9] A number of scholars and childcare practitioners have applied these new insights. For example, sociologist Lee Robins designed a questionnaire for the National Institutes of Mental Health to be administered to children as young as four.[10] Other developmentalists challenge the notion of a single "critical period" in childhood, insisting on the importance of the entire life span.[11] Studies of children in their middle years and of adolescents have shown that individuals appear to be capable of growing and changing throughout life. Few accept the stage theories of development that were advanced by G. Stanley Hall and Erik Erikson.[12] Theories of moral and cognitive development, however, remain popular.[13]

Research has dramatically changed our view of babies by using new technology to measure sensory, perceptual, and cognitive development.[14] We once believed that newborns could not taste, see, discriminate sounds, or experience pain. We now know that babies not only can see at birth but also soon become active visual explorers. Infant research has documented that cognitive and social processes begin very early in life. Indeed, babies are influenced by auditory stimuli even before birth and very soon after birth prefer the sound of the human voice. By one month of age they can elicit social responses from others and soon learn to behave in ways that please their mothers. Two- or three-month-old infants prefer their mother's face to that of strangers, prefer to look at patterned rather than plain stimuli, and can discriminate colors. At three or four months, babies have a primitive sense of numbers, are able to distinguish two objects from three, and can learn, remember, and imitate. Recent research suggests that neurological foundations for rational thinking, problem solving, and general reasoning are largely established by age one.[15] Parents no longer are advised not to play with babies, as they were in the 1920s, when Holt and Watson dominated child-rearing advice; instead they are urged to stimulate their infants. The marketplace has responded with a vast array of toys, books, and television programs designed to foster early cognitive development.

OTHER NEW DIRECTIONS

"Attachment" has been hailed as one of the most important and exciting breakthroughs in child-study theory and research in four decades, and the field has honored the originators of the field, John Bowlby and Mary Ainsworth, accordingly.[16] The basic premise of attachment theory is that the first relationship of the infant, usually with the mother (or other primary caregiver), is of fundamental importance to the child's future well-being. Research within the past few decades has also focused on the important influence of the father, siblings, grandparents, other relatives, and caregivers as well as the influence of birth order and of peer relationships and the continuing importance of attachment throughout life.[17]

As in the 1920s, developmentalists are emphasizing the importance of studying children in their natural environments rather then in laboratories. Urie Bronfenbrenner pioneered in expanding the definition of children's environments to include the school, local community, and other social systems.[18] Barbara Rogoff, writing about the mutual involvement of the child and the social world, argued that they cannot be regarded as "independently definable."[19] Other scholars are looking at child development in other historical periods.[20]

Until the 1950s few investigators examined developmental differences between boys and girls, but since then gender research has overturned popular notions about differences between the sexes and has yielded more precise information about such differences.[21] Resiliency research, which asks how and why many children who face multiple risks come through relatively intact, has become increasingly important. Investigations have focused on children with mentally ill, alcoholic, or drug-abusing parents, as well as on children who experience a host of other chronic adversities such as poverty, marital conflict between parents, and domestic or neighborhood violence.[22] The concept of the child as active participant in his own life emerged during the early decades of child development research and is now receiving extensive attention.[23]

Research on African-American, Hispanic, Native American, and other minority children has lagged in spite of the urgent need for additional knowledge. However, significant progress has occurred during the past fifteen years. Examples of important contributions include the special issue of *Child Development* on minority children edited by Vonnie McLoyd and Margaret Beale Spencer (1990). Similarly, significant new conceptual frameworks for studying minority children have been published, and the National Science Foundation has recently funded several centers to study culture and development.[24] A focus on race, ethnicity, and culture has become one of the highest priorities in developmental research.

The chief theoretical framework of the early decades of child study, the nature-nurture controversy, continues to be of major interest, largely because of the biomedical revolution, especially findings in behavioral genetics and neuroscience.[25] While most developmentalists now acknowledge that nature and nurture are inseparable, studies that elucidate the intricacies of their interaction are relatively new. The most innovative research designs combine genetic and environmental theory and measurement.[26]

The early emphasis by the Children's Bureau on large-scale surveys has a prominent place in the current child sciences. Many developmentalists have helped to create or are using extensive new data sets on children, most of which are in the public domain.[27]

WHAT HAPPENED TO THE CHILD
DEVELOPMENT RESEARCH INSTITUTES
AND THE SRCD?

In spite of all the changes in the field, some remnants of the child development institutes survive. The Berkeley Institute of Child Welfare Research, now the Berkeley Institute of Human Development, has been tracking its subjects for three-quarters of a century.[28] The Institute of Child Development, part of the School of Education at the University of Minnesota, is another important research center that recently celebrated its seventy-fifth anniversary. [29] The Yale Child Study Center, as we have seen, continues its long tradition of clinical studies and child development research.

The institute at Teachers College, Columbia University, failed to survive the Great Depression, and the Iowa Child Welfare Research Station abandoned its original research goals in 1964 and changed its name to the Institute of Child Behavior and Development. It closed ten years later.[30] Two institutes not sponsored by Rockefeller, the Merrill-Palmer and the Fels Institute, carried on for over a half-century. The former became part of the Office of Research and Graduate Studies of Wayne State University in 1982; the latter merged with the Wright State University School of Medicine in 1977.[31]

Although a number of the original child development research institutes no longer exist, several new ones are very active and symbolize the renewed importance of science in the service of children during the late twentieth and early twenty-first centuries. Examples are the Institute for Policy Research at Northwestern University, the Center for Child and Family Policy at Duke University, the Center for Research on Child Wellbeing at Princeton University, and three centers at Columbia University: the National Center for Children in Poverty, the Center for Children and Families, and the Institute for Child and Family Policy.[32]

THE SOCIETY FOR RESEARCH
IN CHILD DEVELOPMENT

The Society for Research in Child Development (SRCD) had almost six thousand members in 2000, according to John W. Hagen, its executive director. Two regional organizations were established in the Southeast and the Southwest. Two new organizations, independent of the SRCD, are the International Society for Infant Studies (ICIS) and the Society for Research on Adolescence (SRA). Pediatricians established the Society for Behavioral and Developmental Pediatrics (SBDP) and the Society for Adolescent Medicine (SAM). The International Society for the Study of Behavioral Development (ISSBD), the first organization to emphasize an international perspective to the study of development, was established in the early 1970s, and the Society for the Study of Human Development (SSHD) was launched in 1998.

The Society for Research in Child Development, like its precursor, the National Research Council Committee on Child Development, still holds biennial conferences. It also publishes *Child Development,* a monograph series, a newsletter, and *Social Policy Reports.* Although the field never achieved the integrated multidisciplinary framework its founders anticipated, the society tries to avoid domination by psychology or any other field, to draw in new disciplines, and to promote exchanges of views and information among scholars and practitioners in diverse fields. A committee founded in 1977 to preserve the sources in the field of child development has expanded to encompass all aspects of this field and the history of childhood and is completing a major oral history of about 150 scholars and pioneers.[33]

One of the two greatest changes in the field within the last half-century has been the entry of more women, who now constitute about 70 percent of SRCD members. SRCD has also worked to enlarge the number of researchers of color, as well as to promote more research on minority children. The Black Caucus of the Society for Research in Child Development was founded in 1973, and it has served as a significant resource for African-American members of the society. Its founders were committed to the promotion of expanded scholarship and understanding of African-American children and families, and in its later years the mission was broadened to include minorities from all groups and nationalities. There has been some discussion of forming an Hispanic Caucus in SRCD. More recently, the Frances Degen Horowitz Millenium Fellows Program, established in 1999, is designed to reach out to undergraduate students of color, to link them with a senior mentor in the society, and to involve them in the society's biennial meetings.

PHILANTHROPY'S CONTINUING ROLE

The second major change for the field of child development is that the federal government has replaced private philanthropy as its chief source of funding. Private foundations continue to play an important role, however, by sponsoring innovative research by public agencies, and even by helping to fund some federal programs, as well as by interpreting and publicizing children's needs.[34] Among the most important philanthropies currently supporting child development research are the Carnegie Corporation, the Annie E. Casey Foundation, the Foundation for Child Development, the William T. Grant Foundation, the Jacobs Foundation, the John D. and Catherine T. MacArthur Foundation, the Packard Foundation, and the Spencer Foundation. The Foundation for Child Development (FCD) can trace its history back to 1908 as the Association for the Aid of Crippled Children. It changed its name in 1972, in order to reflect its commitment to broad social research, advocacy, and action on behalf of children at risk, particularly children from poor families.[35] It is the oldest continuing philanthropy devoted to improving the lives of children through research, policy, and leadership training.

With computer-age millionaires redefining philanthropy, its future role in child development research and social policy cannot be predicted.

CHILD DEVELOPMENT RESEARCH
AND SOCIAL POLICY

At the first meeting of the Society for Research in Child Development in June 1934, members recognized the tension between research and policy by restoring to the society's constitution the service function that had been eliminated by the National Research Council Committee on Child Development. During the early decades of the SRCD's existence, social policy was interpreted almost entirely in terms of parent education and other private-sector activities. For decades, many members opposed involvement in social policy activities because they believed that it would interfere with scientific objectivity.

In 1964, looking beyond the family to professional practitioners working with children, the SRCD began a new series, *Reviews of Child Development Research,* designed to bring research findings about children to the attention of pediatricians, social workers, clinical psychologists, teachers, child psychiatrists, and other childcare specialists. In 1977 the society established its Committee on Child Development and Social Policy, now called the Committee on Policy and Communication. In *Child Development and Social Policy,* editors Harold Stevenson and Alberta Siegel expressed the philosophy underlying the society's activities in this field: "Unless our knowledge about children can begin to exert a stronger influence on the development of policies that influence the lives of our children, we are vulnerable to the charge that we are not meeting our full social responsibility."[36]

In the 1970s the Foundation for Child Development and the William T. Grant Foundation, (led by G. Orville Brim, Jr., and Robert Haggerty respectively), persuaded the society to launch the highly effective SRCD Congressional Fellowship Program, and in the 1990s SRCD established the Executive Branch Fellowship Program as well. More than one hundred individuals in the child sciences have worked as experts in these federal settings. The society opened an Office for Policy and Communications in Washington, D.C., in the 1970s and has increased its commitment to better public policies for children.[37] The *Newsletter* regularly features profiles of federal agencies that support child development research.

The sudden call to developmentalists in the 1960s to help plan Head Start programs and their subsequent interest in Great Society programs reawakened their concern with policy questions and revealed their inexperience in policy formation and implementation.[38] During the mid-1970s, the Bush Foundation of St. Paul, Minnesota, at the urging of one of its board members, Irving B. Harris, consulted several scholars about how they could best help the field of child development.[39] Edward Zigler suggested that there was a great need to train people to understand both how young people develop and how social policy is formed. In 1977–78 the Bush Foundation established centers for this purpose at Yale, the University of Michigan, the University of North Carolina, and UCLA. In 1982 the Bush Foundation renewed its support for another five years and awarded additional funds for activities designed to increase communication among the centers.[40] Efforts to secure permanent support were successful at Yale and resulted in an extension of the center at the University of Michigan into the early 1990s.[41]

THE FATE OF THE CHILD GUIDANCE CLINICS AND OF CHILD PSYCHIATRY

The major European influence on American child psychiatry after World War II was in psychoanalytic theory and practice. Although they were influenced by psychoanalysis, early child guidance clinics were eclectic, drawing their assumptions from behaviorism and a dynamic psychiatry based primarily on Alfred Meyer's psychobiology. By 1960, 60 percent of the guidance clinics were primarily Freudian in orientation, and only 8 percent were entirely non-Freudian. This trend paralleled that in academic psychiatry, where by 1962 half of the department chairmen were members of analytic societies.[42] Bernard Rosenblatt observed: "The larger clinics established training programs in child psychiatry and child psychology, and psychotherapy with children was considered ... the most important part of the training in these disciplines. The method ultimately used was mostly psychoanalytic psychotherapy. Wherever it was possible to appoint an analyst as leader of the child guidance clinic this was done."[43] By 1962 Eveoleen Rexford had concluded that "the modern child guidance clinic is the offspring of a union between the child guidance movement originating in the United States and child analysis brought from Europe."[44]

Anna Freud was impressed with the influences of child guidance on therapeutic work with parents. Her work, in turn, helped to persuade many American psychiatrists of the value of child analysis, which was widely used in psychiatric clinics only after 1950, when play therapy, doll therapy, role-playing games, storytelling, art therapy, projective techniques, and a variety of other new therapeutic methods for use with children were developed, mainly by American therapists.[45] Some clinics also experimented with short-term and group psychotherapy.

Psychoanalytic influences, as well as more experience in working with troubled children, led many therapists to move from their early concern with "everyday problems of everyday children" to the study and treatment of children with severe emotional disturbances. Psychiatric social worker Jesse Taft published the first American text on psychotherapy with children in 1933, and Frederick Allen published the second in 1942. According to Leo Kanner, efforts to classify childhood pathology began in 1943, when he reported the syndrome of early infantile autism, the first recognition of a psychotic disorder peculiar to childhood.[46] The American Psychiatric Association established a section on the psychopathology of childhood in 1943, and in the years that followed Lauretta Bender (1947), Louise Despert (1951), Margaret Mahler (1955), and William Goldfarb (1961), among others, published studies dealing with childhood schizophrenia, autism, and other childhood pathologies.[47]

The extension of therapeutic techniques from child guidance and the study of infants in foundling hospitals led to the identification of a condition called hospitalism. Rene Spitz, who coined the term, defined it as "the evil effect of institutional care on infants placed in institutions from an early age."[48] Childhood depression was ignored for decades, and not officially recognized until 1980.[49] Since then controlled studies by psychiatrists of treatments tailored for depressed children and adolescents have burgeoned.[50]

The Commonwealth Fund's effort to transform child guidance into child psychiatry was advanced in 1959 when the American Academy of Child Psychiatry prevailed over the American Association of Psychological Clinics in requiring that all child guidance clinics have a medical connection.[51] Reacting to criticism of their narrow focus on psychotherapy and their middle-class bias, the clinics began to pay attention in the late 1950s to the relationship between social conditions and behavioral disorders.[52] After 1965 new therapeutic techniques, such as behavior modification therapy, drawn from the psychological laboratory rather than from psychiatry, were introduced. The growing admission of severely disturbed children to psychiatric clinics led to the development of day care and nursery school programs, psychiatric in-patient hospitals, and diagnostic and evaluation centers coordinated by psychiatrists.[53]

Since the 1950s psychiatrists have initiated and collaborated with developmentalists in a significant number of longitudinal and cross-sectional studies. The outstanding example of such collaboration was the long-term partnership

between British psychiatrist John Bowlby and Canadian developmental psychologist Mary Ainsworth, which led to the documentation and elaboration of
attachment theory.[54] During the past quarter-century psychiatrists have collaborated with professionals from other disciplines on numerous important
longitudinal and cross-sectional studies. Psychiatrist Sir Michael Rutter has
been honored for his contribution to developmental research and served as the
president of the Society for Research in Child Development.[55]

THE FEDERAL GOVERNMENT
AND MENTAL HEALTH

David Levy commented in 1952, "If the criterion for success of a program is that
it proves its worth when it is taken over and supported by the community, then
the Commonwealth Fund child guidance program was one of the most successful enterprises in the field of philanthropy."[56] The National Mental Health Act
of 1946, passed one year after the Commonwealth Fund ended its mental-
hygiene program, was the first step in the federal government's adoption and expansion of mental health services and research initiated by the mental hygiene
and child guidance movements. The act authorized the creation in 1949 of the
National Institute of Mental Health (NIMH), which had three objectives almost identical to those of the Commonwealth Fund mental health programs:
research, training, and assistance to the states in developing their own programs.

During World War II, as in World War I, psychiatry gained enormous prestige. The revelation of emotional disturbances in servicemen contributed to the
passage of the National Mental Health Act and to the proliferation of child
guidance clinics.[57]

In the 1950s, as the fields of psychiatry and clinical psychology became increasingly concerned with sociocultural factors affecting mental health, interest
in applying the public health model to mental illness revived, and community
mental health emerged as a new area of specialization. One of its goals was to
shift attention from internal psychological factors to the influence of the sociocultural environment; another was to extend traditional mental health services
to groups that previously had not been served. The Joint Commission on Mental Health and Illness, established by Congress in 1961, recommended substantial federal financing of mental health care that was previously the responsibility of state mental hospitals. Continuous care of the mentally ill within their
communities, many believed, was preferable to improving the state hospital
system.

In 1963 the Community Mental Health Services Act authorized $150 million for the construction of community mental health centers over the next three years. By 1975 over $900 million had been spent or pledged for the community health program). Proponents of the act used a rhetoric strikingly similar to the statement of early child guidance advocates, claiming that as much as two-thirds of the population were in need of mental health evaluation and treatment. According to David Musto, this was perceived not as an intractable problem but rather as a gigantic opportunity to bring about social progress through early detection and treatment of mental illness and the manipulation of the social environment by mental health experts.[58] In 1963 the president of the American Psychiatric Association quoted journalist Philip Wylie in calling attention to the great opportunity now open to psychiatrists: "You can inherit the earth. The only question is 'How Soon?' . . . Never was chaos so great; never was paradise so near the reach of common folks like you and me."[59] But this attempt to achieve "social reform through psychological insight" also proved unworkable. The extension of mental health services to new population groups has far outpaced the discovery of new ways to meet their special needs.[60]

During the late 1960s and the early 1970s, the Joint Commission on Mental Health of Children, a nongovernmental, multidisciplinary, nonprofit organization, concluded from a national study authorized by Congress that psychiatric clinics had failed to help poor families and children and recommended establishment of a national mental health program for children.

MENTAL HEALTH SERVICES OFFERED BY GUIDANCE CLINICS IN THE TWENTIETH CENTURY

According to Irene Josselyn, an attempt was made to substitute the phrase "psychiatric clinic for children" for the term "child guidance clinic," to convey the message that the clinic was a medical facility.[61] The new name did not stick, however, because it failed to acknowledge the contributions of psychologists and social workers. Child guidance is still part of the name of many clinics throughout the country, although several have substituted "center" for "clinic" because "clinic" is frequently associated with service to the poor and because "center" suggests training and research as well as service functions. Some clinics call themselves "centers for children and the family" or some such title but are essentially guidance clinics.[62]

In recent decades, mental health clinics have many sponsors, take many forms, and offer diverse services to children and their families. Community clinics modeled primarily on the Commonwealth Fund demonstration clinics are still widespread. Some have been incorporated into community mental health services; others are part of a mental health facility that serves both children and adults. More clinics are now affiliated with universities or hospitals, and these are the only clinics that sponsor research. Research on the effectiveness of individual interventions continues.[63] With the exception of the St. Louis clinic, all of the original Commonwealth Fund demonstration clinics are still functioning. Several of them, including the Philadelphia Child Guidance Center, have become leading centers for the practice of family therapy.[64] Two of the most renowned early clinics, the Philadelphia Center and the Judge Baker Foundation in Boston, have returned to their original goal of helping disadvantaged families and children. The foundation was renamed the Judge Baker Children's Center in 1993, its seventy-fifth anniversary year. Today it is a clinical research institute.[65]

THE AMERICAN ORTHOPSYCHIATRY ASSOCIATION (AOA)

In spite of the predominance of psychiatrists during the early decades of the American Orthopsychiatry Association (AOA), today they represent only about 740 of the association's seven thousand members. Approximately 2,300 members are psychologists and 2,400 are social workers. The circulation of the *American Journal of Orthopsychiatry* (*AJO*) is now about 9,000.

Child psychiatrists and developmentalists have become increasingly interested in understanding and applying both disciplines. Psychiatrist Robert Emde was elected president of the SRCD in 1990, as was fellow psychiatrist Sir Michael Rutter in 1999. Developmentalist Edward Zigler was elected president of the AOA in 1993. Pediatrician Julius Richmond and psychiatrist David Levy had previously been elected president of both the AOA and the SRCD.

Between 1950 and 1980, the *AJO* doubled the space it devoted to research, largely because of members' interest in neurobiology. Research in child psychiatry, as in adult psychiatry, has increasingly included research in psychopharmacology.

Explicitly in favor of the application of knowledge from its inception, the AOA has remained interested in public policy issues. Unlike *Child Develop-*

ment, the *AJO* has taken public stands on such controversial social issues as poverty, civil rights, contraception, and abortion. Leon Eisenberg and David R. De Maso call this "commitment to the least fortunate members of society, both in terms of clinical services to individuals and of leadership for social change," the *AJO*'s "proudest characteristic."[66]

THE CHILDREN'S BUREAU SINCE 1935:
AN OVERVIEW

During the 1930s there were repeated attempts to divest the Children's Bureau of some of its functions. These efforts failed, but by the end of World War II many questioned the bureau's special status. It was "the only agency in any modern democratic country organized exclusively on a population age-group basis—an admirable administrative device in the eyes of the bureau's particular friends, [but] an anachronism in . . . the eyes of many groups that support a broad Federal welfare program."[67] The Reorganization Act of 1945 provided an opening for those in the Budget Bureau, the Public Health Service, and the Federal Security Administration who believed that government services should be organized by function rather than age. Children's Bureau chief Katherine Lenroot argued that since children had no political power, they needed a powerful federal agency to protect their interests, but President Truman's reorganization plan of 1946 transferred the bureau from the Labor Department to the Federal Security Administration.[68] There it became "one of a number of administrative units under a non-cabinet level" and was stripped of its labor functions.[69] (Since 1913 the chiefs of the bureau had reported directly to the Secretary of Labor, and therefore had enjoyed a large measure of independence.) After thirty-four years of stability, the bureau had experienced four major organizational moves in less than twenty years.[70]

An historian of public health argues that "the bureau was further enfeebled in 1953, when it became a minor unit in the Department of Health, Education and Welfare; went one step farther in 1963 when it was switched to the Welfare Administration and divested of its responsibility for researching child health issues; and culminated in 1969 when President Nixon took away its responsibility for administering maternal and child health programs."[71] It is now a relatively minor agency in the Administration for Children and Families in the Department of Health and Human Services.[72] Lenroot's prediction that children's programs would get lost if they were merged with adult programs turned out to be correct.[73]

WHITE HOUSE CONFERENCES, 1940–1970

Decennial White House Conferences for children were held through 1970.[74] The 1940 conference, "Children in a Democracy," drew attention to inequalities in opportunities for rural children and those in low-income, minority, and migrant families. Only seven hundred people attended the conference, and its work was overshadowed by the onset of World War II.[75]

The mid-century conference focused on how each child could achieve a healthy personality. It publicized the findings of dynamic psychiatry, particularly the theories of psychoanalyst Erik Erikson, and was the first conference in which youth participated. Attended by five thousand delegates, it was hailed as "the largest movement on behalf of children in the history of this country."[76] In its 1954 decision outlawing racial segregation in public schools, the Supreme Court cited the findings of the 1950 conference fact-finding report on the harmful effects of segregation on children.

"Children in a Changing World," the 1960 Golden Anniversary White House Conference on Children and Youth, was attended by more than seven thousand delegates. It focused on American values and the effects of rapid changes in society and the world on the development of children and youth.[77]

The White House Conference for Children and Youth, known as the "Nixon Conference," was divided, for the first time, into two parts, a conference on children up to age thirteen, held in Washington, D.C., in December 1970 and a separate conference on youth aged fourteen to eighteen held in Estes Park, Colorado, in April 1971.[78] Young protesters against the Vietnam War had disrupted the Democratic National Convention in Chicago in 1968, and the potential for similar protests undoubtedly underlay the decision to hold a separate youth conference. The conference on children was attended by 3,700 delegates, the conference on youth by 1,500.

An attempt to continue the tradition of biennial White House conferences for children and youth failed during the Carter administration and has not been tried since, although a White House Conference on Early Childhood was held during the Clinton administration in 1997.

FEDERAL SUPPORT FOR RESEARCH
ON CHILDREN

As we have seen, the initial program of the National Institute of Mental Health (NIMH), established in 1946, was based largely on that of the Commonwealth

Fund. Today NIMH supports studies on cognitive development, social and personality processes in children, and developmental psychopathology. The National Institute of Child Health and Development (NICHD) was established in 1963 as part of the National Institutes of Health to support research on the development of both normal and mentally disabled children. Both the NIMH and the NICHD support intramural as well as extramural programs and multidisciplinary research. The National Science Foundation and the Institute of Education Sciences also fund child development research.[79] All of these federal agencies are of central importance to the fields of the child sciences.

INFORMING THE AMERICAN PEOPLE ABOUT
THE WELL-BEING OF OUR CHILDREN

Although several federal agencies support research on children, none has assumed the responsibility, mandated by the Children's Bureau Act of 1912, "to report on all matters pertaining to the welfare of children and child life among all classes of our people." Julia Lathrop wisely continued to interpret the reporting function to mean keeping the nation fully informed about the status of its children.[80] In recent years, the reporting function is primarily the province of UNESCO and private institutions such as the Brookings Institution, the Annie E. Casey Foundation, the Carnegie Corporation, Child Trends, the Children's Defense Fund, the Foundation for Child Development, the Society for Research in Child Development, and the William T. Grant Foundation.

An *AJO* editorial commented on the inability of NIMH and either federal research agency to publish their results in "user-friendly formats" or "to translate their results into meaningful agendas for action."[81] Perhaps these agencies need to be reminded of the conviction of the first two chiefs of the Children's Bureau that an informed public is essential to the well-being of the nation's children.

HEAD START: FEDERAL INTERVENTION
ON BEHALF OF POOR CHILDREN

Project Head Start was launched in 1965 to provide environmental enrichment for preschool-age children from low-income families in order to improve their physical, mental, and emotional development and, it was hoped, to prevent future poverty among them.[82] The social and scientific climate that led to Head

Start was a mixture of new attitudes and old beliefs. New attitudes pertained primarily to the responsibilities of the federal government and its role in combating poverty. The conviction, widespread in the 1920s, that social reform could be achieved by applying scientific knowledge to early childhood stimulated this comprehensive effort by the federal government to intervene in children's lives. Since the 1920s Americans had learned that poverty was widespread and persistent, with consequences that threatened the nation's social and economic well-being.[83] The civil rights movement of the 1950s and 1960s and the growing concern about poverty fueled the conviction that the federal government should try to reduce social and economic inequality. The Economic Opportunity Act (EOA) was passed in August 1964, early in the Johnson administration. The EOA opened the "war on poverty," and the creation of Head Start was one part.[84]

The entrenched American faith in the power of education to foster equality and the revival of the belief that early childhood is the most important determinant of later behavior were used to justify Head Start. Interest was reawakened in the questions raised by staff of the Iowa Child Welfare Research Station in the 1930s on the response of the IQ to environmental changes. During the 1960s new works challenged the hereditarian traditions that had dominated the 1950s.[85] Many assumed that environmental enrichment for children could work quickly and have permanent effects. Again in the 1960s, as in the 1920s, the stage was set for unrealistic expectations about what a program for children could accomplish.[86]

Until the 1960s few developmentalists had studied the effects on children of their socioeconomic environment. Only 10 percent of the articles in *Child Development* between 1930 and 1959 dealt with this subject.[87] Those developmentalists who did undertake studies of the effects of special interventions to counter environmental risks focused narrowly on cognitive processes. The field then exploded in the 1980s and 1990s, resulting in extensive studies of poverty and children.[88]

The paucity of investigations in the 1960s that might have been useful to the planners of Head Start was partly a consequence of the unfortunate decision by participants in the early child development and child guidance movements to focus on the middle-class child. Although the Children's Bureau was interested in showing the general effects of poverty on children, it was not interested in studying its impact on the development of individual children.

Sargent Shriver, director of the Office of Economic Opportunity from 1965 to 1968, invited child developmentalists to participate in the planning of Head Start although they had had little experience with public policy complexities.[89]

The developmentalists advised the planners to begin with a small pilot project that could provide a foundation of evidence and experience for a national program. Political pressure led to the establishment in 1965 of a summer program for 561,359 children enrolled in 11,068 centers. This was expanded to a year-long program, hastily implemented.[90] Developmentalist Bettye Caldwell confessed, "Many of us were uneasy."[91] Administrator Jules Sugarman commented on how hard it was, in the face of the pressures and enthusiasms of the 1960s, to say, "No, we're not ready."[92] President Johnson contributed to the grandiose expectations by declaring that the eight-week summer program would ensure that "thirty million man-years, the combined lifespan of these youngsters— will be spent productively and rewardingly, rather than wasted in tax-supported institutions or in welfare-supported lethargy."[93] "Impassioned rhetoric flowed like foam at a beerfest in Munich. We were going to accomplish miracles for the children of America," Caldwell recalled.[94]

Developmentalists did help to design a multidisciplinary, multifaceted program aimed at reaching the "whole child," that familiar phrase from the 1920s and 1930s. Lois-Ellin Datta pointed out that the program had to meet each child's individual medical, dental, nutritional, and developmental needs and to encompass cognitive, linguistic, motivational, and social-emotional dimensions.[95] Head Start's social and psychological services were intended to foster the children's social competence and motivation, and because children were perceived in relation to their community as well as their family, the program established links with many community services. Its emphasis on parent participation in its administration and day-to-day activities was one of its most successful components.[96]

The most common criticism of early Head Start was that it promised too much. The lesson of the past, that lasting damage is inflicted when too much is promised, had not been learned. A dozen years after its start, Sandra Scarr and R. A. Weinberger wrote that Head Start was still recovering from "environmentalism run amok."[97] In 1993 Zigler and Styco concluded: "Childhood intervention alone cannot transform lives. . . . and must not be considered more than one piece of the solution to the problem of poverty."[98]

Head Start, nonetheless, became the most successful of the Great Society programs and has survived for more than thirty-five years. It now serves about 35 percent of low-income children. Efforts continue not only to improve current programs but to extend Head Start to other age groups and to all children.[99] In view of the politicization of Head Start throughout its history, its future may depend as much on whether or not it serves political interests as on how much it helps poor young children and their families. Documenting the accomplishments of Head Start has been crucial to its survival.[100] One can only hope that continued evidence of its worth and favorable political circumstances will enable one of the world's most important governmental interventions for children to continue.

WHAT'S AHEAD?

The enterprises that the founders of child study set in motion about a century ago have profoundly affected the ways in which we think about and treat children and their development. With revolutionary advances in technology and methodology on the horizon, no one can predict what the scientific study of children will tell us in the future or where it will lead.

More knowledge about children has not stimulated the new commitment to children the founders hoped for. The United States still lags behind the rest of the industrialized world in providing childcare and adequate food and shelter for poor children, in infant mortality rates, in medical and social support for poor pregnant women, and in paid maternity leave. The passage of the Children's Health Insurance Program (CHIP) in 1997 made an important contribution to child health care. Although the United States continues to lead the world in expenditures for education, it has been reluctant to provide funds for children's other needs. And it is still timid about childcare measures that might limit family autonomy. The belief that "My children are none of your business" still prevails among a substantial portion of the population. Today young children are more likely than any other age-group to be poor, and the ever-increasing number of older American voters should make it even harder to fund the basic services children need.

These comments are meant to be realistic, not pessimistic. It is much easier to find out what should be done for children than to get it done. Only within the past few decades could developmentalists and policy makers be confident that the knowledge base was sound enough to risk significant intervention. Challenges remain because policy decisions require extensive scientific evaluation over the long run. Developmentalists now pay much more attention to social policy issues but need to concentrate more on better communication with policy makers, practitioners, and the public. How can developmentalists compress complicated information into brief, accurate, easily understood statements? Much needed are case studies of how knowledge of children has been applied effectively and how it has been misapplied and misinterpreted.

Currently, many Americans are worried about the future of the nation's children. But history is full of surprises. Achieving social change is almost always a matter of tenacious, long-term effort, unexpected opportunity, or both. Who knows if, or when, a fortuitous coalescence of scientific advance and social circumstance, comparable to that which occurred in the 1920s, will reawaken the nation to the importance of its children? We must hope that if that moment comes, developmentalists, policy makers, and others who care about children will be ready to seize the opportunity.

Notes

INTRODUCTION: THREE MOVEMENTS, ONE GOAL

1. Harold Jones, "The Replacement Problem in Child Analysis," *Child Development* 27(1956): 237. Jones reported that a 1918 survey showed that only three psychologists and two psychiatrists (not identified) studied children exclusively. I am indebted to David Johnson, Executive Director of the Federation of Behavioral, Psychological and Cognitive Sciences for his "educated guess" about the number of behavioral scientists studying children today. He based it on the membership of numerous organizations, with generous allowance for overlap and members not involved in research. The organizations counted included the Society for Research in Child Development, the American Education Research Association, several divisions of the American Psychological Association, and pediatric societies focusing on developmental or behavioral research.

2. Clarke Chambers, *Seedtime of Reform: American Social Services and Social Action, 1918–1933* (Minneapolis, 1963), 30–31.

3. Sydney Halpern, *American Pediatrics: The Social Dynamics of Professionalism, 1880–1980* (Berkeley, 1988), 80–109; Steven L. Schlossman, "Perils of Popularization: The Founding of *Parents' Magazine*," *History and Research in Child Development,* ed. Alice Smuts and John Hagen, Monographs of the Society for Research in Child Development 50 (Chicago, 1986).

4. *National Research Council Directory of Research in Child Development,* ed. James A. Hicks, Reprint and Circular Series of the National Research Council no. 102 (Washington, D.C., 1931); Handbooks of Child Psychology were published in 1931, 1933, 1946, 1954, 1970, and 1983; and Leo Kanner, *Child Psychiatry* (Springfield, Illinois, 1935). For information on the founding of the child development institutes, see chapter 9 and for the child guidance clinics of the 1920s, chapter 12. The American Orthopsychiatry Association (AOA), the organization that represents child guidance professionals, had twenty-six members when it was founded in 1924. The Society for Research in Child Development (SRCD) also began in 1933 with one hundred members. In 1995 the AOA and the SRCD have approximately twelve thousand and five thousand members, respectively. The *American Journal of Orthopsychiatry* and *Child Development* were founded in 1930.

5. Sigmund Freud, "The Analysis of a Phobia in a Five-Year Old Boy in 1909," in Freud, *Collected Papers* (London, 1933) 3: 149–248; and John Anderson, "Methods in Child Psychology," *Handbook of Child Psychology,* ed. Carl Murchison (Worcester, Mass., 1931). See chapter 2 for additional examples of hostility to the study of children.

6. The first child guidance clinic was the Illinois Psychopathic Institute, described by William Healy and Augusta Bronner in their chapter, "The Child Guidance Clinic: Birth and Growth of an Idea," in *Orthopsychiatry, 1923–1948: Retrospect and Prospect,* ed. Lawson G. Lowrey and Victoria Sloane (New York, 1948), 14–34. The first child development institute was the Iowa Child Welfare Research Station, described in Dorothy Bradbury and George Stoddard, *Pioneering in Child Welfare: A History of the Iowa Child Welfare Research Station, 1917–1933* (Iowa City, 1933); and Hamilton Cravens, *Before Head Start: The Iowa Station and America's Children* (Chapel Hill, 1993).

7. The Children's Bureau's budget in 1912 was $25,600, the Iowa Child Welfare Research Station's annual budget was $25,000, and the Illinois Psychopathic Institute's budget was $25,000 for a five-year period.

8. Commonwealth Fund, "Report of the Conference on Juvenile Delinquency," 1921; and Commonwealth Fund Archive, Rockefeller Archive Center, North Tarrytown, New Jersey; and Lawrence K. Frank, *Recent Social Trends: A Report of the President's Research Committee on Social Trends* (New York, 1932), xliv. See also Harold Coe Coffman, *American Foundations: A Study of Their Role in the Child Welfare Movement* (New York, 1936); John C. Burnham, "The New Psychology: From Narcissism to Social Control," in *Change and Continuity in Twentieth-Century America: The 1920s,* ed. John Braemen, Robert E. Bremner, and David Brody (Columbus, Ohio, 1938), 82–92; and Henry May, "Shifting Perspectives on the 1920s," *Mississippi Historical Review* 18 (1956): 405–27.

9. Dorothy Bradbury, *Five Decades of Action: A History of the Children's Bureau* (Washington, D.C., 1962); and Herbert Hoover, "Opening Address," in *White House Conference for Child Health and Protection, 1930: Addresses and Abstracts of Committee Reports* (New York, 1931), 7.

10. Robert Wiebe, *The Search For Order, 1877–1920* (New York, 1967), 169. "Welfare" at this time meant "well-being" in a general sense, with no connotation of charity or aid to the poor. In the early decades, the Laura Spelman Rockefeller institutes were called child welfare research institutes rather than institutes of child development research.

11. Dorothy Ross, *G. Stanley Hall: The Psychologist as Prophet* (Chicago, 1972), 279–308; and David Levy, "Critical Evaluation of the Present State of Child Psychiatry," *American Journal of Psychiatry* 108(1952): 482.

12. Ross, *G. Stanley Hall,* 115–24; Edwin S. Corwin, "The Impact of the Idea of Evolution on the American Political and Constitutional Tradition," in *Evolutionary Thought in America,* ed. Stow Persons (New Haven, 1950), 191; Ralph Barton Perry, *The Thought and Character of William James* (Cambridge, Mass., 1948); Morton G. White, *Pragmatism and the American Mind* (New York, 1973); and Allen Davis, *Spearheads For Reform: The Social Settlements and the Progressive Movement, 1890–1914* (New York, 1967). Among the scientists who helped the women reformers were the eminent psychologist Carl Emil Seashore, who drew up the blueprint for the Iowa Child Welfare Research Station and advised Hillis and her followers on how to conduct their campaigns, and Adolph Meyer and William James, who advised Julia Lathrop and Ethel Dummer to employ William Healy to undertake the clinical study of juvenile delinquents. During the last decade of the nineteenth century and until 1910, Hall had worked with progressive reformers on campaigns for juvenile justice, playgrounds, and better recreation but had refused to participate in efforts to reduce child labor or abolish poverty. After 1910 Hall no longer retained the approval of social justice reformers. Organized motherhood, always Hall's staunchest supporter, remained loyal. Hall the scientist is the subject of chapter 2, and Hall the reformer appears in chapters 2–5. See also Sophonisba Breckinridge, *Women in the Twentieth Century: A Study of Their Political, Economic, and Social Activities* (New York, 1933).

13. Bradbury and Stoddard, *Pioneering in Child Welfare;* Healy and Bronner, "Child Guidance Clinic," 14–20; and Ethel Dummer, "Life in Relation to Time," in *Orthopsychiatry, 1923–1948,* ed. Lowrey and Sloane, 3–13. The role of urban women in Progressive reform is well known, but the campaign of Iowa farm women for the Iowa station and the support of the Children's Bureau by organized farm women during the 1920s, when the Bureau was attacked as a communist organization, suggest that the contribution of rural women to social reform needs further investigation.

14. Robert W. De Forest, "Margaret Olivia Sage, Philanthropist," *Survey* 34(November 1918): 151; Miriam Z. Lansam, "Anna M. Richardson Harkness," *Notable American Women: The Modern Period,* ed. Barbara Sicherman and Carol Hurd (Cambridge, Mass., 1980), 134–35; and *The Merrill-Palmer Institute Report,* 1920–1940 (Detroit, 1941).

15. Bradbury and Stoddard, *Pioneering in Child Welfare;* Leo Kanner, "American Contributions to the Development of Child Psychiatry," *Psychological Quarterly* 35 supplement (1961): 5; and *Child Mental Health in International Perspective,* ed. Henry David (New York, 1972). European women social reformers who led child welfare movements were not nearly as concerned as American women with linking child welfare reform to child study.

CHAPTER 1. SAVE THE CHILD AND SAVE THE NATION

1. Arthur Calhoun, *A Social History of the American Family from Colonial Times to the Present* (New York, 1973), 51; and Anne L. Kuhn, *The Mother's Role in Childhood Education: New England Concepts, 1830–1860* (New Haven, 1947), 26.

2. Linda K. Kerber, "Daughters of Columbia: Educating Women for the Republic, 1787–1806," in *The Hofstadter Aegis: A Memorial,* ed. Stanley Elkins and Erik McKitrick (New York, 1974), 36–59; Linda K. Kerber, "The Republican Mother: Women and the Enlightenment—An American Perspective," *American Quarterly [AQ]* 28(1976): 186–205; and Linda K. Kerber, *Women of the Republic: Intellect and Ideology in Revolutionary America* (Chapel Hill, 1980). I agree with scholars who claim that much of American child-centeredness is rooted in the nation's orientation toward the future. Child labor was not considered a problem until late in the nineteenth century. Norton traces the origins of domesticity during the colonial era. See Mary Beth Norton, *Liberty's Daughters: The Revolutionary Experience of American Women, 1750–1800* (Boston, 1980).

3. Kerber, "Republican Mother," 199; and Benjamin Rush, "Thoughts on Female Education, Accommodated to the Present State of Society, Manners, and Government in the U.S.A." (Philadelphia, 1787).

4. Lois Meek Stolz, Interview by Alice Smuts, transcript in author's possession, 9 December 1976. Mary Ryan discusses the transition from "patriarchal household to feminine domesticity" (Mary P. Ryan, *The Empire of the Mother: American Writing About Domesticity, 1830–1860* (New York, 1982), 19–43). For Rush's ideas on female education and a discussion of other concepts that helped to distinguish the "democratic" from the "aristocratic" lady, see Nancy F. Cott, *The Bonds of Womanhood: "Woman's Sphere" in New England, 1780–1835* (New Haven, 1977), 104–05.

5. Edmund S. Morgan, *The Puritan Family: Religious and Domestic Relations in Seventeenth-Century New England* (New York, 1966); and Gerald F. Moran and Maris A. Vinovskis, "The Great Care of Godly Parents: Early Childhood in Puritan New England," in *History and Research in Child Development,* vol. 50., ed. Alice B. Smuts and John Hagen (Chicago, 1986), 24–37.

6. The ideology of domesticity and the New England movements that sought social reform through the child are discussed by Kuhn and Cott (Kuhn, *Mother's Role in Childhood Education,* 71–97; and Cott, *Bonds of Womanhood,* 63–100). Margolis points out that the existence of a separate feminine domestic realm and the expectation that women would devote most of their time and energy to child rearing dated only from the early nineteenth century and applied only to middle- and upper-class women (Maxine Margolis, *Mothers and Such: Views of American Women and Why They Change* (Berkeley and Los Angeles, 1984), 4, 12.

7. Robert Sunley, "Early-Nineteenth-Century American Literature on Child Rearing," *Childhood in Contemporary Cultures,* ed. Margaret Mead and Martha Wolfenstein (Chicago, 1955), 150–67; Bernard Wishy, *The Child and the Republic: The Dawn of Modern American Child Nurture* (Philadelphia, 1972), 3–49; and Mary Ryan, *Empire of the Mother,* 19–43. Kerber argues: "Even as Americans enlarged the scope, resonance, and power of republicanism they simultaneously discounted and weakened the forces of patriarchy. They recoded the value of women's sphere, validating women's moral influence on their husbands and lovers, ascribing world historical importance to women's maternal role, and claimed for women a nature less sexual and more self-controlled than the nature of men. The ideology of republican womanhood recognized that women's choices and women's work did serve large social and political purposes, and that recognition was

enough to draw the traditional women's 'sphere' somewhat closer to men's 'world,' but to use the ideology of domesticity was also to make a conservative political choice among alternative options" (Linda Kerber, "Separate Spheres, Female Worlds, Woman's Place: The Rhetoric of Women's History," *Journal of American History* [*JAH*] 75 [June 1988]: 20).

8. John Abbott quoted in Phillip Greven, Jr., ed., *Child Rearing Concepts, 1682–1861: Historical Sources* (Itasca, 1973), 133.

9. Barbara Welter, "The Cult of Womanhood, 1820–1860," *AQ* 18(1966): 51–74.

10. Nancy Hewitt, "Beyond the Search for Sisterhood: American Women's History in the 1980s," *Journal of Social History* 10(1985): 302–03, 311.

11. Laura McCall, "The Reign of Brute Force Is Now Over: A Content Analysis of Godey's Lady's Book, 1830–1860," *Journal of Educational Research* [*JER*] 9(1989): 218–36.

12. Ryan, *Empire of the Mother*, 143–57. See especially Kerber's stimulating review on historians' use of the metaphor of "separate spheres" (Kerber, "Separate Spheres," 9–39). Other useful reviews of historians' interpretations of domestic ideology are in Barbara Sicherman, "Review Essay, American Essay," *Signs* 1(1975): 461–85; and Hewitt "Beyond the Search for Sisterhood."

13. Kuhn, *Mother's Role in Education*, 186.

14. Slater brilliantly discusses the shift from Enlightenment to romantic views of child nature (Philip Slater, *Children in the New England Mind: In Death and Life* (Hamden, Conn., 1977)). On romantic reform in America from 1815 to 1865, see John Thomas, "Romantic Reform in America," *AQ* 17(1965): 656–81.

15. Bushnell is quoted in Greven, "Child Rearing Concept," 158–59, 173. See also Horace Bushnell, "Discourses on Christian Nurture," reprint (New York, 1867). Greven's historical sources on child-rearing concepts from 1628 to 1861 present a vivid picture of puritan-evangelical concepts and the transformation of these concepts by Bushnell.

16. Abbott, also convinced of the importance of early childhood, declared that "in a vast majority of cases the first six or seven years decide the character of the man" (John Abbott, *The Mother at Home* (New York, 1833), 159). During the last part of the nineteenth century, the emphasis shifted to the school-age child. Attention to children between two- and seven-years-old did not resume until World War I.

17. In Slater, *Children in the New England Mind*, 93.

18. Cott, *Bonds of Womanhood*, 93–99. Cott argues that the canon of domesticity implied a repudiation of aristocratic models and placed all women on the same level.

19. Kathryn Sklar, *Catharine Beecher: A Study in American Domesticity* (New Haven, 1973). Beecher, a prime example of the Republican Mother, was the most popular author proclaiming the message of the mother's sacred mission, to fulfill through child rearing the promise of the democracy. She preached that wifehood and motherhood were professions to which all other interests of women should be subordinated.

20. Richard Meckel, "Educating a Ministry of Mothers: Evangelical Maternal Associations, 1815–1860," *JER* 2(1982): 403–23. Boylan discusses the role of maternal associations in promoting Sunday schools. The origin and growth of maternal associations must be seen within the context of the extraordinary growth, during the early nineteenth century, of women's benevolent associations and female religious activism (Anne Boylan, *The Ori-*

gins of Evangelical Sunday Schools: The Formation of an American Institution, 1790–1880 (New Haven, 1988)). Among the more important works in a vast literature on this subject are Carroll Smith-Rosenberg, *Religion and the Rise of the American City: The New York City Mission Movement, 1812–1870* (Ithaca, N. Y., 1971); Mary Ryan, "The Power of Women's Networks: A Case Study of Female Moral Reform in Antebellum America," *Feminist Studies* 5 (1979): 66–85; Mary Ryan, *Cradle of the Middle Class,* 1981; Mary Ryan, *Women in the Public: Between Banners and Ballots* (Baltimore, 1990); Nancy Hewitt, *Women's Action and Social Change, Rochester, N.Y., 1822–1872* (Ithaca, N.Y., 1984); and Lori Ginsberg, *Women and the Work of Benevolence: Morality, Politics, and Class in the Nineteenth-Century United States,* (New Haven, 1990). Ginsberg's introduction discusses the specific contributions of many of these works.

21. Meckel, "Educating a Ministry," 402–23. Meckel attributes the overwhelming involvement of women in voluntary religious activities, at this time, to the effects of the Second Great Awakening. He believes that the influence of maternal associations may have been underestimated because they were organized at the local level and often left no lasting records. Cott (*Bonds of Womanhood,* 7, 149–51) argues that the appearance of maternal associations suggests how the perception of motherhood as a social, as well as a personal role led women to seek supportive peer groups. Maternal associations, she speculates, were forerunners of the new women's organizations that grew so rapidly after the Civil War. Kett points out that maternal associations limited their scope to concern for children under ten years of age, since older children were considered the responsibility of men (Joseph Kett, "The Stages of Life, 1790–1840," in *The American Family in Social Historical Perspective,* ed. Michael Gordon [New York, 1983], 233).

22. Kuhn, Cott, and Kerber call attention to the ambiguity of the ideology of domesticity, its potential for either conservative or radical interpretations (Kuhn, *Mother's Role in Childhood Education,* 180–81; Cott, *Bonds of Womanhood,* 203–06; and Kerber, "Republican Mother," 204–05).

23. Anne Scott, *Natural Allies: Women's Association in American History* (Urbana, Ill., 1993), 58–77.

24. Kuhn, *Mother's Role in Childhood Education,* 180–81; Cott, *Bonds of Womanhood,* 203–06; and Kerber, "Republican Mother," 204–205.

25. Barbara Ehrenreich and Deirdre English, *For Her Own Good: 150 Years of Experts' Advice to Women,* (Garden City, N.Y., 1979), 194, quoting Beatrice Forbes-Robertson Hale, *What Women Want: An Interpretation of the Feminist Movement* (New York, 1914), 246.

26. Aileen S. Kraditor, *The Ideas of the Woman Suffrage Movement, 1890–1920* (New York: 1965), 65–67, 257–59.

27. Cott discusses the origins and history of the term "social feminism" and its variants. She argues that "the use of social feminism as an umbrella term neither deals with the broad political spectrum from left to right that both men's and women's politics occupied, nor recognizes that women's loyalties and alliances, outside of feminism, shaped their women-oriented activities" (Nancy Cott, "What's in a Name? The Limits of 'Social Feminism', or Expanding the Vocabulary of Women's History," *JAH* 76 (1989): 809–29). Pernick supports and elaborates on Cott's objections to "social feminism" and suggests the substitution of more precise terms (Martin Pernick, "Letters to the Editor," *JAH* 77 (June

1990): 380–81). Although I agree with their criticisms, I retain the term as used by many of the historians I cite. More recently, Koven and Michel have used the term "maternalism" to cover "ideologies and discourses that exalted women's capacity to mother" and were sometimes adopted by society as a whole (Seth Koven and Sonya Michel, "Womanly Duties, Maternalist Politics, and the Origins of the Welfare States in France, Germany, Great Britain, and the United States," *American Historical Review* 95(1990): 1076–1108). Sklar and other historians who wish to emphasize the contributions of women to the origins of the modern state, use "maternalism" (Kathryn Sklar, "The Historical Foundations of Women's Power in the Creation of the American Welfare States, 1830–1950," in *Mothers of a New World*, ed. Seth Koven and Sonya Michel (New York, 1993)).

28. Nancy Cott discusses three traditions of feminism in the late nineteenth century (Cott, *Grounding of Modern Feminism*).

29. Ethel Sturges Dummer, "Feminism," 30 October 1916, Ethel Sturges Dummer Papers [hereafter, ESD], Elizabeth and Arthur Schlesinger Library on the History of Women in the United States, Radcliffe College, Harvard University, Cambridge, Massachusetts, Box 16.

30. Kraditor, *Ideas of the Woman Suffrage Movement*, 117.

31. Ethel Sturges Dummer to Miss Chamberlain, 16 January 1914, ESD, Box 20; Ethel Sturges Dummer to Emma Lundberg, 24 February 1921, ESD, Box 36.

32. Charles Loring Brace, *The Dangerous Classes of New York City and Twenty Years' Work with Them* (New York, 1872). Brace portrayed neglected city children as a menace to society.

33. Jane Addams, "Why Women Should Vote," *Ladies Home Journal* 27(1909): 69.

34. Jacob Riis, *The Children of the Poor* (New York, 1892); and John Spargo, *The Bitter Cry of the Children* (New York and London, 1906).

35. Mrs. Theodore W. (Alice) Birney, "Address of Welcome" (paper presented at the National Congress of Mothers, New York, 1897).

36. Cora Bussey Hillis quoted in Ginalie Swaim,"Cora Bussey Hillis: Woman of Vision," *Palimpest* 60(1979): 163–77.

37. Ida Tarbell, *The Business of Being a Woman* (New York, 1912), 75, 81.

38. Charles Darwin, *The Origin of Species and the Descent of Man*, Modern Library ed. (New York, 1859), 873; Henry Drummond, *The Lowell Lecture on the Ascent of Man* (New York, 1894), 321; and Margaret Sage, quoted by Irwin G. Wyllie, "Margaret Olivia Slocum Sage, 1828–1918," in *Notable American Women, 1607–1950: A Bibliographic Dictionary*, ed. Edward T. James, Janet Wilson James, and Paul Boyer (Cambridge, Mass., 1971), 223. Margaret Sage practiced what she preached. She founded the Russell Sage Foundation in 1907 with an endowment of $10 million for the improvement of society.

39. The number of married women actually employed was probably much larger than the number shown in nineteenth-century censuses, but white middle-class wives and mothers did not begin to move into the paid labor force in large numbers until World War II. See Robert W. Smuts, "The Female Labor Force: A Case Study in the Interpretation of Historical Statistics," *Journal of the American Statistical Association* 55(1960): 71–79.

40. Sheila M. Rothman, *Woman's Proper Place: A History of Changing Ideals and Practices, 1870 to the Present* (New York, 1978), 19–21.

41. Ruth Schwartz Cowan, *More Work for Mothers: The Ironies of Household Technology from the Open Hearth to the Microwave* (New York, 1983), 100–01.

42. Anne Firor Scott, *Natural Allies, Women's Associations in American History* (Urbana, Ill., 1993), 85–110.

43. Karen J. Blair, *The Clubwoman as Feminist: True Womanhood Redefined, 1868–1914* (New York, 1980), 100–101.

44. Andrea Hofer-Proudfoot, *Des Moines Register,* 22 May 1900.

45. Ruth Bordin, *Women and Temperance: The Quest for Power and Liberty, 1873–1900* (Philadelphia, 1981), xvi.

46. Barbara Leslie Epstein, *The Politics of Domesticity: Women, Evangelism, and Temperance in Nineteenth-Century America* (Middletown, Conn., 1981), 115. See Epstein's volume for a discussion of the origins of the temperance movement.

47. Frances E. Willard, *Do Everything: A Handbook for the World's White Ribboners* (Chicago, 1895).

48. Bordin, *Women and Temperance,* 11–16, 98, 108.

49. Bordin, *Women and Temperance,* 103–04; and Rothman, *Woman's Proper Place,* 46–70.

50. Bordin, *Women and Temperance,* 102–04.

51. Bordin, *Women and Temperance, 149–50.* Epstein attributes the decline of temperance as a feminist movement to its insistence on promulgating conservative moral doctrines. See Epstein, *Politics of Domesticity,* 147–51.

52. William R. Brock, *Investigation and Responsibility: Public Responsibility in the United States, 1865–1900* (New York, 1984), 37–38.

53. Laurence Vesey, *The Emergence of the American University* (Chicago, 1965), 76–77.

54. Mary O. Furner, *Advocacy and Objectivity: A Crisis in the Professionalization of Social Science* (Lexington, Ky., 1975), 317, 324. Furner discusses the controversy over "reform versus knowledge" among social scientists shortly before and after the turn of the century. This controversy also dominated the early years of the movements to establish scientific child study and continues to the present (10–34).

55. Furner, *Advocacy and Objectivity,* 371.

56. Thomas Haskell, *The Emergence of Professional Social Science: The American Social Science Association and the Nineteenth-Century Crisis of Authority* (Urbana, Ill., 1977). The changes behind the decline of the ASSA and the rise of professional social science are discussed in Chapter 4.

57. William Leach, *True Love and Perfect Union: The Feminist Reform of Sex and Society* (New York, 1980), 292.

58. Leach, *True Love and Perfect Union,* 202.

59. Franklin Sanborn, "The Work of Social Science," *Journal of Social Science* [*JSS*] (July 1874), 37.

60. Franklin Sanborn, *JSS* (November 1887): 21; and Franklin Sanborn, *JSS* (May 1880): xxxi.

61. May Wright Sewall, "Domestic Education," *Ballot Box* (September 1881).

62. Leach, *True Love and Perfect Union,* 292–322.

63. Haskell, *Emergence of Professional Social Science,* vi.

64. Robert Bremner, *From the Depths: The Discovery of Poverty in the United States* (New York, 1956), 51–57.

65. Haskell, *Emergence of Professional Social Science,* 138.

66. Kenneth L. Kusmer, "The Functions of Organized Charity in the Progressive Era: Chicago as a Case Study," *JAH* (December, 1973), 677. Kusmer objects to the tendency of Bremner and other historians to treat the charity organization movement as a transitional occurrence rather than a major social movement (657–68). It continued to grow in importance and complexity until the 1930s and was largely responsible for the development of casework theory and the professionalization of social work.

67. Robert Bremner, *From the Depths,* 51–57; and Walter Trattner, *From Poor Law to Welfare State: A History of Social Welfare in America* (New York, 1979), 86–89.

68. Haskell, *Emergence of Professional Social Science,* 102–03.

69. All quotations in this paragraph are found in Kusmer, "Functions of Organized Charity in the Progressive Era," 660–71.

70. Bremner, *From the Depths,* 51–57; Trattner, *From Poor Law to Welfare State,* 86–93; and James Patterson, *America's Struggle Against Poverty* (Cambridge, Mass., 1986), 3–20.

71. Estelle Freedman, "Separatism as Strategy: Female Institution Building and American Feminism, 1870–1930," *Feminist Studies* 5(1979): 518.

72. Allen F. Davis, *Spearheads for Reform: The Social Settlements and the Progressive Movements, 1890–1914* (New York, 1967), 3–8, 12–16. Chosen to second the nomination of Theodore Roosevelt for President of the United States on the Progressive Party ticket in 1912, Addams received as much applause from the delegates as Roosevelt. She played a significant part in writing the party platform and in the campaign. According to Davis, Addams, portrayed as a benevolent "Saint Jane," came to symbolize disinterested virtues and was venerated more than any other American woman (Allen Davis, *American Heroine: The Life and Legend of Jane Addams* [New York, 1973], 104, 146, 47, 189). In 1931 she received the Nobel Prize.

73. Davis, *Spearheads for Reform,* 16–18.

74. Robert C. Reinders, "Toynbee Hall and the American Settlement Movement," *Social Service Review* (March 1982): 39–54.

75. Barbara Miller Solomon, *In the Company of Educated Women* (New Haven, 1985), 109–12.

76. Davis, *American Heroine,* 46.

77. Kathryn Kish Sklar, "Hull House in the 1980's: A Community of Women Reformers," *Journal of Women in Culture and Society* 10 (1985): 663; and Clark A. Chambers, *Paul Kellogg and the Survey: Voices for Social Welfare* (Minneapolis, 1971), 25. Women received only 17 percent of the bachelor's degrees granted in 1890, however, suggesting that many women enrolled in higher education were not pursuing degree programs (United States Commissioner of Education, "Annual Statement of the Commissioner of Education to the Secretary of the Interior" (Washington D.C., 1890)).

78. Jane Addams, *The Second Twenty Years at Hull-House, September 1909 to September 1929* (New York, 1930): 408.

79. Davis, *Spearheads for Reform,* 18–22; and Anne Firor Scott introduction to *Democracy and Social Ethics,* by Jane Addams (Cambridge, Mass., 1964), xxxix, xlvi.

80. Bremner, *From the Depths,* 123–25.

81. Addams, *Second Twenty Years,* 310–13.

82. Jane Addams, "Charity and Social Justice," (paper presented at the NCCC, 1910), 1–2.

83. Jane Addams, *Twenty Years at Hull-House* (New York, 1910), 312.

84. Chambers, *Paul Kellogg and the Survey,* 25–30, 53.

85. Addams, "Charity and Social Justice," 1–5.

86. Martin Bulmer, Kevin Bales, and Kathryn K. Sklar, "The Social Survey in Historical Perspective," in *Social Survey in Historical Perspective, 1880–1940,* ed. Kevin Bales, Martin Bulmer, and Kathryn K. Sklar (Cambridge, 1991), 3. Social investigation, a broader category than social survey, is part of the prehistory of the survey. Social investigation was used to describe statistical investigations and other types of inquiries into social conditions, especially those that had a distinctly moral tone (Bulmer, Bales, and Sklar, "Social Survey in Historical Perspective," 12–13).

87. See Kevin Bales, "Charles Booth's Survey of the Life and Labour of the People of London 1889–1903," in *Social Survey in Historical Perspective,* ed. Bales, Bulmer, and Sklar, 66–110.

88. See Kathryn Sklar, "Hull House Maps and Papers: Social Science as Women's Work in the 1980s," in *Social Survey in Historical Perspective,* ed. Bales, Bulmer, and Sklar; W. E. B. Du Bois, *The Philadelphia Negro: A Social Study* (Philadelphia: University of Pennsylvania Press, 1996); and Steven Cohen, "The Pittsburgh Survey and the Social Survey Movement: A Sociological Road Not Taken," in *Social Survey in Historical Perspective,* ed. Bales, Bulmer, and Sklar. Cohen writes, "To minds shaped by the reform movements of the early twentieth century, the *Pittsburgh Survey* was the most notable example of a new scientific and democratic method to help transform American society from one in which free land had once provided the means for mass democracy and individual opportunity to one in which science . . . would now have to provide such opportunities."

89. John M. Glenn, Lilian Brandt, Frank E. Andrews, *Russell Sage Foundation, 1907–1946* (New York, 1947).

90. Bulmer, Bales, and Sklar, "Social Survey in Historical Perspective," 1–49.

91. Martin Bulmer, "The Decline of the Social Survey Movement and the Rise of American Empirical Psychology," in *Social Survey in Historical Perspective,* ed. Bales, Bulmer, and Sklar, 300.

92. Davis, *American Heroine,* 96.

93. Rosalind Rosenberg, *Beyond Separate Spheres: Intellectual Roots of Modern Feminism* (New Haven, 1982), 239–40; and Ellen F. Fitzpatrick, *Endless Crusade: Women Social Scientists and Progressive Reform* (New York, 1990), 71–75.

94. Sklar, "Hull House Maps and Papers," 135.

95. Sklar quoting Kelley, "Hull House Maps and Papers," 111–12.

96. Sklar, "Hull House Maps and Papers," 115.

97. Sklar, "Hull House Maps and Papers," 112–13.

98. Dorothy Ross, *The Origins of American Social Science* (New York, 1991). Ross explains that experimental psychology and psychiatry emerged from natural sciences, medicine, and biology.

99. Although the term "behavioral sciences" was not introduced until much later, to distinguish psychology and psychiatry from the social sciences, I use it. See chapters 2, 3, and 4

for illustrations of Hall as a transitional figure. Chapters 3 and 4 discuss the growth of women's organizations and their dedication to parent education and welfare reform.

CHAPTER 2. G. STANLEY HALL AND THE CHILD STUDY MOVEMENT

1. Wilhem Wundt, *Outlines of Psychology* (Leipzig, Germany, 1907).
2. For information on the baby biographies and excerpts from Darwin and Preyer's biographies, see William Kessen, *The Child* (New York, 1965). Hall studied his own two babies but did not publish his findings for many years, possibly because one child died. See G. Stanley Hall, "Notes on the Study of Infants," *Pedagogical Seminary* 1 (1891): 127–38.
3. Arnold Gesell, "Charles Darwin and the Study of Child Development," *Child Development* 46 (1939b) 548–50.
4. Charles Darwin, *The Expression of the Emotions in Man and Animals* (London, 1872).
5. Gesell, "Charles Darwin," 550–52.
6. Wilhelm Preyer, *The Mind of the Child* [Die Seele des Kindes], trans. G. Stanley Hall (New York, 1888–89).
7. Millicent Shinn, *Notes on the Development of a Child* (University of California Publications, 1893–99).
8. John C. Burnham, "Millicent Washburn Shinn, 1858–1940." in *Notable American Women, 1607–1950: A Biographical Dictionary*, ed. Edward T. James, Janet Wilson James, and Paul Boyer (Cambridge, Mass., 1971), 285–86.
9. G. Stanley Hall, "A Study of Anger," *American Journal of Psychology* 10 (1899): 516–91.
10. Dorothy Ross, *G. Stanley Hall: The Psychologist as Prophet* (Chicago, 1972), 81–99; and Sheldon White, "G. Stanley Hall: From Philosophy to the Developmental Psychology," in *A Century of Developmental Psychology*, ed. Peter Ornstein, Ross Parke, John Reiser, and Carolyn Zahn-Waxler (1994), 103–27.
11. Ross, *G. Stanley Hall*, 105–07.
12. Lawrence Cremin, *The Transformation of the School: Progressivism in American Education, 1876–1951* (New York, 1962); Carl F. Kaestle and Maris Vinovskis, *Educational and Social Change in Nineteenth-Century Massachusetts* (Cambridge, 1980); and David Tyack, *The One Best System: A History of American Urban Education* (Cambridge, Mass., 1974). Most of these topics are discussed and illustrated in Robert Bremner et al., *Children and Youth in America: A Documentary History, 1866–1932*, vol. 2 (Cambridge, Mass., 1971), 1093–115, 1317–45, 1383–84, 1420–62. For statistics on enrollment, and discussion of changes in education between 1890 and 1930, see Charles H. Judd, "Education," in *Recent Social Trends in the United States: Report of the President's Research Committee on Social Trends*, vol.2 (New York, 1933; reprint, 1970), 325–81. See Ronald D. Cohen, "Child Saving and Progressivism, 1885–1915," in *American Childhood: A Research Guide and Historical Handbook*, ed. Joseph M. Hawes and N. Ray Hiner (Westport, Conn., 1985), 273–98, for standard and revisionist interpretations of American education.
13. Ross, *G. Stanley Hall*, 120–23, 311–12.
14. On the kindergarten movement, see Evelyn Weber, *The Kindergarten Movement: Its Encounter with the Educational Thought in America* (New York, 1969); Elizabeth Dale Ross, *The Kindergarten Crusade: The Establishment of Preschool Education in the United States*

282   Notes to Pages 34–37

(Athens, Ohio, 1976); and Michael S. Shapiro, *Child's Garden: The Kindergarten Movement from Froebel to Dewey* (University Park, Pa., 1983). For the ways in which school texts reflected moral education, see Ruth Miller Elson, *Guardians of Tradition: American Schoolbooks of the Nineteenth Century* (Lincoln, Nebr., 1964).

15. Ross, *G. Stanley Hall,* 115–24.

16. Ross, *G. Stanley Hall,* 117–19.

17. The best and most extensive discussion is in Alexander Siegel and Sheldon H. White, "The Child Study Movement: Early Growth and Development of the Symbolized Child," *Advances of Child Development and Behavior* 17 (1982):233–85. See also John C. McCullers, "The Contents of Children's Minds: A Partial Replication," *Journal of the History of Behavioral Sciences* [*JHBS*] 12 (1971): 169–75; and Ross, *G. Stanley Hall,* 126–29.

18. G. Stanley Hall, "The Contents of Children's Minds upon Entering School," *Princeton Review* 2 (May 1883): 249–72.

19. Ross, *G. Stanley Hall,* 129–39.

20. Hall and James each claimed to have founded the first psychological laboratory in America.

21. Ross, *G. Stanley Hall,* 131–46, 211–12.

22. See Laurence Veysey, *The Emergence of the American University* (Chicago, 1965), 165–70, for ways in which Jonas Clark crippled Clark University and for the hiring of its faculty by the University of Chicago.

23. Ross, *G. Stanley Hall,* 279–80.

24. G. Stanley Hall, "Child Study and Its Relation to Education," in *Health, Growth and Heredity: G. Stanley Hall on Natural Education,* ed. Charles E. Strickland and Charles Burgess (New York, 1965), 76–77.

25. According to Grinder, Hall's genetic psychology is an offshoot of neo-Lamarckian evolutionary doctrine. See Robert E. Grinder, *A History of Genetic Psychology: The First Science of Human Development* (New York, 1967).

26. Ross has suggested that these profound changes in Hall's conception of child study may have been precipitated by the death of his wife and daughter in an accident. Jonas Clark's refusal to provide promised financial support and Hall's professional and personal reverses drained him. Between 1891 and 1895, a period called by Hall "The Great Fatigue," he published no substantive psychological work (Ross, *G. Stanley Hall,* 251–54).

27. Ross, *G. Stanley Hall,* 260–67.

28. Edward L. Thorndike, "G. Stanley Hall, 1846–1924," *National Academy of Sciences Biographical Memoirs* 12 (1928): 140.

29. Littman has described experimental psychology as a "mechanical, materialistic, physical science that safeguarded itself by banishing mind and soul." It was, he continued, an "abstract, impersonal, dehumanized psychology that emphasized man's rational nature and excluded morality, ethics, and the kinds of personal experiences on which the dynamic viewpoint concentrated" (Richard A. Littman, "Social and Intellectual Origins of Experimental Psychology," in *The First Century of Experimental Psychology,* ed. Eliot Hearst [1979], 50). Littman points out that experimental psychology's narrow scope excluded the study of individual differences, motivation, child development, psychosis and neurosis, animal be-

havior, and practical applications. Several nonpsychologists objected to the exclusion of ethics and religion from their disciplines. A group of American economists, for example, rebelled against the tenets of classical American and European political economy, insisting that economics could be both scientific and ethical. They differed from Hall in their emphasis on the welfare of the group rather than the individual, their opposition to laissez-faire, and their belief that state action was necessary to achieve social reform. For the blend of ethics and economics reflected in the goals and activities of early years of the American Economic Association, see Sidney Fine, *Laissez-Faire and the General Welfare State: A Study of Conflict in American Thought, 1865–1901* (Ann Arbor, Mich., 1951), 198–219.

30. Charles Darwin, *The Correspondence of Charles Darwin: Volume 13, 1865* (1865), 1–118.

31. Darwin, *Expression of the Emotions.*

32. In *The Descent of Man,* Darwin demonstrated his belief in the absence of fundamental differences between the mental faculties of man and the higher mammals (Charles Darwin, *The Descent of Man* [1871]). On Darwin as psychologist, see Howard Gruber, *Man: A Psychological Study of Scientific Creativity,* rev. ed. (Chicago, 1981).

33. Hall, "Contents of Children's Minds."

34. Ross, *G. Stanley Hall,* 263. For the questionnaire studies' varied subjects, see Louis N. Wilson, *Bibliography of Child Study, 1898–1912* (New York, 1975).

35. Ross points out that "evolutionary concepts and viewpoints supported and extended at every point the insights of the romantic poets and philosophers, and Hall's own self-awareness of the distinctive needs of childhood" (Ross, *G. Stanley Hall,* 265).

36. Littman, "Social and Intellectual Origins," 42.

37. Quoted in Henry Drummond, *The Lowell Lecture on the Ascent of Man* (New York, 1894).

38. William F. Quillan Jr., "Evolution and Moral Theory," in *Evolutionary Thought in America,* ed. Stow Persons (New Haven, 1950), 409–18.

39. Hall assured popular audiences that "scientific psychology could safely replace religion as the moral guide for such functions as child rearing and education," and he suggested that the role of science as a substitute or a foil for religion "may well account for some of the force and character of American psychology's scientific ideal" (quoted in Dorothy Ross, "The Zeitgeist and American Psychology," *JHBS* 5 (1969): 260–62). See James Turner, *Without God, Without Creed: The Origins of Unbelief in America* (Baltimore, 1985), 67–69, 94, for the belief of Hall and some of his contemporaries that human events reveal a moral purpose.

40. Ross, *G. Stanley Hall,* 89–91.

41. G. Stanley Hall, "The Ideal School as Based on Child Study," *Forum* 32 (1901): 24–39; Ross, *G. Stanley Hall,* 302, 371–79; and Dominick Cavallo, *Muscles and Morals: Organized Playgrounds and Urban Reform, 1880–1920* (Philadelphia, 1981), 57–70.

42. Hall describes the characteristics of children at each age and how schools should adapt to them (Hall, "Ideal School," 24–39). See Chapter 3 for the implications of Hall's recapitulation theory for child-rearing goals and practices.

43. Ross, *G. Stanley Hall,* 370.

44. G. Stanley Hall, *Adolescence: Its Psychology and Its Relations to Physiology, Anthropology, Sociology, Sex, Crime, Religion, and Education* (New York, 1904).

45. Ross, *G. Stanley Hall*, 286–301, 341–56; and Sheldon White, "Child Study at Clark University, 1894–1904," *JHBS* 26 (1990): 131–50.

46. Ross, *G. Stanley Hall*, 286.

47. Ross, *G. Stanley Hall*, 295.

48. Dorothy Bradbury, "The Contribution of the Child Study Movement to Child Psychology," *Psychological Bulletin* 34(1937): 21–38.

49. James Mark Baldwin, *Mental Development in the Child and the Race: Methods and Processes* (New York, 1895); James Mark Baldwin, *Social and Ethical Interpretations of Mental Development: A Study in Social Psychology* (New York, 1897); Robert B. Cairns, "Developmental Theory Before Piaget: The Remarkable Contribution of James Mark Baldwin," *Contemporary Psychology* 25 (1980): 438–40; and Robert B. Cairns, " The Making of a Developmental Science: The Contributions and Intellectual Heritage of James Mark Baldwin," in *Century of Developmental Psychology*, ed Ornstein, Parke, Rieser, and Zahn-Waxler, 127–43.

50. Emily Davis Cahan, "The Genetic Psychologies of James Mark Baldwin and Jean Piaget," *Developmental Psychology* 20, no. 1 (1984): 128–35; and Cairns, "Making of a Developmental Science," 139. James Mark Baldwin was president of the American Psychological Association and co-founder with James McKeen Cattell of three psychological journals.

51. Ross, *G. Stanley Hall*, 269–88.

52. Munsterberg quoted in G. Stanley Hall, *Life and Confessions of a Psychologist* (New York, 1923), 399.

53. Edward L. Thorndike, "G. Stanley Hall, 1846–1924," *National Academy of Sciences Biographical Memiors* 12 (1928): 140.

54. Ross, *G. Stanley Hall*, 268–70.

55. Hall, "Child Study and Its Relation to Education," 78–84, 88.

56. Edward L. Thorndike, "Notes on Child Study," *Columbia University Contributions to Philosophy, Psychology, and Education* 8, no. 3–4 (1901): 20.

57. Alan Costall, "Evolutionary Gradualism and the Study of Development," *Human Development* 29 (1986): 8.

58. Quoted by Arnold Gesell, "The Preschool Child in a Democracy," (Speech, 8 May 1939) Arnold Gesell Papers (including records of the Yale Child Development Clinic) [hereafter, AG], Library of Congress, Washington, D.C., Box 144.

59. John Anderson, *The Psychology of Development and Personal Development* (New York, 1955), 181.

60. Geraldine Jonich, *The Sane Positivist: A Bibliography of Edward L. Thorndike* (Middletown, Conn., 1968), 98. Barr maintains that, after 1900, physicians wanting to conduct medical research found that few objected to their use of children in orphanages as research subjects. See Bernadine Barr, "Spare Children, 1900–1945: Inmates of Orphanages as Subjects of Research in Medicine and in the Social Sciences in America" (Ph.D. diss., Stanford University, 1992).

61. Hall, "Child Study and Its Relation to Education," 78.

62. John B. Watson and Rosalie Raynor, "Conditioned Emotional Reactions," *Journal of Educational Psychology* 3 (1920): 1–14.

63. See the Children's Bureau Records in the National Archives (1914–1940, file 9–1-0–2) for the letters from 1918. During the 1970s there was a movement, especially among minority populations, to restrict scientists from harming or exploiting children who were research subjects; see Robert R. Sears, *Your Ancients Revisited: A History of Child Development* (Chicago, 1975), 63. Parental resistance to outside influence persists. Examples include objections to Head Start as an intrusion by government, the recent growth of the home-schooling movement, and the proposed "parental rights amendment" to the Colorado State constitution, designed to strengthen parents' control over child rearing and public school curricula, which was defeated by voters in 1996.

64. Dupree believes that "the rise of the laboratory is one of the great unwritten chapters in the history of American science. . . . By the turn of the century the dominant home of the American scientific community was the laboratory, a professional habitat from which scientists successfully excluded non-scientists"(A. Hunter Dupree, "The Measuring Behavior of American Scientists," in *Nineteenth-Century American Science,* ed. George H. Daniels [Evanston, Ill., 1972], 22–37).

65. Dupree, "Measuring Behavior," 22–37; and Littman, "Social and Intellectual Origins," 41.

66. Samuel F. Fernberger, "The American Psychological Association: A Historical Summary, 1892–1930," *Psychological Bulletin* 29 (1932): 1–89.

67. Thorndike, "Notes on Child Study," 20.

68. Michael M. Sokal, *An Education in Psychology: James McKeen Cattell's Journals and Letters from Germany and England, 1880–1890* (Cambridge, Mass., 1981); and Edwin Boring, *A History of Experimental Psychology.* 2d ed. (New York, 1950).

69. Edward Thorndike, *A History of Psychology in Autobiography,* 3 (1936), 260.

70. Thorndike, *History of Psychology.*

71. Edward L. Thorndike, *Educational Psychology* (New York, 1903).

72. Robert S. Woodworth, "Edward Lee Thorndike, 1874–1949," in *Biographical Memoirs* 27 (Washington D.C., NAS, 1952), 209–11.

73. Thorndike, *History of Psychology,* 260–63; and Joncich, *Sane Positivist,* 131, 329–30.

74. Ross, *G. Stanley Hall,* 359.

75. Emily Davis Cahan, "John Dewey and Human Development," in *Century of Developmental Psychology,* ed. Ornstein, Parke, Rieser, and Zahn-Waxler, 148–49.

76. Richard Hofstader, "The Child and the World," *Daedalus* 91 (1962): 501–26.

77. John Dewey quoted in Lewis Feuer, "Dewey and the Back to the People Movement," *Journal of the History of Ideas* 17 (1956): 559.

78. Quote from Henry May, *The End of American Innocence: A Study of the First Years of Our Own Time, 1912–1917* (Chicago, 1964), 151.

79. Quote from Ross, *G. Stanley Hall,* 358, 359, 364.

80. Alfred Binet and Theophile Simon, "Application of the New Methods to the Diagnosis of Intelligence Level among Normal and Subnormal Children in Institutions and the Primary Schools," in *The Development of Intelligence in Children,* trans. Elizabeth S. Kite (Vineland, N.J., 1916a),first published in *L'Annee Psychologique* 12 (1905): 245–336; "New Methods for the Diagnosis of the Intelligence of Subnormals," 245–336; "Upon the Necessity of Establishing a Scientific Diagnosis of Inferior States of Intelligence," 245–336;

and Robert Siegler, "The Other Alfred Binet," in *Century of Developmental Psychology,* ed. Parke, Ornstein, and Zahn-Waxler, 175.

81. Theta H. Wolf, *Alfred Binet* (Chicago, 1973).

82. Michael M. Sokal, *Psychological Testing and American Society, 1890–1930* (New Brunswick, N.J., 1987); and Florence Goodenough, *Mental Testing, Its History and Principles,* (New York, 1949).

83. Hall, *Life and Confessions,* 399.

84. Eliot Hearst, ed., *The First Century of Experimental Psychology* (Hillsdale, N.J., 1979), 320.

85. Eliot Hearst, "One Hundred Years of Developmental Psychology," in *First Century,* ed. Hearst, 20.

86. Hearst summarizes structuralism and functionalism. He describes Titchener as an avid disciple of Wundt, who believed that psychology's main task was the "analytical study of the generalized, normal adult mind and that the analysis and description of basic mental elements should precede the study of their function." Boring discusses functionalism as a response to the American frontier. "The pioneer struggles to wrest from nature first his living and then his comforts. Natural selection and the survival of the fittest color his daily thoughts. It is no surprise then that Americans should have taken readily to evolutionary theory nor that it should mold its thinking on many topics with respect to survival and success by means of the concepts of accommodation and adaptation." He asks, "Was not G. Stanley Hall a perpetual settler, clearing the land, building a cabin, and then moving on when the region got congested?"

87. Ralph Barton Perry, *Realms of Value; a Critique of Human Civilization* (Cambridge, 1954), 250.

88. Merle Curti, *The Growth of American Thought* (New York, 1943), 121–23.

89. Quoted by Richard Hofstader, *Social Darwinism in American Thought, 1860–1915* (Philadelphia, 1945), 109.

90. See Samuel Hays, *The Response of Industrialism, 1885–1914* (Chicago, 1957) on how individualistic reformers provided the tone, moral fervor, and energy for Progressivism. All the sources listed contain good discussions of pragmatism, instrumentalism, the differences between the ideas of James and Dewey, and their influence on Progressivism.

91. Edwin S. Corwin, "The Impact of the Idea of Evolution on the American Political and Constitutional Tradition," in *Evolutionary Thought in America,* ed. Stow Persons (New Haven, 1950), 191.

92. Ross, *G. Stanley Hall,* 386–87. Other participants in the 1909 conference included: psychiatrists Carl Gustav Jung and Adolph Meyer; psychologists William Stern and Edward B. Titchener; anthropologist Franz Boas; biologist Herbert Jennings; Carl E. Seashore, who guided the campaign for the Iowa Child Welfare Research Station; Bird Baldwin, its first director; Henry H. Goddard, director of a psychological clinic that tested mental defectives; and James McKeen Cattell.

93. Quoted in Stephen Kern, "Freud and the Emergence of Child Psychology, 1880–1910" (Ph.D. diss., Columbia University, 1970), 217.

94. John C. Burnham, "Psychiatry and American Medicine, 1884–1918," *Psychological Issues* 5, no. 4 (1967): 40, 88, 89; Nathan Hale, *The Beginnings of Psychoanalysis in the United*

States, 1876–1917 (New York, 1971), 332–50; David Shakow and David Rapaport, *The Influence of Freud on American Psychology* (New York, 1964). For the importance of Hall's influence on American acceptance of psychoanalysis, see John C. Burnham, "The New Psychology: From Narcissism to Social Control," in *Change and Continuity in Twentieth-Century America,* ed. Robert Bremner, John Braeman, and David Brody (Columbus, Ohio, 1968), 351–400; and Hale, *Beginnings of Psychoanalysis.*

95. Hall, *Life and Confessions.*

96. Ross, *G. Stanley Hall,* 365.

97. Lewis M. Terman, "Trails to Psychology," *Psychology in Autobiography* 2 (1932): 297– 331.

98. Florence Goodenough and John Anderson, *Experimental Child Study* (New York, 1931), 7. Many additional comments by psychologists on Hall as an inspiration are included in Edward L. Thorndike, *Human Nature and the Social Order* (New York, 1940), 135– 53. For appreciation of Hall as a humanist, see Donald H. Meyer, "The Scientific Humanism of G. Stanley Hall," *Journal of Humanistic Psychology* 1 (1971): 201–13.

99. Thorndike, "G. Stanley Hall."

100. Kessen, *Child,* 151. See also White, "G. Stanley Hall," 122–23 on reappraising Hall's legacy.

CHAPTER 3. SCIENTIFIC CHILD REARING, ORGANIZED MOTHERHOOD, AND PARENT EDUCATION

1. Robert Bremner, John Barnard, Tamara Hareven, and Robert Mennel, eds., *Children and Youth in America: A Documentary History, 1866–1932,* vol. 2 (Cambridge, Mass., 1971), 811–94; Manfred Waserman, "Henry L. Coit and the Certified Milk Movement in the Development of Modern Pediatrics," *Bulletin of the History of Medicine* 46(1972): 359–90; and Manfred Waserman, "The Emergence of Modern Child Health Care and the Federal Government," (Ph.D. diss., Catholic University, 1981). Twenty child health centers in cities with populations over ten thousand existed prior to 1900, 76 by 1909, and 258 by 1914. Many health services for babies and very young children were established in the 1890s but did not spread until the next decade (Lawrence K. Frank, "Childhood and Youth," in *Recent Social Trends,* vol. 2 [New York, 1933], 736). Hall strongly influenced the improvement of health services in public schools (Dorothy Ross, *G. Stanley Hall: The Psychologist as Prophet* [Chicago, 1972], 294–97). For another example of women who put their faith in medical science before it had proved itself, see Judith Walzer Leavitt, "Science Enters the Birthing Room: Obstetrics in America Since the Eighteenth Century," *Journal of American History* [*JAH*] 70(1983): 281– 304.

2. Ginalie Swaim, "Cora Bussey Hillis: Woman of Vision," *Palimpsest* 60(1979): 169. The newspaper articles (May 1900) can be found in the Cora Bussey Hillis Scrapbook Inventory [hereafter, CBH], Iowa State Historical Society, Iowa City, Iowa, Box 2. An exception to the emphasis on motherhood was the preference for scientific home management by followers of the chemist and founder of home economics Ellen Richards (Edward T. James et al., eds. *Notable American Women, 1607–1950: A Biographical Dictionary* [1971], 143–46).

3. These beliefs were expressed repeatedly in campaign literature for a children's bureau, the Iowa Child Welfare Research Station, and child guidance clinics.

4. L. Emmett Holt, *The Care and Feeding of Children,* 12th ed. (New York, 1925), 23. Pediatrics became a recognized medical specialty in 1879, when the American Medical Association established a section on diseases of childhood, and in 1888 the American Pediatric Association was founded. There were only 123 pediatricians in 1923, but they had a powerful influence on other physicians, nurses, and mothers. Siegel and White wrote that since many parents of children with serious mental or physical problems still have trouble knowing what to do and where to find help, it is "easy to imagine the mixture of hope and confusion aroused in late nineteenth-century parents when the word was out that expert help was available and the responsibility to find and use it was theirs" (Alexander Siegel and Sheldon H. White, "The Child Study Movement: Early Growth and Development of the Symbolized Child," *Advances of Child Development and Behavior* 17 [1982]: 69).

5. G. Stanley Hall, "The Ideal School as Based on Child Study," *Forum* 32(1901): 25.

6. G. Stanley Hall, *Life and Confessions of a Psychologist* (New York, 1923), 542. James Turner discusses late-nineteenth-century beliefs that the origins of morality were in human nature and social life and could be revealed by studying the history of civilizations. Hall, he wrote, saw a "moral purpose incarnated in the course of human events" (James Turner, *Without God, Without Creed: The Origins of Unbelief in America* [Baltimore, 1985], 68–69).

7. Ross, *G. Stanley Hall,* 371.

8. G. Stanley Hall, "A Glance at the Phyletic Background of Genetic Psychology," *American Journal of Psychology* [AJP] 19(1908): 151. In this work, Hall wrote, "Just as it was easier to say that fossil shells on the Alps were dropped there by Crusaders, who we know did carry some as charms, than it was to develop the science of palaeontology so it is simpler to say that morbid fears of children are due to early frights, and their anger, pity, water, tree and sky-psychoses to their own infant experiences, to the exclusion of palaeo-atavistic influences." The analogy to "growing pains" is mine, not Hall's, but is suggested by his repeated comments on the transitory nature of childhood emotions.

9. Daniel Walker Howe, "The Social Science of Horace Bushnell," *JAH* 70(1983): 305–22.

10. G. Stanley Hall, "A Study of Anger," *AJP* 10(1899): 516–91; and Ross, *G. Stanley Hall,* 129–31.

11. G. Stanley Hall, "Children's Lies," *AJP* 3(1890): 59–70.

12. Dominick Cavallo, *Muscles and Morals: Organized Playgrounds and Urban Reform, 1880–1920* (Philadelphia, 1981), 92.

13. Hall, "Glance at the Phyletic Background," 211.

14. Mrs. Theodore (Alice) Birney, *Childhood* (Minneapolis, 1905), 2–5, 65. Marden et al. also emphasize the importance of psychology, knowledge of the individual child, and the difference between child and adult nature (Orison Marden et al., *The Uplift Book of Child Culture* [Philadelphia, 1913]: 3–17, 22–26, 37, 61, 145–47).

15. G. Stanley Hall, "Child Study and Its Relation to Education," in *Health, Growth, and Heredity,* ed. Charles E. Strickland and Charles Burgess (New York, 1965), 82–83.

16. C. Anderson Aldrich, "Science and Art in Child Nourishment," *Journal of Pediatrics*

[*JP*] 1(October 1932): 413–34; and Joseph Brennemann, "Psychological Aspects of Nutrition in Childhood," *JP* 1(October 1932): 145–71.

17. Apple discusses the "science" of artificial feeding in the progressive period (Rima D. Apple, "Mothers and Medicine: A Social History of Infant Feeding, 1890–1950," in *Wisconsin Publications in the History of Science and Medicine* [Madison, Wis., 1987]). Articles by pediatricians on unscientific aspects of early approaches to infant feeding and their harmful effects include: C. Anderson Aldrich, "Looking Forward in Pediatrics," *Journal of the American Medical Association* [*JAMA*] 97(1932): 413–34; Brennemann, "Psychological Aspects of Nutrition in Childhood," 145–71; and Grover Powers, "Infant Feeding," *JAMA* 105(1935): 753–61.

18. The first five editions were published in 1894, 1897, 1903, 1906, and 1909. Holt revised his book twelve times before his death in 1924. By 1928 twenty-eight editions had been published. The book was translated into many European languages as well as Chinese. Holt's son continued to revise it after his father's death and also collaborated on his biography (Ronald L. Duffus and Emmet Holt, Jr., *L. Emmet Holt: Pioneer of a Children's Century* [New York, 1940]).

19. C. Anderson Aldrich and Mary Aldrich chastised pediatricians for ignoring babies' individuality. Anderson Aldrich was the leader of a group of humanistic pediatricians in Chicago who tried to counteract the influence of early "scientific" pediatrics (C. Anderson Aldrich and Mary M. Aldrich, *Babies Are Human Beings: An Interpretation of Growth* [New York, 1947]). According to Parmelee, the humanistic approach of the Chicago pediatricians stemmed from the influence of their wives and the mothers of their patients, almost all of whom had been affected by the kindergarten movement (Arthur H. Parmelee, Jr., interview by author, 23 March 1977). Some of the wives, including Mrs. Aldrich, wrote newspaper advice columns on child health and behavior.

20. L. Emmett Holt, *The Care and Feeding of Children,* 12th ed. (New York, 1925). Later research in child development demonstrated the benefits of play and other kinds of stimulation during the early months.

21. L. Emmett Holt, "The General Care of the Baby," in *The Happy Baby,* editorial advisor L. Emmett Holt (New York, 1926), 1–2. Kathleen W. Jones emphasized the influence of poor, urban mothers on Holt in the New York City hospital where he practiced (Jones, "Sentiment and Science: the Late Nineteenth Century Pediatrician as Mother's Advisor," *Journal of Social History* [JSH] 17[1983]: 79–96). Jones and Parmelee are among the few who have called attention to the influence of mothers on pediatricians. Note that most of Holt's "forbidden practices" are among those advocated by pediatricians today. A striking example is today's emphasis on the importance of play and stimulation for the healthy development of babies and young children.

22. Sarah Comstock, "Mothercraft: A New Profession for Women," *Good Housekeeping* (December 1914): 627–78. Thanks to Martin Pernick for calling my attention to this article.

23. Celia Stendler, "Sixty Years of Child Training Practices," *JP* 36(1950): 122–34; and Clarke E. Vincent, "Trends in Infant Care Ideas," *Child Development* 22(1951): 199–210.

24. Jay Mechling, "Advice to Historians on Advice to Mothers," *JSH* 9(1975): 44–63.

25. Martha Wolfenstein, "Trends in Infant Care," *Journal of Orthopsychiatry* 23(1953): 120–

30; Orville G. Brim, Jr., "Changes and Trends in Child Rearing Advice," *Child Study* 36(Fall 1959): 24; and Milton J. E. Senn, "Fads and Facts as the Basis of Child-Care Practices," *Children* 4(1957): 43–47.

26. For discussions about the lack of a clear relationship between changes in child-rearing advice and advances in empirical findings on children, see Brim, "Changes and Trends," 24; and Senn, "Fads and Facts," 43.

27. Max Lerner, *America as Civilization: Life and Thought in the United States Today* (New York, 1957), 562.

28. Theodore Roosevelt, "Address to the First International Congress in America on the Welfare of the Child," under the auspices of the National Congress of Mothers, Washington, D.C., March 1908.

29. Steven L. Schlossman, "Philanthropy and the Gospel of Child Development," in *Private Philanthropy and Public Elementary and Secondary Education: Proceedings of the Rockefeller Archive Center Conference Held on 8 June 1979,* ed. Gerald Benjamin (New York, 1980), 15–32.

30. Sheila M. Rothman, *Woman's Proper Place: A History of Changing Ideals and Practices, 1870 to the Present* (New York, 1981), 99–103.

31. Ross, *G. Stanley Hall,* 283–84.

32. For Hall's influence on kindergarten curricula, see Barbara Beatty, *Preschool Education in America: The Culture of Young Children from the Colonial Era to the Present* (New Haven, 1995), 100. Shapiro presents another view of Hall's relation to the kindergarten movement (Michael S. Shapiro, *Child's Garden: The Kindergarten Movement from Froebel to Dewey* [University Park, Pa., 1983], 107–29).

33. Elvena B. Tillman, "Alice Josephine McLellan Birney, 1858–1907," in *Notable American Women, 1607–1950: A Biographical Dictionary,* ed. Edward T. James, Janet Wilson James, and Paul Boyer (Cambridge, Mass., 1971), 147–48.

34. Steven L. Schlossman, "Before Home Start: Notes Toward a History of Parent Education in America, 1897–1929," *Harvard Educational Review* 46(1976): 443–53.

35. National Congress of Mothers, (Paper presented at the National Congress of Mothers, Proceedings of the First Annual Convention, Washington, D.C., 1897).

36. Schlossman, "Before Home Start," 440–41. For a discussion of Adler's role in child labor reform, see Walter L. Trattner, *Homer Folks: Pioneer in Social Welfare* (New York, 1968), 73, 98. Schlossman calls attention to the vigorous reform efforts of Hannah Schoff in the areas of child labor regulation, compulsory school laws, juvenile courts, vocational training, and other arenas related to crime and poverty in "Before Home Start," 445.

37. Schlossman, "Before Home Start," 443–53.

38. Schlossman, "Before Home Start," 443–54.

39. Mrs. Theodore W. (Alice) Birney, Newspaper clipping, 21 May 1900, CBH, Box 2.

40. CBH (Boxes 1 and 2) includes many examples of activity by the Iowa Congress in behalf of poor women.

41. Schlossman, "Before Home Start," 450–52; and Birney, Newspaper clipping, 21 May 1900.

42. Birney, Newspaper clipping, 21 May 1900. Sophonisba P. Breckinridge observed that the reports and speeches of the National Congress revealed a "faint distrust of the effect on

the child and the home of higher education" (*Women in the Twentieth Century: A Study of Their Political, Social, and Economic Activities* [New York, 1933], 25). Illustrations of the conservatism of the congress are included in Barbara Ehrenreich and Dierdre English, *For Her Own Good: 150 Years of the Experts' Advice to Women* (Garden City, N.Y., 1979), 191–96; Sheila Rothman, *Women's Proper Place: A History of Changing Ideals and Practices, 1870 to the Present* (New York, 1978), 97–132; and Schlossman, *Before Home Start*, 446–48. In 1899 the *New York Tribune* reprinted a cartoon that originally appeared in *Punch,* the British humor magazine. It shows an elegantly dressed woman attempting to persuade a charwoman to attend mothers' club meeting. The charwoman responds, "Well yer leddyship; you're very kind: but I never was a society woman" (Photocopy in CBH, Box 2).

43. The Iowa newspaper press coverage of the National Congress of Mothers, 21–25 May 1900 can be found in CBH, Box 2.

44. Cora Bussey Hillis, Addresses to the Iowa legislature, 28–31 January 1904 and 8 April 1904, CBH, Box 2.

45. Cora Bussey Hillis, "How the Iowa Child Welfare Station Came into Being," Typescript, 1919, CBH, Box 1, Folder 11.

46. Carroll Smith-Rosenberg, *Disorderly Conduct: Visions of Gender in Victorian America* (New York, 1985), 263–64; and Rothman, *Woman's Proper Place,* 64.

47. Ross, *G. Stanley Hall,* 281–83.

48. John Cawelti, "America on Display: The World's Fairs of 1876, 1893, 1993," in *World's Fairs in the Age of Industrialism in America: Essays on Social and Cultural Values,* ed. Frederick Cople Jaher (New York, 1968), 317–63.

49. Rosenberg, *Beyond Separate Spheres.*

CHAPTER 4. SOCIAL WELFARE REFORMERS AND REFORM-MINDED SCIENTISTS

1. Rosalind Rosenberg, *Beyond Separate Spheres: Intellectual Roots of Modern Feminism* (New Haven, 1982), 55.

2. Rheta Childe Dorr, *A Woman of Fifty* (New York, 1924), 55.

3. Carroll Smith-Rosenberg, "Beauty and the Beast, and the Militant Woman: A Case Study of Sex Roles and Social Stress in Jacksonian America," *American Quarterly* 23 (1971): 245.

4. Jill Ker Conway, "Jane Addams: An American Heroine," *Daedalus* 93 (1964): 172.

5. Jane Addams, "Utilization of Women in City Government," in Addams, *Newer Ideals of Peace* (New York, 1907), 180–207

6. Jane Addams, *My Friend Julia Lathrop* (New York, 1935), 70.

7. Jane Addams, *The Spirit of Youth and the City Streets* (New York, 1909), 52–55; and Jane Addams, *Twenty Years at Hull-House* (New York, 1910, Reprint 1957), 355–68.

8. All quotes in the paragraph are by: Sophonisba Breckenridge, *Women in the Twentieth Century: A Study of Their Political, Social, and Economic Activities* (New York, 1933), 3–17.

9. Breckenridge, *Women in the Twentieth Century,* 16, 29.

10. Sarah Platt Decker, quoted by Dorr, *Woman of Fifty,* 118–20.

11. Helen M. Winslow, *A Woman's Club Story* (Boston, 1906), 185–86. One example of the new fervor for social reform were the one million letters clubwomen sent to members of Congress in support of the Pure Food and Drug Act of 1906.

12. Karen J. Blair, *The Clubwoman as Feminist: True Womanhood Redefined, 1868–1914* (New York, 1980), 97.

13. Judge Richard Tuthill, quoted in David Rothman, *The Discovery of the Asylum: Social Order and Disorder in the New Republic* (Boston, 1980), 214.

14. Breckenridge, *Women in the Twentieth Century.*

15. Robert Wiebe, *The Search For Order, 1877–1920* (New York, 1967), 23.

16. Carroll Smith-Rosenberg, *Disorderly Conduct: Visions of Gender in Victorian America* (New York, 1985), 254.

17. Quoted by Blair, *Clubwoman as Feminist,* 113.

18. Jane Addams, "Charity and Social Justice" (paper presented at the NCCC, 1910a) 1–3; and Jane Addams, "The Child at the Point of Greatest Pressure" (paper presented at the NCCC, 1912) 26–30. Refer also to Clarke Chambers, *Seedtime of Reform: American Social Science in Social Action, 1918–1933* (Minneapolis, 1963), 26–30, for a discussion about the emphasis in the 1920s on improving life for all children through constructive educational and welfare programs. Thanks to Professor Chambers for pointing this out to me. The relationship between the first professional social and behavioral scientists and welfare reformers deserves more attention than I can give it here.

19. John Burnham, Interviews with William Healy and Augusta Bronner (Cambridge, Mass. 1960), 457–65. According to Burnham, Progressive psychiatrists and psychologists were unique to America, even though a comparable progressive reform movement occurred in Britain during these same years.

20. Chambers, *Seedtime of Reform,* 30–33, 301, 305; Allen Davis, *Spearheads for Reform: The Social Settlements and the Progressive Movement, 1890–1914* (New York, 1967), 44.

21. Ivy Pinchbeck and Margaret Hewitt, *Children in English Society,* vol. 1 (London 1969), 309–10.

22. Rothman, *Discovery of the Asylum,* 225–28; and Joseph Hawes, *Children in Urban Society: Juvenile Delinquency in Nineteenth-Century America* (New York, 1971), 259.

23. Joseph Lee, *Play in Education* (New York, 1915), viii.

24. Lillian Wald, quoted in Davis, *Spearheads for Reform,* 60.

25. Davis, *Spearheads for Reform,* 60–61.

26. Ronald Cohen, "Child Saving and Progressivism, 1885–1915" in *American Childhood: A Research Guide and Historical Handbook* (Westport, Conn., 1985), 274. After 1920 new public playgrounds tended to be located at public schools rather than in neighborhoods.

27. Dominick Cavallo, *Muscles and Morals: Organized Playgrounds and Urban Reform, 1880–1920* (Philadelphia, 1981), 20, 68–72, 78.

28. Arnold Gesell and Beatrice Gesell, *The Normal Child and Primary Education* (Boston, 1912), 24.

29. Davis, *Spearheads for Reform,* 152.

30. Cavallo, *Muscles and Morals,* 55–70, 76; Stanley Hall and A. Caswell Ellis, "A Study of Dolls," *Pedagogical Seminary* [PS] 4, no. 2 (1896):129–75; and Dorothy Ross, *G. Stanley Hall: The Psychologist as Prophet* (Chicago 1972), 300. The research by Hall and Caswell

Ellis on doll play is still admired. Ross points out that this research went beyond recapitulation theory, showing how a child projects her own feelings and reveals her individuality. George Johnson, Luther Gulick, and Joseph Lee undertook longitudinal studies of the interactions between play and recapitulation.

31. Stanley Hall is quoted in Cavallo, *Muscles and Morals,* 51.

32. Cavallo, *Muscles and Morals,* 60.

33. Cavallo, *Muscles and Morals,* 50, 60, 147–55.

34. Jane Addams quoted by Merle Curti, "Jane Addams on Human Nature," *Journal of the History of Ideas* [JHI] 22 (1961), 252. Schlossman demonstrates how the ambiguity of Hall's ideas enabled them to serve conservative as well as liberal purposes (Steven L. Schlossman, "G. Stanley Hall and the Boys' Club: Conservative Applications of Recapitulation Theory," *Journal of the History of Behavioral Science* 9[1973]: 140–147). See Curti for Hall's influence on Addams's conception of human nature (Merle Curti, "Jane Addams on Human Nature," JHI 22[April-June 1961]: 242, 254, 247).

35. G. Stanley Hall, *Adolescence: Its Psychology and Its Relations to Physiology, Anthropology, Sociology, Sex, Crime, Religion, and Education* (New York, 1904); Ross, *G. Stanley Hall,* 333–40; and Cavallo, *Muscles and Morals,* 90–92.

36. Steven Schlossman, "Hall and Boys' Club," 140–47. Stephen Hardy and Alan Ingham ("Games, Structure, and Agency: Historians on the American Play Movement," *Journal of Social History* 4[1983]: 285–301) discuss different historical interpretations of the play movement. They find that local records show that workers, local citizens, and other groups demanded playgrounds, sometimes joining and sometimes opposing elite reformers, and that there was "consensus on the moral justification for playgrounds but opposition on who would regulate the child's activities within them."

37. Cavallo, *Muscles and Morals,* 66–81, 142–46. See the next chapter for Hall's objections to child labor crusades and a federal children's bureau.

38. Cavallo, *Muscles and Morals,* 111.

39. Ross, *G. Stanley Hall,* 380–81.

40. Hawes, *Children in Urban Society,* 191–221. See Hawes for a discussion of European and American studies of criminology and juvenile delinquency, including the work of Hall's students and colleagues at Clark, who did not heed his advice to study the individual delinquent. Both Hawes and D. Rothman call attention to Hall's emphasis on environmental causes of juvenile delinquency.

41. According to Ross, Hall's stance on the eugenics movement was moderate.

42. Hawes, *Children in Urban Society,* 207, 223–40.

43. David J. Rothman, *Conscience and Convenience: The Asylum and Its Alternatives in Progressive America* (New York, 1980), 210–11.

44. Hall, *Adolescence,* 342.

45. Ben Lindsey, "The Child and the Community," *Journal of Proceedings and Addresses* (1909): 742.

46. Hall, *Adolescence.*

47. G. Stanley Hall, "The Children's Institute of Clark University," *Harper's Magazine* (1910a): 620–24; G. Stanley Hall, "The Child Welfare Conference" PS 17 (1910b): 504; and Ross, *G. Stanley Hall,* 362–64.

48. Ross, *G. Stanley Hall,* 362–63.

49. Hall, "Child Welfare Conference," 504.

50. The undated and unsigned memorandum is in the Iowa Child Welfare Research Station Records of the University of Iowa Archives, Iowa City.

51. Hall, "Children's Institute" 620–24; and Ross, *G. Stanley Hall,* 363–64, 413.

52. Hall, "Child Welfare Conference," 540.

53. Hall, "Children's Institute," 624.

54. Married with three children, a professed socialist, and a professional career woman, Kelley did not fit stereotypes of the settlement house worker. Declaring that "the best child labor law is a compulsory education law," she linked legislation prohibiting child labor to compulsory school attendance laws. She suggested that scholarships be provided for families whose children were compelled to attend school to provide family income. She proposed a consumers' boycott of products made by industries that exploited children, an idea first implemented by the New York Consumers' League, established in 1891. The National Consumers' League, a federation of local and state leagues modeled on the New York league and other state organizations, was established in 1899. Hull-House Maps and Papers was compiled by residents of the settlement as part of the Library of Economics and Politics, edited by Richard T. Ely, professor of economics at the University of Wisconsin.

55. Leslie Diehl, "The Paradox of G. Stanley Hall: Foe of Coeducation and Educator of Women," *American Psychologist* 41(1986): 868–78. At age seventy-eight Hall published a sympathetic portrait of the flapper. The importance of personal freedom, Ross says, "appeared to override the Victorian image of Woman to which he had adhered all of his life." Ethel Dummer asked Hall (November 16, 1920) for a reprint of a chapter from his *Morale: The Supreme Standard of Life and Conduct* (1920), which Dummer found sympathetic to feminism. Hall, in his reply (November 21, 1920), called it "the feminism chapter." Hall also modified his extreme views on laissez-faire in his seventies (Merle Curti, *American Philanthropy Abroad* [New York, 1967], 427). See Diehl for Hall's view of women's role and his ambivalence toward his female graduate students at Clark University.

56. G. Stanley Hall and H. F. Saunders, "Pity," *American Journal of Psychology* 11(1900): 590–91.

57. Ross, *G. Stanley Hall,* 318–19.

58. Julia Lathrop, "The Children's Bureau" (Paper presented at the NCSW, Fort Wayne, Indiana, 1912)

59. Together, Wald and Kelley established the New York Child Labor Committee in 1902 and, two years later, helped to found the NCLC.

60. Lillian Wald, "The Idea of the Federal Children's Bureau" (Paper presented at the NCSW, Philadelphia, 1932), 33.

61. Wald, "Idea of the Children's Bureau," 34.

62. Lillian Wald, *The House on Henry Street* (New York, 1915); and Ronald Duffus, *Lillian Wald: Neighbor and Crusader* (New York, 1938).

63. Kathryn Sklar, *Florence Kelley and the Nation's Work: The Rise of Women's Political Culture, 1830–1900* (New Haven, 1995).

64. Kathryn Sklar, "Hull House Maps and Papers: Social Science as Women's Work in the 1980s," in *The Social Survey in Historical Perspective, 1880–1904,* ed. Martin Bulmer, Kevin Bales, and Kathryn Sklar (Cambridge and, New York, 1991), 111–47.

65. Sklar, "Hull House Maps," 122.

66. Florence Kelley, "The Manufacturers' Program Won't Do," Survey 59 (1928): 344–45; and Dorothy Blumberg, *Florence Kelley: The Making of a Social Pioneer* (New York, 1966), 149, 164.

67. Kathryn Sklar, "Hull House in the 1980s: A Community of Women Reformers," *Journal of Women in Culture and Society* 10(1985): 677.

68. For a history of the child labor movement, see Walter Trattner, *Crusade for the Children: A History of the National Child Labor Committee and Child Labor Reform in America* (Chicago, 1970). Between 1904 and 1906, the NCLC devoted substantial resources to gaining support for the bill to establish a children's bureau.

69. Elvena Tillman, "The Rights of Childhood and the National Child Welfare Movement, 1890–1919" (Ph.D. diss., University of Wisconsin, 1968); and Nancy Weiss, "Save the Children: A History of the Children's Bureau, 1903–1918" (Ph.D. diss., University of California, 1974), 48–81.

70. Florence Kelley, "The Federal Government and Working Children," *Annals of the American Academy of Political and Social Sciences* 27(1906): 290.

71. Homer Folks, "The National Children's Bureau" (Paper presented at the NCCC, 1910), 92.

72. Harold Jambor, "Theodore Dreiser, The Delineator Magazine, and Dependent Children: A Background Note on the Calling of the 1909 White House Conference," *Social Service Review* 32(1958): 37.

73. Dreiser remained the editor until 1910. Weiss points out that although Dreiser played a significant role in arousing sympathy for homeless children and support for convening the 1909 conference, he was concerned primarily with the plight of dependent children and remained uninvolved with the campaign for the Children's Bureau and other broader aspects of child welfare reform.

74. Jambor, "Theodore Dreiser," 37–39.

75. Rothman, *Conscience and Convenience,* 210–11.

76. Jambor, "Theodore Dreiser," 37–39.

77. Jambor, "Theodore Dreiser," 38–39.

78. Robert Bremner, John Barnard, Tamara Hareven, and Rovert Mennel, eds. *Children and Youth in America: A Documentary History, 1866–1932,* vol. 2 (Cambridge, Mass., 1971): 358–67, 761; Grace Abbott, *The Child and the State,* vol 1. (Chicago, 1938), 1–17; and Weiss, "Save the Children" 58–69. Once President Roosevelt was interested in the conference, social workers became involved. How to provide and pay for the care of dependent children had been a controversial issue in the welfare field for many years.

79. Bremner et al., *Children and Youth,* 369–85; and Molly Ladd-Taylor, "Mother-work: Ideology, Public Policy, and the Mothers' Movement, 1830–1930" (Ph.D. diss., Yale University, 1986). The conference's closing banquet was devoted to speeches in favor of the bureau. Wald delivered an eloquent, emotional address citing European nations that were providing better care for their children than the United States was. The private na-

tional agency for children that many conference members wanted, the Child Welfare League of America, funded by the Commonwealth Fund, was established in 1921.

80. Jane Addams, *The Second Twenty Years at Hull-House, September 1909 to September 1929* (New York, 1930), 18.

81. Weiss, "Save the Children," 64.

82. In spite of the conference's statement favoring private assistance, the movement to ensure public aid for mothers followed immediately.

83. See chapter 5 for the 1919 White House Conference and the Epilogue for White House Conferences for children 1930 to 1970.

CHAPTER 5. THE CHILDREN'S BUREAU UNDER JULIA LATHROP

1. Robert Bremner et al., eds., *Children and Youth in America: A Documentary History, 1866– 1932*, vol. 2 (Cambridge, Mass., 1971), 762–64. For a discussion on the campaign, see 757– 74. See also Elvena B. Tillman, "The Rights of Childhood and the National Child Welfare Movement, 1890–1919" (Ph.D. diss., University of Wisconsin, 1968); and Nancy P. Weiss, "Save the Children: A History of the Children's Bureau, 1903–1918" (Ph.D. diss., University of California, 1974). Folks summarizes the opposition to the bureau and the answering arguments (Homer Folks, "The National Children's Bureau" [Paper presented at the NCCC, 1910]). The New York City Bureau of Child Hygiene under Josephine Baker was the first public agency to assume responsibility for maternal and infant welfare.

2. Senator Weldon Heyburn of Idaho in 1911, quoted in Bremner et al., *Children and Youth,* 765.

3. Weiss, "Save the Children," 94.

4. Bremner et al., *Children and Youth,* 764–74.

5. Edward T. Devine, "Children's Bureau Bill Again Before Congress," *Charities and Commons* 21(1919): 1254–55; and Weiss, "Save the Children," 61, 69, 83, 84.

6. Bremner reproduces the text of the law (Bremner et al., *Children and Youth,* 774); Parker and Carpenter discuss the contradiction in the law's instruction to the bureau and how Lathrop tried to resolve it (Jacqueline K. Parker and Edward M. Carpenter, "Julia Lathrop and the Children's Bureau: The Emergence of an Institution," *Social Service Review* 55(March 1981): 60–77). Congress gave the Children's Bureau a broader mandate than it later gave to the Women's Bureau. The Children's Bureau Act did not define childhood, but Lathrop interpreted it to mean children up to sixteen years of age. See Children's Bureau, *Annual Report of the Children's Bureau,* CB Publication (Washington D.C., 1914), 5.

7. Parker and Carpenter, "Lathrop and Children's Bureau,"61.

8. Folks, "National Children's Bureau," 92.

9. Tillman, "Rights of Childhood, 196–97.

10. Parker and Carpenter, "Lathrop and Children's Bureau," 61. Muncy traces the growth of the school and argues convincingly that it acted as an auxiliary staff for the Children's Bureau (Robyn Muncy, *Creating a Female Dominion in American Reform, 1890–1935* [New York 1991], 66–92). She states, "Lathrop's position at the Bureau and Breckinridge's and Abbott's at the School were symbiotic, they empowered each other in the common enterprise of sustaining their reform program."

11. Muncy, *Creating a Female Dominion,* 47–48; and James Johnson, "The Role of Women in the Funding of the United States Children's Bureau," in *"Remember the Ladies": New Perspectives on Women in American History,* ed. Carole V. R. George (Syracuse, 1975), 179–96.

12. In an illuminating discussion of the early years of the bureau, Parker and Carpenter show how Lathrop defined its mission, "selected operating goals from its statutory functions, and utilized a potent constituency" (Parker and Carpenter, " Lathrop and Children's Bureau," 60–77).

13. Parker and Carpenter, "Lathrop and Children's Bureau," 60–77.

14. Julia Lathrop, Letter to Sophia Vogt, 27 June 1916, Children's Bureau Records [hereafter, CB], Central Files, 1914–1940, Record Group 102, 81–95.

15. Hartley quoted by Robyn Muncy (Muncy, *Creating a Female Dominion,* 56).

16. Lathrop's identification with women's organizations went back to the 1890s, when, as a member of the State Board of Charities, she enlisted their help to improve state institutions (Jane Addams, *My Friend Julia Lathrop* [New York, 1935], 170).

17. Julia Lathrop, "The Children's Bureau," *American Journal of Sociology* 8(1912–1913): 318.

18. Jane Addams, *The Second Twenty Years at Hull-House, September 1909 to September 1929* (New York, 1930), 23.

19. Lathrop, "Children's Bureau," 314.

20. Lathrop, "Children's Bureau," 319.

21. Lathrop, "Children's Bureau," 322.

22. Lathrop, "Children's Bureau," 328.

23. In addition to enlisting the GFWC, Lathrop was able to persuade the Daughters of the American Revolution, the Colonial Dames, the Mothers' Congress, and various other important women's associations to assist in the drive for birth registration. By 1914 help came from fifteen hundred women in seventeen states. Although not authorized to collect birth statistics, the bureau persuaded the Census Bureau to suggest that it do so and to develop for it a system for registering births, one example of the way in which it tried to work with other government agencies. See Lathrop, "Children's Bureau," 329.

24. Julia Lathrop, "Federal Safeguards of Child Welfare," *Annals of the American Academy of Political and Social Sciences* 21(1925): 99–100.

25. Grace Abbott, *The Child and the State,* vol. 2 (Chicago, 1938), 613.

26. Children's Bureau, *Annual Report* (1914), 7; and Parker and Carpenter, "Lathrop and Children's Bureau," 62.

27. Addams, *My Friend Julia Lathrop,* 178.

28. Lathrop described the requisites for the subject of the first field investigation: it "must be fundamental to social welfare, of popular interest, and serve a real human need; and from a practical viewpoint it must be work which could be done a small bit at a time and published in installments as each unit was finished," adding that infant mortality met all of these requirements (Children's Bureau, *Annual Report* [1914], 7–8; 1915, 81–82). See also Richard A. Meckel, *Save the Babies: American Public Health Reform and the Prevention of Infant Mortality, 1850–1929* (Baltimore, 1990), 178–82; and Dorothy Bradbury, *Five Decades of Action: A Short History of the Children's Bureau* (Washington D.C., 1964), 7–11.

29. Nine parts of the infant mortality study were completed and published during Lathrop's administration. *Why Do Babies Die?* was the title of the bureau's first research publication. Congress passed the amendment to the Children's Bureau Act on April 17, 1914. See Children's Bureau, *Annual Report* (1915), 74.

30. Molly Ladd-Taylor, *Mother-Work: Women, Child Welfare, and the State, 1890–1930* (Urbana, Ill., 1994), 314–26; Meckel, *Save the Babies,* 178–95; and Grace Abbott, "Ten Years' Work for Children," *North American Review* 218(1923): 191–92.

31. Widespread fear of federal interference with the privacy of the family meant that agents of the bureau had to be extremely cautious during their investigations, ensuring that they always had permission for what they were doing and refraining from asking questions that could offend or damage the reputation of any woman, although this often meant not collecting important data. The infant mortality investigation had a "two-fold effect," Lathrop said, "the effect upon the particular community and a contribution to a body of knowledge of the social causes of unnecessary infant mortality" (Ladd-Taylor, Mother-Work, 316).

32. Meckel, *Save the Babies,* 179.

33. For a discussion of the infant mortality studies that distinguishes information previously known or suspected from radical new discoveries, see Meckel, *Save the Babies,* 180–82.

34. Katherine F. Lenroot, Interview for Social Security Project, Oral History Research Office, Columbia University, 1965, 17.

35. Meckel, *Save the Babies,* 185.

36. Meckel, *Save the Babies,* 180–82.

37. Children's Bureau, *Annual Report* (1914), 11.

38. Molly Ladd-Taylor, *Raising a Baby the Government Way: Mothers' Letters to the Children's Bureau, 1915–1932* (Piscataway, N.J., 1986), 34–36.

39. Alice Phelps, Letter to Julia Lathrop, 19 October 1916, Ethel Sturges Dummer Papers [hereafter, ESD], Elizabeth and Arthur Schlesinger Library, Radcliffe College, Harvard University, Cambridge, Massachusetts, Box 32.

40. Julia Lathrop, Letter to Ethel Dummer, 14 November 1916, ESD, Box 32

41. Ethel Dummer, Letter to Julia Lathrop, November 1916, ESD, Box 32, Folder 634.

42. After the birth, Phelps proposed the establishment of a series of Sunshine Cottages, small hospitals for mothers and babies under the supervision of the bureau. Lathrop rejected the suggestion when Grace Meigs decided that Phelps did not have the ability to execute such a project. The bureau began investigating conditions affecting maternal health in Montana about the same time as its investigations in Wyoming. For the results, see *Children's Bureau, Maternity Care and the Welfare of Young Children in Homesteading County* in Montana (Washington, D.C., 1919). Phelps's letter is reproduced in Ladd-Taylor, Raising a Baby, 49, but there appears to be no published record of Lathrop's and Dummer's roles in helping Phelps and arranging for a public health nurse for Sweetwater.

43. For the importance of Meigs's research, see Meckel, *Save the Babies,* 202–06.

44. Grace L. Meigs, Letter to Ethel Dummer, September 1917.

45. Ethel Dummer, Letter to Julia Lathrop, 14 April 1917.

46. Julia Lathrop, Letter to Katherine Morton, 17 November 1917, ESD, Box 17 and 21 November.

47. T. M. Morton, Letter to Julia Lathrop, 21 November 1917, ESD, Box 32.

48. Julia Lathrop, Letter to Katherine Morton, 21 November 1917, ESD, Box 17 and 21 November.

49. Katherine F. Lenroot, Interview by Social Security Project, Oral History Research Office, Columbia University, New York, New York, 1965, 14–21.

50. Dummer's help in securing information on illegitimacy (including arranging for the translation of Norwegian laws on illegitimacy) and her letters on prostitution and unwed mothers can be traced in the Lathrop-Dummer correspondence (ESD, 1914, Box 32, Folders 632–34). In addition to her support of child guidance and the Children's Bureau, Dummer participated in the 1930 White House Conference for Children and during the 1940s supported courses in child development at Northwestern University. For a discussion of the important work the Children's Bureau initiated under Lathrop, see Susan Tiffin, In *Whose Best Interest? Child Welfare Reform in the Progressive Era* (Westport, Conn., 1982), 173–86.

51. For the bureau's investigations of the juvenile court and juvenile delinquency, see Tiffin, *In Whose Best Interest?*, 215–52. Reports of the investigations and some of their consequences are in Children's Bureau, *Annual Report of the Children's Bureau (1914–1921)*.

52. Grace Abbott, "Ten Years' Work for Children," *North American Review* 218(1923): 194–200.

53. Abbott, "Ten Years' Work," 195–98; Walter L. Trattner, *Crusade for the Children: A History of the National Child Labor Committee and Child Labor Reform* (Chicago, 1970), 133. See also Ladd-Taylor, *Raising a Baby*, for a penetrating analysis of the opposition of many parents to the bureau's administration of the child labor law.

54. The proposed amendment to the Children's Bureau Act stated, "Provided, that such published matter shall be furnished to legislative bodies and boards of health and health officers but not to the general public except on request."

55. Dorothy Bradbury, Interview by author, n.d., 43; and Parker and Carpenter, "Lathrop and Children's Bureau," 60–77.

56. See CB Records, files 4-5-3-1 to 4-6-3-3, for examples of the questions that mothers brought to the bureau. For comments on the scarcity of child rearing literature before 1925, see Sidonea Gruenberg, "Parent Education and Child Welfare in America," *White House Conference* 3(1932).

57. Emily K. Abel, "Correspondence between Julia Lathrop, Chief of Children's Bureau, and a Working-Class Woman, 1914–1915," *Journal of Women's History* 5(1993): 79–83.

58. See Ladd-Taylor, *Raising a Baby*, 11–45. Letters are in CB Records (files 9-1-0-2 and 4-5-3-1 to 4-6-3-3).

59. Gruenberg, "Parent Education," 34.

60. Dorothy Bradbury, Interview by author, n.d., 1, 7, 9.

61. Leona Baumgartner, "Fifty Years' Work for Children," *Pediatrics* 29(1962): 517–19; and Ladd-Taylor, *Raising a Baby*, 13–15.

62. For vivid details of the primitive conditions under which many families lived during the period preceding and following World War I, see Baumgartner, "Fifty Years' Work," 517–19; Dorothy Bradbury, "The Story of Infant Care," Katherine B. Oettinger Papers [hereafter, KBO], Elizabeth and Arthur Schlesinger Library on the History of Women in the

United States, Radcliffe College, Harvard University, Cambridge, Massachusetts, Box 2, n.d.; and Ladd-Taylor, *Raising a Baby,* 13–15.

63. Ladd-Taylor, *Raising a Baby,* 142–47. Request letters are in CB Records, 1940 (files 4-5-3-2; 4-6-3-3).

64. The letters contained many complaints about doctors and medical care (Ladd-Taylor, *Raising a Baby,* 13–19). Lois Meek Stolz believed that one reason for the publication of *Infant Care* (1914) was the bureau's belief that the mothers' pension movement would lead to more children being kept at home and that their mothers would need help with child rearing (Lois Meek Stolz, Interview by Author, 17 December 1978). During the 1914 hearings on the bureau's appropriation, the U.S. Public Health Service charged that the bureau was duplicating its work and referred to a bulletin it had issued, *Care of the Baby.* Lathrop replied that the bureau had undertaken work on its manuals after consulting with the Public Health Service and receiving its assurance that it had not done and did not propose to do the same work. *Care of the Baby* was published in 1913 as part of U.S. Public Health Reports, a document circulated to doctors and specialists in public health. Bradbury reports that by 1915 the Public Health Association perceived the pamphlet's possibilities and began printing more copies (Bradbury, "Story of Infant Care," 11). Between 1915 and 1919, nearly three quarters of a million copies were distributed. From 1922 to 1938 circulation was small.

65. Bradbury, "Story of Infant Care," 10–12.

66. Bradbury, "Story of Infant Care," 13.

67. Bradbury reproduces West's spirited response to the removal of her name from the title page of *Infant Care.* See Bradbury, " Story of Infant Care," 13–15.

68. Katherine F. Lenroot, Interview by Social Security Project, Oral History Research Office, Columbia University, New York, New York, 1965, 70–72.

69. The great Chicago exhibit of 1911 on childcare that settlement workers had helped to arrange offered advice on physical care but nothing on behavior problems. It seems likely that letters helped the bureau to realize how many parents had unanswered questions on psychological care. Bradbury reports that congressmen began sending names of their constituents to the bureau in order that they might receive copies of *Infant Care.* See Bradbury, "Story of Infant Care," 12.

70. For literature by historians who believe that the Children's Bureau childcare manuals reflect middle-class values, see Nancy P. Weiss, "Mother, the Invention of Necessity: Dr. Benjamin Spock's Baby and Child Care," *American Quarterly* 29(1977): 297; Ladd-Taylor, *Raising a Baby,* 12; and Muncy, *Creating a Female Dominion,* 112–18.

71. Nancy P. Weiss, "The Mother-Child Dyad Revisited: Perceptions of Mothers and Children in Twentieth-Century Child Rearing Manuals," *Journal of Social Issues* 34(1978): 29–45.

72. Meckel, *Save the Babies,* 202.

73. Addams, *My Friend Julia Lathrop,* 206.

74. Josephine Baker, "Lessons from the Draft," *Transactions of the American Association for Study and Prevention of Infant Mortality* (1918): 181–88.

75. Children's Bureau, *Annual Report of the Children's Bureau* (1918), 186–94.

76. Children's Bureau, *Annual Report of the Children's Bureau,* 235.

77. The purposes of Baby Week were to emphasize the constructive side of baby care and to reach more middle-class mothers. For an excellent discussion of the bureau's early demonstrations in infant health, see Parker and Carpenter, "Lathrop and Children's Bureau," 60–87.

78. Muncy, *Creating a Female Dominion*, 96–97.

79. Children's Bureau, *Annual Report of the Children's Bureau* (1918), 179.

80. Muncy, *Creating a Female Dominion*, 97–98.

81. The bureau needed the support and assistance of its women volunteers more than ever after the war because Congress had cut its budget and certain patriotic groups had accused the bureau of radicalism. See Muncy, *Creating a Female Dominion*, 99–103.

82. In 1918 the Children's Bureau published an eighty-two-page pamphlet by Mrs. Max West on the preschool child. Hillis, in Iowa, was very active in recruiting women to work for the bureau during Children's Year. Before the war only eight states had child welfare divisions; by 1920 thirty-five states had a child hygiene or child welfare division.

83. Children's Bureau, *Annual Report of the Children's Bureau*, 256–64.

84. Julia Lathrop, "Child Welfare Standards: A Test for Democracy" (Paper presented at the NCSW, Atlantic City, N.J., 1919), 3–9.

85. Lathrop, "Child Welfare Standards," 8–9.

86. Lathrop, "Child Welfare Standards," 5, 7, 9.

87. Julia Lathrop, "Federal Safeguards of Child Welfare," *Annals of the American Academy of Political and Social Sciences* 21(1925): 99–100.

88. Lenroot, Interview, 1965, 13.

89. Abbott was appointed secretary of the conference. To prepare for it, she and Lathrop visited Belgium, France, and England. Representatives of America's major allies in the war attended. "The concept that children's needs have no national boundaries has been a vital part of the outlook of the Children's Bureau from its very inception," Abbott explained. Future chiefs of the bureau were to become active participants in international efforts to help children, first through work with the League of Nations, later with the United Nations.

90. Alice Hamilton, *Exploring the Dangerous Trades: The Autobiography of Alice Hamilton, M.D.* (Boston, 1943), 18.

91. The bureau could not legislate or enforce standards but could see to it that the issues and proposals were presented to states and local communities, which did have those powers. The final report of the conference summarized its recommendations under the following headings: the economic and social basis for child welfare standards, child labor, the health of children and mothers, children in need of special care, and standardization of child welfare standards. A novel feature of the conference, regional conferences in major cities, became permanent at future conferences.

92. Lucy Gillet, Letter to Dr. Dorothy Mendenhall, 9 December 1919, CB Records, Folder 8-6-12-10-2. One correspondent claimed that a bath twice a week was above the maximum for certain pioneer places. Lathrop believed that the leaflet's requirements were closer to the optimum than the minimum.

93. Children's Bureau, *Annual Report of the Children's Bureau*, 144–46.

94. See Children's Bureau, *Annual Report of the Children's Bureau*, 48–49. New Zealand had lowered its infant mortality rate to about half that of the United States in 1915.

95. Meckel, *Save the Babies,* 194–98.

96. Sheila Rothman, "Women's Clinics or Doctors' Offices: The Sheppard-Towner Act and the Promotion of Preventative Health Care," in *Social History and Social Policy,* ed. D. Rothman and S. Wheeler (New York, 1981), 176.

97. Rothman, "Women's Clinics or Doctors' Offices," 175–201; Halpern, *American Pediatrics,* 80, 98–103; and Arthur H. Parmelee, Jr., "History of Pediatrics and Well Child Care"(Manuscript and personal communication, 15 April 1994).

98. Stanley J. Lemons, *The Woman Citizen: Social Feminism in the 1920's,* 2nd ed. (Charlottesville, Va., 1990), 153–80; Muncy, *Creating a Female Dominion,* 193–223; and Meckel, *Save the Babies,* 206–11.

99. Muncy, *Creating a Female Dominion,* 106–07; and Meckel, *Save the Babies,* 211–12.

100. Only the bare details of the events preceding the passage of the Sheppard-Towner Act of 1921 are presented here because there is abundant literature on the act. For additional information, see Muncy, *Creating a Female Dominion,* 105–15; Meckel, *Save the Babies,* 206–11; Ladd-Taylor, *Mother-Work,* 166–96; Lemons, *Woman Citizen,* 155–78; Lela B. Costin, *Two Sisters for Social Justice: A Biography of Grace and Edith Abbott* (Urbana, Ill., 1983), 130–39; Rothman, *Woman's Proper Place,* 136–42; Rothman and Wheeler, *Social History,* 175–202; and Joseph Chepaitis, "The First Federal Social Welfare Measure: The Sheppard-Towner Maternity and Infancy Act, 1918–1932" (Georgetown University, 1968).

101. Muncy, *Creating a Female Dominion,* 88.

102. Louise C. Wade, "Julia C. Lathrop," in *Notable American Women, 1607–1950: A Biographical Dictionary,* ed. Edward T. James, Janet Wilson James, and Paul Boyer (Cambridge, Mass., 1971), 371; and Muncy, *Creating a Female Dominion,* 131, 141, 148–49, 153.

103. Jane Addams, *The Second Twenty Years at Hull-House, September 1909 to September 1929* (New York, 1930), 153–56.

104. Muncy, *Creating a Female Dominion,* 112–17; Jill Ker Conway, "Women Reformers and American Culture, 1870–1930," *Journal of Social History* 5(1971–1972): 164–77; and Ladd-Taylor, *Raising a Baby,* 9–10.

105. Mary R. Beard, "Books by and about Women," *Social Service Review* 10(1936): 350.

106. Beard, "Books by and about Women," 350.

107. Margaret Mahoney, Letter to author, 3 December 1993.

CHAPTER 6. FROM JUVENILE DELINQUENCY RESEARCH TO CHILD GUIDANCE

1. Jane Addams, *The Second Twenty Years at Hull-House, September 1909 to September 1929* (New York, 1930).

2. Reform of the juvenile justice system included the establishment of juvenile courts, detention homes for children and youth, and probation systems. By 1910 almost every city in the United States had a juvenile court, and the improvement of juvenile justice had become one of the most important Progressive reforms. Works that discuss the movements for juvenile justice include Grace Abbott, *The Child and the State,* 2 vols. (Chicago, 1938); Sophonisba P. Breckinridge and Edith Abbott, *The Delinquent Child*

and the Home (New York, 1912); Robert Bremner et al., eds., *Children and Youth in America: A Documentary History, 1866–1932,* 2 vols. (Cambridge, Mass., 1971); Homer Folks, *Care of Destitute, Neglected and Delinquent Children* (New York, 1902); Anthony Platt, *The Child Savers: The Invention of Juvenile Delinquency* (Chicago, 1969); Steven L. Schlossman, *Love and the American Delinquent: The Theory and Practice of "Progressive" Social Justice, 1825–1920* (Chicago, 1977); Robert Mennel, *Thorns and Thistles: Juvenile Delinquency in the United States, 1825–1940* (Hanover, N.J., 1973); Susan Tiffin, *In Whose Best Interest? Child Welfare Reform in the Progressive Era* (Westport, Conn., 1982); Walter I. Trattner, *From Poor Law to Welfare State: A History of Social Welfare in America* (New York, 1979); Murray Levine and Adeline Levine, "The More Things Change: A Case History of Child Guidance Clinics," *Journal of Social Casework* 26(1970):19–34; Sheila M. Rothman, *Woman's Proper Place: A History of Changing Ideals and Practices, 1870 to the Present* (New York, 1978); and Joseph Hawes, *Children in Urban Society: Juvenile Delinquency in Nineteenth-Century America* (New York, 1971).

3. William Healy and Mary T. Healy, *Pathological Lying, Accusations, and Swindling* (Boston, 1915).

4. David J. Rothman, *The Discovery of the Asylum: Social Order and Disorder in the New Republic* (Boston, 1971).

5. Flora J. Cooke, Report to Dr. Helen Koch, September 1944, Ethel Sturges Dummer Papers [hereafter, ESD], Elizabeth and Arthur Schlesinger Library, Radcliffe College, Harvard University, Cambridge, Massachusetts, Box 15.

6. Ethel S. Dummer, Letter to Miss Chamberlin, 16 January 1914, ESD, Box 20.

7. Ethel S. Dummer, Talk on mental hygiene and religion, 1930, ESD, Box 30.

8. Dummer, Talk on mental hygiene and religion.

9. Neither Margaret Olivia Sage, founder of the Russell Sage Foundation, nor Edith Harkness, founder of the Commonwealth Fund, was involved in research.

10. Ethel S. Dummer, Letter to William Healy, 9 April 1920, ESD, Box 30.

11. The scholars at the meeting included psychologists, physicians, sociologists, and settlement workers. See William Healy, Letter to Julia Lathrop, 4 April 1908, ESD, Box 30.

12. Ethel S. Dummer, Papers pertaining to the Research Committee on Delinquency, 1906, ESD, Box 30.

13. William Healy, Letter to Julia Lathrop, 4 April 1908.

14. John C. Burnham, Interviews with William Healy and Augusta Bronner (Cambridge, Mass., Houghton Library, Harvard University, 1960), 6.

15. Burnham, Interviews with Healy and Bronner, 51.

16. For information on the Witmer and Vineland clinics, see Barry Smith, Letter to Lawrence Frank, April 1914, Laura Spelman Rockefeller Memorial Archives [hereafter, LSRM], Rockefeller Archive Center, Pocantico Hills, Sleepy Hollow, New York, Series 30.5, Box 30; Walter E. Fernald, "Growth of the Provision for the Feeble-Minded in the United States," *Mental Hygiene* [*MH*](1917):34–59; John O'Donnell, "The Clinical Psychology of Lightner Witmer: A Case Study of Institutional Innovation and Intellectual Change," *Journal of the History of Behavioral Sciences* [*JHBS*] 15 (1979): 3–17; and David Shakow, "Clinical Psychology: An Evaluation," in *Orthopsychiatry, 1923–1948: Retrospect and Prospect,* ed. Lawson Lowrey and Victoria Sloane (New York: American Orthopsy-

chiatric Association, 1948), 231–33. Shakow explains why Witmer, founder of the first psychological clinic in the world and coiner of the term "clinical psychology," had so little influence on the field of mental hygiene and on clinical psychology. O'Donnell's essay is the best discussion of Witmer's contribution.

17. William Healy and Augusta Bronner, "The Child Guidance Clinic: Birth and Growth of an Idea," in *Orthopsychiatry,* ed. Lowrey and Sloane, 14–34.

18. Healey and Bronner, "Child Guidance Clinic."

19. George E. Gardner, "William Healy, 1869–1963," *Journal of the American Academy of Child Psychiatry* 11(1972):1–29.

20. Joel Hunter reports that after 1919 the term *psychopath* was no longer used by psychiatric clinics for children (Hunter, "The History of Development of Institutes for the Study of Children," in *The Child, the Clinic, and the Court,* ed. Jane Addams (New York, 1925), 204–14). Healy wrote to Dummer, "It would be much better, in my opinion, not to call this a psychopathic institute. Of problems studied many are not at all psychopathic nor do we commit ourselves at all to the idea that all problems of conduct belong in the realm psychopathology." See William Healy, Letter to Ethel Dummer, 12 April 1916, ESD, Box 30.

21. Ethel S. Dummer, "Life in Relation to Time," in *Orthopsychiatry,* ed. Lowrey and Sloane, 3–13.

22. Ethel S. Dummer, Resignation from the Board of the National Probation Association, 28 April 1934, ESD, Box 40. Dummer's most important contribution to education may have been arranging for the publication of a symposium with Herbert Jennings, John B. Watson, Adolph Meyer, and William I. Thomas. Healy's greatest contribution, according to Glueck, was his emphasis on the multiple causes of social behavior. (See Bernard Glueck, "Thomas Salmon and the Child Guidance Movement," *MH* 14[1964]: 318–22). Social workers reached the same conclusion as Healy concerning the multiple causes of emotional disturbances at about the same time. See Annette Garrett, "Historical Survey of the History of the Evolution of Casework," *Journal of Social Casework* [*JSC*] 30(1949): 219–29. For additional illustrations of organic theories, see Arthur E. Fink, *Causes of Crime: Biological Theories in the United States, 1800–1915* (New York, 1962).

23. Burnham, Interviews with Healy and Bronner.

24. Lawson G. Lowrey, "Psychiatry for Children: A Brief History of Developments," *American Journal of Psychiatry* [*AJP*] 108(1944): 375–88.

25. Jon Snodgrass, "William Healy (1869–1963): Pioneer Child Psychiatrist and Criminologist," *JHBS* 20(1984): 332–39.

26. Sheldon S. Glueck, "Special Editorial: Remarks in Honor of William Healy," *MH* 48(1964): 318–22.

27. William Healy, Letter to Ethel S. Dummer, 8 November 1918, ESD.

28. George E. Gardner, "In Memoriam: William Healy, 1869–1963," *Journal of Orthopsychiatry* [*JO*] 34(1964): 960–64. See the bibliography for eight books written by Healy, or Healy and a co-author, between 1925 and 1940. Healy dedicated the 1929 edition of *The Individual Delinquent* to Dummer. After 1940 he published five more books and numerous articles.

29. Gardner, "In Memoriam."

30. Augusta Bronner, Letter to William Healy, 10 January 1923. Mary Richmond, who is credited with providing a scientific base for social work, expressed a similar view (Mary Richmond, *Social Diagnosis* (New York, 1917)). "If we could just have enough facts, we would know what to do." Annette Garrett, "Historical Survey of the History of the Evolution of Casework," *JSC* 30(1949):219–29.

31. Burnham, Interviews with Healy and Bronner, 66–68.

32. Ethel Kawin, "The Contribution of Adolph Meyer to Child Guidance," *MH* 29(1945): 575–90.

33. Theodore Lidz, "Adolph Meyer and the Development of American Psychiatry," *AJP* 123(1966): 320–32; and Franklin G. Ebaugh, "A Tribute to Home," *AJP* 123(September 1966):336–68. Lidz is persuasive in linking Meyer's psychiatry to pragmatism and instrumentalism, a connection also mentioned by Ebaugh.

34. Adolph Meyer, "Mental Abnormalities in Children during Primary Education," *Transactions of the Illinois Society for Child Study* (1895): 48–58; and Adolph Meyer, "What Do Histories of Cases of Insanity Teach Us Concerning Preventive Mental Hygiene During the Years of School Life?" *Psychological Clinic* 2(1908–1909): 89–101.

35. Dorothy Ross, *G. Stanley Hall: The Psychologist as Prophet* (Chicago, 1972), 381.

36. Lidz, "Adolph Meyer," 320–32.

37. Adolph Meyer, *The Commonsense Psychiatry of Adolph Meyer: Fifty-Two Selected Papers,* ed. Alfred Lief (New York, 1948).

38. Lidz, "Adolph Meyer" 321, 324.

39. The literature does not specify Meyer's influence on Healy but mentions that Meyer, as well as James, recommended Healy for the investigation of juvenile delinquency.

40. Lidz, "Adolph Meyer," 321–24.

41. Adolph Meyer, "The Birth and Development of the Mental Hygiene Movement," *MH* 19(1935): 29.

42. Meyer, "Birth and Development."

43. Clifford Beers, *A Mind That Found Itself* (New York, 1908), 17; and Eunice E. Winters, "Adolph Meyer and Clifford Beers, 1907–1910," *Bulletin of the History of Medicine* 43(1969): 414–43.

44. William James, Letter to Adolph Meyer, 24 February 1909.

45. Adolph Meyer, Letter to William James, 26 February 1909.

46. Winters, "Meyer and Beers," 414–43.

47. Earl D. Bond, *Thomas W. Salmon, Psychiatrist* (New York, 1950), 34, 43, 47, 194–98.

48. Salmon P. Chase, n.d. The Salmon papers were unprocessed when I examined them.

49. Margo Horn, *Before It's Too Late: The Child Guidance Movement in the United States, 1922–1945* (Philadelphia, 1989), 19–20.

50. Bernard Glueck, "Thomas Salmon and the Child Guidance Movement," *Journal of Juvenile Research* 13(1929): 80.

51. Henry Goddard, *The Kallikak Family: A Study in the Heredity of Feeblemindedness* (New York, 1912).

52. Hamilton Cravens, "Applied Science and Public Policy: The Ohio Bureau of Juvenile Research and the Problem of Juvenile Delinquency," in *Psychological Testing and American Society,* ed. Michael Sokal (New Brunswick, N. J., 1987), 158–94.

53. Cravens's informative article on the Bureau of Juvenile Research, established in 1914 to study juvenile delinquents, with special reference to the detection of mental retardation and mental abnormalities, emphasizes Goddard's new approach to children as individuals, not simply as members of a group. The new study produced results that contradicted earlier ones. According to Cravens, by 1919 the differences between Goddard and Healy were "minimal." Nevertheless, Goddard continued to associate juvenile delinquency with psychopathology, a stance rejected by Healy in 1915.

54. Glueck, "Salmon and Child Guidance Movement," 79–80.

55. Thomas Salmon, "Some New Problems for Psychiatric Research in Delinquency," *MH* 4(1920): 29–42.

56. Lowrey, "Psychiatry for Children," 380–81; George Stevenson, "The Development of Extra-Mural Psychiatry in the United States," *AJP* 100(1944):147; and John C. Burnham, "The New Psychology: From Narcissism to Social Control," in *Change and Continuity in Twentieth-Century America,* ed. Robert Bremner, John Braeman, and David Brody (Columbus, Ohio, 1968).

57. Stevenson, "Development of Extra-Mural Psychiatry," 147–48.

58. For some consequences of the discovery of shell shock, see Burnham, "New Psychology," 360–63. Seventy-two thousand men were rejected from the army because of neuropsychiatric disorders; over two thousand men were sent home from overseas because of "shell shock."

59. Earl D. Bond, *Thomas W. Salmon, Psychiatrist* (New York, 1950), 78, 79, 108.

60. Thom was a neurologist on the staff of state hospitals before the war and served with the medical corps during the war. His wartime experiences inspired him to work with children. See Eveoleen Rexford, Interview by Alice Smuts, 15 June 1975. Meyer rejected America's post–World War I enthusiasm for psychiatry. See also Adolph Meyer, *The Commonsense Psychiatry of Adolph Meyer: Fifty-Two Selected Papers,* ed. Alfred Lief (New York, 1948).

61. Burnham, Interviews with Healy and Bronner, 163, 65.

62. Murray Levine and Adeline Levine, *A Social History of Helping Services: Clinic, Court, School, and Community* (New York, 1970), 238, 254. Psychiatric social workers were used in the Boston Psychopathic Hospital and in the Henry Phipps Clinic in 1913, when those clinics admitted children for psychiatric treatment. Although psychiatric social work was well established in state hospitals before World War I, the war encouraged its growth. See Emil Southard and Mary J. Jarrett, *Kingdom of Evils* (New York, 1922), on the early days of psychiatric social work at the Boston Psychiatric Hospital, and Lois M. French, *Psychiatric Social Work* (New York, 1940), for a history of the field.

63. William Healy, *The Individual Delinquent: A Textbook of Diagnosis and Prognosis for All Concerned in Understanding Juvenile Offenders* (Boston, 1915), 26, 27.

64. Mary Richmond, *Social Diagnosis* (New York, 1917).

65. Annette Garrett, "Historical Survey of the History of the Evolution of Casework," *JSC* 30(1949): 219, 223, 225.

66. Kathleen Woodroofe, *From Charity to Social Work in the United States and England* (Toronto, 1962), 116, 118–47.

67. Woodroofe, *From Charity to Social Work.* The chapter entitled "The Psychiatric Deluge"

discusses social work's preoccupation with the psychic life of the individual, a "deluge" in the United States but only a "trickle" in England. See also Healy and Bronner, "Child Guidance Clinic", and George S. Stevenson and Geddes Smith, *Child Guidance Clinics: A Quarter Century of Development* (New York, 1934), 56, 59, 62, 63. The Juvenile Psychopathic Institute in Chicago became a county agency in 1914 and part of the state's Department of Public Welfare in 1917. Its name was changed to the Institute for Juvenile Research in 1920. By this time, it offered professional assistance to parents and employed three psychiatrists, six psychologists, and nine social workers.

68. Jessie Taft, "Mental Hygiene and Social Work," in *Social Aspects of Mental Hygiene,* ed. Frankwood E. Williams (New Haven, 1925), 125–28.

69. Bessie Sperry, Interview by author, 1975.

70. Healy and Bronner, "Child Guidance Clinic," 14–34; and George E. Gardner, "In Memoriam: William Healy, 1869–1963," *JO* 34(1964): 960–64.

71. Healy and Bronner, "Child Guidance Clinic," 14.

72. Stevenson and Smith, *Child Guidance Clinics,* 56, 59, 62, 63; and *Judge Baker Guidance Center: Twenty Years of Growth, 1917–1937* (Boston, 1937). Stevenson and Smith, as well as the Judge Baker Guidance Center volume, contrast "single-cause theories" of childhood disturbances, prevalent before the child guidance movement, with examples of "interrelated causes—scientifically explained." The Judge Baker Foundation was renamed the Judge Baker Guidance Center in 1933.

73. Stevenson and Smith, *Child Guidance Clinics;* and *Judge Baker Guidance Center.*

74. Leo Kanner, "Autobiography," Unpublished manuscript (1970), American Psychiatric Association Archives, Washington, D.C.

75. David Levy, "Critical Evaluation of the Present State of Child Psychiatry," *AJP* 108(1952): 482.

76. Stevenson and Smith, *Child Guidance Clinics,* 109, 110.

77. Commonwealth Fund, "Commonwealth Fund Annual Report," 1–62 (1929–1930), 67.

78. *Judge Baker Guidance Center,* 8, 9.

79. Burnham, Interviews with Healy and Bronner.

CHAPTER 7. BETTER CROPS, BETTER PIGS, BETTER CHILDREN

1. Carl Emil Seashore, "Some Reminiscences about the Founding of the Station," typescript 28 April 1933, Historical File, University of Iowa Libraries [hereafter HFIL], Iowa City, Iowa, Box 1. G. Stanley Hall and his colleagues studied normal school-age children primarily in order to improve education. The Iowa Child Welfare Research Station's purpose in studying normal children was to produce a dependable science of child rearing.

2. Dorothy Bradbury and George Stoddard, *Pioneering in Child Welfare: A History of the Iowa Child Welfare Research Station, 1917–1933* (Iowa City, 1933).

3. The presence in Iowa of Carl Seashore, one of the nation's leading psychiatrists, who was willing to guide the women's campaign, certainly contributed to its success.

4. Dale Harris, Interview by author, 17 November 1980. I am indebted to Dale Harris, former director of the Minnesota Institute of Child Development, for calling my attention

to the powerful influence of the land-grant-college tradition on child development research institutes.

5. The Morrill Act of 1862 established the land-grant colleges. The second Morrill Act in 1890 provided an additional endowment.

6. Earl D. Ross, *Democracy's College: The Land Grant Movement in the Formative Stage* (Ames, Iowa, 1942), 141; and A. Hunter Dupree, "The Measuring Behavior of American Scientists," in *Nineteenth-Century American Science,* ed. George H. Daniels (Evanston, Ill., 1972), 22–37. The Hatch Act of 1877 provided for federal land grants to help support the state research stations. The experiment stations brought system and direction to the land-grant colleges and, more than any other factor, ensured their continuation.

7. The Smith-Lever Act not only increased extension work but also fundamentally changed the relationship of the land-grant colleges to the federal government and brought about a closer union of rural communities with the colleges.

8. Alfred Charles True, *A History of Agricultural Education in the United States, 1785–1925* (Washington D.C.: U.S.G.P.O., 1929), 288; A. Hunter Dupree, *Science in the Federal Government: A History of Policies and Activities* (Baltimore, 1986), 181–82; Edward V. Pope, "Extension Service Programs Affecting American Families," *Marriage and Family Living* 20 (August 1858): 270–71; and Sophonisba P. Breckenridge, *Women in the Twentieth Century: A Study of Their Political, Social, and Economic Activities* (New York, 1933), 266–68.

9. Ross, *Democracy's College,* 157–58; and Pope, "Extension Service Programs," 271–73. Ross points out that scientific recognition and analysis of problems of nutrition, sanitation, and household organization and equipment, mainly in the land-grant colleges, led to professional training in these fields. By the 1890s "the peculiar profession of women was being prepared for the opportunities that commercial promotion, consumer protection, and child welfare measures would provide" (Ross, *Democracy's College,* 157–58).

10. Bradbury and Stoddard, *Pioneering in Child Welfare,* 8.

11. At seventeen Laura was able to attend a local college, and until her death she lived, in Hillis's words, a "happy, useful life."

12. Cora Bussey Hillis, " How the Iowa Child Welfare Station Came into Being," Typescript, 1919. Cora Bussey Hillis Scrapbook Inventory [hereafter, CBH], Iowa State Historical Society, Iowa City, Iowa, Box 1, Folder 11.

13. Ginalie Swaim, "Cora Bussey Hillis: Woman of Vision," *Palimpsest* 60(1979): 164. Hillis's third child, Philip, died of meningitis in 1893; her fourth child, Isaac, died of a ruptured appendix in 1903; and Doris, the youngest child, died of scarlet fever on Jan. 1, 1907. By then her surviving children were adults, allowing her freedom to campaign. The two older children, Ellen and Cyrus, survived their parents.

14. Hillis, " How the Station Came into Being," 3.

15. Hillis, " How the Station Came into Being," 3–7.

16. Swaim, "Cora Bussey Hillis," 165–68.

17. Hillis, " How the Iowa Child Welfare Station Came into Being," 8.

18. Hillis, " How the Iowa Child Welfare Station Came into Being," 11, 13.

19. Bradbury and Stoddard, *Pioneering in Child Welfare,* 7–8. When MacLean left the university, he returned correspondence from Hillis, telling her to keep it as proof of her

"mothering" of the idea of a child study laboratory (see Hillis, 24 February 1908; and MacLean, 13 and 19 February 1908, and 1 March 1909).

20. Hillis, " How the Station Came into Being," 7–13.

21. Cora Bussey Hillis, "Iowa Station," Iowa Newspaper Articles, 27 January 1906, CBH, Box 2. Hillis never intimated that a scientific laboratory to study children was her idea, because she believed it would be more readily accepted if people thought that it had broader origins.

22. Julia Lathrop, Letter to Cora B. Hillis, 22 November 1912, CBH, Box 1, Folder 1. Hillis responded to Lathrop's question about the bureau's work for birth registrations by working for the passage of a vital statistics bill for the state. The bill failed, but she led a campaign in Des Moines in 1913 that registered 90 percent of the births in the city.

23. Carl Emil Seashore, "Carl Emil Seashore," in *A History of Psychology in Autobiography*, ed. Carl Murchison (Worcester, Mass., 1930), 225–97; and George G. Stoddard, "Carl Emil Seashore, 1866–1949," *American Journal of Psychology* 62(1949): 452–56.

24. Carl Emil Seashore, *Pioneering in Psychology*, no. 398 (Iowa City: University of Iowa Studies, 1942), 180. Seashore wrote, "Every feature which was outlined in the original plan and argument for the charter is now in operation and no radically new feature has been added"(Seashore, "Some Reminiscences," 7). Ten years of correspondence between Hillis and Seashore reveal a mutual respect and, often, a lively exchange of ideas.

25. Seashore, "Carl Emil Seashore," 257–65; Seashore, *Pioneering in Psychology*, 1–2, 6–38, 140–42; and Stoddard, "Carl Emil Seashore," 456.

26. Cora Bussey Hillis, Letter to Carl Seashore, 18 November 1914, Iowa Child Welfare Research Station Archives [ICWS], State University of Iowa, Iowa City, Iowa.

27. Carl Seashore, Letter to Cora Hillis, 21 November 1914, ICWS.

28. Seashore, "Some Reminiscences," 8.

29. Seashore, *Pioneering in Psychology*, 8.

30. Lawrence K. Frank, "Childhood and Youth," in *Recent Social Trends in the United States: Report of the President's Research Committee on Social Trends*, vol. 2 (New York, 1933; reprint, 1970), 795.

31. Carl Seashore, "A Child Welfare Research Station: Plans and Possibilities of a Research Station for the Conservation and Development of the Normal Child," Typescript, 1915, ICWS.

32. A slightly altered version of this document, intended by Seashore as a tentative outline in 1915, became the charter of the station and also served as a model for constitutions of other child development institutes (Stoddard, "Carl Emil Seashore," 271).

33. Iowa Child Welfare Research Committee, "Minutes December 23, 1914," ICWS; Iowa Child Welfare Research Committee, "Minutes December 7, 1914," ICWS; Seashore, "Some Reminiscences," 9.

34. Hillis, "How the Station Came into Being,", 9.

35. Hillis, "How the Station Came into Being," 6–8; and Carl Emil Seashore, "Origin of the term 'Euthenics,'" *Science* 95(1942): 455–56. Richards, a Vassar professor, invented the term "euthenics." During the 1920s a Department of Euthenics was established at Vassar College.

36. Bradbury and Stoddard, *Pioneering in Child Welfare*, 14–16.

37. Seashore, *Pioneering in Psychology,* 183; and Cora Bussey Hillis, "A Child Welfare Research Station: Practical Reasons for Having One," News story, paper not identified, 11 February 1915, CBH, Box 2, Folder 1.

38. Seashore's emphasis on the importance of early childhood experience in determining future behavior are similar to the beliefs of child-rearing spokesmen of an earlier period, for example, those of Horace Bushnell (Seashore, "Child Welfare Research Station: Plans and Possibilities," 12–13). On optimal child development, see also Seashore's debt to Jane Addams's essay "The Child at the Point of Greatest Pressure," (Paper presented at the NCCC, 1912): 26–30.

39. Seashore, "Some Reminiscences," 4.

40. Seashore, "Some Reminiscences," 6.

41. Seashore, "Some Reminiscences," 5–6.

42. Hillis, "Child Welfare Research Station: Practical Reasons."

43. Zealous friends, devoted to the cause but with only a vague idea of what a research station was, overstated what it might accomplish. Their comments prejudiced legislators and required time and effort to overcome (Hillis, "How the Station Came into Being," 20).

44. Hillis, "Child Welfare Research Station: Practical Reasons."

45. Carl Seashore, "Plan and Purpose of the Child Research Station," ICWS, 1916.

46. Seashore, "Plan and Purpose." According to Seashore, most people associated the study of children with vivisection, but more widespread than the belief that child study was dangerous was the conviction that it simply could not be done. Although efforts were made to overcome these misconceptions, he admitted that at that time assertions about the safety, necessity, and possibility of scientific study of the child had to be taken on faith.

47. Daniel Kevles, *In the Name of Eugenics: Genetics and the Uses of Human Heredity* (New York, 1985), 3–19, 70–73; and Kenneth Ludmerer, *Genetics and American Society: A Historical Appraisal* (Baltimore, 1972), 10–14, 75. Kevles's history of eugenics covers the British and American movements in both their scientific and cultural aspects. Studies of the American eugenics movement include Hamilton Cravens, *The Triumph of Evolution: American Scientists and the Heredity-Environment Controversy, 1900–1941* (Philadelphia, 1978); Mark H. Haller, "Heredity in Progressive Thought," *Social Service Review* 37(1963): 166–76; Robert C. Bannister, *Science and Myth in Anglo-American Social Thought* (Philadelphia, 1979); Carl Degler, *At Odds: Women and the Family in America from the Revolution to the Present* (New York, 1991); Merle Curti, *Human Nature and American Thought* (Madison, Wis., 1980): 272–312; and Martin Pernick, *The Black Stork: Eugenics and the Death of "Defective" Babies in American Medicine and Motion Pictures* (New York, 1996).

48. Ernst Mayr, *The Growth of Biological Thought: Diversity, Evolution, and Inheritance* (Cambridge, Mass., 1982).

49. Cravens, *Triumph of Evolution;* Hamilton Cravens and John C. Burnham, "Psychology and Evolutionary Naturalism in American Thought, 1840–1940," *American Quarterly* 23(1971): 635–57.

50. Haller, "Heredity in Progressive Thought," 166–76.

51. Kevles, *In the Name of Eugenics,* 61–62, 81.

52. Jacqueline K. Parker and Edward M. Carpenter, "Julia Lathrop and the Children's Bureau: The Emergence of an Institution," *Social Service Review* (1981): 71.

53. For information on fitter family contests, see Kevles, *In the Name of Eugenics,* 61–2. On the vogue for baby health contests, see Parker and Carpenter, "Lathrop and Children's Bureau," 71.

54. Blakeslee quoted by Kevles, *In the Name of Eugenics,* 61–62, 81.

55. Ludmerer, *Genetics and American Society,* 79; and Cravens, *Triumph of Evolution.*

56. For evidence of the dominance of hereditarian views in this period, see Ludmerer, *Genetics and American Society,* 79; and Cravens, *Triumph of Evolution,* 58.

57. Bradbury and Stoddard, *Pioneering in Child Welfare,* 28.

58. Cora Bussey Hillis, "Proposal for a Children's Place at the Fair in St. Louis," 19 January 1902, Box 2, Folder 2.

59. Hillis, "Child Welfare Research Station: Practical Reasons."

60. Carl Seashore, "Administration and Scope of the Iowa Child Welfare Research Station," in *University of Iowa Studies,* New Series, vol. 33 (Iowa City, Iowa, 1916).

61. Kevles shows that "eugenics" did not necessarily carry the ugly connotations of a later period but suggested the science of improving the human stock (Kevles, *In the Name of Eugenics,* 3).

62. Hillis, "How the Station Came into Being," 7.

63. Darling later became a Pulitzer prize–winning cartoonist and noted conservationist. See David L. Lendt, *The Life of Jay Norwood Darling* (Des Moines, Iowa, 1984).

64. Bradbury and Stoddard, *Pioneering in Child Welfare,* 19–21. The sheep bill carried the house by a vote of seventy-nine to thirteen; among those voting for it were twenty-seven who had voted against the station.

65. Bradbury and Stoddard, *Pioneering in Child Welfare,* 21.

66. Cravens reports that the Iowa legislature had a peculiar tradition of voting down new appropriations when first introduced ("Inconstancy of the Intelligence Quotient: The Iowa Child Welfare Station and the Criticism of Hereditarian Mental Testing, 1917–1930," Meeting, History of Science Society [Madison, Wis., October 1978], 5).

67. Hillis, "How the Station Came into Being," 22–23.

68. Hamilton Cravens, *Before Head Start: The Iowa Station and America's Children* (Chapel Hill, 1933); and Henry L. Minton, "Iowa Child Welfare Station and the 1940 Debate on Intelligence: Carrying on the Legacy of a Concerned Mother," *Journal of the History of Behavioral Sciences* 20(April 1984): 160–76.

69. Sklar comments on the need for more research on women's reform efforts in the Progressive era (Kathryn Kish Sklar, "Organized Womanhood: Archival Sources on Women and Progressive Reform," *Journal of American History* 75 [June 1988]: 176–83). See Flanagan for the different approaches to reform of women and men club members in Chicago and for the influence of settlement women on businessmen (Maureen A. Flanagan, "Gender and Urban Political Reform: The City Club and the Woman's City Club of Chicago in the Progressive Era," *American Historical Review* 5(1990): 1032–50). Bradbury and Stoddard discuss the women leaders and organizations that participated in the campaign (Bradbury and Stoddard, *Pioneering in Child Welfare,* 14–16). The two male officers of

the association were a president of the Iowa National Bank, who served as auditor, and a representative of the Trade and Labor Assemblies of Des Moines.

70. Ross, *Democracy's College*, 28, 56.

71. The president of Iowa State Agricultural College devoted two-thirds of his opening address in 1858 to the equalization of education for women.

72. Seashore, "Some Reminiscences," 11.

73. Hillis's portrayal of the campaign in altruistic terms does not mean that her motives or those of her colleagues were completely unselfish but that she was shrewd enough to project this impression.

74. Although over two hundred Iowa legislators had to be influenced, Hillis boasted that she had speaking acquaintance with only eleven representatives. She said that this proved that women could yield influence without lobbying.

75. Hillis, "How the Station Came into Being," 10; and Bradbury and Stoddard, *Pioneering in Child Welfare*, 29–30.

76. Hillis, "How the Station Came into Being," 10; and Bradbury and Stoddard, *Pioneering in Child Welfare*, 29–30.

77. Cora Bussey Hillis, Letter to Carl Seashore, 2 August 1918, HFIL.

78. Bradbury and Stoddard, *Pioneering in Child Welfare*, 29–30.

79. Recent historical scholarship on women reformers has devoted increasing attention to the type of social feminism represented by clubwomen. Millions of clubwomen who supported Progressive reform were mothers, and many of them must have shared Hillis's conservative views on women's proper role. Current research on Progressive women reformers is likely to identify other mother-leaders, whose purposes and methods differed significantly from those of reformers who were unmarried professional women.

80. Seashore, *Pioneering in Psychology*, 181–82.

81. For the research skills and abilities necessary to maintain good relations with influential farmers that characterized successful directors of agricultural experiment stations, see Rosalind Rosenberg, *Beyond Separate Spheres: Intellectual Roots of Modern Feminism* (New Haven, 1972), 181–209.

82. Beth Wellman, "Contributions of Bird Thomas Baldwin to Child Development," *Journal of Juvenile Research* 14(1930): 1–7.

83. Baldwin's books on preschool children were published in 1921, 1924, and 1930.

84. Carl Seashore, Letter to Cora Hillis, 17 April 1918, CBH, Box 1.

85. Cora Bussey Hillis, Letter to Baldwin, 7 November 1917, CBH, Box 1.

86. Cora Bussey Hillis, Letter to President Wilson, 12 October 1918, CBH, Box 1.

87. State University of Iowa, "The State University of Iowa Newsletter," 27 December 1919, HFIL; and Cravens, *Before Head Start*, 36–37.

88. Pernick, *Black Stork*, 41–78.

89. Seashore had wanted the aesthetic development of children to be among the first subjects to be studied by the station, but colleagues dissuaded him. Seashore devoted much of his own research to the investigation of children's musical ability (Seashore, *Pioneering in Psychology*, 225–32).

90. Bradbury and Stoddard, *Pioneering in Child Welfare*, 43–44.

CHAPTER 8. THE CHILDREN'S DECADE

1. Other references to the importance of children permeate the popular and scholarly literature of the 1920s. Frank maintains that increased attention to children may have stemmed, in part, from the decreasing ratio of children to adults during the 1920s, which gave parents more time for each child. See Lawrence K. Frank, "Childhood and Youth," in *Recent Social Trends: A Report of the President's Research Committee on Social Trends,* vol. 2 (New York, 1933; reprint, 1970), 756.
2. Clark A. Chambers, *Seedtime of Reform: American Social Action, 1918–1933* (Minneapolis, 1963), 30; and Frank, "Childhood and Youth," 752.
3. Chambers, *Seedtime of Reform,* 13–14.
4. Chambers, *Seedtime of Reform,* 29–58.
5. Julia Lathrop, "Children's Year: The Children's Era," *Survey* 42(3 May 1919): 170.
6. Stanley J. Lemons, "The Sheppard-Towner Act: Progressivism in the 1920's," *Journal of American History* 55(March 1969): 776–86; and James M. Giglio, "Volunteerism and Public Policy Between World War I and the New Deal: Herbert Hoover and the American Child Health Association," *Presidential Studies Quarterly* 13(1973): 430–52.
7. Ray Lyman Wilbur, *White House Conference on Child Health and Protection, 1930: Addresses and Abstracts of Committee Reports* (New York, 1931), 7.
8. Dorothy Bradbury and George Stoddard, *Pioneering in Child Welfare: A History of the Iowa Child Welfare Research Station, 1917–1933* (Iowa City, 1933), 27.
9. Clark A. Chambers, "The Belief in Progress in the Twentieth Century," *Journal of the History of Ideas* [JHI] 19(1958): 198.
10. James Patterson, *America's Struggle Against Poverty, 1900–1985* (Cambridge, Mass., 1986), 3–20.
11. Laura Spelman Rockefeller Memorial, "Child Study Work in the Women's Colleges," LSRM Series 3.5, Box 30.
12. Lewis M. Terman, "The Status of Applied Psychology in the United States," *Journal of Applied Psychology* 5(March 1921): 3–4; Henry L. Minton, "The Iowa Child Welfare Station and the 1940 Debate on Intelligence: Carrying on the Legacy of a Concerned Mother," *Journal of the History of Behavioral Sciences* [JHBS] 20(April 1984): 160–76; Frank Samuelson, "World War Intelligence Testing and the Development of Psychology," *JHBS* 18(1977): 274–82; and Sidney Kaplan, "Social Engineers as Saviors: Effects of World War I on Some American Liberals," *JHI* 17(June 1956): 347–69.
13. Matthew Hale, Jr., *Human Science and the Social Order: Hugo Munsterberg and the Origins of Applied Psychology* (Philadelphia, 1980), 162.
14. John C. Burnham, "The New Psychology: From Narcissism to Social Control," in *Change and Continuity in Twentieth-Century America,* ed. Robert Bremner, John Braeman, and David Brody (Columbus, Ohio, 1968), 351–97; and Grace Addams, "The Rise and Fall of Psychology," *Atlantic Monthly* 153(1934): 82–92.
15. John Anderson, *The Psychology of Developmental and Personal Adjustment,* 84.
16. Burnham, "New Psychology," 351–98.
17. Psychology and anthropology were the only social sciences represented in the National

Research Council. Carl Seashore was appointed chair of the division in 1920, and the following year Bird Baldwin became chair of its newly formed Committee on Child Welfare and Parent Education. The other members were psychologists Helen Woolley and Henry Goddard.

18. Barry D. Karl, "Presidential Planning and Social Science Research: Mr. Hoover's Experts," *Perspectives in American History* 3(1969): 347–412.

19. Ronald C. Tobey, *The American Ideology of National Science, 1919–1930* (Pittsburgh, 1971), 15; and Hunter A. Dupree, *Science in the Federal Government: A History of Policies and Activities* (Baltimore, 1986), 316–23.

20. John B. Watson, *Psychology from the Standpoint of a Behaviorist* (Philadelphia and London, 1919), 1–3.

21. Robert Kargon, *The Maturing of American Science: A Portrait of Science in Public Life Drawn from the Presidential Addresses of the American Association for the Advancement of Science, 1920–1970* (Washington D.C., 1974), 33.

22. Stanley G. Hall, *Life and Confessions of a Psychologist* (New York, 1923).

23. Chambers, "Belief in Progress," *JHI* 19(1958): 198.

24. Henry May, "Shifting Perspectives in the 1920s," *Mississippi Historical Review* 18(December 1956): 405–27.

25. May, "Shifting Perspectives," 410–11.

26. Robert Bremner, *American Philanthropy*, 117–40; and Merle Curti, "American Philanthropy and the National Character," *American Quarterly* 10, no. 4(1958): 420–37.

27. Merle Curti, *American Philanthropy Abroad*, 259–307.

28. The American Red Cross changed during the war from an agency that spent about $500,000 a year to one that could raise and distribute $100 million in a single campaign and $400 million during the war. This "was not viewed as a temporary exigency . . . but as an experience that could be repeated." See Barry D. Karl and Stanley N. Katz, "The American Private Philanthropic Foundation and the Public Sphere," *Minerva* 19, no. 2(1981): 261, 236–70.

29. Karl and Katz, "American Private Philanthropic Foundation," 261.

30. Robert E. Kohler, "Policy for the Advancement of Science: Rockefeller Foundation, 1924–29," *Minerva* 16(1978): 481.

31. Grants for children's programs rose from $6.28 million in 1920 to $12 million in 1930. Adult grants only increased from $16.5 million to $21.5 million during the same period. See Harold Coe Coffman, *American Foundations: A Study of Their Role in the Child Welfare Movement* (New York, 1936), 23, 48.

32. Harvey M. McGhee and Susan L. Abrams, *For the Welfare of Mankind: The Commonwealth Fund and American Medicine* (Baltimore, 1985); and Raymond B. Fosdick, *The Story of the Rockefeller Foundation* (New York, 1952), 192–95.

33. Robert E. Kohler, "Policy for the Advancement of Science—Rockefeller Foundation, 1924–29," *Minerva* 16(1978): 490; and Martin Bulmer and Joan Bulmer, "Philanthropy and the Social Sciences in the 1920s: Beardsley Ruml and the Laura Spelman Rockefeller Memorial," *Minerva* 19 (Autumn 1981): 350.

34. Bulmer and Bulmer, "Philanthropy and Social Sciences," 381–82.

35. Stanley Coben, "American Foundations as Patrons of Science: The Commitment to In-

dividual Research," in *The Sciences in the American Context: New Perspectives,* ed. Nathan Reingold (New York, 1974), 239–40.

36. Beardsley Ruml, "Conditions Affecting the Memorial's Participation in Social Science," Memorandum presented to the Laura Spelman Rockefeller Memorial, 10 July 1922, LSRM, Series 1, Box 1, Folder 9.

37. Kohler, "Policy for Advancement," 481–82.

38. The Bulmers' article offers a lucid analysis of the Memorial's change of direction and its significant effect on the development of the social sciences in the United States. It hails Ruml's memorandum as "one of the most important statements about the social sciences in the United States in the first half of the twentieth century." In seeking to use the resources of a major private philanthropic foundation to strengthen the basic social sciences in the universities, it points out, Ruml entered the field when there were scarcely any other sources of financial support. "The support of the Russell Sage Foundation for the 'survey movement' and Carnegie support of particular projects were much more specialized and were not part of a comprehensive programme. No federal or state government funds were available for social science research. The directions in which Ruml sought change were, moreover, new departures, though in tune with trends already at work." See Bulmer and Bulmer, "Philanthropy and Social Sciences,"361–68.

39. Ruml, "Conditions Affecting Participation," Memorandum presented to the Laura Spelman Rockefeller Memorial, 10 July 1922, LSRM, Series 1, Box 1, Folder 9.

40. Bulmer and Bulmer, "Philanthropy and Social Sciences," 347–407.

41. Lawrence K. Frank, "Varieties of Research," Lawrence K. Frank Papers [hereafter, LKF], National Library of Medicine, History of Medicine Division, Bethesda, Maryland, Box 11 (June 1934), 360.

42. Milton J. E. Senn, *Insights on the Child Development Movement in the United States: Monographs of the Society of Research in Child Development* (Chicago, 1975), 5–6.

43. Lawrence K. Frank, Interview by Jeanne Spiegel, 1966–67, Society for Research in Child Development Archive [hereafter, SRCDA], National Library of Medicine, History of Medicine Division, Bethesda, Maryland, Box 12, Folder 1.

44. Frank's father deserted his mother when he was a small child, and Frank saw him infrequently. His mother became an alcoholic in later life. See Mary Frank Perry, Interview, 19 July 1972, Milton J. E. Senn Oral History Collections in Child Development and Child Guidance [hereafter, Senn OHCD], National Library of Medicine (NLM), History of Medicine Division, Bethesda, Maryland.

45. Bird T. Baldwin, Memorandum to Walter Jesup, 13 September 1920.

46. Cora Bussey Hillis, Letter to Carl Seashore, 27 September 1920.

47. For a description of Hillis's meeting with Vincent Rockefeller and Rockefeller's decision to send foundation representatives to the station, see J.C. Martzell, Letter to Baldwin, 1 December 1920. See Dutton's characterization of Hillis as a great woman, second only to Laura Spelman Rockefeller in her influence on the Laura Spelman Rockefeller Memorial. Her "bold experiment" in applying science to children, he claims, was carefully watched by Rockefeller trustees and their advisers, who thereafter pumped millions of dollars into applied social science (William S. Dutton, "The Rockefeller Story: Man's Greatest Challenge," *Colliers* 127(19 May 1951): 29–30).

48. Hillis to Seashore, 27 September 1920.

49. See Baldwin, Memorandum to Jesup, 13 September 1920; and Bird T. Baldwin, Letter to Frank, 15 March 1923, LSRM, Series 3.5, Box 40, Folder 417. The 1923 grant of $22,500 specified that it must be used for a specific project (LSRM minutes 21 November 1922). Baldwin chose to undertake a longitudinal study of children in rural Iowa (Bird T. Baldwin, Eva Fillmore, and Lora Hadley, *Farm Children: An Investigation of Rural Child Life in Selected Areas of Iowa* [New York, 1930]). The Memorial insisted that the station alter its program before it awarded the grants. The influence between station and Memorial was reciprocal.

50. Minutes of the LSRM meeting (24–27 August 1927, 54–75) include Ruml's comment on rural bias after he failed to persuade the Trustee Committee on Review to approve child development programs in urban centers. "I thought I made a strong case," he said, "when I pointed out that in view of this concentration of population, it would be useful to make a special effort to reach these cities through the administrative unit of the school board." He was told "that there were more eminent men born within fifty miles of the Hanover town pump than within fifty miles of New York," and "asked whether the concentration on the city was worth while if the human product coming out of the cities didn't measure up more satisfactorily." Ruml added, "I didn't ask for the statistics."

51. See Parke et al., eds., *A Century of Developmental Psychology* (Washington D.C., 1994), 15 for a table, "Dimensions of Theory and Research in Developmental Psychology," comparing 1900, the 1950s and 1960s, and the 1990s.

52. Lawrence K. Frank, "Recording on the History of Child Development Centers in the U.S.A.," Senn OHCD (December, 1963).

53. Steven L. Schlossman, "Philanthropy and the Gospel of Child Development," in *Private Philanthropy and Public Elementary and Secondary Education: Proceedings of the Rockefeller Archive Center Conference Held on 8 June 1979,* ed. Gerald Benjamin (New York, 1980), 15–32.

54. Frank, "Recording on History."

55. Beardsley Ruml and Lawrence K. Frank, Transcript of staff meeting, 24–27 August 1927, LSRM, Series 2, Box 3, Folder 41.

56. Frank and Ruml preferred to locate centers for child research and parent education at state universities because they believed them to be important agents for improving their states and also because they wanted to take advantage of their extension facilities. Ruml and Frank commented on the advantages of state universities and land-grant colleges (LSRM 24–27 August 1927). Frank's insistence on autonomous institutes, resisted by faculty and administrators at the Universities of Minnesota and California, delayed their founding. Discussion of the founding of the LSRM institutes is limited to inaccurate information from Frank, a few articles, and Craven's history of the Iowa station. See Frank, "Recording on History,"; Hamilton Cravens, "Child Saving in the Age of Professionalism, 1915–1930," in *American Childhood: A Research Guide and Historical Handbook,* ed. Joseph M. Hawes and N. Ray Hiner (Westport, Conn., 1985; 1993), 15–88; Elizabeth Lomax, "The Laura Spelman Rockefeller Memorial: Some of Its Contributions to Early Research in Child Development," *JHBS* 10(1977): 283–93; Theresa R. Richardson, *The Century of the Child: The Mental Hygiene Movement and Social Policy in the United States*

and Canada (New York, 1989); Schlossman, "Philanthropy and Gospel of Child Development," 15–32; Robert R. Sears, *Your Ancients Revisited: A History of Child Development* (Chicago, 1975); and Milton J. E. Senn, *Insights on the Child Development Movement in the United States: Monographs of the Society of Research in Child Development* (Chicago, 1975). There are many more histories of the early child guidance movement than of the child development movement because the LSRM insisted on a policy of anonymity, while the Commonwealth Fund actively promoted and evaluated its child guidance program.

57. Cravens, "Child Saving," (Westport, Conn., 1985), 415–88.

58. Alice Smuts, "Edna Noble White, June 3, 1879-May 4, 1954," in *Noble American Women, 1607–1950: A Biographical Dictionary,* ed. Edward T. James, Janet Wilson James, and Paul Boyer, Vol. 2 (1980), 728–29.

59. Lawrence K. Frank, "The Beginnings of Child Development and Family Life Education in the Twentieth Century," *Merrill Palmer Quarterly* 7(1962): 1–28.

60. Lester W. Sontag, "The History of Longitudinal Research: Implications for the Future," *Child Development* 42(October 1971): 987–1002; and Lester W. Sontag, Interview by author, 1983; and *Fels at Fifty,* Yellow Springs, Ohio, 1979.

61. Beardsley Ruml, Memorandum, 6 April 1927, LSRM, Series 3.5, Box 31, Folder 329.

62. Lawrence K. Frank, *Spelman Fund of New York Report for 1929–1930* (New York, 1933), 7.

63. Frank, "Childhood and Youth," 792–94; Eduard Lindeman, "Parent Education and Training: Subcommittee on the Family and Parent Education," (Paper presented at the WHC, New York, 1930); and Frank, *Spelman Fund Report 1929–1930,* 34–35.

64. Caroline A. Chandler and Laura L. Dittmann, ed., *Early Child Care: The New Perspectives* (New York, 1968).

65. Chapter 3 discussed the split between the parent education movement launched by the National Congress of Mothers and the 1920s movement supported by the Memorial.

66. Miriam Van Waters, "Philosophic Trends in Modern Social Work," Paper presented at the National Conference of Social Work, Boston, 1930).

67. For the shift from the reform of institutions to reform of the individual, see Burnham, "New Psychology," 396–97; Roy Lubove, *The Professional Altruist: The Emergence of Social Work as a Career, 1880–1930* (Cambridge, Mass., 1965), 85–113; Philip Klein, *From Philanthropy to Social Welfare in America* (San Francisco, 1968), 153–56; Kathleen Woodroofe, *From Charity to Social Work in the United States and England* (Toronto, 1962), 121–33; and Clark A. Chambers, *Paul Kellogg and the Survey: Voices for Social Welfare* (Minneapolis, 1971), 77–94. Howard Odum traces a change in motives for childcare from "pity for his condition or salvaging the child from becoming a pauper in the future" to scientific appreciation of "individual treatment of children with an emphasis placed upon the needs of the child and not the act." The introduction to *Recent Social Trends* states, "Much of what is thought of as heredity is really the family influence on the personality of the child. . . . The potentialities of child development and the responsibility of parenthood make parent education a major problem of the future" (p. xli). Note Frank's comments on the modification of theories about the determining power of heredity and the strengthening of belief in the plasticity of human nature (Lawrence K. Frank, "Childhood and Youth," in *Recent Social Trends,* vol. 2 [1933], 752).

68. John B. Watson, *The Psychological Care of the Infant and Child* (New York, 1928), 12.

69. Watson, *Psychological Care,* 5.

70. Frank, "Childhood and Youth," 752.

71. Frank had three children by his first wife, two by the second, and two by the third. McGraw observed Frank's use of Watsonian methods during a visit to his home in 1925. See Harold Stevenson, Interviews by Helen Lynd, January 1973; and Myrtle McGraw, Interview by author, 1977.

72. Wilbur, *White House Conference, 1930,* 10.

73. Lawrence K. Frank, "Parent Training," LSRM (26 March 1924) Series 3.5, Box 30, Folder 315.

74. Frank, Introduction, in *Recent Social Trends,* xli.

75. Lindeman, "Parent Education and Training," ii.

76. Ernest Groves, "Parent Education," *Annals of the American Academy of Political and Social Sciences* (1932): 216. Cultural lag was the central integrative theme of Frank's *Recent Social Trends.* For another illustration of the use of cultural lag as a framework for research, see Robert S. Lynd and Helen M. Lynd, *Middletown: A Study in Contemporary American Culture* (New York, 1929).

77. Frank wrote, "If we want to produce social progress the solution is to find a technique for reducing cultural lag" (Lawrence K. Frank, "N.T.," LSRM [15 January 1925]). For Frank's views on cultural lag, see Lawrence K. Frank, *Recent Social Trends,* vol. 2 (New York, 1933), 796–98. Frank refers to "unbelievable archaisms" and "astonishing cultural lags" that need to be overcome if social progress is to take place. See Lawrence K. Frank, "European Experience," LKF, 13 March 1929, Box 11. In the 1920s over half of the children in the United States lived in rural areas, and extension services were the best way to reach them.

78. Attention to mothers permeated both the nineteenth century and the 1920s. One interesting exception was the Federated Father's Club of Council Bluffs, Iowa, founded by thirty fathers in 1913 ("Fathers, 1914–1915," n.d., Cora Bussey Hillis Scrapbook Inventory [hereafter, CBH], Iowa State Historical Society, Iowa City, Iowa, Box 2). For the first studies of the impact of the father on the family as a child-rearing system, prompted by massive unemployment during the Great Depression, see Urie Bronfenbrenner and Ann Crouter, "The Evolution of Environmental Models in Research," in *Handbook of Child Psychology,* ed. Paul Mussen and Leonard Carmichael, vol. 1 (New York, 1983), 372. The absence of fathers during World War II stimulated more studies: Lois Meek Stolz, *Father Relations of War-Born Children: The Effects of Postwar Adjustment of Fathers on the Behavior and Personality of First Children Born While Fathers Were at War* (Stanford, Calif. and New York, 1954); John Nash, "The Father in Contemporary Culture and Current Psychological Literature," *Child Development* 36(1965): 261–98; and Michael E. Lamb, "Fathers: Forgotten Contributors to Child Development," *Human Development* 18(1975): 245–66.

79. Lawrence K. Frank, "European Experience," LKF, 13 March, 1929, Box 11.

80. Frank wrote, "It is manifestly absurd for the state to hand out money without any attempt at improving the ways and practices of the home in regard to children whom it is proposed to help. . . . It seems certain that within the next few years efforts will be made

to work out methods of teaching mothers and foster mothers the essentials of wholesome child care which they must adopt as a condition precedent to the receipt of allowances paid to them" {Lawrence K. Frank, "Child Welfare," LSRM [17 October 1925], Series 3.5, Box 30, Folder 315}.

81. Julia Lathrop, "The Highest Education for Women," in *The Fiftieth Anniversary of the Opening of Vassar College* (Poughkeepsie, N.Y., 1915), 81–85.

82. Sheila M. Rothman, *Woman's Proper Place: A History of Changing Ideals and Practices, 1870 to the Present* (New York, 1978), 97–132.

83. Lois Meek Stolz, Interview by author, transcript in my possession, 9 December 1976.

84. Lois Meek Stolz, Interview by author, 17 December 1978, 14–37; and Emily Davis Cahan, "Research and Child Development and the Formation of Social Policy: Historical Precedents and Current Perspectives," Bush Foundation (Minneapolis, Minn., 1992), 240.

85. See Minutes of meeting, 24–27 August 1927, LSRM, Series 3.5, Box 30, 167–70. Stolz reported that child development courses and the nursery school laboratory at Vassar had to be placed under the Institute of Euthenics because the psychology department would have nothing to do with child development. The presidents of Barnard, Wellesley, and Bryn Mawr were among those who opposed the parent education program of the AAUW. Stolz believed that their attitudes reflected intellectual snobbery, rather than feminism. See Lois Meek Stolz, Interview by author, 9 December 1976.

86. Pauline Knapp, Interview by Milton J. E. Senn, 6 April 1971, Senn OHCD.

87. For prejudice against the field of child development among home economists, see Pauline Knapp, Interview by Milton J. E. Senn, 6 April 1971. White was the most influential home economist in the field of child development and a close colleague of Frank. Frank was eager to enlist home economists in his cause because he wanted to tie the nursery school movement to home economics rather than to psychology and because he needed home economists to reach rural families. Breckinridge points out that the number of women enrolled in extension programs tripled between 1920 and 1930, increasing from 210,000 to 640,000 (Sophonisba P. Breckinridge, *Women in the Twentieth Century: A Study of Their Political, Social, and Economic Activities* [New York, 1933], 15).

88. Myrtle McGraw, Interview by author, 9 May 1972, Senn OHCD.

89. LSRM, "Child Study Work in Women's Colleges," n.d., Addenda 3.5, Box 30.

90. Watson, *Psychological Care,* 12.

91. Dale Harris, successor to John Anderson as director of the Minnesota Institute, commented on Anderson's attitude toward parent education, "Although not personally much given to 'application,' he took this obligation very seriously and maintained study groups, publication of leaflets, a weekly newspaper release to many small dailies and weeklies of the state, and an annual training conference for the parent education chairpersons of local and district PTAs. He kept those up until the 1940s and published an extensive evaluation in the mid-1930s. John always thought that Iowa cheated a bit on the promise to Rockefeller by using the annual lecture series to fulfill the parent education obligation. It put on an annual institute of three days, which later dwindled to a couple of lectures per day. See Dale Harris, Correspondence with author, 21 May 1991.

92. Helen Witmer, *The Field of Parent Education: A Survey from the Viewpoint of Research* (New York, 1934).

93. Lois Meek Stolz, Interview by author, 17 December 1978, 14–37.

94. Steven L. Schlossman, "Before Home Start: Notes Toward a History of Parent Education in America, 1897–1929," *Harvard Educational Review* 46(1976): 436–67; Steven L. Schlossman, "The Formative Ear in Parent Education: Overview and Interpretation," in *Parent Education and Public Policy,* ed. Ron Haskins and Diane Adams (Norwood, N. J., 1983), 7–39; Steven L. Schlossman, "Science and the Commercialization of Parenthood: Notes Toward a History of *Parents' Magazine,*" *American Psychological Association Division 7 Newsletter* (Spring 1983): 14–17; and Steven L. Schlossman, "Perils of Popularization: The Founding of *Parents' Magazine,*" in *History and Research in Child Development: Monographs of the Society for Research in Child Development,* ed. Alice Smuts and John Hagan (Chicago, 1986), 65–77.

95. See Beardsley Ruml, Memorandum, 1927, LSRM, Series 3.4, Box 31, Folder 329. Unlike child welfare reform, prewar parent education movement lost momentum following the end of Hall's child study movement in 1910. See Chapter 3 for the split between the Progressive parent education movement led by the National Congress of Mothers and the postwar movement sponsored by the LSRM.

96. L.B. Day, Letter to Beardsley Ruml, 11 March 1927, LSRM, Series 3.4, Box 30, Folder 315.

97. L.B. Day, Letter to Beardsley Ruml, 15 May 1925, LSRM, Series 3.4, Box 30, Folder 315.

98. Arthur Woods, "Committee on Review, 1924–1928," Letter to Beardsley Ruml, n.d., LSRM, Series 3.5, Box 31, Folder 392. For other disparaging comments on parent education by Day, see the minutes of the LSRM August 1927 meeting.

99. Milton J. E. Senn, *Insights on the Child Development Movement,* 69–89; and Milton J. E. Senn, *Speaking Out for America's Children* (New Haven, Conn., 1977), 43–69.

100. Harold Stevenson points out that, although Watson's impact should have been short-lived, it was not, and "child rearing became simply a matter of habit training" (Harold Stevenson, "How Children Learn: The Quest for a Theory," in *HCP,* ed. Paul H. Mussen [New York, 1983], 216). One can perceive Watson's influence in child-rearing pamphlets prepared for the 1930 WHC and in the child-rearing literature of Douglas Thom. For Watson's influence on Wooley, see Helen Russel Wooley, "Eating, Sleeping, Elimination," in *HCP,* ed. Carl Murchinson (Worcester, Mass., 1931).

CHAPTER 9. CHILD DEVELOPMENT RESEARCH

1. Hamilton Cravens, *Before Head Start: The Iowa Station and America's Children* (Chapel Hill, 1933), 68; and Alice Smuts and John Hagen, eds., *History and Research in Child Development* 50, Monographs of the Society for Research in Child Development (Chicago, 1986), 108–11. In spite of his leadership in establishing the Iowa Child Welfare Research Station, Seashore preferred that funds go to traditional psychological research rather than to the Child Welfare Committee. The committee's chief activity was to assist Cora Bussey Hillis's unsuccessful efforts to establish a Children's Palace at the 1926 Philadelphia Exposition.

2. Dorothy McLean, "A Generation of Research," *Child Development* [*CD*] 25 (1954): 3–8;

Smuts and Hagen, *History and Research,* 108–25; and Robert Woodworth, "Report to the Committee on Child Welfare of Results of Questionnaire Sent Out from the Office of the Division of Anthropology," 21 April 1925, Laura Spelman Rockefeller Memorial [hereafter, LSRM], Rockefeller Archive Center, Pocantico Hills, Sleepy Hollow, New York, Series 3.5, Box 30, Folder 320.

3. Smuts and Hagen, *History and Research,* 112–13.

4. In December 1924 the division approved a motion to ask the Memorial to appropriate $40,000 for four years to support the work of the Committee on Child Welfare and Parent Education. The renamed committee was officially recognized on June 30, 1925, but its grant was delayed until January 1926 (Woodworth, "Report to the Committee").

5. Smuts and Hagen, *History and Research,* 113–15.

6. Emily Cahan, "Science, Practice, and Gender Roles in Early American Child Psychology," in *Contemporary Construction of the Child: Essays in Honor of William Kessen* (New Haven, Conn., 1991), 244–45, 255–59. See Cahan's discussion of the association of practical application with women's work and research with men's.

7. Smuts and Hagen *History and Research,* 113–20.

8. Bird T. Baldwin, "Research in Child Development," NRCCCD, First Conference on Research in Child Development, 1925, LSRM, Series 3.5, Box 36, 13.

9. Woodsworth, "Report to the Committee on Child Welfare," 3.

10. Smuts and Hagen, *History and Research,* 116–20.

11. Smuts and Hagen, *History and Research,* 119–26.

12. Society for Research in Child Development. Minutes, 23 June 1933, Society for Research in Child Development Archives [hereafter, SRCDA], National Library of Medicine, History of Medicine Division, Bethesda, Maryland, Box 1, folder 1.

13. For discussion of the differences between child development and child psychology, see Lois Stolz, "Old and New Directions in Child Psychiatry," *Merrill Palmer Quarterly* [*MPQ*] 12 (1963): 221–32; Dale Harris, "The Concept of Development," in *An Experimental Psychology of Development: Pipe Dream or Possibility?* ed. Wallace A. Russell (Minneapolis, 1956), 162–74; and John Anderson, "The Contributions of Child Development to Psychology," *Journal of Consulting Psychology* 6 (1939): 128–34. The terms *child development* and *child psychology* were used interchangeably during the 1920s and 1930s and sometimes still are. See Lawrence Frank, "The Beginnings of Child Development and Family Life Education in the Twentieth Century," *MPQ* 7 (1962): 18; Lawrence Frank, Letter to Charles Merriam, 16 November 1926, LSRM, Series 3.5, Box 30; Lawrence Frank, Letter to Ethel Richardson, 15 April 1927, LSRM, Series 3.5, Box 43, Folder 452; and Lawrence Frank, "The Problem of Child Development," *CD* 6 (1935): 7–12.

14. Herbert Stolz, director of the institute at the University of California, Berkeley, was a physician and parent educator, but psychologist Harold Jones was director of research. Arnold Gesell, director of the Yale institute, was a psychologist and a pediatrician. Helen Woolley, Bird Baldwin, John Anderson, and William Blatz, directors of the institutes at Teacher's College, Columbia, Iowa, Minnesota, and Toronto, respectively, were all psychologists. Psychologist Helen Woolley, director of the institute at Teachers College, was the only female director, possibly reflecting the fact that most early educators and parent

educators were women. She was succeeded by psychologist Lois Meek (later Lois Meek Stolz) in 1930.

15. Lawrence Frank, "Possibilities for a Foundation Program," 13 March 1924, Lawrence K. Frank Papers [hereafter, LKF], National Library of Medicine, History of Medicine Division, Bethesda, Maryland, Box 11; and Frank to Richardson, 15 April 1927..

16. Barbara Biber, Interview with Milton J. E. Senn, 19 July 1972, Milton J. E. Senn Oral History Collection in Child Development [hereafter, Senn OHCD], National Library of Medicine, History of Medicine Division, Bethesda, Maryland.

17. Charles Super, "Secular Trends in Child Development and the Institutionalization of Professional Disciplines," *Society for Research in Child Development Newsletter* (1983), 10–11; Ray Marston, *Directory of Research in Child Development*, Vol.76, Reprint Circular Series of the NRC (Washington D.C., 1927); and Marion Kenworthy, "Social Maladjustments in the Intellectually Normal," *Mental Hygiene* 14 (October 1930): 837–41.

18. Lois Meek Stolz, "Lois Meek Stolz: An American Child Development Pioneer," Interview with Ruby Takanishi, 1978, 37–43, Arthur and Elizabeth Schlesinger Library on the History of Women in America, Radcliffe College, Cambridge, Massachusetts.

19. Stolz interview with Takanishi.

20. Stolz reported that during the 1920s all presidents of nursery schools were engaged in research. In spite of Frank's efforts, the connection between nursery school education and research was later lost (Lois Stolz, Interview by author, 17 December 1976). See also Lawrence Frank, "The Significance of Nursery Schools with Special Emphasis on Their Mental Hygiene Aspects," (Paper presented at the Special Committee Hearing of the New York City Council, re: Nursery Schools, Albany, New York, April 1939a).

21. Margaret MacMillan, *The Nursery School* (New York, 1921); and Harriet Johnson, *Children in the Nursery School* (New York, 1928).

22. Before the 1920s parents assumed that preschool children did not need companionship. One of the more important contributions of nursery school research was to document the many ways in which children profited from the experience. Edna White, "The Objectives of the American Nursery School," *Family* 6 (1928): 50–51; Edna White, "American Nursery School: Its Aims and Opportunities," *Arrow of Pi Beta Phi* 48 (1932): 587–88; and Mary Cover Jones, Interview with author, 16 December 1976.

23. John Anderson, "Methods in Child Psychiatry," in *Handbook of Child Psychology*, ed. Carl Murchison (Worcester, Mass., 1931), 3–28; and John Anderson, "Child Development: An Historical Perspective" *Child Development* 27 (1996): 181–96.

24. Emmett Holt, *The Care and Feeding of Children*, 12th ed. (New York, 1925); and Howard Meredith, *Physical Growth From Birth to Two Years: A Review and Synthesis of North American Research for the Period 1850–1941* (Iowa City, 1943).

25. Materials in Children's Bureau Records (hereafter CBR), National Archives, Washington, D.C., Central File 1914–1940, Record Group 102, file 12–7–3–3-2 illustrate the difficulties that the Children's Bureau had with the determination of height and weight standards. See Bird Baldwin, "Research in Child Development," NRCCCD, First Conference on Research in Child Development, 1925, LSRM, Series 3.5, Box 36; Arnold Gessel, *Infancy and Human Growth* (New York, 1928); Marion Radke-Yarrow and Leon Yarrow, "Child Psychology," *Annual Review of Psychology* 6 (1955): 1–28; Lewis Terman,

Genetic Studies of Genius (Stanford, Calif., 1925); and Beth Wellman, "Physical Growth and Motor Development in Children," in *Handbook in Child Psychology,* ed. Carl Murchison (Worcester, Mass., 1931), 242–77.

26. A significant longitudinal study, the Guidance Study under the direction of Jean Mac-Farlane, was begun at the Berkeley institute in 1927, with a representative sample of infants as research subjects. The Berkeley Growth Study, initiated by Nancy Bayley, began by studying changes in children's growth during their first three years. The Oakland Growth Study at Berkeley, proposed in 1927, was not funded until 1931. Its subjects were two hundred girls and boys, approximately ten years old, who were about to enter an Oakland junior high school. Another major longitudinal study was directed by Lester Sontag of the Fels Institute. See Gerald Kagan and Harold Moss, *From Birth to Maturity* (New York, 1962); Mary Cover Jones et al., *The Course of Human Development,* (Waltham, Mass., 1971); and Lester Sontag, "The History of Longitudinal Research: Implications for the Future," *CD* 42 (October 1971): 987–1002.

27. Harold Jones, NRCCCD, Fourth Conference on Research in Child Development, Unpublished Proceedings (Washington D.C., 1933), 50–52, LSRM, Series 3.5, Box 36.

28. *The Twenty-Eighth Yearbook of the National Society for Education: Preschool and Parent Education,* 1929.

29. Lois Stolz, Interview by author, 17 December 1978.

30. Harold Jones, Third Conference on Research on Child Development, Unpublished Proceedings (Toronto, May 1929) Part 2: 321–23, LSRM, Series 3.5, Box 36.

31. For recent discussions of values permeating developmental psychology, see William Kessen, Sheldon White, and Urie Bronfenbrenner, "Toward a Critical History of Developmental Psychology," *American Psychologist* 41 (November 1986): 1218–30; and Sheldon White, "Psychology as a Moral Science," in *The Child and Other Cultural Inventions,* ed. Frank Kessel and Alexander Siegel (New York, 1983), 1–25.

32. The European authors included such eminent scientists as Jean Piaget, Anna Freud, Charlotte Buhler, and Kurt Lewin. Robert Sears in *Your Ancients Revisited: A History of Child Development* (Chicago, 1975), discusses "handbooks" of psychology from 1931 to 1970 and lists chapter topics and authors for each edition.

33. Lawrence Frank, "European Experiments," 1929, LFK, Box 11.

34. Lawrence Frank, Laura Spelman Rockefeller Memorial (24–27 August 1927), 158–63.

35. The Round Table, "Clinical Aspects of Growth and Development," *American Journal of Pediatrics* 20 (1941): 259–78. Frank said that, except for the Denver Child Research Station directed by pediatrician Alfred Washburn, and Arnold Gesell's clinic, the child study centers established in the late 1920s and 1930s were "largely without medical participation and supervision. . . . The result has been, therefore, that many studies . . . are not well equipped with medical assessments and have not been enlarged by the study of the physical and biological aspects of child growth and development" (Lawrence Frank, "Recording on the History of Child Development Centers in the U.S.A," Senn OHCD, December 1963); see Halpern for ways in which well-baby clinics, height and growth charts, the Sheppard-Towner Act of 1921, and the 1930 White House Conference led to greater emphasis on the normal development of the well child after 1930 (Sydney Halpern, *American Pediatrics: The Social Dynamics of Professionalism, 1880–1980* [Berkeley, 1988]).

36. Stolz, "Lois Meek Stolz," Interview with Ruby Takanishi, 56–58.

37. Lawrence Frank, "Varieties of Research," June 1934, LKF, Box 11. The Washington Child Research Center and Abbott's opposition to it are discussed in chapter 13.

38. Nancy Bayley, Interview by author, 8 December 1976. It is hard to reconcile Seashore's support of the campaign for the Iowa station with his efforts to restrict the activity of the NRC Committee on Child Welfare and his refusal to allow Bayley to study children.

39. Carl Murchison, *A History of Psychology in Autobiography* (Worcester, Mass., 1930). Referring to the contempt for child psychology, Murchison (1931, Preface) wrote, "This attitude of patronage is based almost entirely on a blissful ignorance of what is going on in the tremendously virile field of child behavior. The time is not far distant, if it is not already here, when nearly all competent psychologists will recognize that one half of the whole field of psychology is involved in the problem of how the infant becomes an adult psychologically."

40. Martin Bulmer and Joan Bulmer, "Philanthropy and Social Science in the 1920s: Beardsley Ruml and the Laura Spelman Rockefeller Memorial," *Minerva* 19 (Autumn 1981): 347–405.

41. Milton Senn, *Insights;* Interview by author, 5 June 1976.

42. General Education Board [GEB], "GEB Program in Child Growth and Development," 15 May 1940, Series 1.3, Box 369, Folder 3849.

43. Emily Davis Cahan, *The William T. Grant Foundation: The First Fifty Years, 1936–1986* (New York, 1990).

44. Raymond Fosdick, *Adventures in Giving, the Story of the General Education Board,* (New York, 1962), 260, 264.

45. General Education Board [GEB], Memorandum, 13 April 1933, Series 1.3, Box 369.

46. GEB, "Present Situation in Child Research," Memorandum, 1934, Series 1.3, Box 369. The GEB permitted adolescent studies to include children six years or older if their purpose was to illuminate adolescent growth and development.

47. GEB, "Present Situation in Child Research." Memorandum, 26 May 1934, Series 1.3, Box 369.

48. GEB, Memorandum, 13 April 1933, Series 1.3, Box 369.

49. GEB, Memorandum on plans for a Negro Child Research Center at Atlanta University, 22 December 1936, Series 1.3, Box 369, Folder 3849.

50. GEB, Memorandum, 13 April 1933; and Minutes of meeting, 24–27 August 1927, LSRM, Series 3.5, Box 30: 167–70.

51. Murchison, ed. *Handbook of Child Psychology.*

52. Mary Cover Jones, "My Life with a Longitudinal Study," in *Historical Selections from the 50th Anniversary Meeting,"* Newsletter of SRCD, guest ed. Joy Osofsky and Robert Emde (June 1985): 2–4.

53. Spelman Fund of New York, "Child Study Policy," 1931, RAC, Series 2, Box 3, GEB Series 1.3, Box 369; GEB, Memorandum, 24 March 1938, Series 1.3, Box 369.

54. GEB, "Abstract of Report on the Program in Adolescent Growth and Development," 31 August 1939, Series 1.3, Box 369. Ruml and Frank had discussed ways to divorce the study

of adolescence from reform and avoid conflict with the Commonwealth Fund's child guidance program. For some research findings of the Oakland Growth Study, see M.C. Jones 1971. A significant early publication of the Oakland Growth Study, Herbert Stolz and Lois Stolz, *Somatic Development of Adolescent Boys* (New York, 1951).

55. GEB, Memorandum on Negro Child Research Center; and Lawrence Frank, Memorandum, 17 September 1936, GEB, Series 1.3, Box 369. One notable exception to the lack of study of black children was John Anderson's inclusion of two hundred black families in his 1930 White House Conference survey of 2757 families on the education and training of the young child in the home.

56. GEB, Memorandum, 13 April 1933.

57. GEB, "Present Situation"; GEB, Memorandum, 25 April 1938, Series 1.3, Box 369.

58. GEB, "Present Situation."

59. GEB, Memorandum on Negro Child Research Center.

60. GEB, "Future Administration of Programs in Child Growth and Development," 3 June 1937, Series 1.3, Box 369.

61. GEB, "Abstracts of Report on the Program in Adolescent Growth and Development," 31 August 1939, Series 1.3, Box 369.

62. Murchison, *Handbook* (1931); and Murchison, *Handbook* (1933).

63. Charles Super, "Secular Trends in Child Development and the Institutionalization of Professional Disciplines," *Society for Research in Child Development Newsletter* (1983): 10–11. Eleven of the twenty-two chapters in the 1931 *Handbook of Child Psychology* were by institute authors. After 1960 most authors of articles in *Child Development* were affiliated with psychology departments.

64. Jones reported the results of the survey but did not describe it or identify the psychiatrists and psychologists who were interested in studying children (Harold Jones, "The Replacement Problem in Child Analysis," *CD* 27 (1956): 237).

65. Lawrence Frank, "Recording on the History of Child Development Centers in the U.S.A.," Senn OHCD, December 1963, 5.

66. Rosalind Rosenberg, *Beyond Separate Spheres: Intellectual Roots of Modern Feminism* (New Haven, 1982).

67. Frank, "Recording on the History," 5. Anderson's work with the NRC Committee on Child Development, his articles in the *Handbook of Child Psychology,* his pioneering study *The Young Child in the Home,* and his contributions to theory and methodology establish him as one of the more significant founders of the field of child development. See Murchison, *Handbook* (1931); Murchison, *Handbook* (1933); Murchison, *Handbook* (1935); and John Anderson, "The Young Child in the Home: A Survey of Three Thousand American Families" (Paper presented at the WHC, New York, 1935).

68. Nancy Bayley commented on the "intolerable dullness of the little there was on the child in early psychology texts," and Jones and Stolz agreed. Jones found that Watson introduced "welcome excitement into the field of child psychology," and his lecture at Vassar College persuaded her to enter that field rather than pediatrics (Nancy Bayley, Interview by author, 8 December 1976; Mary Cover Jones, Interview by author, 1976; Lois Meek Stolz, Interview by author, transcript in author's possession, 9 December 1976). See Lois

Meek Stolz, "Old and New Directions in Child Psychiatry," *MPQ* 12 (1963): 221–32 for a discussion of early textbooks on child psychology.

69. Sheldon White, Letter to author, 14 June 1995. Thanks to Sheldon White for the count of male and female authors. He found that eighteen of the articles had male and female coauthors, and the sex of authors of seventeen articles could not be determined because they were signed with initials instead of first names. Thanks to John Hagen for the information on women SRCD members and graduate students.

Growing acknowledgment of women's contributions to the fields of psychology and child development is shown by the increase in biographies and autobiographies of women scientists including autobiographies by developmentalists Mary Ainsworth, Myrtle McGraw, Lois Barclay Murphy, and Mary Wright (Agnes O'Connell and Nancy Filipe Russo, eds., *Models of Achievement: Reflections of Eminent Women in Psychology* (New York, 1983); Robert Karen, *Becoming Attached: The Unfolding Mystery of the Infant-Mother Bond and Its Implications for Later Life* [New York, 1994]). Less recognized than the work of women scientists has been the influence of wives and mothers on male scientists. The leader of humanistic pediatrics, C. Anderson Aldrich, said that his wife should have been listed as coauthor of his books (Letter to Ethel S. Dummer, 26 May 1939, ESD, Box 26).

70. John Hicks, *A Directory of Research in Child Development,* Vol.102: Reprint and Circular Series of the National Research Council, 1931; and Robert Woodworth, "Report to the Committee on Child Welfare of Results of Questionnaire Sent Out from the Office of the Division of Anthropology," 12 April 1925, LSRM, Series 3.5, Box 30, Folder 320.

71. Among the scientists not affiliated with the institutes who were active in the SRCD were anthropologists Margaret Mead and Edward Sapir; sociologists Robert and Helen Merrill Lynd; pediatricians Martha Eliot, Harold Stuart, and C. Anderson Aldrich; biologist E.V. McCollum; and psychiatrist Adolph Meyer. Aldrich and Levy became SRCD presidents. Mead and Frank were close friends, and the Lynds acknowledged Frank's help with *Middletown.* Levy was the first scientist to become president of both the Society for Research in Child Development and the American Orthopsychiatry Association, the professional association for child guidance personnel.

72. Lawrence Frank, "Forces Leading to a Child Development Viewpoint" (Paper presented for Dr. Ruth Wheeler of Vassar College, 28 November 1939, LKF, Box 12).

73. John Anderson, "Methods in Child Psychiatry," in *Handbook of Child Psychology,* ed. Murchison, 3–28; and Arnold Gesell, "Clinical Studies of Child Development" (Paper presented at the NRCCCD, 3rd conference, Toronto, 1929).

74. Senn, *Insights.*

75. Leta Hollingworth declared, "It has become a fashion in educational research to rush forth hastily with a huge load of pencil and paper tests; to spend an hour or two on a hundred children; to rush hastily home to the adding machine, there to tabulate the performance of the children, not one of which has ever been perceived as an individual child" (Leta Hollingworth, *Psychology of the Adolescent* [New York, 1928]).

76. Harold Stevenson, "How Children Learn: The Quest for a Theory," in *HCP,* ed. Paul H. Mussen (New York, 1983), 219, 230.

77. Lawrence Frank, "Varieties of Research," June 1934, LKF, Box 11.

78. Mary Cover Jones, "A Laboratory Study of Fear: The Case of Peter," *Pedagogical Seminary* 31(1924): 308–315; Mary Cover Jones, "The Elimination of Children's Fears" *Journal of Experimental Psychology* (*JEP*) 7 (1924): 382–90; Mary Cover Jones, Interview with author, 1976; John B. Watson and Rosalie Watson, "Studies in Infant Psychology," *Scientific Monthly* 13 (1921): 493–515.

79. Helen Christianson, Mary Rogers, and Blanch Ludlum, *The Nursery School: Adventure in Living and Learning* (Boston, 1961); and Lawrence Frank, "Childhood and Youth," in *Recent Social Trends,* vol. 2 (1933), 751.

80. Stolz, "Lois Meek Stolz," Interview with Ruby Takanishi, 111–23; George Stoddard, Interview, 4 February 1971, Senn OHCD.

81. Harry Hopkins, *Spending to Save: The Complete Story of Relief* (New York, 1936). The decision to administer the program through the public schools meant that preschool children became the responsibility of public education for the first time. Emergency nursery schools were designed to serve children of needy and unemployed families between the ages of two and six, the usual legal age for school entrance. The nursery schools were established in thirty-eight states, the District of Columbia, and the Virgin Islands. Almost three thousand schools were established, ranging from one each in Mississippi and Wyoming to 535 in Ohio. The Advisory Committee prepared and published a series of bulletins to help teachers, administrators, and parents working in the emergency schools and a 1934 *Handbook for Leaders of Parent Education Groups in Emergency Education Programs.* The Children's Bureau was not represented on the Advisory Committee, according to Stolz, because of Grace Abbott's aloofness from nursery schools and antagonism between Harry Hopkins and Abbott. Christianson et al. commented: "For teachers in need of employment and eager to do a constructive piece of work, the emergency nursery school provided an opportunity which challenged them to give of their best. For the parents who bore a heavy burden of anxiety regarding bare physical essentials for their family, contact with the nursery school opened new possibilities for attacking their problems."

Historian Robert Tank pointed out that the emergency nursery schools were neither day nurseries nor true nursery schools but something in between, institutions "designed to safeguard the health and welfare of impoverished children during very hard times." For discussion of nursery schools during World War II, see Barbara Beatty, "The Rise of the American Nursery School Movement: Laboratory for a Science of Child Development" (Paper presented at the SRCD, Biennial Meeting, Indianapolis, 30 March 1955, 185–91); Gilbert V. Steiner, *The Children's Cause* (Washington D.C., 1976), 16–20; Helen Christianson, Mary Rogers and Blanche Ludlum, *The Nursery School;* and Robert Tank. "Young Children, Families, and Society in America since the 1880s: The Evolution of Health, Education, and Child Care Programs for Preschool Children" (Ph.D. diss., University of Michigan, 1980, 359).

82. For an illuminating discussion of the FERA and WPA nursery schools, see Barbara Beatty, *Preschool Education in America: The Culture of Young Children From the Colonial Era to the Present* (New Haven, 1995).

83. Stolz, "Lois Meek Stolz," Interview with Ruby Takanishi, 111–23.

84. Remaining emergency schools were incorporated into centers for children of war work-

ers under the Lanham Act (passed in 1941, but not extended to childcare centers until 1943). In March 1945, 1,481 nursery school centers enrolled 51,229 children. Only the California children's centers survived the program begun under the Lanham Act. Lois Stolz directed the Kaiser Shipyards Child Service Centers from 1943 to 1945

85. Beatty, "Rise of American Nursery School," 185–91.
86. White House Conference, "WHC on Child Health and Protection, 1930: Addresses and Abstracts of Committee Reports" (Paper presented at the WHC, New York, 1932).
87. Stolz, "Lois Meek Stolz," Interview with Ruby Takanishi, 151.
88. Steven Schlossman, "Perils of Popularization: The Founding of *Parents Magazine*," in Smuts and Hagen, *History and Research,* 65–77.
89. "Merchants to the Child," *Fortune* (1931): 71–100.

CHAPTER 10. OUT OF STEP WITH HIS TIMES

1. Hamilton Cravens, *Before Head Start: The Iowa Station and America's Children* (Chapel Hill, 1993); and Elizabeth Lomax, "The Laura Spelman Rockefeller Memorial: Some of Its Contributions to Early Research in Child Development," *Journal of the History of the Behavioral Sciences* 10(1977): 283–93.
2. Unless otherwise stated, all boxes cited in this chapter are from the Arnold Gesell Papers [hereafter, AG], including records of the Yale Child Development Clinic, in the Library of Congress, Washington, D.C. See Arnold Gesell, *Mental Growth of the Pre-School Child: A Psychological Outline of Normal Development from Birth to the Sixth Year, Including a System of Developmental Diagnosis* (New York, 1925); and Louise Bates Ames, Memorandum on meetings with Milton J. E. Senn in January and February 1949 on the status of her employment at the child study center, 13 May 1949, Box 128. Grover Powers, chair of Yale pediatrics, headed a 1947 committee charged with suggesting changes in the scope of the clinic's work and recommending a new director. The committee urged more collaboration between the Yale clinic and other university departments, especially pediatrics, and the appointment of a director more receptive to psychoanalysis. Gesell had refused to participate in interdisciplinary research or permit others to use clinic facilities, and had no respect for Freudian psychology. The story of Gesell's retirement, the changeover to the Yale Child Study Center, and the ensuing bitterness between Senn and Gesell and former members of Gesell's staff is documented in Box 128. See Arnold Gesell correspondence with Milton J. E Senn and Louise Bates Ames, June 1948, AG, Box 128; Arnold Gesell, Memorandum on June interviews with Milton J. E. Senn, and Louise Bates Ames, 13 May 1949. Psychoanalyst Albert J. Solnit succeeded Senn in 1966. Today the Yale Child Study Center is part of the Yale Department of Psychiatry.
3. For a discussion of Gesell's legacy, see Esther Thelen and Karen E. Adolph, "Arnold Gesell: The Paradox of Nature and Nurture," in *A Century of Developmental Psychology,* ed. Ross Parke, Peter Ornstein, John Rieser, and Carolyn Zahn-Waxler (Washington, D.C., 1994), 357–87. An obituary declared Gesell "more famous than the president" ("Gesell Obituary," *New Haven Register* May 29, 1961). He was mentioned in short stories and motion pictures and was the subject of cartoons. *Infant and Child in the Culture*

of Today (1943) sold more copies in England, Russia, and China than in the United States. See Box 13.

4. Gesell, *Mental Growth;* Arnold Gesell, "The Developmental Psychology of Twins," in *Handbook of Child Psychology,* vol. 1, ed. Carl Murchison (Worcester, Mass., 1931), 158–203; Arnold Gesell, "Cinemanalysis: A Method of Behavior Study," *Journal of Genetic Psychology* 47(1935): 3–16; Arnold Gesell and Frances L. Ilg, *Feeding Behavior of Infants: A Pediatric Approach to the Mental Hygiene of Early Life* (Philadelphia, 1937); Walter Miles, "Arnold Lucius Gesell, 1880–1961: A Biographical Memoir," *Biographical Memoirs* 37(1964): 59–67; and Benjamin Spock, *Baby and Child Care* (New York, 1946).

5. See Arnold Gesell, "Clinical Organization for Child Development Research" (paper presented at the 1st meeting of the SRCD 3–4 November 1934), AG, Box 142; and George G. Stoddard, Letter to Kenneth Blackfan, March and April 1931, AG, Box 54. Stoddard wrote that pediatricians were not equipped by training to take over social and behavioral problems. He thought that they should stick to disease and stop trying to control issues of social health.

6. Lawrence Frank, "Recording on the History of Child Development Centers in the U.S.A.," December 1963, Milton J. E. Senn Oral History Collection in Child Development [hereafter, Senn OHCD], National Library of Medicine, History of Medicine Division, Bethesda, Maryland. In this recording, Frank said that it had been expected that the Yale clinic would constitute the genetic branch of the Institute of Human Relations established at Yale University in 1930 and that Gesell would collaborate with the medical school, psychology, and other departments. Gesell, however, "refused to allow any other departments to participate and gave no encouragement for anyone to visit his nursery school or to otherwise collaborate. . . . This was a disappointment to those who had negotiated the institute but nothing could be done about it because the university administration would take no action to ask Dr. Gesell to make his facilities available to others."

7. Arnold Gesell, "The Conditioned Reflex and the Psychiatry of Infancy," *American Journal of Orthopsychiatry* 8(1938): 19–29; and Arnold Gesell, "A Half-Century of Science and the American Child: 50th Anniversary of Child Study Association of America," *Child Study* 16(1938): 35–7, 78–9 (page numbers are from talk manuscript, not published article). Gesell published his criticism of behaviorism but expressed his reservations about psychoanalysis in copious notes (Boxes 54 and 83). He disliked Freud's "dualism," and his deductions about childhood derived from retrospective studies of adults rather than studies of young children.

8. Arnold Gesell, *A History of Psychology in Autobiography,* vol. 4., ed. Edwin G. Boring et al. (Worcester, Mass., 1952), 142.

9. Gesell, *History of Psychology,* 123; and Theodore Buehler, interview by author. Arnold's only son, Judge Gerhard Gesell (of Nixon tapes fame), believed that his father's unique writing style and unusual vocabulary were the result of his having learned to read and write English by studying the Bible and Shakespeare (Gerhard Gesell, interview with the author, 4 April 1978).

10. Autobiographical notes, n.d., Box 229. For extensive handwritten autobiographical notes, often different from the published autobiography (1952), see Box 229. The elder Gesell's photographs are displayed today in Alma and Madison, Wisconsin.

11. Gesell, *History of Psychology* 124. Gerhard spoke of the deep impression the darker side of village life had made on his father, especially his observation of alcoholism, which, he said, made his father a teetotaler for life. Arnold loved Alma, returned often, and chose to be buried there.

12. Gesell, *History of Psychology,* 126. Gerhard Gesell recalled many visits during his childhood to Hall's home. See Box 28 for Gesell-Hall correspondence.

13. Gesell, History of Psychology, 128, 130. Lois Meek Stolz believed that Beatrice had a profound influence on Gesell and recalls her interviewing potential research assistants for the Yale clinic (Lois Meek Stolz, interview by author, 9 December 1976). Robert Yerkes wrote, "I have discovered the handiwork of each of you in The Guidance of Mental Growth in Infant and Child" (letter to Arnold and Beatrice Gesell, 9 December 1930, Box 199).

14. Arnold Gesell and Beatrice Chandler, The Normal Child and Primary Education (Boston, 1912), 3, 27.

15. Gesell, "Half-Century of Science."

16. Gerhard Gesell, interview with author.

17. Gesell, History of Psychology, 137; and Miles, "Arnold Lucius Gesell," 71. Gesell visited the Lightner Witmer clinic and the Vineland Training School in 1909, the same year William Healy visited these clinics to prepare for his study of juvenile delinquents.

18. Arnold Gesell, "Village of a Thousand Souls," *Atlantic Magazine* 80(1913): 11–15. See chapter 8 for Hillis's and Seashore's environmentalism and Seashore's opposition to negative eugenics.

19. Gesell, "Village of a Thousand Souls," 11–15.

20. Gesell, History of Psychology, 127.

21. Gesell, "Village of a Thousand Souls," 11.

22. See chapter 8 for discussion of the eugenics movement and of "negative eugenics."

23. Gesell, "Village of a Thousand Souls," 15. Gesell was saddened by the hostility Alma residents expressed after publication of the 1913 article (Theodore Buehler, interview by author, 16–17 May 1978).

24. Gesell, *Infancy and Human Growth* (New York, 1928), 356.

25. Gesell, "The Preschool Child and the Present-Day Parent," *Proceedings of the Midwest Conference on Parent Education,* 2–6 March 1926, 1.

26. Arnold Gesell, "A Mental Hygiene Service for Preschool Children," *America Journal of Public Health* 12(1922): 1030–33; Arnold Gesell, "The Psychological Significance of the Preschool Period," *Public Health Nurse* 14(1922): 233–34; Arnold Gesell, "The Preschool Child: His Social Significance," *Annals of the American Academy* 105(1923): 277–80; Arnold Gesell, "The Nursery School Movement," *School and Society* 20(1924): 644–52; Arnold Gesell, "The Significance of the Nursery School," *Childhood Education* 1(1924): 11–20; Arnold Gesell, "Experimental Education and the Nursery School," *Journal of Educational Research* 14(1926): 81–87; Arnold Gesell, "Normal Growth as a Public Health Concept," *Public Health Nurse* 18(1926): 394–99; and Arnold Gesell, *Psychological Guidance in Child Adoption.* Children's Bureau Publication 137 (Washington, D.C., 1926). Ineligible for war service, Gesell was able to concentrate on the work of the clinic while many of his colleagues were serving in the armed forces. Gesell's proposals for preschool programs are strikingly similar to those of Head Start in their emphasis on parents, men-

tal health, and education. He argued that preschool programs should be available to all children. Edward Zigler, a founder and one of the most active supporters of Head Start, expressed hope that Head Start programs eventually will encompass all children, eliminating the current unfortunate distinction between poor children and those who are better off (Edward Zigler, Interview by author, 15 May 1996).

27. Gesell, "Normal Growth as Public Health Concept," 399.

28. Gesell, "Normal Growth as Public Health Concept," 398–399.

29. Gesell, "Preschool Child and Present-Day Parent," 2–8.

30. Gesell, "Normal Growth as Public Health Concept," 399. Gesell suggested that periodic developmental exams of preschool children could be accomplished through the upward extension of infant consultation centers.

31. Gesell, "Preschool Child and Present-Day Parent," 6.

32. Gesell, "Preschool Child and Present-Day Parent," 2, 4.

33. William Blatz, 3 August 1931, AG, Box 253; and Arnold Gesell, "The Preschool Child in a Democracy."

34. Arnold Gesell and Elizabeth Evans Lord, "A Psychological Comparison of Nursery School Children from Homes of Low and High Economic Status," *Pedagogical Seminary* 34(1927): 339–56.

35. Gesell, "Normal Growth as Public Health Concept."

36. Gesell and Ilg, *Feeding Behavior of Infants*, 360–62.

37. The study was published in the same year that Frank refused to fund research on children from lower-class homes (Lawrence K. Frank, Letter to Ethel Richardson, 15 April 1927, Laura Spelman Rockefeller Memorial [hereafter, LSRM], Rockefeller Archive Center, Pocantico Hills, Sleepy Hollow, New York, Series 3.5, Box 43, Folder 452). Gesell's positive and optimistic approach after 1921 to the problems of preschool children contrasts sharply with his advocacy of negative eugenics eight years earlier. The transformation is puzzling. Possibly a thorough search of the Gesell papers from 1913 through 1921 might unearth a clue. See Arnold Gesell's commentary on the study in *Infancy and Human Growth*, 371–72.

38. Bird T. Baldwin and Lorie I. Stecher, *The Psychology of the Preschool Child* (New York, 1924); and Gesell, *Mental Growth*.

39. Gesell, *Mental Growth*, 128.

40. Gesell, *Mental Growth*, 355–441. It is unfortunate that more attention cannot be given here to Gesell's system of developmental diagnosis, which many consider to be one of his most significant contributions. See especially Arnold Gesell and Catherine S. Amatruda, *Developmental Diagnosis: A Manual of Clinical Methods and Applications Designed for the Use of Students and Practitioners of Medicine* (New York, 1941).

41. Gesell, *Mental Growth*, 133. The Yale Psycho-clinic did not become the Yale Clinic of Child Development until 1930, when Gesell was assigned to the Board of Permanent Officers of the Medical School.

42. Arnold Gesell, "Clinical Studies of Child Development" (paper presented at the NRC-CCD, 3rd conference, Toronto, 1929).

43. Gesell, "Normal Growth as Public Health Concept," 134. Gesell believed that clinical observation was a corrective to misleading interpretation of experimental results.

44. Arnold Gesell, "Infants Are Individuals," *Child Study* 15(1938): 244–47.

45. Arnold Gesell, "How Science Studies the Child," *Scientific Monthly* 34:3 (1932): 266.

46. The surviving films are now at the Archives of the History of Psychology, University of Akron, Akron, Ohio.

47. Gesell and Ilg, *Feeding Behavior,* 21. Arnold Gesell and Frances L. Ilg define the purpose of the developmental studies at the Yale clinic as "interest in determining the influence of age on the origin of behavior under the conditions of contemporary American culture" (Gesell and Ilg, *Infant and Child,* vol.1, *Child Development: An Introduction to the Study of Human Growth* [New York, 1943], 12). All early developmentalists used age and sex as primary variables in their normative research, but Gesell attached more importance than most to age norms and did not pay much attention to sexual differences. The work on normative development from ages eleven through sixteen was carried on after Gesell left Yale by the Gesell Institute. See Boxes 120 and 121 for the history of the Yale clinic.

48. Leo Kanner, "Arnold Gesell's Place in the History of Psychology and Psychiatry," *Psychological Research Reports* 13(1960–1963): 9. Gesell believed the terms growth and development were synonymous but preferred growth.

49. Lewis M. Terman, Letter to Arnold Gesell, January 1931, AG, Box 210. Gesell's book reviews included four on Jean Piaget. According to John Flavell, Gesell was probably the only psychologist during the 1920s, and one of few during the 1930s, who published comments on Piaget (John Flavell, Interview by author, May 1996).

50. Arnold Gesell, *Infancy and Human Growth* (New York, 1928); Arnold Gesell, "The Developmental Psychology of Twins," in *Handbook of Child Psychology,* vol. 1, ed. Carl Muchison (Worchester, Mass., 1931), 158–203; Arnold Gesell and Helen Thompson, "Learning and Growth in Identical Twins: An Experimental Study by the Method of Co-Twin Control," *Genetic Psychological Monograph* 6(1929), 1–23; and Murchison, *Handbook of Child Psychology,* 209–235.

51. Gesell and Ilg, *Infant and Child;* Gesell and Ilg, *Child from Five to Ten;* and Gesell and Ilg, *Youth.*

52. Gesell and Ilg, *Infant and Child,* 12; and Arnold Gesell, correspondence with Myrtle McGraw, 18 February 1931, 34, AGP, Box 31.

53. Gesell and Ilg, *Infant and Child,* 288–89.

54. Gesell, "Conditioned Reflex," 19.

55. Gesell and Ilg, *Infant and Child,* 46–58.

56. Mrs. Joseph Walden, Letter to Arnold Gesell, 28 July 1938, AG, Box 198. For Gesell's views on the importance of respecting a child's individuality, see Box 146. For his views on democracy within the home and its implications with respect to disciplining children, see Box 159.

57. The quote is one of many comments from parents that Gesell passed on to his editor, Paul B. Hoeber (Arnold Gesell, Letter to Hoeber, 10 December 1945, Box 200).

58. Gesell and Ilg, *Child from Five to Ten;* and Catherine Lowes, Gillian Lowes, and Susan Lowes, Letter to Arnold Gesell, 28 January 1953, Box 31.

59. Gillian Lowes, Letter to Arnold Gesell, 28 January 1953; Arnold Gesell, Letter to Gillian Lowes, 6 February 1953, Box 31; and Gillian Lowes, Letter to Arnold Gesell, 28 February 1953, Box 31.

60. Gesell and Ilg, *Infant and Child,* 68–72.

61. Yale University Clinic of Child Development, *The First Five Years of Life: A Guide to the Study of the Preschool Child* (New York, 1940).

62. Mrs. Joseph Walden, Letter to Arnold Gesell, 15 April 1940, Box 200.

63. Joseph Brennemann, "The Menace of Psychiatry," *American Journal of Diseases of Children* 42(1931): 388; and Hilde Bruch, *Don't Be Afraid of Your Child: A Guide for Perplexed Parents* (New York, 1952), 29.

64. Arnold Gesell, "Maturation and the Patterning of Behavior," in *Handbook,* 2nd ed., ed. Murchison.

65. Gesell, "Democracy Begins at Home," for the 1940 White House Conference, 1940, AG.

66. Gesell, Correspondence with Milton J. E. Senn and Louise Bates Ames, June 1948, 9, AG, Box 128; Gesell and Ilg, *Child from Five to Ten,* 41.

67. Gesell and Ilg, *Child from Five to Ten,* 2.

68. Gesell and Ilg, *Child from Five to Ten,* 4.

69. Helen Thompson, Senn OHCD (1972).

70. Gesell, "Maturation and Patterning of Behavior," 231.

71. Gesell, *Infancy and Human Growth,* 378.

72. Gesell, *Infancy and Human Growth,* 373, 378.

73. Gesell, "Village of a Thousand Souls."

74. Gesell and Ilg, *Infant and Child,* 10.

75. Arnold Gesell, "The Documentation of Infant Behavior and Its Relation to Cultural Anthropology." Address at the 8th American Scientific Congress (Washington, D.C., 1940), AG, Box 145.

76. Helen Thompson, Senn OHCD (1972).

77. Arnold Gesell, "Infants Are Individuals," *Child Study* 15(1938), 244–47.

78. Arnold Gesell. "The Mental Welfare of the Infant," paper presented at Conference at Northeastern Hospital for Women and Children (3 October 1933), AG, Box 142, 8.

79. Gesell, "Half-Century of Science," 7.

80. Gesell, "Half-Century of Science," 12.

81. Helen Thompson, Senn OHCD (1972).

82. Gesell, "Infants Are Individuals," 28.

83. John Watson and Rosalie Watson, "Studies in Infant Psychology," *Scientific Monthly* 13(1921): 493–515.

84. Myrtle McGraw, Senn OHCD, 9 May 1972.

85. Nancy Bayley, Interview by author, 8 December 1976; Mary Jones, Interview by author, 10 May 1976; and Myrtle McGraw, Interview by author, 17 March 1979.

86. Helen Thompson, Senn OHCD (1972).

87. Arnold Gesell, Correspondence with Myrtle McGraw, 6, 9, 19 February 1931.

88. Victor Bergenn, Thomas Dalton, and Lewis Lipsitt, "Myrtle McGraw: A Growth Scientist" *Developmental Psychology* 28(1932): 383.

89. Gerhard Gesell, interview.

90. Arnold Gesell et al., *Psychology of Early Growth,* 9 May 1938.

91. Myrtle McGraw, *Growth: A Study of Johnny and Jimmy,* 1935.

92. Myrtle McGraw, Interview by author, 17 March 1979.

93. Katherine Lenroot, Letter to Arnold Gesell, 29 March 1939, AG, Box 55.

94. Gesell, "Documentation of Infant Behavior."

95. Lois Stolz, "Youth: The Gesell Institute and Its Latest Study," *Contemporary Psychology* 3(1958): 10–15. Stolz's review is a trenchant criticism of Gesell's normative research, particularly on adolescence.

96. Myrtle McGraw, "Maturation of Behavior," in *Manual of Child Psychology,* ed. L. Carmichael (1946), 332–69.

97. Esther Thelen and Karen E. Adolph, "Arnold Gesell: The Paradox of Nature and Nurture" in Parke, *Century of Developmental Psychology,* 357–58.

98. Arnold Gesell, *Infancy and Human Growth* (New York, 1928).

99. Gesell, *Infancy and Human Growth,* 373.

100. Gesell, *Infancy and Human Growth,* 375.

101. Guy Montrose, ed., *The Thirty-Ninth Yearbook of the National Society for the Study of Education: Intelligence, Its Nature and Nurture, Part 1* (Bloomington, Ill., 1940).

102. Montrose, ed., *Thirty-Ninth Yearbook,* 149–150.

103. Arnold Gesell, 1957, AG, Box 49.

104. See Lewis Warren, *Lincoln's Youth: The Indiana Years, 1816–1830* (New York, 1959).

CHAPTER 11. THE CHILD GUIDANCE MOVEMENT

1. Before reading the next two chapters, readers may want to review Chapter 6 for events from 1909 through World War I that led to the child guidance movement of the 1920s.

2. S. V. Clevenger, "Insanity in Children," *American Journal of Neurology and Psychiatry* (1883): 585–601.

3. Eli Rubenstein, "Childhood Mental Disease in America: A Review of the Literature before 1900," *American Journal of Orthopsychiatry* [AJO] 18(1948): 314–21.

4. Leo Kanner, "Emotionally Disturbed Children: A Historical Review," *Child Development* (1962): 99. Benjamin Rush, considered "the first American psychiatrist," briefly discussed insanity in childhood in 1812 and observed that "madness" seldom occurred before puberty (Lewis C. Nolan, "American Psychology from Its Beginnings until World War I," in *American Handbook of Psychology,* ed. Silvano Arierti et al. [New York, 1959], 3–17).

5. A. McGehee Harvey and Susan L. Abrams, *For the Welfare of Mankind: The Commonwealth Fund and American Medicine* (1986), 82.

6. Both the Laura Spelman Rockefeller Memorial and the Commonwealth Fund were supported by Standard Oil fortunes.

7. Miriam Z. Langsam, "Anna M. Richardson Harkness," in *Notable American Women, 1607–1950: A Biographical Dictionary,* ed. Edward T. James, Janet Wilson James, and Paul Boyer, vol. 1 (1971), 134–35.

8. Harvey and Abrams, *For the Welfare of Mankind.*

9. William White, *The Mental Hygiene of Childhood* (New York, 1931), 256–67.

10. White never treated children, but he was one of the few dynamic psychiatrists of his time with a strong interest in children. He emphasized the influence of parental behavior and attitudes on children rather than inherited traits. "What a man shall be depends not so

much on what his grandfather and great-grandfather were as on the manner of his rearing" (White, *Mental Hygiene*).

11. Lawson G. Lowrey, "The Birth of Orthopsychiatry," in *Orthopsychiatry, 1923–1948: Retrospect and Prospect,* ed. Lawson G. Lowrey and Victoria Sloane (New York, 1948), 524–
49. The notable exception to the many signs of interest in the mental hygiene of childhood was the 1919 White House Conference on Child Welfare Standards, sponsored by
the Children's Bureau, whose only attention to mental health was its recommendation
for the psychiatric examination of all atypical or retarded children in schools (Children's
Bureau, *Standards of Child Welfare.* Children's Bureau Publication 60 [Washington,
D.C., 1919]). Only a decade later, however, the 1930 White House Conference for Child
Health and Protection paid unusual attention to mental health.

12. *Commonwealth Annual Report* (1920), 21, 15, 16, 25.

13. Thomas Salmon, "Summary of the Work Plans and Needs of the National Committee
for Mental Hygiene," 6 May 1921, Ethel Sturges Dummer Papers [hereafter, ESD], Elizabeth and Arthur Schlesinger Library on the History of Women, Radcliffe College, Harvard University, Cambridge, Massachusetts, Box 32.

14. Salmon, "Summary."

15. William Healy to Ethel Dummer, 16 March 1921, ESD, Box 30, Folder 580.

16. Healy wrote to Dummer that the Fund's original idea of using the Judge Baker Foundation as a training school had been given up and that he preferred the foundation to remain an independent organization because he favored many different models for psychiatric clinics for children (Healy to Dummer 16 March 1921). The Fund gave the Judge
Baker Foundation $15,000 in 1921 and $7,500 in 1922.

17. Margo Horn, *Before It's Too Late: The Child Guidance Movement in the United States,
1922–1945* (Philadelphia, 1989), 27.

18. Participants in the Lakewood conference included Salmon, Glueck, Bronner, Thurston,
Farrand, J. Prentice Murphy (secretary of the Children's Bureau of Philadelphia), Henry
C. Morrison (educator at the University of Chicago), and Judge Charles Hoffmann.
Commonwealth Fund.

19. Horn, *Before It's Too Late,* 27–30.

20. I am indebted to Horn for her interesting report on Abbott's memo. Abbott is the only
one I could find who opposed the recommendations of the Lakewood conference. Abbott probably was unaware that the Fund, like the Memorial, had a firm policy that excluded their support of social legislation or of social agencies involved in controversial
social action (Horn, *Before It's Too Late,* 27–30).

21. Max Farrand, a Yale historian, was the first general director of the Fund. He served on a
part-time basis from 1919 to 1921.

22. Lowrey, " Birth of Orthopsychiatry," 533–34.

23. Lawson G. Lowrey, "Psychiatry for Children: A Brief History of Developments," *American Journal of Psychiatry* 108(1944): 375–88.

24. Commonwealth Fund, "Report of the Conference on the Prevention of Juvenile Delinquency" (New York, 1921), Commonwealth Fund Archive [CFA], Rockefeller Archive
Center, Pocantico Hills, Sleepy Hollow, New York.

25. Lawrence K. Frank, *Spelman Fund of New York Report for 1929–1930* (New York, 1933).
26. Paul V. Lemkau, *Mental Hygiene in Public Health* (New York, 1949), 29.
27. William Alanson White, "The Origins and First Twenty-Five Years of the Mental Hygiene Movement," *Science* 72(1930):77–81.
28. Maurice R. Davie, "Foreword," in *Social Aspects of Mental Hygiene,* ed. Frankwood E. Williams (New Haven, 1925).
29. Commonwealth Fund, *Commonwealth Fund Annual Report* (1920–1921), 43.
30. See chapter 9 for discussion of the optimism of social reformers in the 1920s and the belief of American business men and others that the nation was entering a "new era." To encourage research and welfare activities on behalf of children, child developmentalists pointed to the achievements of the agricultural and conservation movements; child guidance enthusiasts, to the accomplishments of public health programs.
31. Theresa Richardson, *The Century of the Child: The Mental Hygiene Movement and Social Policy in the United States and Canada* (New York, 1989), 109–12; Horn, *Before It's Too Late,* 27–30; and George Stevenson, "Child Guidance and the National Committee for Mental Hygiene," in *Orthopsychiatry,* ed. Lowrey and Sloane, 57, 64–65. The Commonwealth Fund discussed the misunderstanding with respect to the Fund's relation to the Monmouth County project, declaring, "It is understood that the Laura Spelman Rockefeller Memorial is to pay the expenses for the psychiatric work at this demonstration to be done by the National Committee for Mental Hygiene. This fact was not known when the program [for the prevention of juvenile delinquency] was originally drafted. We understand, however, from Dr. Salmon that the Laura Spelman Foundation's gift will be absolute and unconditional, so that there is no reason why the work so financed, should not be an integral part of the activities included in this program under the Division of Prevention of Delinquency of the Committee for Mental Hygiene. . . . In other words, the work will be conducted precisely as though it were financed by the Commonwealth Fund." Commonwealth Fund, "Report on Conference on Juvenile Delinquency," 6.
32. Frank wrote that the purpose of the child study program was to study normal children. After the Commonwealth Fund closed the second phase of its program in 1932, the General Education board (GEB), which had taken over the LSRM child study programs, sponsored a conference of child guidance psychiatrists in 1933. Smith's unfamiliarity with and skepticism regarding developmental research is shown in his asking Robert Woodbury of the Children's Bureau if he agreed with Smith's unfavorable opinion of developmental research. Woodbury replied that he believed the research to be "important and of high quality," but there is no evidence that Smith changed his mind (Barry Smith, letter to Robert Woodbury, 1922; and Robert Woodbury, letter to Barry Smith, 1922).
33. *Commonwealth Fund Annual Report* (1921–22, 1925–26, 1926–27). The Commonwealth Fund and LSRM were both founded in 1918. Both sponsored child study programs that began in the mid-twenties. Child guidance professionals established their professional society, the American Orthopsychiatry Association, in 1924; child developmentalists, the National Research Council Committee on Child Development, in 1925. Both launched their professional journals in 1930. In 1927 the goals of each foundation's child study programs changed significantly. See chapter 9 for changes in the child development program; chapter 12 for changes in the child guidance program.

34. George Stevenson and Geddes Smith, *Child Guidance Clinics: A Quarter Century of Development* (New York, 1934), 22.

35. *Commonwealth Fund Annual Report* (1921–22) 33; Murray Levine and Adeline Levine, *A Social History of Helping Services: Clinic, Court, School* (New York, 1970), 236–37; Lawson Lowrey, "Psychiatry for Children: A Brief History of Developments," *American Journal of Psychiatry* 108(1944), 375–88; Nina Ridenour, *Mental Health in the United States: A Fifty-Year History* (Cambridge, 1961), 34–35; and Helen Witmer, *Psychiatric Clinics for Children with Special Reference to State Programs* (New York: 1948), 33–34. The history of the program from 1922 until 1927 may be traced through the Commonwealth Fund annual reports, especially the *Fourth Annual Report, 1921–1922*, which summarizes the program, and reports for the years 1925–27, which discuss its achievements. Among the best sources on the Commonwealth Fund's program are Stevenson and Smith, *Child Guidance Clinics;* Witmer, *Psychiatric Clinics;* Helen Witmer, *Psychiatric Interviews with Children* (New York, 1946); Horn, *Before It's Too Late,* 27–30; Levine and Levine, *A Social History of Helping Services* (New York, 1970); Murray Levine and Adeline Levine, *Helping Children: A Social History* (New York, 1992); and Lowrey and Sloane, eds., *Orthopsychiatry.* See Porter Lee and Marion Kenworthy, *Mental Hygiene and Social Work* (New York, 1929), for a history of the Bureau of Children's Guidance. For discussion of the visiting teacher program, see Levine and Levine, *Social History,* 125–43; Thomas and Thomas, *The Child in America: Behavior Problems and Programs* (New York, 1928); Mary Sayles, *The Problem Child in School* (New York, 1925); Jane Culbert, *The Visiting Teacher at Work* (New York, 1929); and E. K. Wickman, *Children's Behavior and Teachers' Attitudes* (New York, 1929). McGehee Harvey and Susan Abrams, "For the Welfare of Mankind: The Commonwealth Fund and American Medicine," 28, 630; provides background on Smith and social worker Marion Scoville, who joined the fund in 1923. Smith, Scoville, and George Stevenson were the chief administrators of the fund's mental hygiene programs through 1940. Glueck resigned from the Bureau of Children's Guidance in 1922. Porter Lee, director of the New York School of Social Work, succeeded him. Stevenson and co-author Smith published the first history of child guidance in 1934.

36. For discussion of the demonstration program, see Stevenson and Smith, *Child Guidance Clinics,* 20–50; Witmer, *Psychiatric Clinics for Children,* 33–34, 236; and Horn, *Before It's Too Late,* 53–69. For articles on specific demonstration clinics, see Lowrey and Sloane, eds., *Orthopsychiatry.* The first book on a child guidance clinic was on the Minneapolis clinic (Smiley Blanton and Margaret Gray Blanton, *Child Guidance* [New York, 1927]). The eight cities in which the clinics were located were, in order of their founding: St. Louis, Norfolk, Dallas, Minneapolis, St. Paul, Los Angeles, Cleveland, and Philadelphia. All but the clinic in Norfolk received enough local support to enable them to become "permanent" clinics. According to Stevenson and Smith, *Child Guidance,* 28, the Norfolk clinic failed because the city did not have an effective network of social agencies.

37. *Commonwealth Fund Annual Report* (1925–26, 1963–4); Levine and Levine, *Social History,* 231–38; Stevenson and Smith, *Child Guidance Clinics,* 22–47; and Horn, *Before It's Too Late.*

38. Stevenson and Smith, *Child Guidance Clinics,* 22–47. For discussion of the significant changes in the demonstration clinics between 1922 and 1935, see Stevenson and Smith,

Child Guidance Clinics, 22, 47; Commonwealth Fund, "Commonwealth Fund Annual Report" (1963–64); Horn, *Before It's Too Late*, 39, 47, 64, 79, 161, 175–76; and Levine and Levine, *Social History*, 231–78.

39. Stevenson and Smith, *Child Guidance Clinics*, 24, 27, 30, 35, 39, 42, 46, and Commonwealth Fund, "Commonwealth Fund Annual Report" 1921–22, 26, discuss the change of policy in accepting referrals from agencies other than courts. The Los Angeles clinic, established in January 1924, had about 10 percent court referrals; the Cleveland clinic, begun in 1924, had less than 8 percent; and the Philadelphia clinic, the last to be established, in 1925, had only 3 percent (Stevenson and Smith, *Child Guidance Clinics*).

40. Stevenson and Smith, *Child Guidance Clinics*, 24–46, 72–3; and *Commonwealth Fund Annual Report* (1921–22), 26.

41. Lee Robins, *Deviant Children Grown Up: A Sociological and Psychiatric Study of Sociopathic Personality* (Baltimore, 1966). Robins's longitudinal study was the product of ten years of research into the adult status, thirty years later, of 524 children who were patients at the St. Louis clinic during its first ten years. She compared these findings with the adult outcomes of a control group of nonpatient school children of the same age, sex, and race and similar intelligence, living in the same neighborhoods as the former patients.

42. Horn, *Before It's Too Late;* Leo Kanner, "Trends in Child Psychiatry," *Journal of Mental Science* 105 (1959), 582–93; and Levine and Levine, *Social History*, 255–63.

43. Commonwealth Fund, "Commonwealth Fund Annual Report" (1922–23), 5.

44. Leo Kanner, *Child Psychiatry* (Springfield, Illinois, 1935). See Kanner, "Trends in Child Psychiatry," 582–85; Horn, *Before It's Too Late*, 47; and Levine and Levine, *Social History*, 255–263; on the shift to middle- and upper-income children. The Levines attributed the sharp decrease in the proportion of poor children in the clinics to the change, stimulated by the demonstration program, from public to private sponsorship of clinics.

45. Only the Twin Cities demonstration clinic was affiliated with a university. Although not formally affiliated with colleges and universities, many clinics did offer lectures and study materials. The Philadelphia clinic later become affiliated with Philadelphia's Children's Hospital and the University of Pennsylvania.

46. Harvey and Abrams, "For the Welfare of Mankind," 34; George Stevenson, "The Development of Extra-Mural Psychiatry in the United States," *American Journal of Psychiatry* 100 (1944): 148; Stevenson and Smith, *Child Guidance Clinics*, 136, 160–61.

47. Marian Warner, "Report on American Child Guidance Clinics," in *Reports of Investigations and Trips: Review of the Years 1926–29*, British Child Guidance File, CFA (1928).

48. Horn, *Before It's Too Late*, 42.

49. Virginia Robinson, *Jessie Taft, Therapist and Social Work Educator: A Professional Biography* (Philadelphia, 1962), 63.

50. *Commonwealth Fund Annual Report* (1926–27). Stevenson and Smith report that children were brought to clinics because of "unacceptable behavior—disobedience, stealing, lying, temper tantrum, truancy, and the like; because of personality problems such as nervousness, inattention and shyness; because of school difficulties—poor work, retardation, indifference to, and so on; or because some crisis in the child's life—transfer from a broken home, for instance—makes it desirable to have a technical analysis of his

capacities and qualities as a guide for constructive action" (Stevenson and Smith, *Child Guidance Clinics,* 55. Murray and Adeline Levine describe changes in the kinds of problems observed in the clinics (Levine and Levine, "The More Things Change: A Case History of Child Guidance Clinics," *JSS* 26 [1970]: 19–34).

51. The case history, labeled "case no. 6302, March 2, 1928, condensed and confidential" and consisting of seven printed reports in a folder with a cover illustrated with a drawing of a boy and man, was given to me in June 1975 by Dr. Nancy Staver, chief psychiatric social worker of the Judge Baker Guidance Center. Dummer relates that her husband suggested that using different colored paper for different parts of the case history would simplify record keeping. Other clinics quickly adopted the technique. Percy's case history is printed on colored sheets that correspond to the different sections of the report. See Ethel Dummer, "Life in Relation to Time," in Lowrey and Sloane, eds., *Orthopsychiatry,* 3–13.

52. Louise Despert, *The Emotionally Disturbed Child Then and Now* (New York, 1951).

53. Leo Kanner, "Origins and Growth of Child Psychiatry," *American Journal of Child Psychiatry* 100 (1944): 139.

54. Anna Freud, *Psychiatric Treatment of Children* (London, 1946); Melanie Klein, *The Psychoanalysis of Children* (London, 1932); and Leo Kanner, Interview by L. Jessnor and W. Weigert, 10 November 1966, American Psychological Association Archives, Washington D.C.

55. When Senn told Dr. Joseph C. Stokes, President of the American Pediatric Society in 1937, that he would be a Commonwealth Fellow at the Philadelphia Child Guidance Clinic, Stokes replied, "Tell me the truth, Milton. Aren't you doing this because there is mental illness in your family and not because you think that you should learn more about the emotional nature of childhood?" Milton Senn, Interview with Milton J. E. Senn, 12 September 1980, Washington D.C.

56. Senn, Interview, 12 September 1980, Washington, D.C.

57. David Levy, "Critical Evaluation of the Present State of Child Psychiatry," *American Journal of Psychiatry* 108 (1952): 481.

58. Levy, "Critical Evaluation," 481–88.

59. The other psychiatrists in the group were Healy, Lowrey, Thom, Levy, Glueck, Douglas Thom, and V. V. Anderson, now regarded as the founders of the American Orthopsychiatric Association (AOA). Minutes of the first meeting are in the University of Minnesota Social Welfare Archive.

60. Lawson Lowrey, "The Birth of Orthopsychiatry," in Lowrey and Sloane, eds., *Orthopsychiatry,* 190–208; Levy, "Critical Evaluation," 481–94; and Leon Eisenberg and David Ray De Maso, "50 Years of the AJO: An Overview and Introduction," in *AJO Annotated Index, Vols. 1–50, 1930–80* (New York, 1985), viii–xxix.

61. Eisenberg and De Maso, "50 Years of the AJO," ix, x.

62. William Healy, Book Review of *The Envelope* by James Plant, *AJO* 21(1951): 210–12.

63. Levy, "Critical Evaluation," 483.

64. David Shakow, "The Development of Orthopsychiatry: The Contributions of Levy, Menninger, and Stevenson," *AJO* 38 (1968): 804–09.

65. Stevenson and Smith, *Child Guidance Clinics,* 56.

66. Earl Bond, *Thomas W. Salmon, Psychiatrist* (New York, 1950), 218.

67. Douglas Thom, *Habit Clinics for Child Guidance,* U.S. Department of Labor, Children's Bureau Publication 135, revised edition (Washington D.C., 1938).

68. Witmer, *Psychiatric Clinics,* 116, 207–09.

69. Eveolyn Rexford, Interview with author, 15 June 1975.

70. Douglas Thom, *Everyday Problems of the Everyday Child* (New York, 1928), 12–4.

71. See chapter 13 for Thom's views on child rearing.

72. Douglas Thom, *Child Management,* Children's Bureau Publication 143 (Washington, D.C., 1925, rev. eds. 1928 and 1937).

73. *Commonwealth Fund Annual Report* (1921–23), 37; (1925–26), 30–49; (1926–27), 33–47; Stevenson and Smith, *Child Guidance Clinics,* 70, 135–40; and Witmer, *Psychiatric Clinics for Children,* 390–91. A New Orleans clinic was supported by a father whose son had had successful treatment in a clinic before losing his life in the war. In seeking sponsors, clinics sought freedom from public control and a close association with a single agency; Stevenson and Smith, *Child Guidance Clinics,* 135.

74. *Commonwealth Fund Annual Report* (1926–27), 36–37. The Bureau of Children's Guidance excluded psychiatrists from its training program, but fourteen received training in other guidance clinics.

75. *Commonwealth Fund Annual Report* (1925–26), 37–40; (1926–27), 39–40.

76. *Commonwealth Fund Annual Report* (1925–26), 40–43; (1926–27), 41–43.

77. *Commonwealth Fund Annual Report* (1926–27), 43, 45–47.

78. *Commonwealth Fund Annual Report* (1926–27), 41–43.

79. Smith wrote that the "adjustment of the individual" was "the main goal and the main criterion" of the program's success.

CHAPTER 12. CHILD GUIDANCE BECOMES CHILD PSYCHIATRY

1. Commonwealth Fund, *Commonwealth Fund Annual Report* 1–62 (1926–27), 46–47; *Commonwealth Fund Annual Report* 1–62 (1928), 50; and Margo Horn, *Before It's Too Late: The Child Guidance Movement in the United States, 1922–1945* (Philadelphia, 1989).

2. Fredrick H. Allen, "Certification in Child Psychiatry," in *Positive Aspects of Child Psychiatry* (1963), 213–30; and "Certification in Child Psychiatry under the American Board of Psychiatry and Neurology," *American Journal of Psychiatry* 117 (1971). Child psychiatry as practiced in the guidance clinics did not represent all of child psychiatry. There was also hospital child psychiatry as practiced in America and Britain. Child guidance psychiatry, however, did represent the unique American approach to the study and treatment of children's emotional problems. The term *child psychiatry* was officially recognized in 1937 at a meeting of the International Congress of Mental Health.

3. *Commonwealth Fund Annual Report* (1928), 34, 46, 59.

4. See Murray Levine and Adeline Levine, *A Social History of Helping Services: Clinic, Court, School, and Community* (New York, 1970), 249. The transition from environmental manipulation to psychotherapy was uneven, starting in some clinics before 1927 and lingering in others until the mid-1930s. Treatment methods differed substantially from clinic to clinic and during the transition period many clinics used both techniques.

5. George S. Stevenson and Geddes Smith, *Child Guidance Clinics: A Quarter-Century of Development* (New York, 1934), 123–24, 129.

6. Lawson G. Lowrey, "Orthopsychiatric Treatment," in *Orthopsychiatry, 1923–1948: Retrospect and Prospect*, ed. Lawson G. Lowrey and Victoria Sloane (New York, 1948), 549.

7. Lowrey, "Orthopsychiatric Treatment," 541.

8. See *Commonwealth Fund Annual Report* (1926–27), 46–47; 1930–31, 37–38; 1932–33, 42; and A. McGehee Harvey and Susan L. Abrams, *For the Welfare of Mankind: The Commonwealth Fund and American Medicine* (Baltimore, 1985), 49, 56–59. By 1930 the fund's interest had shifted to the problem of psychiatric education in general, which included the training of child guidance psychiatrists. Determining the significance of psychiatric practice for the whole field of psychiatry was one manifestation of the fund's new interest in developing an expert elite in scientific research and professional education. It established a special division on psychiatric education in 1930.

9. *Commonwealth Fund Annual Reports* (1928–29), 34, 46, 59; (1932–33), 56; and Stevenson and Smith, *Child Guidance Clinics*, 127.

10. Helen Witmer, *Psychiatric Clinics for Children with Special Reference to State Programs* (New York, 1940), 12, 162–65, 174–75.

11. For definition and discussion of indirect and direct therapy, see Lowrey, "Orthopsychiatric Treatment," 537–39.

12. Stevenson and Smith, *Child Guidance Clinics*, 68.

13. Witmer, *Psychiatric Clinics*, 45–46.

14. Stevenson and Smith, *Child Guidance Clinics*, 55–56; and Horn, *Before It's Too Late*, 161.

15. Fredrick H. Allen, "Psychiatry and Social Work in Cooperation," in *Positive Aspects of Child Psychiatry* (New York, 1935), 186; and Helen Witmer, *Psychiatric Interviews with Children* (New York, 1946), 9.

16. Stevenson and Smith, *Child Guidance Clinics*, 91.

17. Witmer, *Psychiatric Clinics*, 9–10.

18. David Levy, "Attitude Therapy," *American Journal of Orthopsychiatry* [*AJO*] 7 (1937): 103–13; and Witmer, *Psychiatric Interviews with Children*, 1, 10.

19. George Stevenson, "Mental Hygiene of Childhood," *Annals of the American Academy of Political and Social Sciences* [*AAAPSS*] 212 (1940): 135.

20. Lowrey, "Orthopsychiatric Treatment," 536–37.

21. Stevenson and Smith, *Child Guidance Clinics*, 156–58.

22. David Levy, "Critical Evaluation of the Present State of Child Psychiatry," *AJP* 108 (1952): 484–85.

23. Lowrey, "Orthopsychiatric Treatment," 536–37.

24. Nina Ridenour, *Mental Health in the United States: A Fifty-Year History* (Cambridge, 1961), 43–49.

25. Lowrey, "Orthopsychiatric Treatment," 541.

26. Witmer, *Psychiatric Interviews with Children*. Of the nine interviews reported, four were between 21 and 24 pages in length, five were longer than 25 pages, and one was 73 pages long. See chapter 11 for "Percy's Story."

27. Witmer, *Psychiatric Interviews with Children*, 259–332.

28. Witmer, *Psychiatric Interviews with Children*, 259.

29. Witmer, *Psychiatric Interviews with Children,* 290, 327.

30. Allen discusses the concept of differentiation in Levy, "Critical Evaluation," 492–93.

31. Witmer, *Psychiatric Interviews with Children,* 261–62.

32. Witmer, *Psychiatric Interviews with Children,* 263.

33. Helen Witmer summarizes the results of the treatment in *Psychiatric Interviews with Children,* 329–31. Remember that treatment methods differed substantially from clinic to clinic.

34. Fredrick H. Allen, "Developments in Child Psychiatry in the United States," *American Journal of Public Health* 8 (1948): 1202.

35. Witmer, *Psychiatric Clinics,* 10

36. Witmer, *Psychiatric Interviews with Children,* 177.

37. Witmer, *Psychiatric Clinics,* 357.

38. Helen Witmer, "A Comparison of Treatment Result in Various Types of Child Guidance Clinics," *AJO* 5 (1935): 351–61; and Witmer, *Psychiatric Clinics,* 77.

39. Horn, *Before It's Too Late,* 177. Horn, questioning why psychotherapy continued to prosper as a treatment method while failing to deliver what it promised, concludes that "only the psychodynamic model offered psychiatrists an enterprise that could properly be called therapeutic." For the observation that providing therapy also enhanced the status of social workers, see Witmer, *Psychiatric Clinics,* 77. Horn analyzed a sample of 179 case records from the Philadelphia Child Guidance Clinic between 1925 and 1944 and gives many examples of losses resulting from the intense emphasis on psychotherapy (Horn, *Before It's Too Late,* 155–78). For another discussion of the consequences of the change from environmental manipulation to psychotherapy, see Lawson G. Lowrey, "Trends in Psychotherapy," *AJO* 9 (1939): 669–70.

40. Witmer, *Psychiatric Clinics,* 264–65, 359.

41. Adolph Meyer, *The Commonsense Psychology of Adolph Meyer,* 451; and Fredrick H. Allen, "Psychiatric Work with Children: Some Present Day Trends," *American Journal of Diseases of Children* [*AJDC*] 44 (1932): 166.

42. Horn *Before It's Too Late,* 140.

43. Meyer, *Commonsense Psychology,* 450–51.

44. Meyer, *Commonsense Psychology,* 529, 530.

45. Meyer, *Commonsense Psychology,* 455.

46. Witmer, *Psychiatric Clinics,* 177; and Levine and Levine, *Social History of Helping Services,* 18–34.

47. Lowrey, "Orthopsychiatric Treatment," 526.

48. James Plant, "Child Psychiatry," *AJP* 94 (1937): 669.

49. Witmer, *Psychiatric Clinics,* 365.

50. Plant, "Child Psychiatry," 665–69.

51. Witmer, *Psychiatric Clinics,* 275.

52. Allen, "Developments in Child Psychology," 1201–1202.

53. Allen, "Psychiatry and Social Work in Cooperation," 176, 186.

54. Leo Kanner, *Child Psychiatry* (Springfield, Ill., 1935), 81.

55. Witmer, *Psychiatric Clinics,* 264–87, 375.

56. David F. Musto, "Whatever Happened to Community Health?" *Public Interest* 39 (1975): 57.

57. *Commonwealth Fund Annual Report* (1929–30).

58. Stevenson and Smith, *Child Guidance Clinics,* 147.

59. Stevenson and Smith, *Child Guidance Clinics,* 146–54.

60. Arnold Gesell, "The Doctrine of Development in Child Guidance," in Lowrey and Sloane, *Orthopsychiatry,* 213–16; and Stevenson and Smith, *Child Guidance Clinics,* 146–54.

61. Stevenson and Smith, *Child Guidance Clinics,* 150.

62. For information on the barriers to cooperation between developmentalists and child psychiatrists, see Milton J. E. Senn, *Insights on the Child Development Movement in the United States,* Monographs of the Society of Research in Child Development (Chicago, 1975), 65–68.

63. For the history of the institute, see Lawson G. Lowrey and Geddes Smith, *The Institute for Child Guidance, 1927–1933* (New York, 1933).

64. David Levy, *Maternal Overprotection, Maternal Deprivation* (New York, 1943), 4.

65. Levy, *Maternal Overprotection,* 5.

66. Levy, *Maternal Overprotection,* 11; and David Levy, Interview, 31 March 1969, Milton J. E. Senn Oral History Collection in Child Development [hereafter, Senn OHCD], National Library of Medicine, History of Medicine Division, Bethesda, Maryland.

67. Lowrey, "Orthopsychiatric Treatment," 524–49.

68. For a discussion of Lowrey and Harry Bawkin on the effects of institutional care on children, see Bernadine Barr, "Spare Children, 1900–1945: Inmates of Orphanages as Subjects of Research in Medicine and in the Social Sciences in America" (Ph.D. diss., Stanford University, 1992).

69. Stevenson and Smith, *Child Guidance Clinics,* 151.

70. Lowrey and Smith, *Institute for Child Guidance,* 55–61; and Levine and Levine, *Social History of Helping Services,* 261.

71. Harvey and Abrams, *For the Welfare of Mankind,* 183–86.

72. See Burton J. Rowles, *The Lady at Box 99: The Story of Miriam Van Waters* (Greenwich, Conn., 1962), 162–69 for Van Waters's description of Dummer and her support of Van Waters's work. Van Waters, who received advanced degrees in psychology and anthropology from Clark University, stressed the importance of parental attitudes and behavior in producing happy, healthy children. Thomas Salmon first used the tem *preventorium* to describe an imaginary institution to be run by boys for the correction of their parents. Van Waters's *Youth in Conflict* (1926) reflected the reform goals of the early child guidance movement.

73. Joseph Brennemann, "Pediatrics, Psychology, and the Child Guidance Movement," *Journal of Pediatrics* [*JP*] 2 (1933); 1–26.

74. David Levy, "The Beginnings of the Child Guidance Movement," *AJO* 38 (1968): 803; and Stevenson and Smith, *Child Guidance Clinics,* 86.

75. Leo Kanner, "The Development and Present Status of Psychiatry in Pediatrics," *JP* 11 (1937): 418–35.

76. Sydney A. Halpern, *American Pediatrics: The Social Dynamics of Professionalism, 1880–1980* (Berkeley, Calif., 1988), 51.

77. Borden S. Veeder, "Trend of Pediatric Education and Practice: President's Address," *AJDC* 50, no.1 (July 1935): 1–10; Harold Kniest Faber and Rustin McIntosh, *History of the American Pediatrics Society, 1887–1975* (New York, 1966), 93–124; and Halpern, *American Pediatrics*, 73–75, 85, 95–99. Many pediatricians during the 1920s feared that pediatrics would not survive as a specialty because of the falling birth rate and competition from government and child welfare services, psychiatrists, psychologists, and social workers.

78. Lester Evans, "The Commonwealth Fund: A Thirty-Six-Year Perspective, 1923–1959," Commonwealth Fund Archives [hereafter, CFA], Rockefeller Archive Center, Pocantico Hills, Sleepy Hollow, New York, n.d.

79. Milton J. E. Senn, Interview by author, 5 June 1976.

80. Kanner, *Child Psychiatry*, 22.

81. *JP* (1936): 553.

82. Julius Richmond, Interview by author, 19 October 1993, Society for Research in Child Development Archive [hereafter, SRCDA], National Library of Medicine, History of Medicine Division, Bethesda, Maryland. Senn reported that some pediatricians were so resistant to answering questions from parents about child rearing that they removed chairs from their treatment rooms to discourage discussion (Milton J. E. Senn, Interview by author, 5 June 1976).

83. Benjamin Spock, Interview by Senn, November 1974, Senn OHCD.

84. White House Conference [WHC], "Psychology, Psychiatry, and Pediatrics: The Problem," (paper presented at Section 1, Medical Service, Subcommittee C, Report of the Subcommittee on Psychiatry and Psychology, New York, 1932). Pediatrician Bronson Crothers chaired the subcommittee. Members included Levy, Plant, Richards, Douglas Thom, and John Anderson. The subcommittee report was based on correspondence with two hundred pediatricians, psychologists, and psychiatrists.

85. WHC, "Psychology, Psychiatry, and Pediatrics," 64.

86. Esther Loring Richards, "Special Psychiatric Problems in Childhood," *Journal of the American Medical Association* 95 (1930): 10–11.

87. WHC, "Psychology, Psychiatry, and Pediatrics," 21. It was reported that 39 percent of school children in Monmouth County needed psychiatric treatment.

88. WHC, "Psychology, Psychiatry, and Pediatrics," 46.

89. WHC, "Psychology, Psychiatry, and Pediatrics," 22. Recall that British observers of American child guidance clinics expressed similar objections.

90. Milton J. E. Senn, "Fads and Facts as the Bases of Child-Care Practices," *Children* 4 (1957); 46–47.

91. Joseph Brennemann, "The Menace of Psychiatry," *AJDC* 42 (1931): 377.

92. James Plant, "The Promise of Psychiatry," *AJDC* 44 (1932): 1320.

93. Halpern, *American Pediatrics*, 82.

94. Ira S. Wile, "The Pediatrician and Behavior Problems of Children," *Archives of Pediatrics* 47 (1930): 676–96; and Halpern, *American Pediatrics*, 82–4.

95. Halpern, *American Pediatrics*, 93; and Faber and McIntosh, *History of Pediatrics Society*, 274.

96. Levy, "Critical Evaluation," 488.

97. See Levy, "Critical Evaluation," 484–85 for his reservations about lay psychotherapy.

98. Leo Kanner, "Supplying the Psychiatric Needs of a Pediatric Clinic," *AJO* 2 (1932):400–410.

99. *Commonwealth Fund Annual Report* (1933–34), 23.

100. Stevenson and Smith, *Child Guidance Clinics,* 110.

101. *JP* (1936): 549–67.

102. *Commonwealth Fund Annual Report* (1963), 26, 30. For information on the Commonwealth Fund's sponsorship of British child guidance clinics see *Commonwealth Fund 1928–1933.*

103. John Bowlby, Interview by author, 6, 12, and 23 June 1977; and Robert Gillespie, Interview by author, 1 July 1977 (transcript in Tavistock Clinic Library, London).

104. Michael Fordham, Interview by author, 5 July 1977.

105. Mildred Creak, Interview by author, 1977 (transcript available in Tavistock Clinic Library, London). At the invitation of John Bowlby, who had trained at the London Child Guidance clinic in the 1930s, I interviewed seventeen psychiatrists and psychiatric social workers and other professionals in England and Scotland who had participated in or were knowledgeable about the early British movement. The tapes and transcripts of these interviews, conducted during the summer of 1977, are in my possession and also in the Tavistock Clinic in Hampstead, but copies soon will be available at the RAC and the History of Medicine Division of the National Library of Medicine, Bethesda, Maryland. My comments on British child guidance are drawn from these interviews.

106. John Bowlby, Interview by author, 6, 12, and 23 June 1977.

107. *Commonwealth Fund Annual Report* (1934–35), 35; and *Commonwealth Fund Annual Report* (1933–34), 23.

108. Horn, *Before It's Too Late,* 94.

109. Harvey and Abrams, *For the Welfare of Mankind,* 618. For a discussion of the fund's cutbacks in mental health in favor of investment in medical research and education, see pages 83 and 145–202.

110. *Commonwealth Fund Annual Report* (1931–32), 42. Note the parallel between the Laura Spelman Rockefeller Memorial's termination of its child development programs in 1929 and the Commonwealth Fund's withdrawal of funds for child guidance clinics in 1932.

111. Horn, *Before It's Too Late,* 92; and Stevenson and Smith, *Child Guidance Clinics,* 166–67.

112. Lowrey, "Orthopsychiatric Treatment," 529.

113. Horn, *Before It's Too Late,* 92–93.

114. William C. Richards and William J. Norton, *Biography of a Foundation: The Story of the Children's Fund, 1929–54* (Ann Arbor, Mich., 1957).

115. Ridenour, *Mental Health,* 102; and William Couzens, Letter to William Norton, 1 June 1931, Children's Fund Papers [hereafter, CFP], Bentley Historical Library, University of Michigan, Ann Arbor, Michigan, Box 11.

116. William Couzens, Letter to William Norton, 25 October 1939, CFP, Box 11. Thanks to

Susan Harrari (personal communication, 1985), who provided the information on the Couzens-Norton correspondence from her research in the Children's Fund Papers.

117. Stevenson and Smith, *Child Guidance Clinics,* 139.

118. *Commonwealth Fund Annual Report* (1930–33), 43.

119. *Commonwealth Fund Annual Report* (1930–33), 43.

120. Witmer, *Psychiatric Clinics for Children with Special Reference to State Programs,* 371. In 1935, 617 community clinics (located by the National Committee for Mental Hygiene, 56) accepted children as patients in 1935, an increase of 147 over 1927. Only 235 of these, however, used a child guidance team. A directory of clinics compiled by the National Committee in 1940 showed them still increasing.

121. Witmer, *Psychiatric Clinics,* 56–57, 245. No city of under 150,000 had a full-time child guidance clinic. Of the first fifty cities ranked by population, twenty-seven had full-time, and twenty-three part-time, clinics. In 1935 fifteen states had no clinics, and in nine others the state made no contribution to psychiatric services for children. Private sources supported 30 percent of psychiatric services for children; municipalities and county governments provided the funds for most of the remaining 10 percent. Three clinics were supported by the federal government.

122. Levy, "Critical Evaluation," 482.

123. Horn, *Before It's Too Late,* 182–84, briefly discusses the consequences of the Commonwealth Fund's child guidance program, with emphasis on what went wrong. Except for a few generalizations, she does not report developments after 1940. For discussion of some of the later developments in child guidance and mental hygiene programs, see Ridenour, *Mental Health. The CFHS, 1918–1962* alludes to the profound influence of American child guidance on British child psychiatry with only the brief comment that the development of child guidance work was rapid in England after World War II. Horn (*Before It's Too Late*) and Harvey and Abrams (*For the Welfare of Mankind*) limit their histories to the fund's activities in the United States, omitting its support of British child guidance.

124. Levy, "Critical Evaluation," 483.

125. *Commonwealth Fund Annual Report* (1930–31), 4–5.

126. Allen, "Developments in Child Psychiatry," 1201.

127. Leo Kanner, "American Contributions to the Development of Child Psychiatry," *Psychiatric Quarterly (Supplement)* 35(1961): 7.

128. Leo Kanner, "Centrifugal Forces in Personality Development," *American Journal of Psychoanalysis* 19(1959): 123–33; and Leo Kanner, "Child Psychiatry in the Framework of Western Society," *Acta Paedopsychiatrica* 24 (1967): 2–10.

129. Noel Hunnybun, Interview with author, 17 July 1977.

130. Stevenson and Smith, *Child Guidance Clinics,* 122.

131. *Commonwealth Fund Annual Report* (1930–33), 48.

132. Celia Stendler, "Sixty Years of Child Training Practices," *JP* 36 (1950): 122–34.

133. See, for example, three titles by Mary B. Sayles: *Three Problem Children: Narratives from a Child Guidance Clinic* (New York, 1924), *The Problem Child in School* (New York, 1925), and *The Problem Child at Home* (New York, 1928). The Judge Baker Foundation also used case histories in its annual reports and other publications.

134. Ridenour, *Mental Health,* 110.

135. Leon Eisenberg and David Ray De Maso, "Fifty Years of the *AJO:* An Overview and Introduction," in *AJO Annotated Index, Vols. 1–50, 1930–80,* vii–xxix (New York, 1985), xx.

136. Sol Cohen, "The Mental Hygiene Movement, the Commonwealth Fund, and Public Education, 1921–1933," in *Private Philanthropy and Public Elementary and Secondary Education; Proceedings of the Rockefeller Archive Center Conference Held on June 8, 1979,* ed. Gerald Benjamin (New York, 1980), 42.

137. WHC, "Psychology, Psychiatry, and Pediatrics," 32–33.

138. Milton J. E. Senn, Interview by author, 5 June 1976.

139. Bernard Rosenblatt, "Historical Perspectives of Treatment Modes," in *Perspectives in Child Psychopathology,* ed. Herbert E. Rie (Chicago, 1971), 52.

140. Rosenblatt, "Historical Perspectives," 52.

CHAPTER 13. THE CHILDREN'S BUREAU UNDER GRACE ABBOTT

1. Chapter 5 discusses the Children's Bureau under Julia Lathrop (1912–1921). President William Howard Taft, while not an active supporter, did not impede the bureau's work, and President Woodrow Wilson cooperated actively. The Department of Labor provided a hospitable home; by 1921 it was calling the bureau its "brightest jewel."

2. William Leuchtenberg, *The Perils of Prosperity, 1914–1932* (Chicago, 1958), 8.

3. Lela B. Costin, *Two Sisters for Social Justice: A Biography of Grace and Edith Abbott* (Urbana, Ill., 1983), 42.

4. See James Patterson, *America's Struggle Against Poverty, 1900–1985* (Cambridge, Mass., 1981), 20, 23, 26, 31–34. He discusses changing attitudes toward poverty in the early twentieth century and quotes Herbert Hoover: "We shall soon with the help of God be in sight of the day when poverty will be banished in the nation" (p. 15).

5. Jane Addams, *The Second Twenty Years at Hull-House, September 1909 to September 1929* (New York, 1930).

6. Addams, *Second Twenty Years,* 155.

7. Addams, *Second Twenty Years,* 152–159.

8. See Children's Bureau, *Annual Report of the Children's Bureau* (Washington, D.C., 1921–1934).

9. Gilbert V. Steiner, *The Children's Cause* (Washington, D.C., 1976), 59.

10. Edith Abbott, "Grace Abbott: A Sister's Memories," *Social Service Review* 13(1939): 351.

11. Abbott, "Grace Abbott," 357.

12. Costin, *Two Sisters for Social Justice,* 20, 39, 69.

13. Abbott, "Grace Abbott," 355–77.

14. Abbott, "Grace Abbott," 380–81.

15. *Hammer vs. Dagenhart* 247 US 251 (1918).

16. Abbott, "Grace Abbott," 380.

17. Costin, *Two Sisters for Social Justice,* 98.

18. Abbott, "Grace Abbott," 392.

19. Costin, *Two Sisters for Social Justice,* 100.

20. Abbott, "Grace Abbott," 49.

21. Grace Abbott, "Public Protection of Children" (paper presented at the National Congress of Social Work [NCSW], Toronto, 1923).

22. See chapter 5 for discussion of the passage of the Sheppard-Towner Act.

23. Richard A. Meckel, *Save the Babies: American Public Health Reform and the Prevention of Infant Mortality, 1850–1929* (Baltimore, 1990).

24. Costin, *Two Sisters for Social Justice,* 139; Molly Ladd-Taylor, "'Grannies' and 'Spinsters': Midwife Education under the Towner-Sheppard Act," *Journal of Social History* 22(1988): 255–75; and Molly Ladd-Taylor, *Mother-Work: Women, Child Welfare and the State, 1890–1930* (Urbana, Ill., 1994): 182–84.

25. Grace Abbott, "The Midwife in Chicago," *American Journal of Sociology* 20(1915): 684–89. Ladd-Taylor ("Grannies and Spinsters") reports that 24,899 midwives enrolled for 2,300 courses given by Sheppard-Towner nurses.

26. Meckel, *Save the Babies,* 212–13.

27. Costin, *Two Sisters for Social Justice,* 39–40; and J. Stanley Lemons, *The Woman Citizen: Social Feminism in the 1920's* (Urbana, Ill., 1973), 153–80.

28. Meckel, *Save the Babies.* For examples of how Sheppard-Towner professionals tried to serve minority mothers, see Ladd-Taylor, *Mother-Work,* 180–84; and Robyn Muncy, *Creating Female Dominion in American Reform, 1890–1935* (New York, 1991), 114–20, 163–64.

29. Nancy F. Cott, *The Grounding of Modern Feminism* (New Haven, 1987), 111–13; and Muncy, *Creating Female Dominion,* 129–31.

30. Ladd-Taylor, *Mother-Work,* 188; and Muncy, *Creating Female Dominion,* 125, 129–31.

31. Meckel, *Save the Babies,* 218. Most of the bills introduced between 1928 and 1932 proposed that the Public Health Service share responsibility with the Children's Bureau for the administration of maternal and child health programs. On the antagonism between the health service and the bureau, see Muncy, *Creating Female Dominion,* 142–46.

32. Ladd-Taylor, *Mother-Work,* 170.

33. Ladd-Taylor reports that African-American infant mortality was reduced from 108 to 106 per 1,000 live births between 1921 and 1928, compared to a reduction from 72 to 64 for whites (Ladd-Taylor, *Mother-Work,* 188). Maternal mortality was not reduced significantly.

34. David J. Rothman and Stanton Wheeler, eds., *Social History and Social Policy* (New York, 1981), 188–94; and Meckel, *Save the Babies,* 217–18.

35. Arthur H. Parmelee Jr., Interview by author, 10 April 1994.

36. Sydney A. Halpern, *American Pediatrics: The Social Dynamics of Professionalism, 1880–1980* (Berkeley, 1988), 90–102.

37. Sheila M. Rothman, *Woman's Proper Place: A History of Changing Ideals and Practices, 1870 to the Present* (New York, 1978), 136–53; D. Rothman and Wheeler, *Social History and Social Policy,* 187; and Ladd-Taylor, *Mother-Work,* 190.

38. Meckel, *Save the Babies,* 218.

39. S. Rothman, *Woman's Proper Place,* 142–50; and D. Rothman and Wheeler, ed., *Social History and Social Policy,* 187–97. Not all pediatricians opposed the extension of public services to mothers and children. Many who had participated in the infant welfare move-

ment and the campaigns to pass and extend Sheppard-Towner remained staunch supporters of the Children's Bureau during the 1930 White House Conference and for many
years thereafter. Numerous examples of their support may be found in the Martha May
Eliot Papers [hereafter, MME], Elizabeth and Arthur Schlesinger Library on the History
of Women, Radcliffe College, Harvard University, Cambridge, Massachusetts.

40. Dorothy Bradbury, Interview by author, n.d.; and Martin Pernick, Interview by author,
8 June 1995. Publications of the Children's Bureau completed or started during Abbott's
administration are listed in the Children's Bureau annual reports from 1922 to 1937. According to Martin Pernick, an authority on early educational films in the fields of health
and welfare, the Children's Bureau was among the most active promoters of film for parent education and propaganda purposes.

41. The panel of experts, initiated by Lathrop shortly before she retired, reviewed all the subsequent literature for parents. By the mid-1930s the bureau was allowing specialists to set
standards for prenatal care and to control the content of its publications, *Prenatal Care*
and *Infant Care*. Pregnancy was portrayed as a pathological condition and tended to be
seen as a medical problem rather than a normal occurrence.

42. Martha May Eliot, *Infant Care*, CB Publication (Washington, D.C., 1929, rev. ed. 1933),
2.

43. White House Conference for Child Health and Protection (WHC), "WHC on Child
Health and Protection 1930: Addresses and Abstracts of Committee Reports" (paper presented at the WHC, New York, 1931).

44. Douglas Thom, *Habit Clinics for the Child of Preschool Age: Their Organization and Practical Value*. CB Publication 135 (Washington, D.C., 1924, rev. ed. 1933).

45. Douglas Thom, *Everyday Problems of the Everyday Child* (New York, 1928); Douglas
Thom, *Are You Training Your Child to Be Happy? Lesson Material in Child Management*,
prepared by Blanche C. Weill with the approval of Douglas Thom, CB Publication 197,
202 (Washington, D.C., 1930, 1939).

46. Leta Hollingworth, *Psychology of an Adolescent* (New York, 1928). *Child Management* was
24 pages in 1925, 43 pages in 1927, and 107 pages in 1937. For Abbott's beliefs about the
importance of psychiatric work for preschool children, see Papers of Grace and Edith
Abbott [hereafter, Abbott Papers], Department of Special Collections, Regenstein Library, University of Chicago, Chicago, Illinois, Addenda 2, Box 2.

47. John B. Watson, *The Psychological Care of the Infant and Child* (New York, 1928), 5.

48. Douglas Thom, *Child Management*, CB Publication 143 (Washington, D.C., 1925, rev.
eds. 1928 and 1937), 41(1925), 14(1937).

49. Thom, *Child Management*, 25.

50. WHC, "Psychology, Psychiatry, and Pediatrics: The Problem" (paper presented at Section 1, Medical Service, Subcommittee C, Report of the Subcommittee on Psychiatry
and Psychology, New York, 1932), 15. A 1930 WHC leaflet, "Habits That Make or Mar,"
part of the series on habit training, gives numerous examples of ways in which a child's
early training determines his adult behavior, for example, that "a child who is allowed to
follow his own whims in the matter of food will later have finicky habits that make him
difficult to fit in at a dinner party" (Thom, *Are You Training Your Child to Be Happy? Lesson Material in Child Management*, 3).

51. Leo Kanner, *In Defense of Mothers: How to Bring Up Children in Spite of the More Zealous Psychologists* (Springfield, Ill., 1941); Hilde Bruch, *Don't Be Afraid of Your Child: A Guide for Perplexed Parents* (New York, 1952); and Stella Chess, Alexander Thomas, and Herbert G. Birch, *Your Child Is a Person: An Approach to Parenthood Without Guilt* (New York, 1965).

52. WHC, "Proceedings of the WHC on Child Health Protection 1930, Section 3, Education and Training" (paper presented at the WHC, New York, 1932), 27. See Caldwell and Richmond for how child-rearing theories influence child rearing advice (Betteye Caldwell and Julius B. Richmond, "Child Rearing Practices and Their Consequences," *Children* 9(1962): 73–78).

53. Statistics on the distribution of *Child Management* from 1929 to 1934 are cited in annual reports of the Children's Bureau for those years.

54. Dorothy Bradbury, *Five Decades of Action: A Short History of the Children's Bureau* (Washington, D.C., 1964), 22.

55. Children's Bureau, *Annual Report of the Children's Bureau*, CB Publication (Washington D.C., 1922); and Emma O. Lundberg, *Unemployment and Child Welfare: A Study Made in a Middle-Western and an Eastern City During the Industrial Depression of 1921 and 1922*, CB Publication 125 (Washington, D.C., 1923).

56. Grace Abbott, "Fundamental Questions Now Before Us" (paper presented at the NCSW, 1922), 21–24.

57. Children's Bureau, *Foster Home Care for Dependent Children*, CB Publication 136 (Washington, D.C., 1926); Children's Bureau, *The Work of Child Placing Agencies: A Social Study of Ten Agencies Caring for Dependent Children (Part 1). Health Supervision of Children Placed in Foster Homes (Part 2)*, CB Publication 171 (Washington, D.C., 1927); and Emma O. Lundberg, *Administration of Mother's Aid in Ten Localities with Special Reference to Health, Housing, and Recreation*, CB Publication 184 (Washington, D.C., 1928).

58. Robert Morse Woodbury, *Maternal Mortality: The Risk of Death in Childbirth from All Diseases Caused by Pregnancy and Confinement*, CB Publication 158 (Washington, D.C., 1926).

59. Elizabeth Carpenter Tandy, *Comparability of Maternal Mortality Rates in the United States and Certain Foreign Countries: A Study of the Effects of Variations in Assignment Procedures, Definitions of Live Births, and Completeness of Birth Registration*, CB Publication 229 (Washington, D.C., 1935).

60. Robert Morse Woodbury, *Maternal Mortality in Fifteen States*, CB Publication 223 (Washington, D.C., 1933).

61. Walter L. Trattner, *Crusade for the Children: A History of the National Child Labor Committee and Child Labor Reform* (Chicago, 1970), 133–36, 162.

62. Children's Bureau, *Child Labor in the United States—Ten Questions Answered*, CB Publication 114 (Washington, D.C., 1924); Grace Abbott, *The Child and the State*, 2 vols. (Chicago, 1938); Abbott, "Grace Abbott," 386–87.

63. Twenty-six publications of the Children's Bureau on the subject of child labor between 1922 and 1934 include: Children's Bureau, *The Welfare of Children in Bituminous Coal Mining Communities in West Virginia*, CB Publication 117 (Washington, D.C., 1923); Children's Bureau, *Administration of Child Labor Laws*, CB Publication 12, 17, 41, 85, 133

(Washington, D.C., 1926); Harriet Anne Byrne, *Child Labor in Representative Tobacco-Growing Areas*, CB Publication 155 (Washington, D.C., 1926); Alice Channing, *Child Labor in Fruit and Hop Growing Districts of the Northern Pacific*, CB Publication 151. (Washington, D.C., 1926); Edith Scott Gray, *Industrial Accidents among Employed Minors in Wisconsin, Massachusetts, and New Jersey*, CB Publication 152 (Washington, D.C., 1926); Nettie Pauline McGill, *Children in Street Work*, CB Publication 188 (Washington, D.C., 1928); Nettie Pauline McGill and Ella Arvilla Merritt, *Children in Agriculture*, CB Publication 187 (Washington, D.C., 1929); Children's Bureau, *Child Labor in New Jersey*, CB Publication 174, 185, 192, 199 (Washington, D.C., 1927; 1928; 1931); Ellen Nathalie Matthews, *Children in Fruit and Vegetable Canneries*, CB Publication 198 (Washington, D.C., 1930); Children's Bureau, *Children Engaged in Newspaper and Magazine Selling and Delivering*, CB Publication 227 (Washington, D.C., 1935); and Alice Channing, *Employment of Mentally Deficient Boys and Girls* CB Publication 210 (Washington, D.C., 1932).

64. Abbott, "Grace Abbott," 421.
65. Abbott, "Grace Abbott," 425.
66. Trattner, *Crusade for the Children*, 204–07.
67. One study of delinquency by William Healy addressed its scientific validity. Another was on older delinquents in Chicago, and another was a two-part investigation of the institutional treatment of delinquent boys. The studies included investigations of courts in specific cities and states and examination of legal aspects, standards, and treatment of children who violated federal laws. By 1927 the bureau had completed a plan for uniform reporting of statistics on delinquency, dependency, and neglect.
68. Children's Bureau, *Welfare of Children in Bituminous Coal Mining Communities;* and Marguerite G. Rosenthal, "The Children's Bureau and the Juvenile Court: Delinquency Policy, 1912–1940," *Social Service Review [SSR]* 60(1986): 306–08.
69. Katherine Lenroot and Emma O. Lundberg, *Juvenile Courts at Work*, CB Publication 141 (Washington, D.C., 1925).
70. Rosenthal, "Children's Bureau and Juvenile Court," 309.
71. Children's Bureau, *Facts about Juvenile Delinquency: Its Prevention and Cure*, CB Publication 215 (Washington, D.C., 1932).
72. Children's Bureau, *Annual Report of the Children's Bureau*, CB Publication (Washington, D.C., 1934).
73. Rosenthal declares that "the bureau was moving toward acceptance of the idea that delinquency, rather than being a problem that grew out of a troubled community structure, was a matter of very individual maladjustment whose antecedents could be found in faulty personal situations" ("Children's Bureau and Juvenile Court," 310). This view was not in accord with Lathrop's and Abbott's repeated statements that poverty is the root of children's problems.
74. Children's Bureau publications that deal with the issues mentioned include: Ruben Oppenheimer and Lulu L. Eckman, *Laws Relating to Sex Offenses Against Children*, CB Publication 145 (Washington, D.C., 1925); Emelyn Foster Peck, *Adoption Laws in the United States*, CB Publication 148 (Washington, D.C., 1925); Children's Bureau, *Illegitimacy as a Child Welfare Problem*, Part 2, CB Publication 75 (Washington, D.C., 1921); Children's

Bureau, *Standards of Legal Protection for Children Born Out of Wedlock,* CB Publication 77 (Washington, D.C., 1921); Children's Bureau, *Illegitimacy as a Child Welfare Problem,* Part 3: *Methods of Care in Selected Urban and Rural Communities,* CB Publication 128 (Washington, D.C., 1924); Children's Bureau, *Children of Illegitimate Birth and Measures for their Protection,* CB Publication 166 (Washington, D.C., 1927); Children's Bureau, *The Welfare of Infants of Illegitimate Birth in Baltimore as Affected by a Maryland Law of 1916 Governing the Separation from Their Mothers of Children under Six Months Old,* Part 1, CB Publication 144 (Washington, D.C., 1925); Children's Bureau, *Children of Illegitimate Birth and Measures For Their Protection,* CB Publication 166 (Washington, D.C., 1927); Alice Madora Donahue, *Children of Illegitimate Birth Whose Mothers Have Kept Their Custod,.* CB Publication 190 (Washington, D.C., 1928); Edith Abbott and Sophonisba Breckinridge, *The Administration of the Aid-to-Mothers Law in Illinois,* CB Publication 82 (Washington, D.C., 1921); Emma O. Lundberg, *State Commissions for the Study and Revision of Child Welfare Laws,* CB Publication 131 (Washington, D.C., 1924); and Children's Bureau, *Laws Relating to Interstate Placement of Dependent Children,* CB Publication 139 (Washington, D.C., 1924). Abbott's interest in the law also was reflected in the bureau's annual reports. As early as 1924, the bureau began to report child welfare activities of state child welfare commissions and to review state child welfare legislation. Reports of child welfare legislation in other countries were added in 1925.

75. Children's Bureau, *Foster Home Care for Dependent Children,* CB Publication 136 (Washington, D.C., 1926); and Children's Bureau, *The Work of Child Placing Agencies: A Social Study of Ten Agencies Caring for Dependent Children,* Part 1. *Health Supervision of Children Placed in Foster Homes (Part 2),* CB Publication 171 (Washington, D.C., 1927).

76. Alfred Kadushin, *Child Welfare Services* (New York, 1967), 49–52.

77. Arnold Gesell, *Psychological Guidance in Child Adoption,* CB Publication 137 (Washington, D.C., 1926).

78. Helen Russell Wright, *Children of Wage Earning Mothers,.* CB Publication 102 (Washington, D.C., 1922); and Clara Mortenson Beyer, *Children of Working Mothers in Philadelphia,* Part 1: *The Working Mothers,* CB Publication 204 (Washington, D.C., 1931).

79. Abbott, "Grace Abbott," 394–95.

80. Lawrence K. Frank, Letter to Louise Stanley, 2 September 1924, Laura Spelman Rockefeller Memorial [hereafter, LSRM], Rockefeller Archive Center, Pocantico Hills, Sleepy Hollow, New York, Series 3.5, Box 25, Folder 275.

81. Stanley wrote Frank that the Federal Board for Vocational Education would collaborate with the proposed Washington Center but did not mention the Children's Bureau (Frank, Letter to Louise Stanley).

82. Martha May Eliot, Oral History, 1973–1978, MME.

83. Lois Meek Stolz, Interview by author, transcript in author's possession, 9 December 1976.

84. Lois Meek Stolz, Interview by author, 17 December 1978. Stolz said, "Grace Abbott was an autocratic and brilliant woman who knew just what you should do and what the Children's Bureau should do. . . . If anything was going to be done for children, the Children's Bureau would do it" (Stolz, Interview by author, 1976). Both Bradbury and Stolz believed that a major reason for the failure of the research center was that its director, Mandel Sher-

man, wanted to do research himself rather than encourage government centers to do it. Grace Abbott was enthusiastic about nursery schools if they were not also research laboratories. See, for example, her article, "What is the Future of the Day Nursery?" *Child Health Bulletin* 3(1927): 33–36. Abbott's fears may have been stimulated by Watson's article on his experiments with babies, which many developmentalists also found objectionable (John B. Watson and Rosalie Watson, "Studies in Infant Psychology," *Scientific Monthly* 13(1921): 493–515). The research at the Washington center, observational and not experimental, was unlikely to harm children, but Abbott's reservations about exposing the bureau to anything that could possibly damage its reputation are understandable.

85. WHC, "WHC on Child Health and Protection 1930: Addresses and Abstracts of Committee Reports."

86. Edith Abbott, Personal correspondence, Letter to Unidentified, n.d., Special Collections Research Center, University of Chicago Library, Series 2, Box 12; and Costin, *Two Sisters for Social Justice,* 168.

87. WHC, "WHC on Child Health and Protection 1930," 25.

88. Ray Lyman Wilbur, *White House Conference on Child Health and Protection 1930: Addresses and Abstracts of Committee Reports* (New York, 1931), 1–13, 15–25.

89. The conference was organized into four main sections: Medical Service, Public Health and Administration, Education and Training, and the Handicapped. Assembled under the main sections were seventeen committees and one hundred and fifty subcommittees.

90. WHC, "WHC on Child Health and Protection 1930: Addresses and Abstracts of Committee Reports," vii.

91. WHC, "WHC on Child Health and Protection 1930: Addresses and Abstracts of Committee Reports," vi–vii.

92. One of the most significant of the original investigations undertaken for the conference was John Anderson's "Survey of the Education and Training of Your Child in the Home," *1930 WHC, 1931,* 156–59, published in 1936 as *The Young Child in the Home* (John Anderson, "The Young Child in the Home" (Paper presented at the WHC, Section 3, Education and Training Committee on the Infant and Preschool Child, New York, 1936). Data were collected on 2,757 families and 3,520 children over one year of age. Black families were included in the sample.

93. Secretary of Labor Davis's impassioned defense of the bureau placed him in opposition to most other members of President Hoover's cabinet and to the President himself.

94. WHC, "WHC on Child Health and Protection 1930: Addresses and Abstracts of Committee Reports," vii; and Bradbury, *Five Decades of Action.*

95. WHC, "WHC on Child Health and Protection 1930: Addresses and Abstracts of Committee Reports," 6.

96. WHC, "WHC on Child Health and Protection 1930: Addresses and Abstracts of Committee Reports," 16.

97. WHC, "WHC on Child Health and Protection 1930: Addresses and Abstracts of Committee Reports," 16.

98. Edith Abbott, Personal correspondence, Letter to Unidentified; and Costin, *Two Sisters for Social Justice,* 171.

99. Edith Abbott, Personal correspondence, Letter to Unidentified.

100. Grace Abbott, *New York Times,* 4 November 1930, 14.
101. WHC, "WHC on Child Health and Protection 1930: Addresses and Abstracts of Committee Reports," 32.
102. Costin, *Two Sisters for Social Justice,* 172–75.
103. Robert Bremner, John Barnard, Tamara Hareven, and Robert Mennel, eds., *Children and Youth in America: A Documentary History, 1866–1932,* Vol. 2 (Cambridge, Mass. 1971), 1083.
104. The Children's Charter is reproduced in Bremner et al., *Children and Youth in America: A Documentary History, 1866–1932,* 106–07.
105. Grace Abbott, "The Child," *American Journal of Sociology* [*AJS*] 37(1931).
106. WHC, "Proceedings of the WHC on Child Health Protection 1930, Section 3, Education and Training," 27.
107. Lorena Hickok surveyed the effects of the Depression for the Federal Emergency Relief Administration and the Works Projects Administration (WPA).
108. WHC, "WHC on Child Health and Protection 1930: Addresses and Abstracts of Committee Reports," 7–11, 36–39; and Louis J. Covotsos, "Child Welfare and Social Progress: A History of the United States Children's Bureau, 1912–1935"(Ph.D. diss., University of Chicago, 1976), 263.
109. Bremner et al., *Children and Youth in America,* 794–95; and Grace Abbott, "Improvement in Rural Public Relief: The Lessons of the Coal Mining Communities," *Social Service Review* 6(June 1932): 183–222.
110. Glen Steele, *Family Welfare: Summary of Expenditures for Relief, General Family Welfare and Relief, Mothers' Aid, Veterans' Aid, Microfilm from Social Statistics in Child Welfare and Related Fields, Annual Report for Registration Area for 1930,* CB Publication 209 (Washington, D.C., 1976). See also MME for effects of the monthly reports (n.d., Box 31, Folder 440–44). When the President's committee requested the bureau's help, the bureau already had established a system for collecting information and making contacts that enabled it to assemble relief statistics rapidly. In July 1930, in order to determine the extent and kinds of treatment provided for children by local social programs, it took over a cooperative plan for obtaining social statistics in certain metropolitan areas initiated by the National Association of Community Chests and Councils in cooperation with the University of Chicago. The bureau supplemented information from this source with relief statistics furnished by the Russell Sage Foundation for cities of one hundred thousand population or more.
111. Children's Bureau, *Annual Report of the Children's Bureau,* CB Publication (Washington, D.C., 1931); Children's Bureau, *The Promotion of the Welfare and Hygiene of Maternity and Infancy for 1929,* CB Publication 203 (Washington, D.C., 1931); and Children's Bureau, *Trends, Problems and Policies in Relief Statistics,* CB Publication 212 (Washington, D.C., 1932).
112. Grace Abbott, *New York Times,* 4 November 1930, 14.
113. Abbott, *New York Times,* 4 November 1930, 14.
114. Edith Abbott, Professional papers, 1931, RL, Addenda 2, Box 3; Emma A. Winslow, *Trends in Different Types of Public and Private Relief in Urban Areas, 1929–1935,* CB Publication 237 (Washington, D.C., 1937).

115. Abbott, Professional papers.

116. Abbott, *New York Times, 4 November* 14.

117. Abbott, "The Child," 952–55; Grace Abbott, "The Child," *AJS* 38(1932): 880–88; and Grace Abbott, "Children of the Depression" (paper presented at the Annual Meeting of the Association for the Prevention of Tuberculosis of the District of Columbia, 20 November 1933).

118. J. Prentice Murphy, "Children in the New Deal," *Annals of the American Academy of Political and Social Sciences* 176 (November 1934): 121–30.

119. Grace Abbott, "Some Effects of the Depression on the Nutrition of Children," *Child Welfare News,* 12 July 1933. See J. Prentice Murphy for a summary of worsening conditions for children during the first years of the Depression, (Murphy, "Children in the New Deal," 121–30). See also Glen H. Elder, who used data from the Oakland Growth Study, Institute of Human Development, Berkeley, California, collected for a totally different purpose, to examine ways in which the Depression changed the lives of families and influenced the development of children (Glen H. Elder, *Children of the Great Depression: Social Change in Life Experience* [Chicago, 1974]).

120. Wilbur, *White House Conference, 1930,* section 4, 72–79.

121. Children's Bureau, *Juvenile Court Statistics, 1929, Based on Information Supplied by 96 Courts,* CB Publication 208 (Washington, D.C., 1932), 5–9; and Steele, *Family Welfare.*

122. Children's Bureau, *Annual Report of the Children's Bureau,* CB Publications (Washington, D.C., 1933, 1934).

123. Katherine F. Lenroot, *Children of the Depression: A Study of 259 Families in Selected Areas of Five Cities,* CB Publication 237 (Washington, D.C., 1931).

124. Katherine F. Lenroot, Transcript of Interview, 1965, Social Security Project, Oral History Research Office, Columbia University, New York, New York.

125. Martha May Eliot, "Child Health Recovery Program," *Public Health Nursing* 26(1934): 817; and Covotsos, "Child Welfare and Social Progress," 271–79.

126. Covotsos, "Child Welfare and Social Progress," 280–82.

127. Costin, *Two Sisters for Social Justice,* 179–83.

128. Grace Abbott, "Federal Regulation of Child Labor, 1906–1938," *SSR* 13(1939): 404.

129. Edwin E. Witte, August 17, 1934, quoted in Costin, *Two Sisters for Social Justice,* 222.

130. Costin, *Two Sisters for Social Justice,* 221–24. The Social Security Act became law on 14 August 1935. Material on Abbott's role may be found in the Abbott Papers (Addenda 2, Box 4) and in MME (Box 4, series 5, Folders 329–35).

131. Martha May Eliot, "The Children's Titles in the Social Security Act: Origins and Development of the Health Services," *Children* 7(1960): 135–42; and Katherine F. Lenroot, "The Children's Titles in the Social Security Act: Origins and Development of the Health Services," *Children* 7 (July–August 1960): 127–30. Mary Irene Atkinson, *Child* (1936), discusses the concept behind the provisions for child welfare services in the Social Security Act. See Meckel for the maternity and infancy provisions of the Social Security Act and some of the ways in which they differed from the Sheppard-Towner Act (Meckel, *Save the Babies,* 222–25).

132. Lenroot, "Children's Titles in Social Security Act," 127–30. Lenroot pointed out that, before the Social Security Act, the emphasis in aid to dependent children programs was

on service, but under the Social Security Act technical and legal questions of eligibility were foremost in the administration of the programs (Lenroot, Transcript of Interview, 106–08).

133. Costin, *Two Sisters for Social Justice,* 222–24.

134. Costin, *Two Sisters for Social Justice,* 224.

135. Lenroot, Transcript of Interview, 106–08.

136. Grace Abbott, "New Measures of Values," *Journal of the National Institute of Social Science* (May–December 1934): 16–29.

137. Costin, *Two Sisters for Social Justice,* 233–35.

EPILOGUE: WHAT HAPPENED TO THE EARLY MOVEMENTS?

1. Robert R. Sears, *Your Ancients Revisited: A History of Child Development* (Chicago, 1975).

2. Harriet L. Rheingold, "The First Twenty Years of the Society for Research in Child Development" in *History and Research in Child Development,* vol. 50 in Monographs of the Society for Research in Child Development, ed. Alice Smuts and John Hagen Smuts (Chicago, 1986).

3. Sheldon White, "The Rise in Developmental Psychology: Retrospective Review of Cognitive Development in Children: Five Monographs of the Society for Research in Child Development," *Contemporary Psychology* 36(1991): 469–73.

4. Edith Grotberg, "Child Development," in *Two Hundred Years of Childhood,* ed. Edith Grotberg (Washington, D.C., 1976), 403–04.

5. Charles M. Super, "Secular Trends in Child Development and the Institutionalization of Professional Disciplines," *Society for Research in Child Development Newsletter* (1983): 10–11. Super's analysis of nearly 500 articles published in *Child Development* from 1930 to 1979 documents the movement of developmental research from multidisciplinary institute to disciplinary departments.

6. Sheldon White and Deborah Phillips, "Designing Head Start: Roles Played by Developmental Psychologists" (paper presented at the conference on Social Sciences and Policy Making, University of Michigan, 13–14 March 1998), 14.

7. Ross Parke, Peter Ornstein, John J. Rieser, and Caroline Zahn-Waxler, eds., *A Century of Developmental Psychology* (Washington, D.C., 1994). For detailed discussions of theory and methodology in child development research, see the four Handbooks of Psychology published since World War II: Leonard Carmichael ed., *Manual of Child Psychology* (New York, 1946); Leonard Carmichael, ed., *Manual of Child Psychology* (New York, 1954); Paul H. Mussen, ed., *Carmichael's Manual of Child Development* (New York, 1979); Paul H. Mussen, ed., *Handbook of Child Psychology* (New York, 1983). See also Parke et al., *Century of Child Psychology,* particularly for its general introduction and its chapters and bibliographies on outstanding developmentalists. I am indebted to the contributors for information and insights.

8. Jerome Bruner, *Under Five in Britain* (London, 1980), 73–74.

9. Ross Parke et al., "The Past as Prologue: An Overview of a Century of Developmental Psychology," in Parke et al., *Century of Developmental Psychology,* 12–13.

10. Lee Robins, Interview by author, October 1993.

11. Paul B. Baltes, David L. Featherman, and Richard M. Lerner, eds., *Life-Span Development and Behavior,* vol. 8 (Hillsdale, N.J. 1987); P. Lindsay Chase-Lansdale, Kathleen Kiernan, and Ruth J. Friedman, eds., *Human Development Across Lives and Generations: The Potential for Change* (New York, 2004); and Michael Rutter and Marjorie Rutter, eds., *Developing Minds: Challenge and Continuity Across the Life Span* (New York, 1993).

12. Erik Erikson, *Childhood and Society* (New York, 1950).

13. Lawrence Kohlberg, *Psychology of Moral Development: The Nature and Validity of Moral Stages,* (San Francisco, 1984); Carol Gilligan, *In a Different Voice: Psychological Theory and Women's Development,* 2nd ed. (Cambridge, Mass., 1993); John Flavell, "Cognitive Development: Past, Present, and Future," in Parke et al., *Century of Developmental Psychology,* 569–88.

14. T. Field, *Infancy* (Cambridge, 1991); J. D. Osofsky, ed., *Handbook of Infant Development,* 2nd ed. (New York, 1987); and Amanda L. Woodward and Jessica A. Sommerville, "Twelve-Month-Old Infants Interpret Action in Context," *Psychological Science* 11, no.1 (2000): 73–76.

15. Judy Rosenblith, *In the Beginning: Development from Conception to Age Two* (Newbury Park, Calif. 1992), 364–75, 477; Flavell, "Cognitive Development," 573; Barbara Rogoff, "Developing and Understanding of the Idea of a Community of Learners," *Mind, Culture, and Activity* 1(1994): 209–29; and Barbara Rogoff, "Cognition as a Collaborative Process" in *Cognition, Perception, and Language,* ed. W. Damon, vol. 2, *Handbook of Child Psychology* (New York, 1998), 679–749.

16. Mary Ainsworth, "The Development of Infant-Mother Attachment," in *Reviews of Child Development Research* 3, ed. Bettye Caldwell and H.N. Riccuti (Chicago, 1973); John Bowlby, *Child Care and the Growth of Love* (London, 1953); Inge Bretherton, "The Origins of the Attachment Theory: John Bowlby and Mary Ainsworth" in Parke et al., *Century of Developmental Psychology;* Jude Cassidy and Phillip R. Shaver, *Handbook of Attachment: Theory, Research, and Clinical Applications* (New York, 1999); and Robert Karen, *Becoming Attached: The Unfolding Mystery of the Infant-Mother Bond and Its Implications for Later Life* (New York, 1994).

17. Rebekah Levine Coley, "(In)visible Men: Emerging Research on Low-Income, Unmarried, and Minority Fathers," *American Psychologist* 56, no. 9 (2001): 743–53; Ross Parke, *Fatherhood,* The Developing Child Series (Cambridge, Mass., 1996); Judy Dunn, *Sisters and Brothers,* The Developing Child Series (Cambridge, Mass., 1985); P. Lindsay Chase-Lansdale et al., "Young African-American Multigenerational Families in Poverty: The Contexts, Exchanges, and Processes of Their Lives," in *Coping with Divorce, Single Parenting, and Remarriage: A Risk and Resiliency Perspective,* ed. E. Mavis Hetherington (Malwah, N.J., 1999); Willard Hartup, "Social Relationships and Their Developmental Significance," *American Psychologist* 44 (1989): 120–26; and E. Hesse, "The Adult-Attachment Interview: Historical and Current Perspectives," in *Handbook of Attachment: Theory, Research, and Clinical Applications,* ed. Jude Cassidy and Phillip R. Shaver (New York,, 1999).

18. Urie Bronfenbrenner, *The Ecology of Human Development* (Cambridge, Mass., 1979); and Urie Bronfenbrenner, "Ecology and the Family as a Context for Human Development: Research Perspectives," *Developmental Psychology* 22(1986): 723–42.

19. Barbara Rogoff, *Apprenticeship in Thinking: Cognitive Development in Social Context* (New York, 1990); Barbara Rogoff, "Cognition as a Collaborative Process," in *Cognition, Perception, and Language,* ed. W. Damon, vol. 2, *Handbook of Child Psychology* (New York, 1998), 679–749; and John Flavell, "Cognitive Development," 579.

20. Glen Elder, *Children of the Great Depression: Social Change in Life Experience* (Chicago, 1974).

21. Susan C. Crockenberg, "Rescuing the Baby from the Bathwater: How Gender and Temperament (May) Influence How Child Care Affects Child Development," *Child Development* 74, no. 4 (2003): 1034–38; Jaclynne Eccles, "Gender Roles and Women's Achievement," *Psychology of Women Quarterly* 11(1987): 135–71; Mary Cover Jones et al., *The Course of Human Development* (Waltham, Mass., 1971), 252–58; Eleanor Maccoby and Carol N. Jacklin, *Psychology of Sex Differences* (Stanford, 1974); Eleanor Maccoby, "Gender Relationships: A Developmental Account," *American Psychologist* 45(1990): 513–20; and Eleanor Maccoby, *The Two Sexes: Growing Up Apart, Coming Together,* The Family and Public Policy Series (Cambridge, Mass., 1998).

22. R. J. Friedman and P. Lindsay Chase-Lansdale, "Chronic Adversities," in *Child and Adolescent Psychiatry,* 4th ed., ed. Michael Rutter and Eric A. Taylor (Malden, Mass., 2002), 261–76; Norman Garmezy and John Rolf, eds., *Risk and Protective Factors in the Development of Psychopathology* (Cambridge, Mass., 1990); Norman Garmezy and Michael Rutter, eds., *Stress, Coping, and Development in Children* (New York, 1983); Michael Rutter and Paul Casaer, eds., *Biological Risk Factors for Psychosocial Disorders* (New York, 1991); Emmy Werner and Ruth S. Smith, *Overcoming the Odds: High-Risk Children from Birth to Adulthood* (Ithaca, 1992); and Marc A. Zimmerman and Revathy Arunkumar, "Resiliency Research: Implications for Schools and Policy," *Social Policy Report* 8, no. 4 (1994): 18.

23. Eleanor J. Gibson, *Principles of Conceptual Learning and Development* (New York, 1969); Eleanor J. Gibson, *Odyssey in Learning and Perception* (Cambridge, Mass., 1991); Rogoff, *Apprenticeship in Thinking;* and Arnold J. Sameroff, "Developmental Systems and Family Functioning," in *Exploring Family Relationships with Other Social Contexts,* ed. Ross D. Parke and Sheppard G. Kellam (Hillsdale, N.J., 1994), 199–214.

24. Cynthia Garcia Coll et al., "An Integrative Model for the Study of Developmental Competencies in Minority Children," *Child Development* 65, no. 5(1996): 1891–1914; and (*http://www.nsf.gov*).

25. Michael Rutter, "Nature, Nurture, and Development: From Evangelism Through Science Toward Policy and Practice," *Child Development* 73, no. 1 (2002): 1–21; and Jack P. Shonkoff and Deborah Phillips, National Research Council (U.S.). Board on Children Youth and Families, National Research Council (U.S.), and Institute of Medicine (U.S.). *From Neurons to Neighborhoods: The Science of Early Childhood Development* (Washington, D.C., 2000).

26. Avshalom Casp, et al., "Role of Genotype in the Cycle of Violence in Maltreated Children," *Science* 297, no. 5582 (2002): 851–54; Avshalom Caspi,et al., "Influence of Life Stress on Depression: Moderation by a Polymorphism in the 5-HTT Gene," *Science* 301, no. 5631 (2003): 386–89; David Reiss et al., "Genetic Probes of Three Theories of Maternal Adjustment: II. Genetic and Environmental Influences," *Family Process* 40, no. 3

(2001): 261–72; and Eric Turkheimer et al., "Socioeconomic Status Modifies Heritability of IQ in Young Children," *Psychological Science* 14, no. 6 (2003): 623–68.

27. P. Lindsay Chase-Lansdale et al., "Children of the National Longitudinal Survey of Youth: A Unique Research Opportunity," *Developmental Psychology* 27, no. 6 (1991): 918–31; P. Lindsay Chase-Lansdale et al., "Mothers' Transitions from Welfare to Work and the Well-Being of Preschoolers and Adolescents," *Science* 277, no. 5612 (2003): 1548–52; Jeanne Brooks-Gunn et al., "Depending on the Kindness of Strangers: Current National Data Initiatives and Developmental Research," *Child Development* 71, no. 1 (2000); NICHD Early Child Care Research Network, "Does Quality of Child Care Affect Child Outcomes at Age 4 _?" *Developmental Psychology* 39, no. 3 (2003): 451–469; and M. S. Resnick et al., "Protecting Adolescents from Harm: Findings from the National Longitudinal Study on Adolescent Health," *Journal of the American Medical Association* 278, no. 10 (1997): 823–32.

28. John Clausen, *American Lives: Looking Back on the Children of the Great Depression* (New York, 1993).

29. Willard Hartup et al., *Child Psychology in Retrospect and Prospect,* vol. 32 in *In Celebration of the 75th Anniversary of the Institute of Child Development: The Minnesota Symposia on Child Psychology* (Mahwah, N.J., 2002). In 1981 John Bowlby was the recipient of the Distinguished Scientific Contributions to Child Development Award from the Society for Research in Child Development. Mary Ainsworth received the same award in 1983.

30. Hamilton Cravens, *Before Head Start: The Iowa Station and America's Children* (Chapel Hill, 1993), 249–50.

31. The welfare programs formerly associated with the Minnesota Child Development Institute have been moved to the De Paul campus of the University of Minnesota. Thanks to John Hagen and Harold Stevenson for information on the status of the child development institutes today.

32. For information on the last years of the Iowa station, see Cravens, *Before Head Start,* 249–50. Thanks to Trudy Siemski, Merrill-Palmer Institute, for current information on the program. Several land-grant universities, including Michigan State, Pennsylvania State, and Cornell, offer child development programs that, like the original institutes in Iowa and Minnesota, emphasize service to the community. These efforts have had limited success, according to Hagen, because funding has not been adequate to cover the high costs of service programs.

33. Smuts and John W. Hagen, *History and Research.* For a broad overview of the opportunities in the vibrant fields of child and family policy, see A Web Guide to Careers in Child and Family Policy: *http://www.sesp.northwestern.edu/CFP* by Rachel S. Gordon and P. Lindsay Chase-Lansdale.

34. Robins, Interview, October 1993.

35. Foundation for Child Development, *Annual Report* (New York, 1999).

36. Harold Stevenson and Alberta E. Siegel, eds., *Child Development and Social Policy,* vol. 1 (Chicago, 1984), xii.

37. J. Lawrence Aber and Lonnie R. Sherrod, eds., *SDRC Newsletter* (Winter 1999): 2.

38. White and Phillips, "Designing Head Start"; and Edward Zigler and Susan Muenchow,

Head Start: The Inside Story of America's Most Successful Educational Experiment (New York, 1992).

39. P. Lindsay Chase-Lansdale, Rachel A. Gordon, and K. McLain, "The Irving B. Harris Graduate School of Public Policy Studies: An Overview and Personal Reflection," *Zero to Three*, Special Issue in Honor of Irving B. Harris, vol. 18, no. 5 (1998).

40. Emily Davis Cahan, *Research and Child Development and the Formation of Social Policy: Historical Precedents and Current Perspectives* (Bush Foundation: Minneapolis, 1992), 67–68, 73–76.

41. For additional information, consult *SRCD Newsletter* 40 (1977), Special Issue on History, ed. A. W. Siegel and W. W. Hartup.,3.Thanks to John Hagen for an update on the oral history.

42. E. Larkin Phillips, "Some Features of Child Guidance Practice in the United States," *Clinical Psychiatry* 13 (1957): 43; and Saul Rosenzweig, "A Brief Semicentennial Survey of Child Guidance Practices, 1909–1959," *Journal of Genetic Psychology* 112 (1968): 109–16.

43. Bernard Rosenblatt, "Historical Perspectives on Treatment Modes," in *Perspectives in Child Psychopathology*, ed. Herbert E. Rie (Chicago, 1971), 66.

44. Eveoleen Rexford, "Child Psychology and Child Analysis in the United States Today," *Journal of the American Academy of Child Psychiatry* 1(1962): 365–84.

45. Anna Freud, *Psychiatric Treatment of Children* (London, 1946); Anna Freud, "The Child Guidance Clinic as a Center of Prophylaxes and Enlightenment," in *Recent Developments in Psychoanalytic Child Therapy*, ed. Joseph Weinrib (New York, 1961), 25–38; Anna Freud, *Normality and Pathology in Childhood* (New York, 1965); and Selma Kramer and Calvin F. Settlage, "On the Concept and Technique of Child Analysis," *Journal of the American Academy of Child Psychiatry* 1(1962): 509–24.

46. Leo Kanner, "Autistic Disturbances of Affective Contact," *Nervous Child* 2(1943): 217–50.

47. See Lauretta Bender, "Childhood Schizophrenia," *American Journal of Orthopsychiatry* [*AJO*] 17(1947): 40–56; Louise J. Despert, *The Emotionally Disturbed Child Then and Now* (New York, 1991); Margaret Mahler, "On Child Psychosis and Schizophrenia: Autistic and Symbiosis Child Psychosis," *PSH* 10(1955); and William Goldfarb, *Childhood Schizophrenia* (Cambridge, 1961). The Bush Foundation, established in 1953 and one of the nation's forty largest philanthropies, has supported programs primarily in Minnesota and North and South Dakota. The program in child development and social policy was one of only two major nonregional programs that the foundation sponsored. One impetus for the program occurred when Irving B. Harris, a major philanthropist for child development research, practice, and policy, joined the board of the Bush Foundation in the 1970s. The principal advisors to the Bush Foundation on the child development and social policy program were Urie Bronfenbrenner, Julius Richmond, Sheldon White, and Edward Zigler. For detailed information on the Bush Centers, see Cahan, *Research and Formation of Social Policy*, 120,198. Between 1978 and 1982, 254 doctoral, postdoctoral, and professional fellows completed training at the four Bush Centers for Child Development and Social Policy. About half went on to pursue academic careers, and half entered nonacademic positions. Thank you to Cahan for sharing her manuscript.

48. Rene Spitz, "Hospitalism," *Psychoanalytic Study of the Child* [*PSOC*] 1(1945): 53; and

Rene Spitz, "Anaclitic Depression: An Inquiry into the Genesis of Psychiatric Conditions in Early Childhood," *PSOC* 2(1946): 331–42. For an overview of work and bibliography related to childhood psychopathology, including childhood depression, see Leon Eisenberg and David Ray De Maso, "50 Years of the *AJO:* An Overview and Introduction," in *AJO Annotated Index, Vols. 1–50, 1930–80* (New York, 1985), viii–xxix.

49. Daniel Goleman, "Childhood Depression May Herald Adult Depression," *New York Times,* 11 January 1994.

50. Alan E. Kazdin and Paul L. Marciano, "Childhood and Adolescent Depression," in *Treatment of Childhood Disorders,* 2nd ed., ed. Eric J. Mash and Russell A. Barkley. (New York, 1998).

51. Leon Eisenberg, Interview by author, 19 October 1993.

52. Edmund W. Gordon, "Impact of Interest in Sociocultural Factors and Community Mental Health," in Rie, *Perspectives in Child Psychopathology,* 387–409.

53. Selma Kramer and Calvin F. Settlage, "On the Concept and Technique of Child Analysis," *Journal of the American Academy of Child Psychiatry* 1(1962): 509–24.

54. Mary Ainsworth, *Infancy in Uganda: Infant Care and the Growth of Love* (Baltimore, 1967); Mary Ainsworth, *Patterns of Attachment: A Psychological Study of the Strange Situation* (Hillsdale, N.J., 1978); Ainsworth, "Development of Attachment,"; Mary Ainsworth and John Bowlby, "An Ethological Approach to Personality Development," *American Psychologist* 46(1991): 331–41; Mary Ainsworth and John Bowlby, *Research Strategy in the Study of Mother-Child Separation* (Paris: Courrier de la Centre Internationale de l'Enfance, 1953); John Bowlby, *Maternal Care and Child Health,* World Health Organization Monograph Series (Geneva, 1951); John Bowlby, *Child Care and the Growth of Love* (London, 1953); John Bowlby, *Attachment and Loss,* vol. 1: *Attachment* (New York, 1969), vol. 2: *Separation: Anxiety and Anger* (New York, 1973); and vol. 3: *Loss: Sadness and Depression* (New York, 1980); John Bowlby, *The Making and Breaking of Affectional Bonds* (London, 1979); and John Bowlby, *A Secure Base: Clinical Application of Attachment Theory* (New York, 1988).

55. Rutter, "Nature, Nurture, and Development."

56. David Levy, "Critical Evaluation of the Present State of Child Psychiatry," *American Journal of Psychiatry* [*AJPsychiatry*] 108 (1952): 481–94. Others who studied the effects of institutional life on children were William Goldfarb, Margaret Ribble, and child guidance pioneers Lawson Lowrey and David Levy. Spitz published his work on early deprivation in 1945 and in 1946 describing a condition he called "anaclitic depression."

57. George Mora, ed., *Recent American Psychiatric Development (since 1930),* ed. Silvano Areti, vol. 1, *American Handbook of Psychology* (New York, 1965), 45–46.

58. David F. Musto, "Whatever Happened to Community Health?" *Public Interest* 39(1975): 55.

59. Philip Wylie is quoted by Musto in "Whatever Happened to Community Health?"55.

60. Musto, "Whatever Happened to Community Health?" 70–71; and John R. Weisz et al., "Bridging the Gap Between Laboratory and Clinic in Child and Adolescent Psychotherapy," *Journal of Consulting and Clinical Psychology* 63(1995): 688–701. See Margo Horn, *Before It's Too Late: The Child Guidance Movement in the United States, 1922–1945* (Philadelphia, 1989), 184–86, for her conclusions about the effects of the Commonwealth

Fund child guidance program on American society. Horn explicitly states that her emphasis is primarily on the negative consequences.

61. Irene Josselyn, "Child Psychiatric Clinics: Quo Vadimus," *AACP* 3(1964): 721.

62. See Leon Eisenberg, "Child Psychiatry: The Past Quarter Century," *AJO* 39(1969): 389 on "why the promissory note of prevention" issued during the early years of the movement has not been redeemed. Thanks to Rose Maruko and Connell O'Brien of the Philadelphia Child Guidance Clinic for helping me to understand changes in nomenclature during telephone interviews (Personal communication, 18 and 22 September 1995).

63. Albert Cain, Interview by author, 14 September 1995; and Robin V. Weersing and John R. Weisz, "Community Clinic Treatment of Depressed Youth: Benchmarking Usual Care Against CBT Clinical Trials," *Journal of Consulting and Clinical Psychiatry* 70, no.2 (2002): 299–310.

64. Salvador Minuchin et al., eds., *Families in the Slums* (New York, 1967); and Salvador Minuchin et al., eds., *Families and Family Therapy* (Cambridge, 1974).

65. I am grateful to Alfred Cain, clinical psychologist at the University of Michigan, and Connell O'Brien of the Philadelphia Child Guidance Center for helping me to understand present trends in research and treatment in child psychiatry (Interviews with author).

66. Eisenberg and De Maso, "50 Years of the *AJO*," xiv–xvii.

67. E. Drexel Godfrey, Jr., *The Transfer of the Children's Bureau* (New York, 1952), 18. Thanks to Sylvia Williams for the information on the AOA and its journal.

68. Katherine F. Lenroot, Transcript of Interview, Social Security Project, Oral History Research Office, Columbia University, New York, New York (1965), 153–59.

69. Richard A. Meckel, *Save the Babies: American Public Health Reform and the Prevention of Infant Mortality, 1850–1929* (Baltimore, 1990).

70. Godfrey, *Transfer of Children's Bureau,* 17–29; and Vince L. Hutchins, "Maternal Health and Child Health Bureau," (November 1994): 697–99.

71. Meckel, *Save the Babies,* 226.

72. *SRCD Newsletter* (Winter 1999): 305.

73. Lenroot, Transcript of Interview, 15.

74. Rochelle Beck, "White House Conferences on Children: An Historical Perspective," *Harvard Educational Review* 43(1973): 653–68; Katherine F. Lenroot, "Summing Up Previous White House Conferences," *The Child* 14(October 1949): 52–54; and Katherine Oettinger, "The Growth and Meaning of White House Conferences on Children and Youth," *Children* 7 (January-February 1960): 3–8.

75. WHC, *Proceedings of the WHC on Children in a Democracy.* CB Publication 266. (Washington, D.C., 1940).

76. WHC, "Proceedings of the Mid-Century WHC on Children and Youth," (Washington, D.C., 1950); and Helen Witmer and Ruth Kotinsky, *Personality in the Making: The Fact Finding Report of the Mid-Century Conference on Children and Youth* (New York, 1952).

77. WHC, "Proceeding: Golden Anniversary Conference on Children and Youth," (Washington, D.C., 1960); and Lori D. Ginsberg, *Women and the Work of Benevolence: Morality, Politics and Class in the Nineteenth-Century United States* (New Haven, 1990).

78. WHC, "Report to the President: WHC on Children," (Washington, D.C., 1971). For material on attempts to reorganize the Children's Bureau from 1930 to 1935, see the

MME Papers, Series 5, Box 18, Folders 250–53. The conference for children was for those up to age thirteen.

79. Edith Grotberg, "Child Development," in *Two Hundred Years of Childhood*, ed. Edith Grotberg (Washington, D.C., 1976), 403–04.

80. Julia Lathrop, "The Children's Bureau," *American Journal of Sociology* 8 (1912–1913): 322.

81. Ellen Bassuk, "In Support of Children and Youth: Encouraging Research Dissemination," *AJO* 65, no. 2(1995), 172–73.

82. Edward Zigler and Karen Anderson, "An Idea Whose Time Had Come: The Intellectual and Political Climate for Head Start," in *Project Head Start: A Legacy of the War on Poverty*, ed. *Edward Zigler and Jeanette Valentine* (New York, 1979), 3, 13.

83. Michael Harrington, *The Other America: Poverty in the United States* (New York, 1962).

84. Catherine J. Ross, "Early Skirmishes with Poverty: The Historical Roots of Head Start," in Zigler and Valentine, *Project Head Start:* 36–39; Zigler and Valentine, *Project Head Start;* and Zigler and Muenchow, *Head Start. Project Head Start* discusses the historical background of Head Start, the philosophy underlying the design of the program, its evolution, and the evaluation of Head Start during its early years.

85. J. McVicker Hunt, *Intelligence and Experience* (New York, 1961); and Benjamin S. Bloom, *Stability and Change in Human Characteristics* (New York, 1964).

86. Zigler and Anderson, "Idea Whose Time Had Come," 3–13.

87. Charles M. Super, "Secular Trends in Child Development and the Institutionalization of Professional Disciplines," *Society for Research in Child Development Newsletter* (1983): 10.

88. Jeanne Brooks-Gunn et al., *Neighborhood Poverty*, 2 vols. (New York, 1997); P. Lindsay Chase-Lansdale and Jeanne Brooks-Gunn, *Escape from Poverty: What Makes a Difference for Children?* (New York, 1995); Greg J. Duncan and Jeanne Brooks-Gunn, *Consequences of Growing Up Poor* (New York, 1997); and Susan E. Mayer, *What Money Can't Buy: Family Income and Children's Life Chances* (Cambridge, Mass., 1997).

89. White and Phillips, "Designing Head Start," (1998).

90. Zigler and Anderson, "Idea Whose Time Had Come," 3, 14, 98.

91. Bettye Caldwell, "A Decade of Early Intervention Programs: What We Have Learned," *AJO* 44(1974): 495.

92. Zigler and Valentine, *Project Head Start*, 115.

93. President Johnson quoted by Zigler and Anderson, "Idea Whose Time Had Come," 16.

94. Caldwell, "Decade of Intervention Programs," 495–96.

95. Lois-Ellen Datta, "Research as Head Start's Informing Vine," in *Proceedings, 1991 Conference, Plenary Session, New Directions in Child and Family Research: Shaping Head Start in the 1990s,* ed. R. Robinson et al. (Washington, D.C., 1992), 17.

96. Zigler and Anderson, "Idea Whose Time Had Come," 16, 74–75.

97. Sandra Scarr and R. A. Weinberger, "Rediscovering Old Truths; or, a Word by the Wise Is Sometimes Lost," *AP* 32(1977): 681.

98. Edward Zigler and Sally J. Styfco, *Head Start and Beyond* (New Haven, 1993), 491.

99. Edward Zigler, "Reinstituting the White House Conference on Children," *AJO* 73(1993).

100. Edward Zigler and Sally J. Styfco, "Using Research and Theory to Justify and Inform Head Start Expansion," *Social Policy Report* 7, no. 2 (1993): 4–5.

Index

AAUW, 32, 55, 151, 152–53, 319

Abbott, Edith, 84, 101, 193–94, 228, 229, 242, 244, 249, 296n10, 335n20

Abbott, Grace: on aid to dependent children, 250–51; and child labor, 92, 229, 239; as Children's Bureau chief, 30, 93, 101, 163, 193, 226–51, 327n81; death of, 251; education of, 228; family background and youth of, 228; illnesses of, 249, 251; and immigrants, 228–29; on juvenile courts, 240; leadership style of, 229, 352n84; and National Conference of Social Work (NCSW), 229, 230; and nursery schools, 327n81, 353n84; as pacifist, 226; on poverty, 238, 247–48; and President's Committee on Economic Security, 249–50; resignation of, from Children's Bureau, 249; and settlement house movement, 229; at University of Chicago, 249, 251; and Washington Child Research Center, 242, 352–53n84; and White House Conferences on children, 242, 242–46, 301n89

Abbott, John, 16, 275n16

Addams, Jane: and Abbott sisters, 229; on adolescence, 67–68; and child welfare reform, 21, 64, 65, 100; and Children's Bureau, 77, 83; on civic housekeeping, 63; on juvenile delinquency, 103; on Lathrop, 101–2; on local government, 85; and Meyer, 109; as pacifist, 226; and playground movement, 67, 68; and presidential nomination of T. Roosevelt, 279n72; scholarship on, 101; and settlement house movement, 25, 27, 28; on social work in 1920s, 227; on women's clubs, 104

Adler, Felix, 55, 56

Adler, Herman, 203, 215

Adolescence, 39, 57, 67–69, 165–66, 235, 324n46, 324–25n54. *See also* Juvenile delinquency

Adoption, 240, 241

Advisory Committee on Emergency Nursery School Education, 170, 327n81

African Americans, 97, 166, 231, 255, 257, 325n55, 348n33, 353n92

Agricultural experiment stations and extension service, 118–19, 319n87

Agriculture Department, U.S., 99, 119, 241–42

Aid to dependent children, 250–51, 355–56n132

Ainsworth, Mary, 254, 261, 326n69, 359n29

Aldrich, C. Anderson, 218, 289n19, 326n69, 326n71

Allen, Frederick, 210–13, 260

AMA, 231, 242, 250, 288n4

American Academy of Pediatrics, 219, 260

American Association of University Women (AAUW), 32, 55, 151, 152–53, 319

American Journal of Orthopsychiatry, 6, 203, 263–64, 266, 272n4

American Medical Association (AMA), 231, 242, 250, 288n4

American Orthopsychiatry Association (AOA), 6, 203–4, 263–64, 272n4, 326n71, 336n33, 339n59

American Pediatric Society, 52, 218–19, 288n4

American Psychiatric Association, 203, 207, 260, 262

American Psychological Association, 36, 43, 154, 284n50

American Red Cross, 144, 314n28

American Social Science Association (ASSA), 24–28, 32, 41–42

Anderson, John, 47, 157, 160, 167, 319n91, 321n14, 325n55, 325n67, 344n84, 353n92

Annie E. Casey Foundation, 257, 266

AOA. *See* American Orthopsychiatry Association (AOA)

ASSA, 24–28, 32, 41–42

Atlanta University, 166

Attachment theory, 254, 261

Babies. *See* Infants

Baker, Harvey H., 114–15, 116

Baker, Josephine, 95, 99, 296n1

Baldwin, Bird, 134, 135, 146, 155–57, 160, 180, 286n92, 314n17, 316n49, 321n14

Baldwin, James Mark, 40, 41, 67, 68, 78, 146, 253, 284n50

Bayley, Nancy, 163, 323n26, 324n38, 325n68

Beard, Mary, 102

Beecher, Catherine, 18, 275n19

Beers, Clifford, 110–11

Behaviorism, 175, 208–9, 215, 236, 329n7. *See also* Conditioning; Watson, John B.

Bender, Lauretta, 260

Berkeley Institute of Child Welfare Research, 147, 165–67, 255, 316n56, 321n14, 323n26

Binet, Alfred, 44

Birney, Alice, 21, 51–52, 56, 57, 121

Birth registrations, 85–86, 238, 297n23, 309n22

Blacks. *See* African Americans

Blatz, William, 161, 179, 321n14

Boas, Franz, 42, 48, 286n92

Boring, E. G., 154, 286n86

Bowlby, John, 220, 254, 261, 345n105, 359n29

Breckinridge, Sophonisba P., 84, 228, 290–91n42, 296n10, 319n87

Brennemann, Joseph, 185, 218

Bronfenbrenner, Urie, 254, 360n47

Bronner, Augusta, 109, 114, 193, 335n18

Bruch, Hilda, 185, 236

Bruner, Jerome, 253

Burnham, John, 65, 292n19

Bush Foundation, 259, 360n47
Bushnell, Rev. Horace, 17, 51, 310n38

Caldwell, Bettye, 268
Carnegie Corporation, 257, 266
Cattell, James McKeen, 43, 44, 143,
    284n50, 286n92
Census Bureau, 81, 82, 247, 297n23
Chess, Stella, 236
Chicago Juvenile Protective Association,
    20, 104, 105
Chicago School of Civics and Philan-
    thropy, 84, 105, 296n10
Child analysis, 259–60
Child Development, 6, 167, 168, 203, 255,
    256, 267, 272n4, 325n63, 356n5
Child development institutes, 146–48,
    158–64, 166–70, 173, 255–56, 316n56,
    319n91, 321–22n14, 345n110. See also
    Iowa Child Welfare Research Station;
    Yale Clinic of Child Development
Child development research: in academic
    settings, 252; on adolescence, 165–66,
    324n46, 324–25n54; and child develop-
    ment institutes, 158–64, 166–70, 255–
    56; and Children's Bureau, 241–42; co-
    twin control technique, 174, 183; and
    Commonwealth Fund, 216; cross-sec-
    tional studies, 160, 169, 260–61; early
    consequences of philanthropic child
    study programs, 167–70; in Europe,
    162; focus and topics of, 160–62, 253–
    55; and General Education Board
    (GEB), 164–67; Gesell's contributions
    to, 174; goals and purposes of, 7–9, 116,
    154, 156–57; and Laura Spelman Rock-
    efeller Memorial (LSRM), 10, 145, 153–
    54, 158–64; obstacles to, 151–52, 154;
    prenatal and infant research, 165, 253–
    54; and social policy, 258–59; training
    fellowships in, 156, 157; and women,
    156, 163, 257. See also Iowa Child Wel-
    fare Research Station; Longitudinal

studies; National Research Council
    Committee on Child Development
    (NRCCD); Society for Research in
    Child Development (SRCD)
Child guidance movement: affiliations
    and sponsors of clinics, 198, 338n45,
    340n73; British observers on U.S.
    movement, 198–99; case records from,
    199–201, 210–12, 339n52; and Com-
    monwealth Fund, 10–11, 106, 111, 115,
    165, 196–99, 205–8, 213–14, 219–22,
    261, 317n56, 324–25n54, 345n110; con-
    tributions of, to child and adult psychi-
    atry, 222–25; court referrals to child
    guidance clinics, 197, 338n39; critics of,
    213; definition of, 3; early child guid-
    ance clinics, 84, 140, 272n6; in Europe,
    10–11, 259–60; evolution of child psy-
    chiatry from, 8, 207–8; founding of, 2;
    funding for, 220, 221; goals of, 7, 116,
    212–14, 340n79; in Great Britain, 219–
    20, 346n123; habit clinics for preschool
    children, 204–5, 235; and Judge Baker
    Foundation, 114–16; legacy of, 222; lo-
    cations of child guidance clinics, 197,
    221, 337n36, 346n121; Meyer's influence
    on, 109–11; in 1930s, 220–21; and pedi-
    atrics, 163, 174–75, 198, 216–19, 323n35,
    326n71; problems of children treated at
    child guidance clinics, 199–201, 338–
    39n50; and psychoanalytic theory,
    259–60; and psychotherapy, 209–13,
    260, 340–41n4, 342n39; and research,
    214–16; shift from behaviorism to dy-
    namic psychiatry in, 208–10; 1950s,
    259–63; statistics on, 3, 140, 205, 220,
    221, 346nn120–121; and sympathetic
    approach to troubled children, 201–3;
    team approach in clinics, 115–16, 193,
    210, 221, 223, 346n120; timeline on, 5–
    6; and treatment of parents, 209–10.
    See also Child psychiatry
Child labor: and Grace Abbott, 229; and

Child labor (*continued*)
 Children's Bureau, 91, 92, 227, 229,
  230, 238–39; constitutional amendment on, 227, 238, 239; in Great Depression, 239; and Hall, 69; laws on,
  74, 92, 227, 229, 230, 238; research on,
  238–39; strike by children, 239; and
  White House Conferences on children,
  77; and women reformers and women's
  organizations, 64, 290n36, 294n54. *See
  also* National Child Labor Committee
  (NCLC)
Child Labor Act, 92, 229, 230, 238
Child psychiatry: in Britain, 346n123; case
  history in, 210–12; compared with
  adult psychiatry, 202–3; contributions
  of child guidance to, 8, 207–8, 222–23;
  need for, 344n87; in 1950s and 1960s,
  259–61; in nineteenth century, 191; and
  pediatrics, 217–19; principles of, 211;
  and psychoanalytic theory, 259–60;
  purpose of, 213; recognition of, as official subspecialty of psychiatry, 207,
  340n2; settings for, 340n2; shift from
  behaviorism to dynamic psychiatry in,
  208–10; textbook on, 219; training in,
  217, 219, 341n8; and treatment of parents, 209–10. *See also* Child guidance
  movement
Child psychology, 154, 162, 163, 167–68,
  324n39, 326n69. *See also* Child development headings
Child rearing: before Civil War, 16–19;
  and corporal punishment, 51; dissemination of literature on, 18–19; in early
  America, 15, 53; and Enlightenment, 17;
  farming and automobile analogies for,
  50, 53, 122, 127; Gesell on, 183–86; Hall
  on, 50–52; Holt on, 50, 52–54, 93, 149,
  234, 254, 289n18; literature on, in late
  1920s and 1930s, 171–72, 234–37; and
  parent education, 54–56; scientific
  child rearing, 49–50, 52–54, 120–21,

149–50; Watson on, 128, 149, 254,
  318n71, 320n100. *See also* Motherhood;
  Parent education
Child Study Association of America, 55,
  56, 152
Child study movement, 2–3, 5, 8, 30, 34–
  48, 60, 61, 78, 127, 146, 307n1
Child Welfare Bulletin, 139
Children: agricultural analogies on, 50,
  53, 122, 127; conservation analogy for,
  128; legal issues concerning, 240–41,
  250; moral character of, 17–18; musical
  abilities of, 136, 312n89; population statistics on, 243; precocity of, 253–54;
  psychopathology of, 260; ratio of
  adults to, 313n1; resiliency of, 254–55;
  romantic views of, 17, 34, 38, 46, 50,
  283n35. *See also* Child rearing; Infants;
  Preschool children
Children's Bureau, U.S.: Abbott as chief
  of, 30, 93, 101, 163, 193, 226–51, 327n81;
  and birth registrations, 85–86, 238,
  297n23, 309n22; budget and staff for, 4,
  75, 83, 87, 96, 101, 140, 227, 230, 272n7,
  301n81; and child labor, 91, 92, 227,
  229, 230, 238–39; critics and opponents of, 42, 71–72, 81–82, 226–28,
  242–45, 301n81; and definition of children, 296n6; Eliot as chief of, 249;
  founding of, 3, 61, 73, 78, 82–83, 140;
  and Hoover, 242–47, 353n93; infant
  mortality research by, 8, 85, 86–88,
  95, 238, 297n28, 298n29, 298n31; and
  juvenile courts, 239–40; juvenile
  delinquency research by, 91, 239–40,
  351n67, 351n73; Lathrop as chief of, 9,
  30, 71, 83–102, 226, 229, 234, 237, 266;
  law on, 81–83, 87, 230, 296n6, 299n54;
  and legal issues concerning children,
  240–41, 250; Lenroot as chief of, 91,
  188, 249–51, 264; letters to, 88–89, 92–
  93, 300n64, 300n69; loss of functions
  of, since 1935, 264; maternal mortality

research by, 88–91, 95, 238; and New Deal, 228, 246–49; and norms on physical development of children, 160; and nursery schools, 327n81; and parent education, 92, 92–95; and preschool children, 96, 301n82; proposal for, 73–75, 77, 295n79; and psychological guidance for parents, 235–37; publications and films of, 88, 93–95, 98–99, 205, 234–37, 300n64, 301n82, 301n92, 349nn40–41; purpose of, 3, 7, 75, 82–83, 229–30, 237; reporting function of, 92, 233–37, 266; research by, 4, 7, 10, 72, 84, 86–92, 116, 237–42, 246–48, 297n28, 298n31, 354n110; resignation of Lathrop from, 101; and rural areas, 88–90, 96, 99, 273n13; and Sheppard-Towner Act, 91, 96, 99–101, 227, 230–33; and Social Security Act Title V, 250; supporters of, 77, 82; timeline on, 5–6; and unemployment, 237–38, 246–48; and White House Conference on Child Health and Protection (1930), 227, 242–46; and White House Conference on Child Welfare Standards (1919), 97–99, 301n91; and women's organizations, 84–86, 96, 297n23; and World War I, 95–96, 301n89

Children's Bureau Act, 81–83, 87, 230, 266, 296n6, 299n54

Children's Defense Fund, 266

Children's Fund of Michigan (CFM), 7, 164, 221

Children's Health Insurance Program (CHIP), 269

Children's Institute (Clark University), 69–71

Children's Year, 92, 95–96, 135, 140, 301n82

CHIP, 269

Civic housekeeping, 63

Clark University, 35–36, 44, 46, 47, 69–73, 110, 146, 176, 293n40, 343n72

Columbia University, 40, 42–44, 56, 145, 165, 188, 219, 256. *See also* Teachers College child development institute

Committee on Child Development. *See* National Research Council Committee on Child Development (NRCCD)

Commonwealth Fund: and British child guidance clinics, 219–20; and child development research, 216; and child guidance clinics, 10–11, 106, 111, 115, 165, 194–96, 196–99, 205–8, 213–14, 219–22, 261, 317n56, 324–25n54, 335n16, 345n110; and child health programs, 217; and child study programs, 4, 86, 105; and Child Welfare League of America, 296n79; endowment for, 334n6; founding of, 9–10, 192, 336n33; goals of, 194, 335n20, 340n79; and juvenile delinquency prevention, 116, 192–94, 196–97, 205–6; and Laura Spelman Rockefeller Memorial (LSRM), 194–96, 336n31, 336n33; and parent education, 148, 208; and psychiatric education, 219, 341n8; publications of, 224; and research, 214–16, 303n9; on schools' role, 204; Smith as director of, 194, 206, 208; timeline on, 5, 6; and Visiting Teacher Program, 205

Community Mental Health Services Act, 262

Conditioning, 42, 149, 153, 169, 170, 235. *See also* Behaviorism

Conway, Jill Ker, 63

Cornell University, 45, 74, 165, 219, 359n32

Costin, Lela B., 229

Cott, Nancy F., 18, 275n18, 276n21, 276n27

Creak, Mildred, 220

Crime, psychopathology of, 111–12

Cultural lag, 143, 149–51, 318n76–77

Daniels, Amy L., 136

Darling, Jay Norwood ("Ding"), 131, 311n63

Darwin, Charles, 22, 32, 37–38, 45, 283n32

Datta, Lois-Ellin, 268

Davis, Allen, 66, 279n72

Davis, James J., 245, 353n93

Decker, Sarah Platt, 64

Delinquency. *See* Juvenile delinquency; Juvenile justice system

Despert, Louise, 201, 260

Developmental psychology, 160, 215. *See also* Child development research

Devine, Edward, 73, 75

Dewey, John, 29, 40, 43–46, 48, 67, 68, 109, 145, 189

Domesticity, 16–22, 57. *See also* Motherhood

Dorr, Rheta Childe, 62

Dreiser, Theodore, 76–77, 295n73

Drummond, Henry, 22, 38

Dummer, Ethel: and American Orthopsychiatry Association, 203; and child development courses, 299n50; and child guidance clinics, 102, 105, 339n51; and Children's Bureau, 9, 89–91, 105; and elementary schools, 107, 304n22; family of, 104; on feminism, 20; funding of research by, 104–5, 216; and Hall, 294n55; and Judge Baker Foundation, 335n16; and juvenile delinquency research, 9, 104, 105, 108, 109, 273n12, 304n28; and Juvenile Protective Association, 104, 105; and term *psychopath,* 304n20; and Van Waters, 343n72; and White House Conferences on children, 299n50

Education. *See* Higher education for women; Kindergartens; Nursery school movement

Educational psychology, 42–44, 48

Eliot, Martha, 94, 157, 234, 242, 249–50, 326n71

Emotions, 32, 38, 46, 51, 288n8

Employment of children. *See* Child labor

Employment of women, 22, 59–60, 64, 70, 74, 277n39

Environment versus heredity, 18–19, 130, 152, 175, 177–80, 182, 186–90, 215, 255, 317n67

Erikson, Erik, 253, 265

Eugenics, 70, 125, 128–30, 135, 177–78, 180, 293n41, 311n61, 331n37

Euthenics, 125, 130

Evolutionary theory, 37–38, 44–46, 283n35

Experimental psychology, 31–33, 35–38, 42–45, 145, 147, 282–83n29. *See also* Psychology

Farmers' Institutes, 121, 122

Farrand, Max, 335n18, 335n21

Federal Emergency Relief Administration (FERA), 170, 250, 354n107

Federation for Child Study, 55, 152

Fels Institute, 148, 164, 256, 323n26

Feminism, 19–21, 24–26, 65, 70, 133, 151, 276–77n27, 294n55, 312n79

FERA, 170, 250, 354n107

Foster care, 77, 241, 319n80

Foundation for Child Development (FCD), 257, 258

Frank, Lawrence K.: career of, 145, 164, 165; and child development research, 158–60, 162–63, 167, 168, 188, 241–42, 324–25n54, 331n37, 336n32; on child rearing, 16; and Children's Bureau research, 241–42; on cultural lag, 150, 151, 318nn76–77; and General Education Board (GEB), 165, 166–67; on heredity versus environment, 317n67; and home economics, 319n87; and Laura Spelman Rockefeller Memorial (LSRM), 4, 145–48, 152, 153, 155, 158–59, 162–63, 195, 241, 316n56; marriages and children of, 149, 318n71; and National Research Council Committee on Child Development, 155, 156; and nursery school movement, 159, 322n20; on outstanding development of 1920s, 194–95; on parent education, 159, 318–19n80; parents of, 145, 315n44; on preventive politics, 195; on ratio of children to adults, 313n1; and Spelman Fund, 164; and Yale Clinic of Child Development, 175, 329n6

Freedman, Estelle, 27

Freud, Anna, 202, 259–60

Freud, Sigmund, 2, 46–47, 51, 78, 105, 109, 208, 329n7. *See also* Psychoanalysis

Froebel, Friedrich, 34, 67

Fuller, Margaret, 218

Functionalism, 43–45, 46, 286n86

Galton, Francis, 43, 44, 128

Gender research, 254

General Education Board (GEB), 6, 164–67, 195–96, 324n46, 336n32

General Federation of Women's Clubs (GFWC), 24, 63–64, 85–86, 96

Genetic psychology, 36, 38–41, 45

Gesell, Arnold: on adoption, 241; books and films by, 174, 176, 180, 181–85, 189, 190, 236, 328–29n3; career of, 176, 177; on child development as discipline, 174–75, 217; child-rearing advice by, 183–86; childhood and early adulthood of, 175–77; and clinical observation, 181, 331n43; contributions of, 174, 182–83; and correlation of physical and mental growth in children, 160; on democracy, 175, 182, 187, 188, 190; and developmental diagnosis, 174, 180, 188, 331n40; education of, 47, 176–77, 321n14; and Gesell Institute, 174, 332n47; and Hall, 176, 189; and heredity versus environment, 175, 177–80, 182, 186, 187–90; Lincoln biography by, 190; on maturation, 186–87; on nursery schools, 179; personality of,

187–88; on playground movement, 67; and preschool children, 178–82, 330–31n26, 331n37; on scope of clinical medicine, 215; writing style of, 329n9; and Yale Clinic of Child Development, 78, 160, 173, 175, 178–82, 328n2, 329n6. *See also* Yale Clinic of Child Development

Gesell, Beatrice Chandler, 67, 176, 330n13

Gesell, Gerhard, 176, 188, 329n9, 330nn11–12

Gesell Institute, 174, 332n47

Glueck, Bernard, 111–12, 193, 196, 304n22, 335n18, 337n35, 339n59

Goddard, Henry H., 44, 112, 129, 177, 286n92, 306n53, 314n17

Goldfarb, William, 260, 361n56

Goodenough, Florence, 47

Great Britain, 198–99, 222, 223, 346n123

Great Depression, 30, 164, 170–71, 220–21, 228, 232, 239, 246–49, 354n110, 355n119

Guidance Study, 166, 323n26

Gulick, Luther, 67, 293n30

Habit clinics, 204–5, 235

Hagen, John W., 256, 326n69, 359nn31–32

Hall, G. Stanley: on adolescence, 39, 57, 67, 68, 69; and applied psychology, 142; autobiography of, 47; baby biographies by, 281n2; career of, in experimental psychology, 35–36, 37, 42; on child welfare reform, 65; on child rearing, 50–52; and child study movement, 2–3, 5, 8, 30, 34–48, 60, 78, 127, 146, 307n1; and Children's Institute at Clark University, 69–71; critics of, 40–42; death of, 47, 176; and deaths of wife and daughter, 282n26; early career of, in psychology, 32–34; on emotions, 38, 46, 51, 288n8; and eugenics movement, 293n41; and evolutionary theory, 37–

Hall, G. Stanley (*continued*)
38, 44, 46, 283n35; on feminism, 70,
294n55; final years of, 46–47; and genetic psychology, 36, 38–41, 45; and
Gesell, 176, 189; and health services in
schools, 287n1; influence of, on National Congress of Mothers, 57; on juvenile delinquency, 68–69, 293n40;
and kindergarten movement, 55; and
Laura Spelman Rockefeller Memorial
(LSRM), 146; legacy of, 47–48; on
mental testing, 44; and Meyer, 110; and
parent education, 148, 169; on pity, 71;
and play and recreation movement, 66,
67, 68, 292–93n30; on potential of social sciences, 143; on science and religion, 283n39; and scientific pedagogy,
33, 34–36; and social Darwinism, 33–
34, 69, 70–71; and social reform, 9,
60–61, 68–69, 273n12; on stage theory
of child development, 51, 52, 253
Hamilton, Alice, 98
Handbook of Child Psychology, 162, 163,
165, 167, 325n63, 325n67, 356n7
Harding, Warren G., 101, 140
Harkness, Anna M. Richardson, 9–10,
192
Harris, Dale, 307–8n4, 319n91
Harris, Irving B., 259, 360n47
Harrison, Elizabeth, 55
Harvard University, 33, 165, 166, 217, 219
Head Start, 171, 174, 179, 258–59, 266–
69, 285n63, 330–31n26, 363n84
Health services for children, 96, 99–101,
140, 217, 227, 230–33, 250, 287n1,
298n42. *See also* Public health; Shep-
pard-Towner Maternity and Infant
Protection Act (1921)
Healy, William: and American Orthopsy-
chiatry Association, 203, 339n59; books
by, 104, 108–9, 304n28; and child psychiatric clinics, 114–16, 192, 193, 199,
202, 335n16; contributions of, 304n22;

education of, 106; family background
and youth of, 106; Freud's influence
on, 47; juvenile delinquency research
by, 9, 44, 103–9, 113–14, 273n12, 305n39,
306n53, 330n17, 351n67; lack of academic status for, 217; on *psychopathic*
as term, 304n20
Hearst, William Randolph, 56
Heredity versus environment, 130, 152,
175, 177–80, 182, 186–90, 215, 255,
317n67
Hewitt, Nancy, 17
Higher education for women, 15, 21, 27–
28, 57, 133, 163, 279n77, 312n71, 319n85
Hillis, Cora Bussey: and birth registrations, 309n22; on child rearing, 49–50,
120–21; and child welfare reform generally, 57, 59, 140; and Children's Palace
at Philadelphia Exposition (1926), 135,
320n1; and Children's Year, 301n82;
death of, 135; deaths of children of, 59,
120, 308n13; family background and
youth of, 119–20; and Iowa Child Welfare Research Station, 9, 10, 59, 78, 117,
119–28, 130–35, 145–46, 152, 273n12,
308–9n19, 309n21, 312nn73–74; leadership skills of, 133–34, 315n47; mothers' club manual by, 21; and National
Congress of Mothers, 56, 120, 121–22;
and Seashore, 130, 133, 146, 309n24
Hispanics, 231, 255, 257
Hofer-Proudfoot, Andrea, 22
Hollingworth, Leta, 235, 326n75
Holt, L. Emmett, 50, 52–54, 93–95, 149,
204, 234, 254, 289n18
Home economics, 64, 119, 147, 151, 287n2,
319n87
Hoover, Herbert: on child health, 234;
and child study generally, 1; and Children's Bureau, 242–47, 353n93; and
Iowa Child Welfare Research Station,
135, 146; on poverty, 141, 149, 246,
347n4; and research on U.S. social

trends, 142, 164; and Sheppard-Towner Act, 232; and White House Conference on Child Health and Protection (1930), 4, 140, 149, 242–47
Hopkins, Harry, 170, 327n81
Horn, Margo, 193, 212, 335n20, 342n39, 346n123, 361–62n60
Hospitalism, 260
Hull House. *See* Settlement house movement
Hull-House Maps and Papers (HHMP), 29, 74, 177–78

ICIS, 256
Ilg, Frances, 183, 332n47
Illegitimacy, 91, 216, 241
Illinois, 56, 63, 84, 109–10, 215, 272nn6–7, 297n16
Immigrants, 27–28, 33, 94, 98, 228–29
The Individual Delinquent (Healy), 104, 108–9, 304n28
Infant mortality, 8, 70, 75, 85–88, 95, 99, 145, 232, 238, 297–98nn28–29, 298n31, 301n94, 348n33
Infants: baby biographies, 31–32, 55, 281n2; baby contests, 122, 129; Baby Week, 92, 95, 96, 301n77; feeding of, 52–53, 54, 217; health of, 99–101, 140, 227, 230–33, 250; research on, 165, 188–89, 253–54
Institute of Child Guidance, 208, 210, 215, 216, 220
Intelligence. *See* Mental testing
International Society for Infant Studies (ICIS), 256
International Society for the Study of Behavioral Development (ISSBD), 256
Iowa, 56, 126, 132
Iowa Child Welfare Research Station: budget and funding for, 131, 135, 140, 145–46, 272n7, 316n49; campaigns for, 121–23, 125–28, 130–32, 312nn73–74; closing of, 256; and colleges, 122–25; directors and staff of, 134, 136, 170, 321n14; early years of, 134–36; environmental bias of, 130, 152; founding of, 3, 5, 9, 117–18, 140, 272n6; goals and purpose of, 3, 134, 146, 152, 307n1; and Hillis, 9, 10, 59, 78, 117, 119–28, 130–35, 145–46, 152, 273n12, 308–9n19, 309n21, 312nn73–74; law on, 131–32, 311n64; name chosen for, 125; and nursery school laboratories, 10; organization of women in support for, 121–22; and parent education, 319n91; and preschool children, 136, 146, 180; reasons for Iowa location of, 118–19; research and training by, 135–36, 170, 267, 312n89, 316n49; and Rockefeller Foundation, 145–46, 315n47; and rural women, 132–34, 273n13; and Seashore, 123–28, 130, 132–36, 152, 273n12, 307n3, 309n24, 312n89; State University of Iowa committee on, 124–25
Iowa State College of Agriculture and Mechanic Arts, 122, 132–33, 312n71
ISSBD, 256

James, William: death of, 78; on experimental psychology, 37, 38; and functionalism, 44–46; and habit-training, 204; and Hall, 33, 37, 41; and Healy's study of juvenile delinquents, 105, 273n12, 305n39; on mental hygiene, 111; and Meyer, 109, 111; on play and recreation, 67, 68; and Thorndike, 42, 43
Johns Hopkins University, 35, 37, 43, 110, 149, 157, 218, 219
Johnson, Lyndon B., 267, 268
Jones, Harold, 161, 271n1, 321n14, 325n64, 325n68
Jones, Mary Cover, 159, 170
Josselyn, Irene, 262
Judge Baker Foundation, 109, 114–16, 193, 199–201, 211–13, 263, 307n72, 335n16, 346n133

Jung, Carl Gustav, 220, 286n92

Juvenile delinquency: and Grace Abbott, 229; Addams on, 103; causes of, 108, 113, 240; Children's Bureau's research on, 91, 239–40, 351n67, 351n73; and Commonwealth Fund, 116, 192–94, 196–97, 205–6; Goddard on, 112, 306n53; Hall on, 68–69, 293n40; Healy's research on, 9, 44, 103–9, 113–14, 273n12, 305n39, 306n53, 330n17, 351n67; prevention of, 65, 116, 192–94, 196–97, 205–6, 250; scientific research on, 68–69, 293n40. *See also* Juvenile justice system

Juvenile justice system, 57, 59, 60, 65, 69, 84, 103, 104, 229, 239–40, 290n36, 302n2. *See also* Juvenile delinquency

Juvenile Protective Association, 20, 104, 105

Juvenile Research Bureau, 112, 306n53

Kanner, Leo, 115, 182, 214, 216, 219, 236, 260

Kelley, Florence, 30, 73–75, 82, 100, 101, 229, 294n54

Kenworthy, Marion, 196

Kevles, Daniel, 310n47, 311n61

Kindergartens, 23–24, 33, 34, 49, 55, 65, 159

Klein, Melanie, 202

Kraditor, Aileen, 20

Kuhn, Anne, 17

Labor Department, U.S., 74, 242, 264, 347n1, 353n93

Labor laws. *See* Child labor; Employment of women

Land-grant colleges, 118–19, 132–33, 308nn4–7, 308n9, 316n56, 359n3. *See also* specific universities

Lanham Act, 171, 328n84

Lathrop, Julia: and Abbott sisters, 229; achievements of, 101–2; Addams's bi-ography of, 101–2; advisors for, 273n12; career of, 63, 84, 101; as Children's Bureau chief, 9, 30, 71, 83–102, 226, 229, 234, 237, 266; critics of, 71–72, 226; death of, 101; and Hall's Children's Institute, 71; on higher education for women, 151; and Hillis's work in Iowa, 122; leadership style of, 229; and Meyer, 109; on pity, 71; and psychiatry, 240; resignation of, from Children's Bureau, 101; and scientific findings, 25; and women's organizations, 84–86, 96, 297n16, 297n23

Laura Spelman Rockefeller Memorial (LSRM): anonymity policy of, 144, 317n56; charter of, 144; and child development institutes, 47, 146, 147–48, 158–64, 166, 173, 272n10, 316n56, 345n110; and child study programs, 4, 16, 86, 118, 145, 195–96, 198; and Commonwealth Fund, 194–96, 336n31, 336n33; dissolution of, 157, 163; endowment for, 144, 334n6; founding of, 10, 336n33; goals of, 153–54, 155, 194; and Hall's child study movement, 146; and Iowa Child Welfare Research Station, 118, 146, 316n49; and National Research Council Committee on Child Development, 321n4; in 1920s, 47, 144–48; and parent education, 47, 148, 152–54, 156; research funded by, 10, 145, 153–54, 158–59, 162–63; staff of, 152; timeline on, 5, 6; and Yale Clinic of Child Development, 147, 173, 175, 181. *See also* Frank, Lawrence K.; Ruml, Beardsley

Lee, Joseph, 66, 68, 293n30

Lenroot, Katherine, 88, 91, 98, 102, 188, 239–40, 249–51, 264, 355–56n132

Levine, Samuel, 218–19

Levy, David, 202, 208–9, 215, 219, 222, 261, 263, 339n59, 344n84, 361n56

Lewin, Kurt, 170

Lindeman, Eduard, 149–50

Locke, John, 45, 55, 66
Longitudinal studies, 160–61, 164–66, 169, 197–98, 216, 218, 260–61, 323n26, 338n41. *See also* Child development research
Lowell, Josephine Shaw, 27
Lowes, Catherine, 184–85
Lowrey, Lawson C., 107, 192, 203, 208, 213, 215, 339n59, 361n56
LSRM. *See* Laura Spelman Rockefeller Memorial (LSRM)
Lundberg, Emma, 239–40
Lynd, Helen Merrill, 149, 326n71

MacBride, Thomas H., 123, 124
MacLean, George F., 122, 308–9n19
Mahler, Margaret, 260
Mahoney, Margaret, 102
Mann, Mrs. Horace, 60
Maternalism, 277n27
Maturation, 186–87
May, Henry, 44, 143
McCall, Laura, 17
McCollum, E. V., 157, 326n71
McGraw, Myrtle, 152, 187, 188, 189, 318n71, 326n69
Mead, George Herbert, 29, 109
Mead, Margaret, 48, 326n71
Meckel, Richard, 18, 87, 88, 233, 276n21
Medicine. *See* Health services for children; Pediatrics
Meek, Lois. *See* Stolz, Lois Meek
Meigs, Grace, 89–90, 95, 298n42
Mendenhall, Dorothy, 94
Menninger, Karl, 203
Mental health services, 261–63. *See also* Child guidance movement; Child psychiatry
Mental hygiene movement, 78, 84, 109–14, 192, 195, 212–13, 224, 236
Mental retardation, 112, 129, 177
Mental testing, 43, 44, 48, 78, 106, 113, 129, 135, 142

Merrill-Palmer Institute, 10, 146, 147, 164, 256, 359n32
Meyer, Adolph: on child guidance movement, 213; and dynamic psychiatry, 208, 259; Freud's influence on, 47, 286n92; and habit-training, 204; and Hall, 48; and Healy, 105, 107, 305n33; influence of, on child guidance movement, 109–11; and National Committee for Mental Hygiene (NCMH), 212–13; naturalistic methods of, 41; and pragmatism and instrumentalism, 305n33; and Society for Research in Child Development (SRCD), 326n71; symposium including, 304n22; trainees of, 210, 213; and women reformers, 273n12
Midwives, 230
Minnesota Child Development Institute. *See* University of Minnesota
Mitchell, Lucy Sprague, 145
Morton, Katherine, 90, 91
Motherhood: and child-rearing advice in nineteenth century, 18–19, 150; Christian motherhood, 18; after Civil War, 19–20; before Civil War, 16–18, 150; and domestic education, 150–51; Hall on, 50–52; Holt on, 50, 52–54, 93, 149, 289n18; in late-nineteenth century, 20–22; and maternal mortality, 88–91, 95, 238; organized motherhood and parent education, 54–56; public motherhood for unmarried professional women, 59–60; Republican Mother, 15–16, 21, 57, 65, 274–75n7, 275n19; scientific motherhood, 49–50, 52–54; and separate spheres doctrine, 16–17, 19, 274n6; and social feminism, 19–20, 151, 312n79. *See also* Child rearing; Mothers' clubs; National Congress of Mothers; Parent education
Mothers' clubs, 18–19, 21, 49, 55, 57, 275n20, 276n21

Mothers' pension movement, 77, 247, 250–51, 296n82, 300n64, 318–19n80
Muncy, Robyn, 96, 296n10
Munsterberg, Hugo, 40–41

National Child Labor Committee (NCLC), 56, 75, 82, 83, 104, 238, 295n68
National Committee for Mental Hygiene (NCMH), 78, 84, 111–13, 116, 191–93, 195, 196, 208, 336n31
National Conference of Charities and Corrections (NCCC), 26, 28
National Conference of Social Work (NCSW), 97, 114, 229, 230, 238, 246
National Congress of Mothers, 21, 22, 48–51, 53, 55–60, 120–22, 127, 151, 290–91n42, 297n23
National Consumers' League, 64, 74, 75, 294n54
National Council on Parent Education, 152, 156
National Education Association (NEA), 34, 35, 36, 39, 47
National Institute of Child Health and Development (NICHD), 266
National Institute of Mental Health (NIMH), 261, 265–66
National Institutes of Health, 253, 266
National Mental Health Act (1946), 261
National Probation Association (NPA), 107, 239
National Research Council (NRC), 6, 47, 136, 142, 252, 313–14n17
National Research Council Committee on Child Development (NRCCD): and Children's Palace at Philadelphia Exposition (1926), 135; conferences of, 157, 161–62, 243, 256; founding of, 155, 336n33; funding for, 166, 321n4; membership of, 156, 157; publications of, 157, 166; purpose and functions of,

156–57, 168, 258; topics addressed by, 161–62; and White House Conference on Children and Youth (1930), 157, 243
National Science Foundation, 255, 266
Native Americans, 231, 255
Nature-nurture controversy, 130, 152, 175, 177–80, 182, 186–90, 215, 255, 317n67
NCCC. See National Conference of Charities and Corrections (NCCC)
NCLC. See National Child Labor Committee (NCLC)
NCMH. See National Committee for Mental Hygiene (NCMH)
NCSW. See National Conference of Social Work (NCSW)
NEA. See National Education Association (NEA)
New Deal, 228, 246–49
New Woman, 62–63, 70
New York, 27, 82, 95, 99, 196, 294n54, 296n1
NICHD. See National Institute of Child Health and Development (NICHD)
NIMH. See National Institute of Mental Health (NIMH)
Nixon, Richard, 264, 265
Northwestern University, 256, 299n50
NPA. See National Probation Association (NPA)
NRC. See National Research Council (NRC)
NRCCD. See National Research Council Committee on Child Development (NRCCD)
Nursery school laboratories, 10, 124, 136, 146, 147, 242
Nursery school movement, 145, 159, 170–71, 179, 319n87, 322n20, 322n22, 327n81, 327–28n84, 353n84

Oakland Growth Study, 165–66, 323n26, 355n119

Parent education: and agricultural extension service, 119, 319n87; and Children's Bureau, 92–95; and Commonwealth Fund, 148, 208; and cultural lag, 149–51; in early twentieth century, 54–56; and Hall, 148, 169; and Laura Spelman Rockefeller Memorial (LSRM), 47, 148, 152–54, 156, 319n91; and mothers' clubs, 18–19, 21, 49, 55, 275n20, 276n21; in 1920s, 148–53; philanthropy for, 10, 153–54. *See also* Child rearing

Parents' Magazine, 2, 153, 171

Pediatrics, 48, 50, 52–54, 78, 98, 100, 163, 174–75, 198, 204, 216–19, 231–33, 245, 288n4, 289n19, 289n21, 323n35, 326n71, 329n5, 344n77, 344n82, 348–49n39

Peirce, Charles, 109

Perkins, Frances, 145, 249, 250

Pernick, Martin, 135, 276n27, 349n40

Phelps, Alice Cutting, 88–91, 298n42

Philadelphia Child Guidance Clinic, 202, 210, 212, 263, 338n39, 338n45, 339n55, 342n39

Philanthropy, 3–4, 6, 7, 9–10, 26–28, 83, 143–48, 167–70, 257–58, 279n66. *See also* specific foundations

Phillips, Deborah, 253

Piaget, Jean, 40, 162, 253, 332n49

Pittsburgh Survey, 29, 74

Plant, James, 203, 213, 218, 344n84

Play and recreation movement, 60, 65, 66–68, 292n26, 293n36

Poverty: Dummer's reactions to, 104; Frank's refusal to fund research on, 331n37; Gesell's study of, 179–80, 188; Hall on, 71; Hoover on, 141, 149, 246, 347n4; human frailty as cause of, 27; and infant mortality, 8, 87–88; and juvenile delinquency, 108, 113; Lathrop and Abbott on, 227, 238, 247–48, 351n73; and National Congress of Mothers, 57, 58; and "new psychology,"

227; in 1920s, 141–42; and settlement house movement, 27–28; social survey of, 28–29; studies of, in 1980s and 1990s, 267; and unemployment, 237–38, 246–48. *See also* Settlement house movement

Pragmatism, 45–46

Preschool children: benefits of companionship for, 322n22; and Children's Bureau, 96, 301n82; and General Education Board (GEB), 165; and Gesell, 178–82, 330–31n26, 331n37; habit clinics for, 204–5, 235; and Iowa Child Welfare Research Station, 136, 146, 180; mental growth of, 180; research on, in 1920s and early 1930s, 158–59; Seashore on, 127. *See also* Nursery school movement

Preyer, Wilhelm, 32, 35

Prostitution, 91, 129

Psychiatric social work, 47, 199, 205, 209, 210, 219, 220, 222, 224, 260, 306n62. *See also* Social work

Psychiatry: contributions of child guidance to, 222–23; development of, compared with child psychiatry, 202–3; Meyer's influence on, 109–11; in 1920s, 142; in nineteenth century, 191; and pediatrics, 217–19; and progressivism, 65, 292n19; and psychoanalytic theory, 259; training of psychiatrists, 210, 340n74, 341n8; during World War I, 112; during World War II, 261. *See also* Child psychiatry; Psychoanalysis; and specific psychiatrists

Psychoanalysis, 174, 175, 215, 259–60, 329n7. *See also* Freud, Sigmund

Psychology: applied psychology, 142–43; developmental psychology, 160, 215, 252–53; as discipline, 30, 31; educational psychology, 42–44, 48; and functionalism, 45; genetic psychology,

Psychology (*continued*)
36, 38–41, 45; Hall's early career in, 32–
34; and National Research Council,
313–14n17; in 1920s, 142–43; and progressivism, 65, 292n19; structural psychology, 45; training of psychologists,
210. *See also* Child psychology; Experimental psychology; Mental testing;
specific psychologists

Psychopathology: of children, 260; of
crime, 111–12; *psychopath* as term,
304n20; of soldiers, 112–13, 261, 306n58

Psychotherapy, 209–13, 260, 340–41n4,
342n39. *See also* Child guidance movement; Child psychiatry

Public health, 73, 89–90, 96, 99–101,
336n30. *See also* Health services for
children

Public Health Service, U.S., 86, 227, 244,
264, 300n64, 348n31

Rank, Otto, 208

Rankin, Jeannette, 100

Recreation. *See* Play and recreation movement

Republican Mother, 15–16, 21, 57, 65,
274–75n7, 275n19

Resiliency of children, 254–55

Reviews of Child Development Research,
258

Rexford, Eveoleen, 259

Richards, Esther L., 218, 344n84

Richmond, Julius, 217, 218, 263, 360n47

Richmond, Mary, 113–14, 305n30

Riis, Jacob, 21

Robins, Lee, 198, 253, 338n41

Rockefeller, John D., 10, 144, 152

Rockefeller, Vincent, 145–46

Rockefeller Foundation, 111, 144, 145–46,
163, 164–67, 192, 244, 315n47. *See also*
Laura Spelman Rockefeller Memorial
(LSRM)

Rogoff, Barbara, 254

Romanticism, 17, 34, 38, 46, 50, 283n35

Roosevelt, Franklin D., 228, 239, 249

Roosevelt, Theodore, 55, 73, 75–77, 81,
82, 122, 245, 279n72, 295n78

Rosenberg, Rosalind, 62

Rosenblatt, Bernard, 225, 259

Rosenthal, Marguerite, 240, 351n73

Ross, Dorothy, 37, 44, 51, 282n26, 283n35,
293n30, 294n55, 308n9

Rothman, David, 69, 293n40

Rothman, Sheila, 60, 99–100

Ruml, Beardsley, 144–48, 152–56, 162,
165, 206, 315n38, 316n50, 316n56, 324–
25n54

Rush, Benjamin, 16, 334n4

Russell Sage Foundation, 9, 27, 69, 83,
145, 277n38, 303n9, 315n38, 354n110

Rutter, Sir Michael, 261, 263

Ryan, Mary P., 17

Sage, Margaret Olivia, 9, 22, 277n38,
303n9

Salmon, Thomas, 111–12, 192–93, 204,
335n18

Sapir, Edward, 48, 326n71

Sarr, Sandra, 268

Schlossman, Steven L., 68, 290n36,
293n34

Sears, Robert, 252

Seashore, Carl Emil: career of, 123; on
child conservation, 128; children of,
123; at Clark University conference
(1909) featuring Freud, 286n92; environmental bias of, 130; euthenics, 125,
130; family background of, 123; and
Hillis, 130, 133, 146, 309n24; and Iowa
Child Welfare Research Station, 123–
28, 130, 132–36, 152, 273n12, 307n3,
309n24, 312n89; and musical abilities of
children, 136, 312n89; and National Research Council Committee on Child
Development, 155, 320n1; and negative
eugenics, 178; on preschool children,

127; on public attitude toward improving children, 117; on scientific study of children, 128, 142, 310n46; and women reformers, 133, 273n12; and women's involvement in child development research, 163, 324n38

Senn, Milton J. E., 153, 164, 173–74, 202, 217, 218, 328n2, 339n55, 344n82

Settlement house movement, 27–28, 29, 60, 62, 63, 66, 73, 84, 177–78, 229

Sewall, May Wright, 25

Sheppard-Towner Maternity and Infant Protection Act (1921), 5, 6, 91, 96, 99–101, 102, 140, 227, 230–33, 250

Sherbon, Florence Brown, 124–26

Shinn, Millicent, 32, 55

Siegel, Alberta, 258

Sing Sing study, 111–12

Skinner, B. F., 169

Sklar, Katherine, 29, 30, 74, 75, 277n27

Smith, Barry, 194, 195, 206, 208, 336n32, 337n35, 338–39n50, 340n79

Smith, Geddes, 209, 214–15, 223–24

Smith, Mary Roberts, 59

Smith College, 113

Smith-Lever Act, 99, 119, 308n7

Smith-Rosenberg, Carroll, 59–60, 64–65

Social Darwinism, 33–34, 45, 69, 70–71

Social feminism, 19–20, 65, 151, 276–77n27, 312n79

Social Policy Reports, 256

Social sciences, 3, 8–9, 24, 30, 60–61, 65, 142–43, 145, 315n38. *See also* Child development research; Psychology

Social Security Act, 4, 96, 228, 249–51, 355–56nn130–32

Social surveys, 28–30, 65, 74, 169, 227, 241, 246

Social work, 26, 28, 69, 78, 113–14, 152, 207–8, 217, 227, 240, 295n78, 304n22, 307n67. *See also* Psychiatric social work

Society for Adolescent Medicine (SAM), 256

Society for Behavioral and Developmental Pediatrics (SBDP), 256

Society for Research on Adolescence (SRA), 256

Society for Research in Child Development (SRCD): awards by, 359n29; Black Caucus of, 257; conferences of, 256; current programs of, 256–57; founding of, 6, 157, 272n4; Governing Council of, 168; membership of, 256, 272n4, 326n71; in 1940s, 252; officers of, 261, 263; public information provided by, 266; publications of, 256, 258; and social policy, 258

Society for the Study of Child Nature, 55

Society for the Study of Human Development (SSHD), 256

Sontag, Lester, 148, 323n26

Spelman Fund of New York, 164, 165

Spencer, Margaret Beale, 255

Spitz, Rene, 260, 361n56

Spock, Benjamin, 174, 217

SRA. *See* Society for Research on Adolescence (SRA)

Standards of child welfare, 97–99, 301n91

Stanford University, 160, 219

Stanley, Louise, 151, 241–42, 352n81

State University of Iowa, 117, 122, 123–25, 163, 165. *See also* Iowa Child Welfare Research Station

Stecher, Lorie I., 180

Stendler, Celia, 224

Stevenson, George S., 208, 209, 214–15, 220–24, 337n35, 338–39n50

Stevenson, Harold, 153, 169, 258, 320n100, 359n31

Stoddard, George, 170–71, 329n5

Stolz, Lois Meek, 16, 161, 170, 188–89, 242, 300n64, 319n85, 322n14, 322n20, 325n68, 328n84, 330n13, 334n95, 352–53n84

Stratton, George, 161–62

Stuart, Harold, 165, 326n71

Styco, Sally J., 268
Sugarman, Jules, 268
Swaim, Ginalie, 49

Taft, Jesse, 114, 199, 260
Taft, William Howard, 81–84, 347n1
Talbot, Emily, 32
Tarbell, Ida, 21
Teachers College child development institute, 147, 152, 156, 164, 167, 170, 256, 321n14
Temperance movement, 23–24, 278n51
Terman, Lewis, 44, 47, 48, 72, 160, 182
Thelen, Esther, 189
Thom, Douglas, 113, 198, 204–5, 235–37, 306n60, 320n100, 339n59, 344n84, 349n50
Thomas, William I., 105, 216, 304n22
Thompson, Helen, 183, 186, 188
Thorndike, Edward L., 37, 40–44, 47, 48, 67, 68, 169, 204
Titchener, Edward B., 45, 286n86, 286n92

Unemployment, 237–38, 246–48
University of California at Berkeley, 147, 165–67, 255, 316n56, 321n14, 323n26
University of Chicago, 29, 36, 40, 84, 109, 144, 228, 249, 251, 296n10, 354n110
University of Minnesota, 147, 167, 219, 255, 316n56, 319n91, 321n14, 359n31
University of Toronto, 147, 179, 219, 321n14

Van Waters, Miriam, 105, 148, 216, 343n72
Vassar College, 141–42, 151, 319n85, 325n68
Vygotsky, Lev, 40

Wald, Lillian, 66, 67, 73–75, 82, 100, 101, 295n79
Washburn, Alfred, 216, 323n35
Washington Child Research Center, 163, 242, 352n81, 352–53n84

Watson, John B.: career of, 149; on child rearing, 128, 149, 254, 318n71, 320n100; and conditioning, 42, 149, 153, 169, 170, 187, 235; and habit-training, 204; on maternal affection, 54; on psychology's aims, 143; on remaking of children, 152; and research on babies and children, 42, 145, 158, 187, 353n84; significance of, 169, 325n68; symposium including, 304n22
WCTU, 23–24, 63, 133, 135
Webb, Beatrice, 64
Weinberger, R. A., 268
Welter, Barbara, 16–17
West, James, 76–77
West, Mrs. Max, 94, 234, 301n82
White, Edna Noble, 10, 147, 151, 319n87
White, Sheldon H., 252, 253, 288n4, 326n69, 360n47
White, William Alanson, 47, 192, 195, 334–35n10
White House Conference on Children and Youth (1909), 5, 69, 76–78, 295nn78–79
White House Conference on Children and Youth (1919), 5, 97–99, 229, 242, 301n91, 335n11
White House Conference on Children and Youth (1930), 4, 6, 140, 149, 157, 217–18, 227, 235–36, 242–46, 299n50, 301n89, 325n55, 353n89
White House Conference on Children and Youth (1940–1970), 188, 190, 265
White House Conference on Early Childhood, 265
Wilbur, Lyman, 242–44, 246
Willard, Frances, 23–24
William T. Grant Foundation, 164, 257, 258, 266
Wilson, Woodrow, 83, 95–97, 135, 140, 242, 347n1
Winslow, Helen, 64
Witmer, Helen, 209, 210

Witte, Edwin E., 249–50

Woman's Christian Temperance Union (WCTU), 23–24, 63, 133, 135

Woman's Committee of the Advisory Committee of the Council of National Defense, 96

Women: alliance between female reformers and male behavioral scientists, 3, 8–9, 30, 60–61, 65; antebellum women, 16–18; and child development research, 156, 163, 168, 257, 326n69; employment of, 22, 59–60, 64, 70, 74, 277n39; as flapper, 294; moral superiority of, 22, 60, 63; New Woman, 62–63, 70; as philanthropists, 9–10; as physicians, 233; research on young women in trouble with the law, 216; in rural areas, 88–90, 96, 99, 132–34, 273n13; and scientific child study, 8–9; and separate spheres doctrine, 16–17, 19, 62–63, 274n6; and social surveys, 29–30; suffrage for, 19, 20, 21, 24, 133; and true womanhood, 16–17, 62. See also Feminism; Higher education for women; Motherhood; Women's organizations; and specific women

Women's organizations: Addams on, 104; and Children's Bureau, 84–86, 96, 297n23; after Civil War, 22–24; cultural pursuits by, 63, 64; and Iowa Child Welfare Research Station, 126; and Lathrop, 84–86, 96, 297n16;

mothers' clubs, 18–19, 21, 49, 55, 57, 275n20, 276n21; and Sheppard-Towner Act, 231; and social feminism, 312n79; and social reform, 63–65, 72, 84–86; and World War I, 96. See also specific organizations

Woodroofe, Kathleen, 114

Woodworth, Robert, 155–57, 169

Woolley, Helen, 152, 167, 168, 242, 314n17, 321–22n14

Works Project Administration (WPA), 170, 354n107

World War I, 44, 91, 92, 95–96, 112–13, 131–32, 141, 143–44, 252, 301n89, 314n28

World War II, 252, 261

WPA, 170, 354n107

Wundt, Wilhelm, 31, 37, 45, 286n86

Wylie, Philip, 262

Wyoming, 88–90, 298n42

Yale Clinic of Child Development, 78, 147, 160, 167, 173–75, 178–82, 255, 323n35, 328n2, 329n6, 332n47

Yale University, 41–42, 165, 166, 177, 219, 259

Yearbook of the National Society for Education, 161

Zigler, Edward, 259, 263, 268, 331n26, 360n47